D1610982

SYMPTOMS OF DEPRESSION

Recent titles in the

Wiley Series on Personality Processes

Irving B. Weiner, *Editor*
University of South Florida

Symptoms of Depression *edited by Charles G. Costello*
Handbook of Clinical Research and Practice with Adolescents *edited by Patrick H. Tolan and Bertram J. Cohler*
Internalizing Disorders in Children and Adolescents *edited by William M. Reynolds*
Assessment of Family Violence: A Clinical and Legal Sourcebook *edited by Robert T. Ammerman and Michel Hersen*
Handbook of Clinical Child Psychology (Second Edition) *edited by C. Eugene Walker and Michael C. Roberts*
Handbook of Clinical Behavior Therapy (Second Edition) *edited by Samuel M. Turner, Karen S. Calhoun, and Henry E. Adams*
Psychological Disturbance in Adolescence (Second Edition) *by Irving B. Weiner*
Prevention of Child Maltreatment: Development and Ecological Perspectives *edited by Diane J. Willis, E. Wayne Holden, and Mindy Rosenberg*
Interventions for Children of Divorce: Custody, Access, and Psychotherapy *by William F. Hodges*
The Play Therapy Primer: An Integration of Theories and Techniques *by Kevin John O'Connor*
Adult Psychopathology and Diagnosis (Second Edition) *edited by Michel Hersen and Samuel L. Turner*
The Rorschach: A Comprehensive System. Volume II: Interpretation (Second Edition) *by John E. Exner, Jr.*
Play Diagnosis and Assessment *edited by Charles E. Schaefer, Karen Gitlin, and Alice Sandgrund*
Acquaintance Rape: The Hidden Crime *edited by Andrea Parrot and Laurie Bechhofer*
The Psychological Examination of the Child *by Theodore H. Blau*
Depressive Disorders: Facts, Theories, and Treatment Methods *by Benjamin B. Wolman, Editor, and George Stricker, Co-Editor*
Social Support: An Interactional View *edited by Barbara R. Sarason, Irwin G. Sarason, and Gregory R. Pierce*
Toward a New Personology: An Evolutionary Model *by Theodore Millon*
Treatment of Family Violence: A Sourcebook *edited by Robert T. Ammerman and Michel Hersen*
Handbook of Comparative Treatments for Adult Disorders *edited by Alan S. Bellack and Michel Hersen*
Managing Attention Disorders in Children: A Guide for Practitioners *by Sam Goldstein and Michael Goldstein*
Understanding and Treating Depressed Adolescents and Their Families *by Gerald D. Oster and Janice E. Caro*
The Psychosocial Worlds of the Adolescent: Public and Private *by Vivian Center Seltzer*
Handbook of Parent Training: Parents as Co-Therapists for Children's Behavior Problems *edited by Charles E. Schaefer and James M. Briesmeister*
From Ritual to Repertoire: A Cognitive-Developmental Approach with Behavior-Disordered Children *by Arnold Miller and Eileen Eller-Miller*
The Practice of Hypnotism. Volume 2: Applications of Traditional and Semi-Traditional Hypnotism: Non-Traditional Hypnotism *by Andre M. Weitzenhoffer*
The Practice of Hypnotism. Volume 1: Traditional and Semi-Traditional Techniques and Phenomenology *by Andre M. Weitzenhoffer*
Children's Social Networks and Social Supports *edited by Deborah Belle*
Advances in Art Therapy *edited by Harriet Wadeson, Jean Durkin, and Dorine Perach*
Psychosocial Aspects of Disaster *edited by Richard M. Gist and Bernard Lubin*
Handbook of Child Psychiatric Diagnosis *edited by Cynthia G. Last and Michel Hersen*
Grief: The Mourning After—Dealing with Adult Bereavement *by Catherine M. Sanders*
Problem-Solving Therapy for Depression: Theory, Research, and Clinical Guidelines *by Arthur M. Nezu, Christine M. Nezu, and Michael G. Perri*
Peer Relationships in Child Development *edited by Thomas J. Berndt and Gary W. Ladd*
The Psychology of Underachievement: Differential Diagnosis and Differential Treatment *by Harvey P. Mandel and Sander I. Marcus*
Treating Adult Children of Alcoholics: A Developmental Perspective *by Stephanie Brown*

SYMPTOMS OF DEPRESSION

Edited by

Charles G. Costello

University of Calgary

A WILEY-INTERSCIENCE PUBLICATION

JOHN WILEY & SONS, INC.

New York • Chichester • Brisbane • Toronto • Singapore

Library of Congress Cataloging-in-Publication Data

Symptoms of depression / [edited by] Charles G. Costello.
p. cm. — (Wiley series on personality processes)
Includes index.
ISBN 0-471-54304-7 (cloth : alk. paper)
1. Depression, Mental. 2. Symptomatology. I. Costello, Charles G., 1929– . II. Series.
[DNLM: 1. Depression. 2. Depressive Disorders. WM 171 S98987]
RC537.S94 1993
616.85'27—dc20
DNLM/DLC
for Library of Congress 92-18109

Printed in the United States of America

91 92 10 9 8 7 6 5 4 3 2 1

Contributors

Lyn Y. Abramson, PhD
Professor of Psychology
University of Wisconsin-Madison
Madison, Wisconsin

Lauren B. Alloy, PhD
Professor of Psychology
Temple University
Philadelphia, Pennsylvania

Roy F. Baumeister, PhD
Professor of Psychology
Case Western Reserve University
Cleveland, Ohio

Christine Z. Bernet, BA
Doctoral Candidate
Department of Psychology
San Diego State University
San Diego, California

Rosalind D. Cartwright, PhD
Professor of Psychology
Rush-Presbyterian St. Luke's Medical Center
Chicago, Illinois

Marylene Cloitre, PhD
Assistant Professor of Psychology
New School for Social Research
New York, New York

Charles G. Costello, PhD
Professor of Psychology
University of Calgary
Calgary, Alberta, Canada

Lisa A. Feldman, PhD
Assistant Professor of Psychology
The Pennsylvania State University
University Park, Pennsylvania

Ian H. Gotlib, PhD
Professor of Psychology and Psychiatry
Northwestern University
Evanston, Illinois

David Healy, MD, MRCPsych.
Director, Academic Sub-department of Psychological Medicine
University of Wales College of Medicine
North Wales Hospital
Denbigh, Clwyd, Wales

Rick E. Ingram, PhD
Professor of Psychology
San Diego State University
San Diego, California

Brenda R. Johnson, PhD
Adjunct Professor of Psychology
San Diego State University
San Diego, California

Martin M. Katz, PhD
Professor of Psychology
Montefiore Hospital and
Medical Center
Albert Einstein College of Medicine
Bronx, New York

Eric Klinger, PhD
Professor of Psychology
University of Minnesota
Morris, Minnesota

Gerald I. Metalsky, PhD
Associate Professor of Psychology
Lawrence University
Appleton, Wisconsin

George C. Patton, MD, MRCPsych.
Consultant Psychiatrist and
Academic Associate
Royal Melbourne Hospital
Victoria, Australia

June P. Tangney, PhD
Assistant Professor of Psychology
George Mason University
Fairfax, Virginia

Herman M. van Praag, MD
Professor of Psychiatry
Montefiore Hospital and
Medical Center
Albert Einstein College of
Medicine
Bronx, New York

Fraser N. Watts, PhD
Research Clinical Psychologist
Medical Research Council Applied
Psychology Unit
Cambridge, England

Paul Willner, PhD
Professor of Psychology
City of London Polytechnic
London, England

Series Preface

This series of books is addressed to behavioral scientists interested in the nature of human personality. Its scope should prove pertinent to personality theorists and researchers as well as to clinicians concerned with applying an understanding of personality processes to the amelioration of emotional difficulties in living. To this end, the series provides a scholarly integration of theoretical formulations, empirical data, and practical recommendations.

Six major aspects of studying and learning about human personality can be designated: personality theory, personality structure and dynamics, personality development, personality assessment, personality change, and personality adjustment. In exploring these aspects of personality, the books in the series discuss a number of distinct but related subject areas: the nature and implications of various theories of personality; personality characteristics that account for consistencies and variations in human behavior; the emergence of personality processes in children and adolescents; the use of interviewing and testing procedures to evaluate individual differences in personality; efforts to modify personality styles through psychotherapy, counseling, behavior therapy, and other methods of influence; and patterns of abnormal personality functioning that impair individual competence.

IRVING B. WEINER

University of South Florida
Tampa, Florida

Preface

The fourth edition of the *Diagnostic and Statistical Manual of Mental Disorders* (DSM-IV) is scheduled for publication in 1994. An effort will be made to put the diagnoses and their criteria on a firmer basis of research data than that which was used for earlier editions of the manual. Unfortunately, the entry point for most of the research that will be reviewed will have been the diagnostic categories of previous editions of the DSM or similar diagnostic systems. The Gordian knots that form the diagnostic categories of these systems are so arbitrary, complex, and controversial that it is unlikely the research data will provide a very sound basis for DSM-IV.

I believe that we are in a *reculer pour mieux sauter* situation. We should not try to construct diagnoses and their criteria by reviewing the confusing data of research using diagnostic systems that were previously constructed in a similar manner. Rather, we should research specific symptoms and, when we have gained thorough knowledge of their nature, we should then begin to investigate their interrelationships and search for the underlying process that explains those interrelationships. In this way we are likely to arrive at more valid syndromes and thus etiologically base diagnoses. Clinicians and researchers may then be able to detect the presence of syndromes associated with these diagnoses by measuring the underlying process. Consequently, the syndromes will be detected more simply, directly, and reliably than current syndromes that are sought in brave attempts to measure a host of complex symptoms in brief interviews.

I hope the close examinations of the symptoms of depression in this book, by revealing their complexity, will give psychopathologists pause before they embark on research into depression using DSM or similar diagnoses as an entry point. I also hope that the thorough reviews of our current knowledge about the symptoms will help researchers who wish to discover the nature of these symptoms and their interrelationships.

Herb Reich and his staff, particularly Peter Brown, at John Wiley & Sons, and Nancy Marcus Land of Publications Development Company of Texas have produced this book with such amiability, efficiency, and speed that I have stopped complaining about the misery, inefficiency and sluggishness of academic publishing. I am very grateful to them.

Calgary, Alberta
October 1992

CHARLES G. COSTELLO

Contents

CHAPTER 1

The Advantages of the Symptom Approach to Depression

CHARLES G. COSTELLO

INTRODUCTION

The advantages of researching *symptoms* of depression rather than *syndromes* of depression are (a) current psychiatric diagnostic systems produce data of questionable reliability and validity; and (b) syndromes, as they are currently identified, are such intricate yet loosely defined concepts that the professional who finds significant environmental and biological correlates of the syndromes does not know what causal mechanisms are involved or even where to look for them.

I will first review articles that have reported the findings of studies that were specifically designed to investigate the reliabilities and validities of three well known structured interviews and their diagnostic systems. These diagnostic systems, by definition, take a categorical approach to psychopathology. I will not discuss the issues involved in research that takes a dimensional approach to the assessment of psychopathology and that collects data using questionnaires. A recent, thorough discussion of these issues can be found in Clark and Watson (1991).

It seems to be generally accepted that the three standardized psychiatric interviews to be discussed (Schedule for Affective Disorders and Schizophrenia [SADS], Endicott & Spitzer, 1978; Present State Examination [PSE], Wing, Cooper, & Sartorius, 1974; and the Diagnostic Interview Schedule [DIS], Robins, Helzer, Croughan, & Ratcliff, 1981), and the diagnostic systems associated with them (Research Diagnostic Criteria [RDC], Spitzer, Endicott, & Robins, 1978; [D-CATEGO], Wing et al., 1974; Diagnostic and Statistical Manual of Mental Disorders [DSM-III and DSM-III-R], American Psychiatric Association, 1980, 1987), produce more reliable identification of psychiatric syndromes and diagnoses than do unstructured clinical interviews. That is no doubt true, but the evidence for their reliability in a more absolute sense is not compelling because most of the studies are methodologically poor and the findings are inconsistent.

Although for the most part, I will simply note the methodological problems of the studies reported, I will describe the better designed studies in more detail. But first I will review the issues surrounding the concept and measurement of reliability.

THE CONCEPT AND MEASUREMENT OF RELIABILITY

Of the three forms of reliability that have been identified by psychometricians—internal, test-retest, and interrater—the most important form that needs to be established for psychiatric interviews, whether for measurement of current symptoms or lifetime symptoms, is the interrater form. Test-retest reliability is an important additional measure when the interviewer i. measuring lifetime symptoms.

Internal reliability is particularly important when measuring the homogeneity of a set of items designed to measure, in a dimensional manner, a single construct such as neuroticism. It would not seem quite so relevant for the data obtained from psychiatric interviews when such data are treated in a categorical manner to produce polythetic classifications. The data from such classifications may, of course, be treated in a dimensional manner, to generate, for instance, total symptom scores. But the primary purpose of such interviews is to assign diagnoses to people, and it is their reliability in this respect that is my concern here. For those readers who believe that internal consistency of psychiatric diagnoses is a legitimate concern, there is a recent good review by George, Blazer, Woodbury, and Mason (1989).

Good test-retest reliability over periods longer than about a week, though important for the measurement of lifetime symptoms, cannot reasonably be expected when measuring symptoms of psychopathological disorders such as depression *for the period immediately before each interview* because such symptoms do not remain stable. Therefore, I will document these studies but will not examine them in any detail.

In studies of the interrater reliability of interviews, one research design shows videotaped interviews to raters individually or in groups. The second design involves one rater interviewing the subject and one or more other raters observing. In the third design, the subject is interviewed twice by two different interviewers.

Three problems that are common to the videotape design and the observer design are (a) subjects are interviewed only once, and therefore the extent to which variability in their reports may contribute to unreliability is not measured; (b) sources of unreliability due to differences in the styles of interviewers are not measured; (c) the interviewer on the videotape, or the interviewer who is being observed in the observer design, may inadvertently cue observers as to how a symptom should be rated. For instance, the point at which the interviewer pauses to rate a symptom or the phrasing of probe questions following an initial question can give away the rating the interviewer has decided on (see Grove, Andreason, McDonald-Scott, Keller, & Shapiro, 1981), for a fuller discussion of these problems).

These three problems do not exist for the interrater design that involves two separate interviews per subject. However, as I noted previously, the time interval between interviews may present problems. When measuring current symptoms, the interval must be short, even when the subject is instructed to consider the same period in both interviews, otherwise aspects of interrater reliability may become confused with whatever is being measured in long-interval, test-retests. My review of the literature categorizes any study that examined the comparability of data from two independent interviews *administered within a 1-week period* as a test of interrater reliability although the study may be described by its authors as a test-retest reliability study (e.g., Semler et al., 1987). I will also review studies where the interval between two independent interviews was greater than 1 week if they were measuring lifetime symptoms and diagnoses.

When short intervals between two interviews are used in measurements of current symptoms or lifetime symptoms, subjects in the second interview may try to repeat from memory what they said in the first interview. Unfortunately, I found only one study (Semler et al., 1987) where an attempt was made to overcome this problem by instructions aimed at ensuring that the subjects understood the purpose of the second interview. Subjects should be told that the purpose of a second interview is not to find out how well they remember what they said in the first interview but to give them another opportunity to report on their experiences and behaviors for the same period that preceded and was covered in that first interview.

An interrater reliability study involving two separate interviews is truly a reliability study when the two interviewers have the same amount of training and experience with the interview procedure and when they independently use exactly the same interview and rating procedures. Some studies, described as reliability studies by the authors themselves or by others, compare data from a structured interview administered by laypeople or mental health professionals with data from the second administration of the same interview by mental health professionals (usually a psychiatrist) who are permitted to use any supplemental probes deemed necessary to obtain adequate information for a decision on the presence or absence of a symptom or for making a diagnosis (e.g., Helzer et al., 1985; Robins et al., 1981; Robins, Helzer, Ratcliff, & Seyfried, 1982). But such studies are validity studies rather than reliability studies. In passing, it is perhaps worth noting that they are peculiar validity studies in that they seem to use the clinically souped-up interviews to provide gold standard data against which to evaluate data from structured interviews that were initially designed to be improvements over unstructured clinical interviews.

Once the researcher has obtained the data in an adequately designed reliability study, he or she faces the problem of how to analyze them. A simple measure of the percentages of subjects on which two raters agree is inadequate because it does not correct for chance agreement. The *k* statistic (Cohen, 1960) is the best available measure of overall agreement because it does correct for chance agreement. Two things must be kept in mind, however, when interpreting *k:* First, the same *k* may result from different patterns of relationships between the diagnoses of two raters. Raters may agree primarily on the absence of symptoms or on the presence of symptoms. If the pattern of results is not presented, the researcher does not know which it is. Therefore, as well as presenting the *k*'s reported in the studies reviewed, I will also, where possible, present data on the percentage of agreement concerning the presence of a diagnosis, which, it seems to me, are the particularly crucial data. The second factor to remember is that the value of *k* is affected by the base rate of the psychopathological disorders in the population from which the study sample has been drawn, and therefore the user must be careful about generalizing the findings to new populations (see Shrout, Spitzer, & Fleiss, 1987, and Spitznagel & Helzer, 1985, for thorough discussions of these issues).

Finally, when generalizing findings on reliability, apart from taking into account differences between populations in base rates, it is also necessary to take into account the distinctiveness of the disorders in the sample studied and in the population to which generalizations are being made. The more unequivocal the diagnoses in a population, the higher the reliability is likely to be.

RESEARCH DATA ON RELIABILITY OF SYNDROMES OF DEPRESSION

Schedule for Affective Disorders and Schizophrenia (SADS) and Research Diagnostic Criteria (RDC)

Nine articles have reported on the interrater reliability of one or other version of the SADS and the RDC (Andreason et al., 1982; Bromet, Dunn, Connell, Dew, & Schulberg, 1986; Endicott & Spitzer, 1978; Fendrich, Weissman, Warner, & Mufson, 1990; Hesselbrock, Stabenau, Hesselbrock, Mirkin, & Meyer, 1982; Mazure & Gershon, 1979; Prusoff, Merikangas, & Weissman, 1988; Spitzer, Endicott, & Robins, 1978; Weissman & Meyers, 1978).

All or part of the reliability data reported in six of these articles is not adequate for the following reasons:

1. The videotape procedure was used (Andreason et al., 1982; Hesselbrock et al., 1982).
2. The observer procedure was used (Spitzer et al., 1978 [the patient studies labeled "A" and "B" and the study of the first-degree relatives of the patients in Study B]; Endicott & Spitzer, 1978 [in which the authors presented further analyses of data obtained from the sample of Study B patients in Spitzer et al., 1978]; Weissman & Myers, 1978).
3. Data are reported on summary scale scores but not on the assignment of subjects to diagnostic categories (Endicott & Spitzer, 1978). The reliability of assignment to diagnostic categories for the subjects whose data are reported in this study was analyzed and reported in Spitzer et al. (1978; see discussion following this list).
4. The first interviewer in a test-retest reliability study of lifetime diagnoses was not blind with respect to the previous diagnoses each subject had received (Mazure & Gershon, 1979).

Coming to the studies that are relatively free of methodological problems, one of the studies reported in Spitzer et al. (1978) involved two independent SADS interviews of 60 psychiatric inpatients. The interviews were separated by a day or two. Although no data were provided on the qualifications or training of the two interviewers, the interview appears to have been given in the same manner at each session. The *k* for the lifetime diagnosis of major depressive disorder was 0.71 and for a present episode of the disorder 0.90. Unfortunately, the percentage of agreement on the presence of a diagnosis was not presented, nor were the raw data presented that would have permitted the calculation of such percentages.

Fendrich et al. (1990) reported the data for lifetime DSM-III diagnoses obtained in two interviews 2 years apart in a sample of 150 offspring aged 6 to 23 years, using the Schedule for Affective Disorders and Schizophrenia for School Aged Offspring, Epidemiologic Version (K-SADS-E; Orvaschel, Puig-Antich, Chambers, Tabrizi, & Johnson, 1982). Of the offspring, 81 were from 41 depressed parents and 69 were offspring of 30 normal parents. The same interviewer saw 62 of the subjects at both interviews. The *k* values for the lifetime diagnosis of major depressive disorder for those seen by the same interviewer and those seen by a different interviewer were 0.66 and 0.58 respectively. Neither percentages of agreement on presence of a diagnosis nor data permitting their calculation were reported.

Bromet et al. (1986) measured the reliability of a diagnosis of lifetime major depression for a community sample of 391 women interviewed on two occasions 18 months apart, both interviews covering the period before the first interview. The reliability data did not differ significantly for the 261 women who were seen by the same interviewer at both interviews and the 131 women who were interviewed by different interviewers. Of the 144 women diagnosed at either interview as having had an RDC episode of major depression in the period before the first interview, only 38% were so diagnosed at both interviews.

The 143 subjects in the Prusoff et al. (1988) study consisted of 54 probands with a lifetime diagnosis of major depression, 33 normal control probands, 44 spouses and 12 offspring over 17 years of age. Two independent interviews with the SADS-L were administered, the time interval between the interviews being 3 to 6 years (M = 4.7 years). The percentage of agreement on the presence of a lifetime diagnosis and the k value for major depression were 81% and 0.80. The comparable figures for depressive personality were 33% and 0.45.

In summary, there are no very convincing data on the reliability of the SADS and RDC. Most of the studies have methodological problems or do not present sufficient data to determine in what respects the data are reliable. One study of lifetime diagnoses (Prusoff et al., 1988) reported good reliability for major depression, but this was probably because the sample was not a diagnostically heterogeneous one. When a diagnostically heterogeneous community sample was investigated (Bromet et al., 1986), the reliability for lifetime major depression was poor.

Present State Examination (PSE), Index of Definition (ID), and CATEGO

Eight studies were specifically designed to measure the interrater reliability of the PSE. Unfortunately, none of them permit any conclusions on the reliability for the syndromes of depression produced nor, for that matter, for any other syndromes. The methodological problems are as follows:

1. The videotape procedure was used for two samples in Wing, Birley, Cooper, Graham, and Isaacs (1967) and in one sample in each of Lesage, Cyr, and Toupin (1991), Luria and Berry (1980), and Wing, Nixon, Mann, and Leff (1977). It was also used in Luria and McHugh (1974).
2. The observer procedure was used for three samples in Wing et al. (1967), and for one sample in each of Kendell, Everett, Cooper, Sartorius, & David (1968), Luria and Berry (1980), and Lesage et al. (1991). It was also used in Cooper, Copeland, Brown, Harris, & Gourlay (1977).
3. Data are reported on the reliability of scores for various sections of the PSE but not on the reliability of assignment of subjects to diagnostic categories (Kendell et al., 1968; Luria & McHugh, 1974; Cooper et al., 1977; Wing, Nixon, Mann, & Leff, et al., 1977; Sturt, Bebbington, Hurry, & Tennant, 1981).
4. Independent PSE interviews were conducted, but psychiatric history data other than that provided by the PSE were available to the raters (two samples in Wing et al., 1967).

5. Independent PSE interviews were conducted, but the time intervals between the interviews were not reported (one sample in Wing et al., 1967).

In summary, despite the frequent use of the PSE and its associated classification systems, no good data on its reliability have been provided by studies specifically designed for that purpose.

Diagnostic Interview Schedule (DIS) and Composite International Diagnostic Interview (CIDI)

Reliabilities of data from studies that are relatively free of methodological problems were reported in five articles on the DIS. In Burnam, Karno, Hough, Escobar, and Forsythe's (1983) study, a Spanish version of the DIS was administered to 61 psychiatric outpatients on two occasions 1 week apart by two independent interviewers. The percentage of agreement on presence of a lifetime diagnosis and the associated k values were 50% and 0.49 for major depressive episode and 25% and 0.16 for dysthymia.

Anthony and Dryman (1987) compared initial DIS lifetime diagnoses with 1-year follow-up diagnoses. They found that 322 (61%) of 529 subjects who had a lifetime diagnosis of major depression at the first interview were not so diagnosed at the second interview.

Helzer, Spitznagel, and McEvoy (1987) examined the 1-year reliability for the lay-administered DIS lifetime diagnoses in 370 subjects selected from the St. Louis ECA sample. My calculations based on the data they presented in their Table 1 (p. 1071) indicated that only 43% of those with a lifetime diagnosis of major depression at the first interview had the same diagnosis at the second interview.

Wells, Burnham, Leake, and Robins (1988) compared the data on the DIS lifetime diagnoses of depressive disorders for 230 subjects at the Los Angeles site of the ECA program. The diagnoses were obtained in two face-to-face full DIS interviews 1 year apart and in a telephone administration of the depression section of the DIS given an average of 3 months after the second full DIS interview. The percentage agreement between the two full DIS interviews with respect to the lifetime diagnoses of major depression was only 38%. The comparable figure for dysthymia was 34%. The percentage agreement between the second full DIS interviews and the telephone interviews for lifetime diagnoses of major depression was 38%. The comparable figure for dysthymia was 36%.

Vandiver and Sher (1991) reported the test-retest reliability over a 9-month period for lifetime diagnoses in 486 college students. They found that only 38% of students receiving a lifetime diagnosis of major depression at the first interview received the same diagnosis at the second interview 9 months later. The comparable percentage agreement between the two interviews for dysthymia was 30%.

In summary, the data on DIS lifetime diagnoses of major depression and dysthymia indicate poor reliability. Averaging the five studies, the percentage agreement on the presence of a lifetime diagnosis of major depression is only 46%. Averaging the three studies that reported data on the presence of a lifetime diagnosis of dysthymia indicated only 30% agreement.

The field trials of the CIDI (Cottler et al., 1991; Wittchen et al., 1991) have used the observer design, and for the reasons noted previously, the reliability data reported are of questionable value.

The study by Semler et al. (1987) in which the CIDI was administered to 60 psychiatric inpatients during two independent intervals with a time interval between the interviews of 1 to 4 days has two strong features in its design: (a) The patients were "instructed to regard both interviews as independent—that is, to answer all questions comprehensively on both occasions and not to consider the second interview a continuation of the first"; (b) the four interviewers involved were all given equally thorough training. One weakness of the design was the short interval between interviews since it was the reliability of lifetime diagnoses that was investigated. The percentages of agreement for a DSM-III lifetime diagnosis and the associated k's were 64% and 0.66 for a major depressive disorder and 33% and 0.47 for a dysthymic disorder. For the subclassifications of affective disorder, the values were bipolar disorder—29%, 0.47; major depressive disorder, single episode—29%, 0.40; major depressive disorder, recurrent—29%, 0.33; atypical bipolar disorder—0% agreement.

The data reported for all the structured interviews and their associated systems could hardly lead to the conclusion that the evidence for the reliability of the current and lifetime diagnoses of depression and its subclassifications is impressive. Unfortunately, researchers too often assume that such reliability has been established. But even if the data on reliability were more reassuring, the question of validity remains.

RESEARCH DATA ON THE VALIDITY OF SYNDROMES OF DEPRESSION

If the reliability of the data on syndromes of depression is not impressive, the level of agreement between the data produced by different psychiatric interviews, that is, their *concurrent validity,* is even less impressive. Five recent studies have presented data concerning the differentiation of depression from normality and other psychopathological conditions. Brockington, Helzer, Hillier, and Frances (1982), in their investigation of 125 inpatients, found that, using k, the concordance between a combined PSE/CATEGO neurotic/retarded classification and SADS/RDC major depressive disorder was 0.51.

Dean, Surtees, and Sashidharan (1983), in their investigation of a community sample of women, found that when the CATEGO system and the RDC system were applied to the syndrome data obtained by their standardized interview, only 65% of the 51 women diagnosed as depressed by one or other of the systems were diagnosed as depressed by both systems.

Sashidharan (1985), in an investigation of inpatients and outpatients, found only a 42% (17 out of 41) agreement between RDC major depression and the CATEGO combined classification of *R* (Retarded) and *D* (Psychotic) depression.

Van den Brink et al. (1989) found that, in their study of 175 psychiatric outpatients, only 58% of 80 cases of depression were diagnosed as depressed by both the CATEGO system and DSM-III criteria.

Hesselbrock et al. (1982) did find good concordance between the SADS-L and DIS for current depression ($k = .74$) and lifetime depression ($k = .72$). However, an "editor" system was used for both interviews to review the interview protocol for completeness, to resolve questionable codes, and to review the diagnosis. The editors were the first two authors of the article. It is possible that they were not blind to the diagnosis based on one interview when deciding on a diagnosis based on the second interview.

Because of the paucity of validity data on syndromes of depression, the remainder of this section will go beyond studies that used one or more of the structured interviews discussed thus far and will include studies that have used more clinical, unstructured approaches.

One approach to the concurrent validity of the data on depression produced by diagnostic systems such as the DSM is to examine the extent to which they agree in identifying subclasses of depression. For instance, Zimmerman, Coryell, Pfohl, and Stangl (1985) examined four definitions of endogenous depression: DSM-III; RDC; Feinberg and Carroll (FC; Feinberg & Carroll, 1982); and Newcastle (Carney, Roth, & Garside, 1965). Whereas 66% of the patients met the RDC criteria and 62% the Feinberg and Carroll criteria for definite endogenous depression, 44% were DSM-III melancholics and 37% were endogenous by the Newcastle criteria. The chance-corrected agreement between the systems was DSM-III versus RDC, $k = 0.69$; DSM-III versus FC, $k = 0.40$; DSM-III versus Newcastle, $k = 0.18$; FC versus Newcastle, $k = 0.32$. Other researchers who have presented similar data indicating the lack of agreement between the diagnoses of endogenous depression produced by different systems are Davidson, Turnbull, Strickland, and Belyea (1984); Katschnig, Nutzinger, and Schanda (1986); and Philipp, Maier, and Benkert (1986).

The lack of agreement between systems for diagnosing endogenous depression is not surprising in view of the differences between the systems as outlined by Zimmerman et al. (1985) and by Davidson et al. (1984). The DSM-III and RDC definitions are phenomenological definitions based solely on the presence or absence of a specified set of depressive symptoms. The Newcastle and FC definitions include judgments about precipitating and associated psychological stress. The Newcastle scale also includes judgments of premorbid personality, whether or not the patient blames other people for the depression; and whether the patient has a history of prior depressive episodes. The Newcastle and FC definitions also include depressive delusions as criteria, whereas RDC and DSM-III have a separate diagnostic classification for the presence or absence of psychosis.

The poor concurrent validity of the different methods of diagnosing depression and its subclassifications suggests that their construct validities are poor. Significant findings usually occur in studies of comparisons between those diagnosed as depressed and those who do not have a psychopathological condition. Significant findings are much less common when comparisons are made between depressed individuals and those who satisfy diagnostic criteria for another psychopathological disorder. For instance, there is no clear evidence of abnormalities that are peculiar to depression in investigations of either cognitive processes (Beidel & Turner, 1986) or, with perhaps the exception of sleep patterns (see Chapter 12 of this book), physiological processes (Golden & Janowsky, 1990).

Another manner in which researchers have tested the validity of the diagnoses of depression is by testing predictions concerning differences between individuals diagnosed as having different kinds of depression. In a thorough study of the validity of the endogenous subclassification of depression, Zimmerman, Coryell, Pfohl, and Stangl (1986) predicted that patients with endogenous depression in contrast to nonendogenous depressives would (a) have a higher degree of affective disorder in their first-degree relatives; (b) have a lower likelihood of alcoholism in their first-degree relatives; (c) have a lower degree of antisocial personality in their first-degree relatives; (d) be older; (e) be more severely ill; (f) be less likely to make a nonserious suicide attempt during the index episode; (g) have lower rates of premorbid personality disorder; (h) have lower frequencies of stressful life events during the year before hospital admission; (i) have less cognitive distortion; (j) have lower frequency of marital separation and divorce; (k) have better social support; (l) have a greater likelihood of biological abnormality on such tests as the dexamethasone suppression test (DST), thyrotropin-releasing hormone stimulation test, or reduced latency to rapid eye movement (REM) sleep; (m) have a better response to somatic therapies. The predictions were tested using the four definitions of endogenous depression listed earlier: DSM-III, RDC, Newcastle, and Feinberg and Carroll. Only 3 of the 13 predictions were confirmed for each of the four definitions: the lower likelihood of alcoholism in the first-degree relatives of endogenous depressives, the greater severity of their illness, and their lower rates of nonserious suicide attempts during the index episode.

There are inconsistent findings with respect to variables that are generally believed to characterize endogenous depressives; namely, family history of depression, presence of biological abnormalities, low rates of stressful life events, and a better response than that of nonendogenous depressives to somatic therapy (Zimmerman et al., 1986; Zimmerman & Spitzer, 1989).

One problem that has bedeviled attempts to establish the construct validity of data on depressive syndromes is the difficulty of distinguishing syndromes of depression from syndromes of anxiety. For instance, Blazer et al. (1988) did a cluster analysis of the symptoms of 406 respondents reporting depressive symptoms in the Piedmont region of North Carolina sample of the ECA project. They identified a syndrome that included symptoms nearly identical to the symptoms associated with the DSM-III classification of major depression, but the syndrome also included anxiety symptoms. The problem of differentiating anxiety from depression also appears in ratings of overall intensity of these conditions based on the interview assessment of symptoms. The review of the data by Clark and Watson (1991) indicated that the correlations ranged from .40 to .45.

It seems then that diagnoses of depression produced by current diagnostic systems are of uncertain reliability and poor validity. The poor validity of the syndrome data produced by standardized interviews is probably due to the poor validities of the symptom data themselves. This, in turn, is probably because the measurement of each symptom is usually based on a short answer to a short question or on brief, unsystematized observations.

Although there is some variability between studies, it seems that symptoms of depression can be rated fairly reliably on the basis of data obtained in structured interviews that permit probing and clinical judgment (Cicchetti & Prusoff, 1983; Endicott, Cohen, Nee, Fleiss, & Sarantakos, 1981; Paykel, 1985; Verghese, Burrows, Foenander, Stevenson, & Davies, 1976). But the test-retest reliabilities of symptom data for the DIS, a nonclinical structured interview, are not good. In the Wells et al. (1988) article, referred to previously, data were reported for lifetime symptoms of depression in 230 individuals who were given a face-to-face full DIS interview and a telephone administration of the depression section of the DIS an average of 3 months later. My calculations of the percentage of agreement with respect to the *presence* of lifetime symptoms based on the data presented in their Table 1 (p. 214) produced the following results: sad or depressed, 73%; loss of appetite, 50%; loss of weight, 53%; gained weight, 39%; trouble falling asleep, 44%; sleeping too much, 38%; moving all the time, 15%; talking or moving slower, 34%; interest in sex low, 27%; tired out, 32%; worthless or guilty, 57%; trouble concentrating, 41%; thoughts slow, 28%; thoughts of death, 41%; wanted to die, 54%; thoughts of suicide, 61%; attempted suicide, 73%; hopelessness, 41%; crying spells, 48%.

There is also poor agreement between the ratings for symptoms generated by clinical structured interviews and nonclinical structured interviews. Farmer, Katz, McGuffin, and Bebbington (1987) examined the degree of agreement between ratings for symptoms produced by the PSE (a clinical structured interview) and the CIDI (a nonclinical structured interview). The overall percentage of agreement and *k* values for the symptoms of depression were as follows: inefficient thinking, 63%, .20; poor concentration, 63%, .21; brooding, 58%, .11;

loss of interest, 58%, .03; depressed mood, 77%, .49; hopelessness, 70%, .21; suicidal plans, 83%, .07; morning depression, 73%, .37; social withdrawal, 62%, .07; self-depreciation, 80%, .56; lack of self-confidence, 67%, .28; ideas of reference, 65%, .01; guilty ideas of reference, 77%, .24; pathological guilt, 70%, .29; loss of weight, 87%, .27; delayed sleep, 72%, .36; subjective anergia plus retardation, 72%, .26; early waking, 78%, .48; loss of libido, 58%, .15. The only k values that were significant ($p < .05$ were those for depressed mood, morning depression, self-depreciation, and early waking.

But, whatever the reliability of symptom data, the data may not be valid. For instance, Mazure, Nelson, and Price (1986) examined the concordance between the ratings of symptoms of depression based on observation and interrogation during a semistructured interview administered to 31 depressed inpatients and the ratings of the corresponding behaviors observed by nurses during a concurrent 3-day period. The four symptom ratings based on observation of behavior during interview were significantly correlated with the nurses' ratings: lack of responsiveness, $r = .695$; motor retardation, $r = .528$; agitation $r = .476$; speech retardation, $r = .471$. But only 5 of 12 symptom ratings made by the interviewers on the basis of patients' reports were significantly correlated with the nurses' ratings. Four of the seven symptoms, for which the correlations were not significant, were difficulty falling asleep, $r = .100$; early morning awakening, $r = .337$; loss of energy, $r = .275$; decreased concentration, $r = .148$. These symptoms are generally considered important in the diagnosis of depression and its subclassifications.

Because, as Wing (1988) has noted and the authors of the chapters in this book demonstrate, symptoms are quite complex and their assessment is not likely to be a straightforward and noncontroversial matter, the validity data do not look that good even when researchers focus their assessments on just one specific symptom. As might be expected, this is certainly a problem when measures of specific symptoms of depression use questionnaires and similar self-report measures. For instance, Zuckerman and Lubin (1985) found that in a patient sample, two measures of depressed mood, the Profile of Mood States (POMS; McNair, Lorr, & Droppleman, 1971) and the Multiple Affect Adjective Checklist (MAACL; Zuckerman & Lubin, 1965) had a low intercorrelation ($r = .32$), indicating poor convergent validity. On the other hand, within each measure the corrleation of the measures of depressed mood with the measures of anxious mood was high—for POMS, $r = .77$, and for MAACL, $r = .78$, indicating poor discriminant validity. As Clark and Watson (1991) have argued, it may not be possible to assess depressed mood independently of other negative mood states such as anxiety because of a shared general negative affect component. This would suggest that symptom-oriented research should start with symptoms of depression that can be measured independently of other phenomena.

Even when an interview is used to measure a specific symptom, the data have questionable validity. For instance, Szabadi, Bradshaw, and Besson

(1976) found that, though speech retardation in the form of speech pause time was detectable by objective measures in their depressed patients, it was not observable by trained clinicians. It is probably asking too much to expect patients themselves to be able to give reliable reports concerning their motor behavior. As Robins (1989) noted:

> It is not common to have thought about whether one has moved or talked more slowly than normal for a period of two weeks or more. To answer that question one has to decide within the very brief interval that social convention allows between question and response what is normal for oneself, whether there was ever a period different from that normal pattern, and how long that different period lasted. (p. 62)

Other research has cast doubt on the validity of patients' reports of their symptoms. Watts & Sharrock (1985) developed an hour-long structured interview devoted entirely to the assessment of concentration in depressed patients. They found that only some of the reports of concentration problems were significantly correlated with some of the objective task performance measures of concentration. Kahn, Zarit, Hilbert, and Niedereke (1975) investigated the relationship between memory complaint and impairment in a group of 153 subjects (aged 50 to 91 years), 113 of whom were psychiatric patients. They found that the more depressed the subject was, as measured by the Hamilton Rating Scale for Depression, the more complaints of memory they reported in interview. However, there were no significant relationships between the level of complaint and actual performance on a number of memory tasks or between the degree of depression and actual performance. Similarly, O'Connor, Pollitt, Roth, Brook, and Reiss (1990) found that in a community sample of elderly depressed persons whose mean age was greater than 80 years, the Pearson correlation coefficients between total memory *complaint* and total memory *performance* score was .01. It is interesting to note that the correlation was just as low for normal people, −.05. Watts, MacLeod, and Morris (1988) found that an imagery formation technique improved the objective memory of nonendogenous depressives for a passage of prose but did not have an effect on the patient's subjective estimates of their memory. The complexity of both the subjective and objective aspects of memory and concentration that are supposedly being measured in the few minutes or seconds assigned to them in psychiatric interviews becomes clear on reading Watts's Chapter 6 in this book.

CONCLUSIONS

Despite the valiant efforts of many psychopathologists, the evidence for the reliabilities and validities of current psychiatric interviews and their associated diagnostic systems is not very good. But even if the reliability and validity data were better, there would still be the following disadvantages in taking a syndrome approach to research on depression:

1. The syndrome approach introduces the problem of confounding. For instance, there is confounding in studies that attempt to investigate the relationships between dysphoric mood and cognition by comparing the cognitive processes of people with a diagnosis of depression and nondepressed people since these people differ from one another in a number of respects other than current mood state (Blaney, 1986).
2. The question of whether the phenomena of mood disorders differ qualitatively from normal phenomena is an important one. However, it is not easy to research the question using a syndrome approach because, though there are apparent normal counterparts of symptoms such as dysphoria (sadness), there are no apparent normal counterparts of complex syndromes such as major depression.
3. Research with animal models of psychiatric disorders appears to have been most helpful where there is a distinct, dominant symptom of the disorder. For instance, research on the conditioning and extinction of avoidance responses, though it has by no means provided a final understanding of the etiology of phobias (Costello, 1970; McNally, 1987), has helped to establish the foundations of the effective behavioral approaches to their treatment.

   The promise of the research on learned helplessness (Seligman, 1975) is more apparent when the research findings are used in an attempt to understand some symptoms of depression rather than a syndrome of depression. For instance, it has been demonstrated that:

   > Uncontrollable shocks moderate monoamine activity in the nucleus accumbens but not in the substantia nigra and, in parallel fashion, experience with uncontrollable shocks reduces the rate of self-stimulation at the nucleus accumbens but not at the substantia nigra. Moreover, this is reversible with dimethylimipramine, an antidepressant. (Overmier & Hellhammer, 1988, p. 185).

   These effects of uncontrollable shocks on the CNS sites for the rewarding effects of self-stimulation suggest that the learned helplessness experimental procedure may assist in the understanding of the symptom of anhedonia.

   On the other hand, when the learned helplessness experiment is considered as a model of a syndrome of depression, the argument is not so convincing: Willner (1985), on the basis of his extensive review of the literature, concluded that it was not entirely clear which type of depression learned helplessness models; Overmier & Hellhammer's (1988) review of the same literature led to the conclusion that learned

> helplessness is a model of reactive depression; Healy (1987) concluded that the evidence supported the hypothesis that learned helplessness is a model of endogenous depression. The problem with trying to model depression as a syndrome, as Healy (1987) has noted, is that depression may have a number of etiologies, be phenomenologically disparate, have a number of different substrates, and be differentially responsive to a number of treatments. The condition in humans that we call depression may also manifest itself in a different way in nonhuman species (Hinde, 1976).

The investigation of symptoms of depression should not become an end in itself. The goal of such research should be to establish the syndromes of depression on a firm research footing. Researchers focusing on symptoms would have done only half their work if they had nothing to contribute to our understanding of the nature of syndromes of depression. As Willner (1985) noted, researchers have demonstrated that dopa increases motor behavior but they have not found a cure for any of the depressive illnesses.

The importance of syndromes becomes clear when we consider how treatments such as antidepressant medications work. Antidepressants do not have common acute neurochemical and acute behavioral effects. The biochemical effects of an antidepressant are multiple and are often opposed or unrelated to those induced by other antidepressants. Antidepressants are not euphoriants and do not have some immediate effect on a specific behavior. Rather, the antidepressants appear to work by having an effect on some basic neurophysiological disturbance that underlies a number of interrelated behavioral problems—in other words, a syndrome (Healy, 1987).

On the other hand, it is unlikely that we will ever understand how antidepressant drugs affect clusters of symptoms if we do not investigate their effects on each symptom. In Chapter 4 of this book, Willner presents experimental data indicating the differential effects of antidepressant drugs on two symptoms of depression—anhedonia and social dysfunction.

The pursuit of syndromes of depression must continue then. However, because of the likely complexity of the syndromes and of the symptoms that constitute them, we may be biting off more than we can chew if more research time is not spent on the investigation of specific symptoms and their interrelationships. Kendler (1990) has pointed out some of the problems of developing a psychiatric nosology on a scientific basis when the entry point of research is a currently defined syndrome. One problem is that researchers may agree on what symptoms define a syndrome but disagree in their theories as to the underlying nature of the syndrome. As Kendler put it, the researcher "*cannot* address the validity of a psychiatric disorder where there is disagreement about its proper construct. That is, data can only provide an answer if there is an agreement about what the question is" (p. 970). Kendler gives as an example the debate about the proper construct for schizotypal personality disorder:

> Two positions have been articulated, which may be termed "familial" and "clinical." The familial position defines schizotypal personality disorder as a nonpsychotic schizophrenia-like syndrome that occurs commonly in relatives of schizophrenics and uncommonly in other individuals. . . . The clinical construct for schizotypal personality disorder assumes that this syndrome should describe patients seen in the clinic who, despite absence of classic symptoms of psychoses, nonetheless have substantial schizophrenialike symptoms. (p. 971)

These two constructs would require two different methods of validation. Eventually it will be necessary to gain knowledge on how a number of symptoms may arise together or in close temporal proximity and how one therapeutic agent may remove them all. But an understanding of the functional relationships between symptoms would seem to be impossible without a thorough knowledge of the nature of the symptoms themselves.

Even when we do naturalistic, quasi-experimental studies, monitoring the changes in one or two symptoms and investigating the causes of those changes would seem to be a much easier task than attempting to monitor the changes in a syndrome and determining the factors associated with those changes.

Should we decide to take a symptom approach, the question then arises as to which symptoms we should choose to investigate. If we are doing animal research, objective symptoms such as motor retardation will be more amenable to investigation than subjective ones such as poor concentration. But, in general, our selection of symptoms for study should be determined by our theories concerning the role played by the symptoms in the diathesis, etiology, and pathogenesis of psychiatric syndromes. But we will not be able to develop promising theories of the role played by symptoms until we have a more thorough knowledge of the symptoms themselves. It is for this reason that the authors of the following chapters of this book thoroughly and critically review our current knowledge of each symptom of depression.

REFERENCES

American Psychiatric Association. (1980). *Diagnostic and statistical manual of mental disorders* (3rd ed.; DSM-III). Washington, DC: Author.

American Psychiatric Association. (1987). *Diagnostic and statistical manual of mental disorders* (3rd ed.-rev.; DSM-III-R). Washington DC: Author.

Andreason, N. C., McDonald-Scott, P., Grove, W. M., Keller, M. D., Shapiro, R. W., & Hirschfeld, R. M. A. (1982). Assessment of reliability in multicenter collaborative research using a videotape approach. *American Journal of Psychiatry, 139,* 876–882.

Anthony, J. C., & Dryman, A. (1987, September). *Analysis of discrepancy in lifetime diagnosis of mental disorders: Results from the NIMH Epidemiologic Catchment Area Program.* World Psychiatric Association, Section on Epidemiology and Community Psychiatry, Reykjavik, Iceland.

Beidel, D. C., & Turner, S. M. (1986). A critique of the theoretical bases of cognitive-behavioral theories and therapy. *Clinical Psychology Review, 6,* 177–197.

Blaney, P. H. (1986). Affect and memory: A review. *Psychological Bulletin, 99,* 229–246.

Blazer, D., Swartz, M., Woodbury, M., Manton, K., Hughes, D., & George, L. K. (1988). Depressive symptoms and depressive diagnoses in a community population. *Archives of General Psychiatry, 45,* 1078–1084.

Brockington, I. F., Helzer, J. E., Hillier, V. F., & Frances, A. F. (1982). Definitions of depression: Concordance and prediction of outcome. *American Journal of Psychiatry, 139,* 1022–1027.

Bromet, E. J., Dunn, L. O., Connell, M. M., Dew, M. A., & Schulberg, H. C. (1986). Long term reliability of diagnosing lifetime major depression in a community sample. *Archives of General Psychiatry, 43,* 435–440.

Burnam, M. A., Karno, M., Hough, R. L., Escobar, J. I., & Forsythe, A. B. (1983). The Spanish Diagnostic Interview Schedule: Reliability and comparison with clinical diagnoses. *Archives of General Psychiatry, 40,* 1189–1196.

Carney, M. W. P., Roth, N., & Garside, R. F. (1965). The diagnosis of depressive syndromes and the prediction of ECT response. *British Journal of Psychiatry, 111,* 659–674.

Cicchetti, D. V., & Prusoff, B. A. (1983). Reliability of depression and associated clinical symptoms. *Archives of General Psychiatry, 40,* 987–990.

Clark, L. A., & Watson, D. (1991). Tripartite model of anxiety and depression: Psychometric evidence and taxonomic implications. *Journal of Abnormal Psychology, 100,* 316–336.

Cohen, J. (1960). A coefficient of agreement for nominal scales. *Educational and Psychological Measurement, 20,* 37–46.

Cooper, J. E., Copeland, J. R. M., Brown, G. W., Harris, T., & Gourlay, A. J. (1977). Further studies on interviewer training and inter-rater reliability of the Present State Examination (PSE). *Psychological Medicine, 7,* 517–523.

Costello, C. G. (1970). Dissimilarities between conditioned avoidance responses and phobias. *Psychological Review, 77,* 250–254.

Cottler, L. B., Robins, L. N., Grant, B. F., Blaine, J., Towle, L. H., Wittchen, H.-U., & Sartorius, N. (1991). The CIDI-core substance abuse and dependence questions: Cross-cultural and nosological issues. *British Journal of Psychiatry, 159,* 653–658.

Davidson, J., Turnbull, C., Strickland, R., & Belyea, M. (1984). Comparative diagnostic criteria for melancholia and endogenous depression. *Archives of General Psychiatry, 41,* 506–511.

Dean, C., Surtees, P. G., & Sashidharan, S. P. (1983). Comparison of research diagnostic systems in an Edinburgh community sample. *British Journal of Psychiatry, 142,* 247–256.

Endicott, J., Cohen, J., Nee, J., Fleiss, J., & Sarantakos, S. (1981). Hamilton Depression Rating Scale: Extracted from regular and change versions of the Schedule for Affective Disorders and Schizophrenia. *Archives of General Psychiatry, 38,* 98–103.

Endicott, J., & Spitzer, R. L. (1978). A diagnostic interview: The Schedule for Affective Disorders and Schizophrenia. *Archives of General Psychiatry, 35,* 837–844.

Farmer, A. E., Katz, R., McGuffin, P., & Bebbington, P. (1987). A comparison between the Present State Examination and the Composite International Diagnostic Interview. *Archives of General Psychiatry, 44,* 1064–1068.

Feinberg, M., & Carroll, B. J. (1982). Separation of subtypes of depression using discriminant analysis: Part 1 (separation of unipolar endogenous depression from non-endogenous depression). *British Journal of Psychiatry, 140,* 284–391.

Fendrich, M., Weissman, M. M., Warner, V., & Mufson, L. (1990). Two-year recall of lifetime diagnoses in offspring at high and low risk for major depression. *Archives of General Psychiatry, 47,* 1121–1127.

George, L. K., Blazer, D. G., Woodbury, M. A., & Mason, K. G. (1989). Internal consistency of DSM-III diagnoses. In L. N. Robins & J. E. Barrett (Eds.), *The validity of psychiatric diagnoses* (pp. 99–121). New York: Raven Press.

Golden, R. N., & Janowsky, D. S. (1990). Biological theories of depression. In B. B. Wolman & G. Stricker (Eds.), *Depressive disorders: Facts, theories and treatment methods.* (pp. 3–21). New York: Wiley.

Grove, W. M., Andreason, N. C., McDonald-Scott, P., Keller, M. B., & Shapiro, R. W. (1981). Reliability studies of psychiatric diagnosis. *Archives of General Psychiatry, 38,* 408–413.

Healy, D. (1987). The comparative psychopathology of affective disorders in animals and humans. *Journal of Psychopharmacology, 1,* 193–210.

Helzer, J. E., Robins, L. N., McEvoy, L. T., Spitznagel, E. L., Stoltzman, R. K., Farmer, A., & Brockington, I. F. (1985). A comparison of clinical and Diagnostic Interview Schedule diagnoses: Physician re-examination of lay-interviewed cases in the general population. *Archives of General Psychiatry, 42,* 657–666.

Helzer, J. E., Spitznagel, E. L., & McEvoy, L. (1987). The predictive validity of lay Diagnostic Interview Schedule diagnoses in the general population. *Archives of General Psychiatry, 44,* 1069–1077.

Hesselbrock, V., Stabenau, J., Hesselbrock, N., Mirkin, P., & Meyer, R. (1982). A comparison of two interview schedules: The Schedule for Affective Disorders and Schizophrenia-Lifetime and the National Institute for Mental Health Diagnostic Interview Schedule. *Archives of General Psychiatry, 39,* 674–677.

Hinde, R. A. (1976). The use of differences and similarities in comparative psychopathology. In G. Serban & A. Kling (Eds.), *Animal Models in Human Psychobiology* (pp. 187–202). New York: Plenum.

Kahn, R. L., Zarit, S. H., Hilbert, N. M., & Niedereke, G. (1975). Memory complaint and impairment in the aged: The effect of depression and altered brain function. *Archives of General Psychiatry, 32,* 1569–1573.

Katschnig, H., Nutzinger, D., & Schanda, H. (1986). Validating depressive subtypes. In H. Hippius, G. Klerman, & N. Matussek (Eds.), *New results in depression research* (pp. 36–43). New York: Springer-Verlag.

Kendell, R. E., Everitt, B., Cooper, J. E., Sartorius, N., & David, M. E. (1968). The reliability of the "Present State Examination." *Social Psychiatry, 3,* 123–129.

Kendler, K. S. (1990). Towards a scientific psychiatric nosology: Strengths and limitations. *Archives of General Psychiatry, 47,* 969–973.

Lesage, A. D., Cyr, M., & Toupin, J. (1991). Reliable use of the Present State Examination by psychiatric nurses for clinical studies of psychotic and nonpsychotic patients. *Acta Psychiatrica Scandinavica, 83,* 121–124.

Luria, R. E., & Berry, R. (1980). Teaching the Present State Examination in America. *American Journal of Psychiatry, 137,* 26–31.

Luria, R. E., & McHugh, P. R. (1974). Reliability and clinical utility of the "Wing" Present State Examination. *Archives of General Psychiatry, 30,* 866–871.

Mazure, C., & Gershon, E. S. (1979). Blindness and reliability in lifetime psychiatric diagnosis. *Archives of General Psychiatry, 43,* 451–456.

McNair, D. M., Lorr, M., & Droppleman, L. F. (1971). *Manual for the Profile of Mood States (POMS).* San Diego, CA: Educational and Industrial Testing Service.

McNally, R. J. (1987). Preparedness and phobias: A review. *Psychological Bulletin, 101,* 283–303.

O'Connor, D. W., Pollitt, P. A., Roth, M., Brook, P. B., & Reiss, B. B. (1990). Memory complaints and impairment in normal, depressed, and demented elderly persons identified in a community survey. *Archives of General Psychiatry, 47,* 224–227.

Orvaschel, H., Puig-Antich, J., Chambers, L. W., Tabrizi, M. A., & Johnson, R. A. (1982). Retrospective assessments of prepubertal major depression with the Kiddie-SADS-E. *Journal of the American Academy of Child and Adolescent Psychiatry, 21,* 392–397.

Overmier, J. B., & Hellhammer, D. H. (1988). The learned helplessness model of human depression. *Animal Models of Psychiatric Disorder, 2,* 177–202.

Paykel, E. S. (1985). The Clinical Interview for Depression: Development, reliability and validity. *Journal of Affective Disorders, 9,* 85–96.

Philipp, M., Maier, W., & Benkert, O. (1986). Dimensional classification as an instrument for biological research in endogenous depression. In H. Hippius, G. Klerman, & N. Matussek (Eds.), *New results in depression research* (pp. 145–155). New York: Springer-Verlag.

Prusoff, B. A., Merikangas, K. R., & Weissman, M. M. (1988). Lifetime prevalence and age of onset of psychiatric disorders: Recall four years later. *Journal of Psychiatric Research, 22,* 107–117.

Robins, L. N. (1989). Diagnostic grammar and assessment: Translating criteria into questions. *Psychological Medicine, 19,* 57–68.

Robins, L. N., Helzer, J. E., Croughan, J., & Ratcliff, K. S. (1981). National Institute of Mental Health Diagnostic Interview Schedule: Its history, characteristics and validity. *Archives of General Psychiatry, 38,* 381–389.

Robins, L. N., Helzer, J. E., Ratcliff, K. S., & Seyfried, W. (1982). Validity of the Diagnostic Interview Schedule, Version II: DSM-III diagnoses. *Psychological Medicine, 12,* 855–870.

Sashidharan, S. P. (1985). Definitions of psychiatric syndromes—comparison in hospital patients and general population. *British Journal of Psychiatry, 147,* 547–551.

Seligman, M. E. P. (1975). *Helplessness: On depression, development and death.* San Francisco: Freeman.

Semler, G., Wittchen, H-U., Josche, K., Zaudig, M., von Geiso, T., Kaiser, S., von Cranach, N., & Pfister, H. (1987). Test-retest reliability of a standardized psychiatric interview (DIS/CIDI). *European Archives of Psychiatry and Neurological Sciences, 236,* 214–222.

Shrout, P. E., Spitzer, R. L., & Fleiss, J. L. (1987). Quantifications of agreement in psychiatric diagnosis revisited. *Archives of General Psychiatry, 44,* 172–177.

Spitzer, R. L., Endicott, J., & Robins, E. (1978). Research Diagnostic Criteria: Rationale and reliability. *Archives of General Psychiatry, 35,* 773–782.

Spitznagel, E. L., & Helzer, J. E. (1985). A proposed solution to the base rate problem in the Kappa statistic. *Archives of General Psychiatry, 42,* 725–728.

Sturt, E., Bebbington, P., Hurry, J., & Tennant, C. (1981). The Present State Examination used by interviewers from a survey agency: Report from the MRC Camberwell Community Survey. *Psychological Medicine, 11,* 185–192.

Szabadi, E., Bradshaw, C. M., & Besson, I. A. O. (1976). Elongation of pause-time in speech: A simple objective measure of motor retardation in depression. *British Journal of Psychiatry, 129,* 592–597.

van den Brink, W., Maarten, W. J., Koeter, W. J., Ormel, J., Dijkstra, W., Giel, R., Slooff, C. J., Tamar, D., & Wohlfarth, M. A. (1989). Psychiatric diagnosis in an outpatient population. *Archives of General Psychiatry, 46,* 369–372.

Vandiver, T., & Sher, K. J. (1991). Temporal stability of the Diagnostic Interview Schedule. *Psychological Assessment: A Journal of Consulting and Clinical Psychology, 3,* 277–281.

Verghese, A., Burrows, G., Foenander, G., Stevenson, J., & Davies, B. (1976). Observer variation and depressive phenomenology. *Psychological Medicine, 6,* 587–590.

Watts, F. N., MacLeod, A. K, & Morris, L. (1988). A remedial strategy for memory and concentration problems in depressed patients. *Cognitive Therapy and Research, 12,* 185–193.

Watts, F. N., & Sharrock, R. (1985). Description and measurement of concentration problems in depressed patients. *Psychological Medicine, 15,* 317–326.

Weissman, M. M., & Myers, J. K. (1978). Affective disorders in a U.S. urban community: The use of Research Diagnostic Criteria in an epidemiological survey. *Archives of General Psychiatry, 35,* 1304–1311.

Wells, K. B., Burnham, M. A., Leake, B., & Robins, L. N. (1988). Agreement between face-to-face and telephone-administered versions of the depression section of the NIMH Diagnostic Interview Schedule. *Journal of Psychiatric Research, 22,* 207–220.

Willner, P. (1985). *Depression: A psychobiological synthesis.* New York: Wiley.

Wing, J. K. (1988). Abandoning what? *British Journal of Clinical Psychology, 27,* 325–328.

Wing, J. K., Birley, J. L. T., Cooper, J. E., Graham, P., & Isaacs, A. D. (1967). Reliability of a procedure for measuring and classifying "present psychiatric state." *British Journal of Psychiatry, 113,* 499–515.

Wing, J. K., Cooper, J., & Sartorius, N. (1974). *The measurement and classification of psychiatric symptoms.* Cambridge: Cambridge University Press.

Wing, J. K., Nixon, J. M., Mann, S. A., & Leff, J. P. (1977). Reliability of the PSE (ninth edition) used in a population study. *Psychological Medicine, 7,* 505–516.

Wittchen, H.-U., Robins, L. N., Cottler, L. B., Sartorius, N., Burke, J. D., & Regier, D. (1991). Cross-cultural feasibility, reliability and sources of variance of the Composite International Diagnostic Interview (CIDI). *British Journal of Psychiatry, 159,* 645–653.

Zimmerman, M., Coryell, W., Pfohl, B., & Stangl, D. (1985). Four definitions of endogenous depression and the dexamethasone suppression test. *Journal of Affective Disorders, 8,* 37–45.

Zimmerman, M., Coryell, W., Pfohl, B., & Stangl, D. (1986). The validity of four definitions of endogenous depression: II. Clinical, demographic, familial and psychosocial correlates. *Archives of General Psychiatry, 43,* 234–244.

Zimmerman, M., & Spitzer, R. L. (1989). Melancholia: From DSM-III to DSM-III-R. *American Journal of Psychiatry, 146,* 20–28.

Zuckerman, M., & Lubin, B. (1965). *The Multiple Affect Adjective Checklist.* San Diego, CA: Educational and Industrial Testing Service.

Zuckerman, M., & Lubin, B. (1985). *Manual for the Multiple Affect Adjective Checklist—Revised.* San Diego, CA: Educational and Industrial Testing Service.

CHAPTER 2

Dysphoria

DAVID HEALY

INTRODUCTION

Any model of depression must be able to account for the central affective disturbances in the illness. This is not merely a question of explaining why a person might feel sad and low but also of accounting for the nature of the mood disturbance. There are three issues: the severity of the disturbance, the distinct quality of the affective changes in depression, and their diurnal variation. Unfortunately for the purposes of this chapter, dysphoria itself and the questions of its severity, distinct quality, and diurnal variation are among the most neglected areas of research in depression.

This chapter will focus on these issues in three ways. First, aspects of the literature pertinent to the severity, distinct quality, and diurnal variation of depressed mood will be reviewed. Second, some data pertinent to each of these questions will be provided. Third, a model that might account for the data and observations from the literature will be offered. However, given the present state of our knowledge about depressive dysphoria, readers should regard the literature review, the data, and the suggested model with considerable caution, that is, as little more than notes.

SEVERITY OF DEPRESSED MOOD

Psychological theories have had some limitations in explaining the severity of the mood disturbance in depression. For example, the learned helplessness hypothesis suggests that affective changes follow associatively from expected loss of control (Maier & Seligman, 1976): "Depressive affect is a consequence of learning that outcomes are uncontrollable" (Abramson, Seligman, & Teasdale, 1978, p. 60). The only elaboration on this is to suggest that the intensity of the affect correlates with the desirability or aversiveness of the outcome (Abramson et al., 1978), which runs directly counter to clinical experience, in which there is often "no correlation between the severity of the precipitating event and the severity of the subsequent self-reproach" (Schneider, 1959, p. 52).

This issue may be clarified to some extent by appealing to a traditional distinction between mood and emotion. Although both may be subsumed under the term *affect,* they have frequently been distinguished semantically and clinically (Healy, 1987). In some sense, mood is to emotion as climate is to weather. Alternatively, mood, like the pedals of an organ, may color the emotional tune, whereas the emotions correspond to the variety of melodies that may be played (Healy, in press).

The physiological accompaniments of emotions tend to be relatively nonspecific and do not differ dramatically from the normal range of physiological variation (Lyons, 1980), in contrast to the physiological components of endogenomorphic depression. These vary dramatically from the norm with major neurovegetative and neuropsychological changes, which have a temporal stability and autonomy.

Biological hypotheses, by focusing on neurobiological disruption, might seem better equipped to explain a severity of affective disturbance that is independent of the precipitating event's aversiveness. There is, however, a further possibility, which is that both biological and psychological factors play a part in generating the affective changes found in depression.

Healy and Williams (1988) proposed that the pertinent biological disturbance might involve a disruption of circadian rhythms; this model is described later in this chapter. In favor of such a proposal is that jet lag and shift work maladaptation syndromes, which clearly do involve circadian rhythm disturbances, are characterized by a pervasive dysphoria (Healy & Waterhouse 1991). A problem with this proposal, however, is that the affective changes found in these conditions do not have the severity associated with depression.

This discrepancy may be resolved by a further aspect of the Healy and Williams (1988) proposal, in which it was suggested that the development of dysphoria, anergia, apathy, and neurovegetative disturbances consequent on circadian rhythm disruption would introduce uncontrollability into the most intimate areas of personal functioning. The learned helplessness proposal that the severity of the affective disturbances found in depression should correlate with perceived uncontrollability might apply to this further uncontrollability, as opposed to the uncontrollability of whatever environmental disruption triggered the disorder. Healy and Williams (1988) proposed that biological disturbances, particularly if they have a mild but pervasive quality, might mobilize cognitive distortions and in so doing intensify a depressive disorder and contribute to its chronicity (see also Williams, 1985; Healy, 1990).

There is some evidence in favor of this suggestion. In a recent study carried out by the author and colleagues (Williams, Healy, Teasdale, White, & Paykel 1990), 44 of 49 patients who met criteria for major depressive disorder (33 endogenous subtype, 7 possibly endogenous, and 4 nonendogenous) completed a Dysfunctional Attitude Questionnaire (DAQ; Burns, 1980) on admission to treatment, after 6 weeks of treatment and 6 months after their first admission. Despite the endogenomorphic features of the subjects' disorders, a high DAQ score predicted persistence of the disorder at 6 weeks despite effective biological treatment (Williams et al., 1990).

Persistence of the index disorder in individuals with high DAQ scores was not simply a matter of selecting individuals who were more likely to be chronic by virtue of having had a greater number of previous episodes or a longer duration of illness before admission to treatment, because controlling for these factors did not alter the findings. Nor was it a matter of the less endogenomorphic subjects having a greater amount of cognitive distortion and becoming more severely and chronically depressed as a consequence, because high DAQ scores were found in subjects who scored both high and low on the Newcastle Diagnostic Index (Carney, Roth, & Garside, 1965) and in both groups predicted persistence of the depressive episode (Williams et al., 1990).

Peselow and colleagues have reported a related set of findings (Peselow, Robins, Block, Barouche, & Fieve, 1990). In their study of 112 patients they found that depressed subjects had higher DAQ scores than normals and that these scores fell with drug treatment. The higher the DAQ score, the poorer the response to treatment.

Such findings are consistent with Teasdale's (1988a) suggestion that endogenous changes in mood may affect cognitive aspects secondarily but that it is the degree to which these dysfunctional cognitions are affected that then renders a person vulnerable to persistent depression or future relapse. The more an individual under the influence of pervasive dysphoria turns to global negative self-judgments, the harder it will be for them to escape from their depressed mood.

Returning to the distinctions between mood and emotion outlined earlier, these findings suggest that the more people become emotional about being depressed, the deeper the pit they dig for themselves. In this case, the emotions would be sadness, guilt, and misery. But if sadness, guilt, and misery are negative emotions overlaid on but not intrinsically part of depressed mood, we are left with the question of the nature of specifically depressive dysphoria and the problem that any attempt to characterize it is likely to be compounded by its penumbra of negative emotions (Healy, 1990).

Two aspects of the dysphoria found in depression, however, appear to pertain to its core nature; its so-called distinct quality and its seeming intrinsic variability. I will consider these next, before offering a specific proposal regarding the nature of depressive dysphoria.

DISTINCT QUALITY OF MOOD

Current operational criteria for major depressive disorders, which supposedly are theoretically neutral, note that the dysphoria found in endogenomorphic depressions is distinct from the sadness or unhappiness that is the normal reaction to adversity (Carney, et al., 1965; Spitzer, Endicott, & Robins, 1978). There are, however, a number of paradoxes about this. One is that despite its distinctiveness, there have been notable difficulties in specifying its peculiar quality. A further paradox is that despite difficulties in specifying the precise nature of this distinct quality, rating its presence on an instrument such as the Clinical Interview for Depression produces higher interrater reliability than is found for almost any other symptom of depression (Paykel 1985).

In one of the few attempts to pinpoint what is distinctive about depressive dysphoria in contrast to normal sadness, Ramos-Brieva and colleagues (1987) isolated a number of features of depressed mood that appeared to mark it out from the normal reactions of sadness in response to psychological stresses. Taking a cognitive behavioral approach, they established that the dysphoria of depression is characterized by associated constructs of tiredness, internality, uncontrollability, invariability of emotional reactivity, lack of hope, inexplicability, the loss of a sense of courage, and a sense that this state was unusual.

While these findings are almost certainly true, it is difficult to consider them in terms of the distinction between moods and emotions, outlined earlier. Do they refer to the actual quality of mood as found in depression or do they refer to the cognitive-emotional reactions mobilized by depressive dysphoria? Another attempt to characterize depressive dysphoria that aimed explicitly, insofar as was possible in a pilot study, at avoiding associated cognitive constructs was carried out in the study of dysfunctional attitudes (Williams et al., 1990).

In this study, a Quality of Mood Questionnaire and Checklist was also delivered to 39 of the 49 subjects recruited. (The first 10 subjects were missed owing to a delay in preparing the scale.) A checklist of adjectives was drawn up, constructed from the categories on hope, pain, sadness, and bitterness in *Roget's Thesaurus*. In the final list, however, all explicit references to the usual descriptors for depressed mood were omitted. This led to the exclusion of the words hopelessness, sadness, guilt, misery, and so on. The words were then grouped into 6 groups based on broad similarity of meaning, as follows:

1.	2.	3.
heavy	fetid	dismayed
numb	bitter	disquieted
frozen	sour	bothered
paralyzed	stale	burdened
dopey	flat	disgusted
drugged	insipid	dispirited
deadened	poisonous	afflicted
clumsy	blighted	oppressed
sluggish	nauseated	wretched

4. awful	5. exhausted	6. raw
horrid	listless	bruised
harrowing	blank	aching
black	empty	tender
tormented	out of sorts	brittle
gloomy	purposeless	tightened up
forlorn	wilted	boring
somber	dull	sore
desolate	powerless	suffocating
bleak	washed out	unbearable

Before seeing these lists, subjects were invited to describe their own mood using the first words that came to mind, with an emphasis on how they actually thought they felt rather than on their attitude to either the future or the past. Following this description in their own words, they were invited to circle the words that "capture some aspect of how your mood feels." No limit was put on the number of words that could be checked. It was hoped that the pattern of words endorsed by subjects would provide a characterization of depressed mood, in much the same way that individuals with pains in different bodily locations and pathologies endorse different descriptors on Pain Questionnaires (Melzack & Wall, 1982).

The words from the list that were endorsed most frequently were as follows:

Dispirited (20).
Sluggish; wretched (19).
Empty; washed out; awful; bothered; dull (18).
Listless; tightened up (17).
Exhausted; gloomy (16).
Burdened (15).
Desolate; powerless; purposeless (14).

It would certainly seem that the words endorsed most frequently in the survey are not the words that people who are simply miserable or unhappy would be likely to offer spontaneously. Dispirited, sluggish, empty, and washed out suggest a somewhat different state from the normal experience of sadness. To find out whether there is any specificity of such descriptors to depressive dysphoria, further studies would have to be carried out with individuals having other clinical conditions and in extraclinical situations with subjects following adverse events.

However, a list such as this raises a great many problems. A number of the words are open to several interpretations. Terms such as dull and boring were intended to characterize a mood state, just as they can be used to describe a pain; but they may also have been taken by the individual to describe themselves. A word such as purposeless may describe an experience or an existential situation.

Ideally, it would also be useful to have some estimate of the natural frequency of use of these words in the regional population from which these subjects were drawn. For example, it is likely that words such as awful, washed out, wretched, and empty occur naturally with much greater frequency than dispirited, listless, and sluggish. This natural bias may have colored the selection of words.

Finally the grouping of words into clusters may have affected endorsement. For what it is worth, however, words in the *listless* cluster, which appears broadly to describe a loss of motivation, were endorsed 138 times; words in the *dispirited* cluster, 114 times; words in the *gloomy* cluster, 104 times; the *sluggish* cluster, 86 times; the *raw* cluster, 83 times; and the *bitter* cluster, 47 times.

Of interest also were the words that were least often checked. Some of these were quite surprising. The *bitter* cluster of words was based on the author's impression that many individuals endorse the poetry of Gerald Manley Hopkins as a penetrating description of depressed or desolate states. His imagery tends to focus on the bitter taste of the self in the desolate state. However, in this study, other than the word bitter itself, which was checked 13 times, related words were endorsed least frequently. In particular the words sour and poisonous received no endorsements at all and words such as fetid (1), blighted (2), insipid (5), and stale (5) received very few endorsements.

More surprisingly, perhaps, the words horrid (3), harrowing (1), somber (5), and out of sorts (6) also received few endorsements. The words that might be seen as being the most explicit descriptors of pain were also endorsed infrequently—raw (9), bruised (6), aching (8), tender (3), suffocating (5), and sore (2), with even unbearable only being endorsed on 10 occasions.

All subjects were also rated on Paykel's Clinical Interview for Depression (Paykel, 1985a), which has a distinct quality of mood subscale. This 7-point scale is rated in response to the question "Now I would like to compare the feelings of depression you have had recently with times in the past when you have felt depressed—the ordinary feeling of depression that everybody gets from time to time when things are going badly. What I want to ask is if this feeling is like those feelings or different from them—not just more severe but a different kind of feeling." Ratings of 1 are given for no difference, 2 for minimal differences, 3 for probable but mild differences, 4 for definite moderate differences, 5 for marked differences, 6 for severe differences, and 7 for extreme differences.

Of the 39 subjects, 17 rated a 5; 15, a 4; 6, either 3 or 2; and 1, a 6. Comparing the results of those subjects who rated either a 5 or 6 with the remainder, there was no statistically significant difference in the frequency of words endorsed.

As mentioned earlier, prior to checking the words that best described their mood, depressed subjects were asked to write down the first words that came to mind to describe their mood. This led to a variety of descriptions ranging from one or two words to one or two pages of comments. Broadly speaking, the descriptions fell into four categories. The commonest primary description was of the experience of lethargy and inability to do things, whether because of tiredness, a specific inability to summon up effort, a feeling of being inhibited, or an inability to envisage the future. These all seemed closely linked.

The next most common description was of a sense of detachment from the environment. This could involve being detached to the point where the appearances of things seemed altered, such as reporting that even the colors of things were changed—typically in the direction of being less clear, less vivid. More commonly, however, the experience of detachment was in terms of being unable to interact with others. This experience ranged from an experience bordering on the form of dissociation found in anxiety to the experience of isolation and loneliness. In the main, however, the experiences of these subjects seemed to differ from those found in dissociative anxiety states.

The next most common descriptor of the mood was of physical changes that were described in terms of feeling that the subject was coming down with a viral illness, either influenza or glandular fever, along with descriptions of aches and pains and, in particular, headaches or numbness of the head or tight bands around the head or a feeling of a balloon being inflated within the head. A number of subjects described a combination of any two of these sets of descriptions or indeed all three.

In addition to the drawbacks to this study previously outlined, a number of further problems become apparent in this section of the study. There was no attempt to standardize for level of intelligence or sociocultural background. It seems highly likely that the sophistication of the description provided would correlate in some way with sociocultural background. This is likely also to apply to a number of the words endorsed in the lists section of the questionnaire.

THE DEPRESSIVE EXPERIENCE OF TIME

One further aspect of depression contributes to the distinctive experience that is depression: the altered awareness of the passage of time commonly experienced by depressed subjects but rarely asked for clinically and even more infrequently investigated systematically. Intuitively, a change in the experience of time, such that time appears to be passing more slowly, seems likely to be linked into the listlessness and anergia that appears typical of depressive dysphoria. It might also play some part in generating the specifically depressive form of dissociation that appeared to emerge from subjects' descriptions of their own mood state.

There is a long tradition of recognition that time passes slowly in depression (Strauss, 1928). Two factors could be involved here, either of which could be deranged. One may be an alteration in the ability to make judgments about objective time and the other specific alterations in the experience of time. The latter, in turn, involves an awareness of both the constancy and continuity of time (time awareness) and the direction of time (time perspective).

As regards objective time judgment in depression, a number of studies have found this to be normal (Bech, 1975; Kitamura & Kumar, 1983; Lehmann, 1967; Melges & Fougerousse, 1966; Mezey & Cohen, 1961). Others have found time judgment to be disturbed although differences in method and terminology make these studies difficult to compare (Dilling & Rabin, 1967; Kuhs et al., 1989; Tysk, 1984; Wyrick & Wyrick, 1977).

Whereas objective time judgment has been found to be normal in the preceding studies, a number of these same studies have found that it characteristically *feels* slower (Bech, 1975; Kitamura & Kumar, 1983; Lehmann, 1967; Mezey & Cohen, 1961; Wyrick & Wyrick, 1977). Slowing of time may represent a kind of temporal anaesthesia (Jaspers, 1959), or it may be delusional or dissociative (Hamilton, 1985).

Initial suggestions were that the slowing of time would be linked to psychomotor retardation (Lewis, 1932; Mezey & Cohen, 1961). This was not confirmed by Bech (1975). Authors, who have not found an association between slowing of time experience and psychomotor retardation, have tended to find one with global severity of the depressive syndrome (Bech, 1975; Kitamura & Kumar, 1982). Most recently, Blewett (1992) has reported an association between altered time experience and both retardation and severity of a depressive episode. All these studies are complicated, however, by a further observation reported by Blewett: When investigated closely, 75% of individuals reporting abnormally slowed time experience stated their experience of the passage of time fluctuated from hour to hour.

A further level of complexity exists because there appears to be some difference between time perception of events that do not exceed 5 seconds—"the psychological present"—and time estimation for longer intervals in which memory processes play a part. In general, there appears to be a greater amount of error in retrospective time judgments, where subjects are told after the time interval that they must estimate its duration, than in prospective time judgments (Hicks, Miller, & Kinsbourne, 1976; Hicks, Miller, Gaes, & Biermann, 1977). Furthermore, the content of the time interval influences judgments, suggesting that what is perceived is not an estimation of time but rather of internal or external events taking place in time (Fraisse, 1984).

Such findings raise the Heisenbergian prospect that the depressive experience of time might be altered by the act of investigating it. This would apply also to the distinct quality of depressive dysphoria, if as seems possible, an altered experience of time contributes to or stems from the same basic disturbance that gives rise to depressive dysphoria.

DIURNAL VARIATION OF MOOD

One of the most enigmatic clinical features of depressed mood is its diurnal variation, which is prototypically worst in the morning and ameliorates during the day. The neglect of the detailed nature of affect by both psychological and biological hypotheses of depression conveniently avoids this issue. How could stable persistent attributions simultaneously persist over weeks or months and fluctuate so dramatically over short periods? Conversely, why should postulated abnormalities of central amines, for example, not lead to a dysphoria of invariant quality (or quantity)?

As well as the long-standing association between morning dysphoria and endogenomorphic depression, there has been an association between evening dysphoria and neurotic depression. In a recent prospective study of this issue, however, Carpenter, Kupfer, and Frank (1986) were unable to confirm this finding. They specifically found that individuals who had an evening dysphoria had a higher incidence of decreased appetite than those with morning dysphoria. They also found that individuals with clear diurnal variation of mood, with either morning or evening dysphoria, tended on the one hand to have longer episodes of depressions but on the other to experience a more rapid clinical response to treatment than those with no marked diurnal variation at all. Finally, Carpenter et al. (1986) found that morning dysphoria appeared particularly associated with retardation and an absence of agitation.

There is some debate about the stage of a depressive episode in which diurnal variation is most typically found. Beck (1967) has suggested that it occurs more frequently in severe depression than in minor stages of depression, whereas Huston (1967) suggested that it appears more frequently in the minor stages of depression. A study by Waldmann (1972) indicated that diurnal variation may be lost in the most severe stages of a depressive episode, which throws up the possibility that diurnal variation may be absent initially, appear at moderate levels of intensity, and disappear again at the severest levels of intensity.

In favor of the suggestion that diurnal variation of mood is likely to present in mild depressions and be lost as the disorder becomes more severe are studies by Middelhoff (1967) and Waldmann (1972), which found that diurnal variation of mood was present in a substantial proportion of individuals during symptom-free intervals. It did not, therefore, only appear with the onset of depression, although the number of people affected with diurnal variation increased with the onset of a depressive episode.

However, all these proposals are compromised by a number of studies suggesting that this prototypical feature of depression has no typical presentation. Stallone, Huba, Lawlor, and Fieve (1973) looked intensively at a small group of patients and found that diurnal variation is not a stable pattern for individuals. In some cases, it may be present at one point of an illness and absent later on, for no obvious reason. When present, it is so for variable lengths of time during the day, even in individuals who believe themselves to have a typical and consistent pattern of mood variation.

In another study using a similar intensive design, Tolle and Goetze (1987) found that the typical diurnal variation of morning dysphoria is irregular and intraindividually unstable. They questioned 63 depressed subjects, among which were 35 endogenomorphic depressives, over a total of 273 days and found an unexpected lack of pattern to the daily course of the depressive state. They concluded that daily rhythms in mood are polymorphic. Reliable regularities cannot be established either intraindividually or in subgroups of subjects. In fact, they found that a constant state of mood during the day was the most frequent finding with typical diurnal variation being noted in only about one third of the patients. However, within this relatively constant state, they noted that there appeared to be a number of ultradian rhythms regarding which reliable data is virtually nonexistent. There must be some doubt as to whether these can be investigated properly in view of the numerous situational variables likely to influence mood during the course of the day.

Of the 39 subjects who completed forms on the quality of their mood, the diurnal variation of their mood was also assessed with a set of questions that retrospectively appear biased toward detecting morning dysphoria. The questionnaire asked subjects whether their mood varied during the day; if it did, subjects were asked whether it was worse in the morning, and if so, at what time it improved and why they thought it improved when it did.

Nine subjects reported that their mood was invariant, 24 reported that they were worse in the morning, 2 that they were worse in the evening, and 4 that the period of maximum dysphoria could be at any point during the day. (A particularly interesting description of diurnal variation was given by one subject who found that his mood was worse physically in the morning but mentally in the evening.)

Of those who had morning dysphoria, 11 said that it typically cleared up by noon, 9 that the time in which it cleared could vary markedly, and 4 that it cleared only by the evening.

Of those with morning dysphoria, 13 attributed their worse mood in the morning to the thought of the day ahead—either its tedious length or a sense of dread or anxiety at the prospect of having to meet people or do things. A further 10 attributed the problem to either poor sleep or the experience of brooding or ruminating while asleep, so that they woke up with the concerns of the previous day still preoccupying them.

Subjects were then invited to say what caused their mood to improve. Of the 11 subjects who perceived their mood as typically lifting by noon, 8 attributed this improvement to being active, whether doing work or meeting people—getting going, while dreaded, was perceived as beneficial. A further

2 subjects agreed that being active and meeting others helped, but they accounted for the benefits in terms of activity providing a distraction. One subject attributed the improvement to the prospect of the day ending.

Of the 9 subjects whose mood cleared at variable times, 4 accounted for the improvement in terms of activity, 1 explained it in terms of the prospect of the day ending, and 4 offered no opinion. Of the 4 subjects who perceived their mood as improving only in the evening, 2 attributed the improvement to activity and 2 to the imminent end of the day.

PAIN AND DEPRESSION

Melzack and Wall (1982) in *The Challenge of Pain,* their seminal work, note that older theories of pain regarded it as "an emotion—the opposite of pleasure—rather than a sensation" (p. 215). Klein (1974) and Blumer and Heilbronn (1982) noted that either pain or an inability to experience pleasure is central to depression. Klein (1974) noted furthermore that "By pleasure centre, we do not mean a distinct anatomical location but rather point to a vulnerable *functional organisation* that may be impaired by the pathophysiology of depression . . . accompanied by disinhibition of . . . a pain centre" (p. 449).

This prescient formulation seems borne out by current studies suggesting that one and the same center may mediate both reward and punishment. The degree of pleasure and unpleasure seems to be a function of the patterning of the stimulation rather than a result of stimulation alone (Gloor, 1978; Melzack & Wall, 1982).

Melzack and Wall (1982) argue that all pain necessarily implies a change in the activity of the central nervous system. Although pain may be initiated by nociception, the changes underpinning it outlast this event and may become self-sustaining or be perpetuated by a loss of the normal patterning of incoming sensations following peripheral deafferentation, as happens in pains associated with phantom limbs, causalgia, and neuralgias. They pointed to the lack of a pain center in the brain, stating that it is "virtually certain that all the brain plays a role in pain" (Melzack & Wall, 1982, p. 162), leading to the hypothesis that the central component of pain is associated with a disruption of the normal "continuous patterning of impulses in a dynamically changing nervous system" (Melzack & Wall, 1982, p. 177).

Recognition of an association between a pain and depression is increasing, with aches and pains of various sorts being reported as ubiquitous in depression (Blacker & Clare, 1987; Blumer & Heilbronn, 1982; Garvey, Schaffer, & Tuason, 1982; Matthews, Weinman, & Mirabi, 1981). This association has led to the concept of masked depression, with pain regarded as a depressive equivalent (Lopez-Ibor, 1972), or in some cases "chronic pain without a somatic cause is depression" (Blumer & Heilbronn, 1984, p. 406).

Blumer and Heilbronn (1982) reported that a subgroup of chronic-pain sufferers has neurovegative disturbances typical of depression, such as insomnia, anorexia, loss of libido, anergia, and a painful state that responds to antidepressants or electroconvulsive therapy (Blumer & Heilbronn, 1982). Of those who respond to antidepressants, a high proportion have sleep electroencephalogram changes typical of major depressive disorders and nonsuppression of cortisol in response to dexamethasone challenge (Blumer, Zorick, Heilbronn, & Roth, 1982). Of particular interest in this regard are observations that patients with bipolar affective disorders, compared with normals, have elevated pain thresholds; that is, they are relatively insensitive to experimental painful stimuli (Davis, Buchsbaum, & Bunney, 1979). This is in contrast to findings from patients labeled *psychoneurotic,* who have lowered pain thresholds (Davis et al., 1979). Such observations argue against a psychodynamic or cognitive explanation of the dysphoria experienced in endogenomorphic depressions and indicate that something is happening in the pain systems of depressed people.

A converging line of evidence in support of common cerebral substrates for pain and depression can be derived from the empirical use of antidepressants for pain, which has led to pharmacological interest in the analgesic properties of antidepressants (Feinmann, 1985; Walsh, 1983). Antidepressant analgesia has only recently been recognized and is rather unusual. It is not associated with an antiinflammatory activity, effectiveness in common animal tests for analgesia, or relief for the usual pains stemming from peripheral injuries. It is present, however, in central pain states resulting from deafferentation (Feinmann, 1985). Conversely, there have been claims that some opiates that have hitherto been thought of as analgesics, particularly effective on the central neuropsychological aspects of pain, possess antidepressant properties (Davis, 1983). This may simply represent a modern rediscovery of what had been known prior to the introduction of tricyclics—that opiates ameliorate but do not cure major depressive disorders (Kuhn, 1970).

If we postulate that the central dysphoria of affective disorders involves disturbances of those systems that we ordinarily think of as mediating pain, it becomes understandable that some patients should insist that their condition is the physical one of pain and deny being depressed. There may be no need to postulate that they are using their pain as a defense against psychological truths or that such depressions happen only in patients of alexithymic disposition, as Blumer and Heilbronn (1982) argued. Indeed, one might quibble with the designation of this condition as "masked depression par excellence" and suggest instead that it be recognized as naked depression. Transcultural studies led Angst (1973) to a similar conclusion: There may be "no fundamental difference between masked depression and the culture independent core . . . of depressive illness . . . . Indeed our classic concept of depression would appear itself to be culturally dependent . . . and possibly needs to be unmasked" (p. 271).

Distinct Quality of Mood

While the subjects who completed the Quality of Mood Questionnaire outlined on page 26 were offered the chance to describe their mood in terms of pain but did not do so, a number of aspects of depressive dysphoria might be accounted for by an identification between pain and depression. In the first place, it would account for this dysphoria appearing to have a character that differs clearly from that of unhappiness and sadness. This character would seem liable to generate the emotional responses of sadness and unhappiness.

Second, the *pain* words in the Quality of Mood Checklist referred to a variety of pain types, many of which would be unlikely to be endorsed if depressive pain was a distinct pain-type. There are, for example, a number of other dysphoric/painful states, such as shift-work maladaptation syndrome or viral states such as influenza, that would not lead to a high rate of endorsement of words in the pain cluster. It remains to be established whether specific descriptors of these dysphoric states would show any overlap with those words chosen by our depressed subjects.

Finally, the description of pain states depends to a great extent on context. If we have a wound to point to, or can point to a clear organ system, this often suffices to convey what we mean. The lack of such a context in depression may be responsible for the seeming lack of "insight" found in most subjects.

Diurnal Variation of Mood

An identification between pain and depressive dysphoria might also help account for the diurnal variation of mood found in depression. Pain sensitivity is known to fluctuate diurnally (Grevert, Albert, Inturrisi, & Goldstein, 1983). However, there is a further possibility here in that Melzack and Wall (1982) noted that pain may be influenced by other sensations, by activity, and by a variety of central neuropsychological factors. The demonstration of these influences led to their gate-control theory of pain.

The diurnal variation in pain sensitivity is influenced by eating or some activity associated with eating and by processes related to stress-induced analgesia (Bodnar, Kelly, Brutus, & Glusman, 1980; McGivern & Berntson, 1980; Puglisi-Allegra, Castellano, & Oliverio, 1982). One possibility, therefore is that depressed individuals are "in pain," a pain which has a tendency to remit during the day but which can also be modulated by activities, just as most other pains can. If this is the case, it is likely that in the severest cases of depression, as patients become progressively more psychomotor retarded, diurnal variation of mood would be lost.

A further piece of evidence can be brought to bear on this issue. Naloxone, an opiate antagonist, can frequently modify gate-control influences on pain sensitivity (Melzack & Wall, 1982). Of particular significance in this regard is the finding that high doses of naloxone, which have ambiguous effects on normal volunteers (Grevert et al., 1983; Pickar, Cohen, Naber, & Cohen, 1982) and benefit schizophrenics (Cohen, Pickar, & Cohen, 1985) are intensely dysphoric to depressed patients (Cohen et al., 1984). In this last study, naloxone was given to depressed subjects at 0930 hours. The researchers did not relate its effects to an antagonism of the improvement of mood that might have been underway at the time of measurement, but this is one possible explanation of their findings.

CIRCADIAN RHYTHMS AND DEPRESSION

Thus there are some grounds for pushing for an identification between depressive dysphoria and pain. If we accept this identification for the sake of argument, we are left with the question, What gives rise to the pain that is depression?

Circadian rhythms are an important source of patterning of neural activity (indeed, perhaps the origin of such patterning) (Healy, 1993). Their abolition would be equivalent to a functional deafferentation, because the feedback from various programmed changes, both peripheral and central, no longer happens or is pathological. A plausible postulate then is that a disruption of rhythmicity may be painful or pervasively dysphoric; it is in jet lag or shift work (Healy & Waterhouse 1991).

A number of recent studies have provided evidence that circadian rhythms are disturbed in depression (Souetre et al., 1989; Tsujimoto, Yamada, Shimoda, Hanada, & Takahashi, 1990; see Healy & Waterhouse, 1991). In general, hypotheses of how this disturbance of rhythms arises have implied a dysfunction of some central clock, which it has been proposed gives rise to the periodic or seasonal nature of affective disorders and clinical features such as early morning wakening and diurnal variation of mood (Healy & Waterhouse 1990). Such proposals were broadly consistent with older stereotypes of the affective disorders, according to which the endogenomorphic nature of the clinical picture was taken to imply that the illness had an endogenous aetiology, that it led to hospitalization by virtue of its severity, that it was liable to persist for more than a year, and that it was not open to modification by psychosocial influences.

There has, however, been a shift in the clinical picture of the affective disorders in recent years. It now appears that depressions with endogenomorphic features and that are responsive to antidepressant treatments are likely to have been precipitated by psychosocial changes (Hirschfeld, 1981; Paykel, 1985b). It also seems that the majority of antidepressant-responsive depressions are relatively mild and that they present in primary care with complaints of a physical dysphoria, listlessness, and anergia rather than unhappiness and guilt (Blacker & Clare, 1987). Finally, there is now good evidence that even depressions with endogenomorphic features respond to therapy programs that involve the induction of motivated activity (Healy & Waterhouse, 1991; Teasdale, 1988b).

This emerging picture is consistent with another type of circadian rhythm disorder. Circadian rhythms disturbances may arise from two sources; one a disturbance of endogenous clock function and the other an alteration of routines, especially social routines, that leads to changes in the pattern of zeitgeber (time-giver) influences on internal rhythms (Healy & Waterhouse, 1990). The prototypes of this latter type of disorder are jet lag and shift work maladaptation syndromes. These are precipitated by environmental disruptions. They involve physiological disturbances and impairments of well-being that bear notable similarities to the disturbances enshrined in current operational criteria for affective disorders, and they respond to therapy programs that involve the induction of motivated activity (Healy & Waterhouse, 1991).

In a recent study of 40 trainee nurses who undertook shift work for the first time, involving an 8-week spell of night work (Minors, Healy, & Waterhouse, in press) found that 31 subsequently complained of loss of energy, 23 of loss of interest and enjoyment, 27 of impaired concentration, 30 of disturbed sleep, and 26 of altered appetite. There were, in addition, a host of other psychosomatic complaints. On looking at the attributions of these subjects, it was found that while most regarded their altered hours of working as the principal contributing factor and expected a return to normality after leaving shift work, there was a marked shift toward perceiving the neurovegetative changes as being uncontrollable. These changes were also almost uniformly perceived as being severe and bothersome.

These findings are consistent with the Healy and Williams (1988) proposal that the introduction of uncontrollability into intimate areas of personal functioning might lead to severe emotional reactions. The differences between shift work and depression are, first, that individuals doing shift work have a clear culturally sanctioned attribution for the origin of their distress, and second that shifts end, whereas the disruptions of social routines that precipitate depression may not end so smoothly or indeed the disorder itself may engender further disorganization of social routines (Healy & Waterhouse, 1991).

The significance of these findings regarding shift work maladaptation syndrome is that they indicate that shift work potentially provides a model for the affective disorders. In terms of the subject matter of the present chapter, a more detailed analysis of the dysphoria that pervades this syndrome might help establish the extent of its resemblance to depressive dysphoria. If they were significantly similar, aspects of dysphoria such as altered experiences of the passage of time as well as diurnal variation and influences thereon would be open to exploration in a controlled fashion, as would be the interaction between dysphoric mood and emotional attributions.

Whether or not there is an identity between shift work maladaptation syndrome and the affective disorders, such work seems necessary given that depression is associated with disturbances of circadian rhythms. In that case it must, besides a core pathology, have a set of secondary features stemming from circadian dysrhythmia, consequent on social dislocation. As these latter will involve dysphoria, to establish the precise nature of depressive dysphoria, it would seem necessary to dissect out from it any contributing dysphoria from other sources.

REFERENCES

Abramson, L., Seligman, M. E. P., & Teasdale, J. (1978). Learned helplessness in humans: Critique and reformulation. *Journal of Abnormal Psychology, 87,* 49–74.

Angst, J. (1973). Masked depressions viewed from the cross-cultural standpoint. In P. Kielholz (Ed.), *Masked depressions* (pp. 269–274). West Berlin: Hans Huber.

Bech, P. (1975). Depression: Influence on time estimation and time experience. *Acta Psychiatrica Scandinavica, 51,* 42–50.

Beck, A. T. (1967). *Depression: Clinical, experimental and theoretical aspects.* New York: Harper & Row.

Blacker, R. E., & Clare, A. (1987). Depressive disorder in primary care. *British Journal of Psychiatry, 140,* 737–751.

Blewett, R. E. (1992). Abnormal time experience in depression. *British Journal of Psychiatry, 161,* 195–200.

Blumer, D., & Heilbronn, M. (1982). Chronic pain as a variant of depressive disease. *Journal of Nervous and Mental Diseases, 170,* 381–394.

Blumer, D., & Heilbronn, M. (1984). Chronic pain as a variant of depressive disease—A rejoinder. *Journal of Nervous and Mental Diseases, 172,* 405–407.

Blumer, D., Zorick, F., Heilbronn, M., & Roth, T. (1982). Biological markers for depression in chronic pain. *Journal of Nervous and Mental Diseases, 170,* 425–428.

Bodnar, R. J., Kelly, D. D., Brutus, M., & Glusman, M. (1980). Stress-induced analgesia: Neural and hormonal determinants. *Neuroscience and Biobehavioural Reviews, 4,* 87–100.

Burns, D. D. (1980). *Feeling good: The New Mood Therapy.* New York: Signet, New American Library.

Carney, M. W. P., Roth, M., & Garside, R. F. (1965). The diagnosis of depressive syndromes and the prediction of ECT response. *British Journal of Psychiatry, 111,* 659–674.

Carpenter, L. L., Kupfer, D. J., & Frank, E. (1986). Is diurnal variation a meaningful symptom in unipolar depression? *Journal of Affective Disorders, 11,* 255–264.

Cohen, M. R., Cohen, R. M., Pickar, D., Sunderland, T., Muelle, E., & Murphy, D. L. (1984). High dose nalaxone in depression, *Biological Psychiatry, 19,* 825–832.

Cohen, M. R., Pickar, D., & Cohen, R. M. (1985). High dose nalaxone administration in schizophrenia. *Biological Psychiatry, 20,* 573–575.

Davis, G. C. (1983). Endorphins and pain. *Psychiatric Clinics of North America, 6,* 473–487.

Davis, G. C., Buchsbaum, M. S., & Bunney, W. E. (1979). Analgesia to painful stimuli in affective illness. *American Journal of Psychiatry, 136,* 1148–1151.

Dilling, C. A., & Rabin, A. I. (1967). Temporal experience in depressive states and schizophrenia. *Journal of Consulting Psychology, 31,* 604–608.

Feinmann, C. (1985). Pain relief by antidepressants: Possible models of action. *Pain, 23,* 1–8.

Fraisse, P. (1984). Perception and estimation of time. *Annual Review Psychology, 35,* 1–36.

Garvey, M. J., Schaffer, C. B., & Tuason, V. B. (1982). Relationship of headaches to depression. *British Journal of Psychiatry, 143,* 544–547.

Gloor, P. (1978). Inputs and outputs of the amygdala: What the amygdala is trying to tell the rest of the brain. In K. E. Livinstone & D. Hornykiewicz (Eds.), *Limbic mechanisms* (pp. 189–209). New York: Plenum.

Grevert, P., Albert, L., Inturrisi, C. E., & Goldstein, A. (1983). Effects of 8-hour naloxone infusion on human subjects. *Biological Psychiatry, 18,* 1375–1392.

Hamilton, M. (1985). *Fish's Clinical Psychopathology.* (2nd ed.). Bristol, England: Wright.

Healy, D. (1987). The comparative psychopathology of human and animal affective disorders. *Journal of Psychopharmacology, 1,* 198–210.

Healy, D. (1990). *The Suspended Revolution: Psychiatry and Psychotherapy Re-Examined.* London: Faber & Faber.

Healy, D. (1993). *Images of uncertainty: Trauma, neurosis and hysteria.* Images of Trauma: From hysteria to post-traumatic stress disorder. London: Faber and Faber.

Healy, D., & Waterhouse, J. M. (1990). Circadian rhythms and affective disorders: Clocks or rhythms? *Chronobiology International, 7,* 4–11.

Healy, D., & Waterhouse, J. M. (1991). Reactive rhythms and endogenous clocks. *Psychological Medicine, 21,* 557–564.

Healy, D., & Williams, J. M. G. (1988). Dysrhythmia, dysphoria, and depression: The interaction of learned helplessness and circadian dysrhythmia in the pathogenesis of depression. *Psychological Bulletin, 103,* 163–178.

Hicks, R. E., Miller, G. W., Gaes, G., & Biermann, K. (1977). Concurrent processing demands and the experience of time in passing. *American Journal of Psychology, 90,* 431–446.

Hicks, R. E., Miller, G. W., Kinsbourne, M. (1976). Prospective and retrospective judgments of time as a function of amount of information processed. *American Journal of Psychology, 89,* 719–730.

Hirschfeld, R. M. (1981). Situational depression: Validity of the concept. *British Journal of Psychiatry, 139,* 297–305.

Huston, P. E. (1967). Psychotic depressive reactions. In A. M. Freedman & H. I. Kaplan (Eds.), *Comprehensive Textbook of Psychiatry.* Baltimore: Williams & Wilkins.

Jaspers, K. (1959). *General psychopathology* (M. V. Hamilton, Trans.) Manchester, England: Manchester University Press.

Kitamura, T., & Kumar, R. (1982). Time passes slowly for patients with depressive state. *Acta psychiatrica Scandinavica, 65,* 415–420.

Kitamura, T., & Kumar, R. (1983). Time estimation and time production in depressive patients. *Acta Psychiatrica Scandinavica, 68,* 15–20.

Klein, D. F. (1974). Endogenomorphic depression: A conceptual and terminological revisions. *Archives of General Psychiatry, 31,* 447–454.

Kuhn, R. (1970). The imipramine story. In F. J. Ayd & B. Blackwell (Eds.), *Discoveries in biological psychiatry* (pp. 205–217). Philadelphia: Lippincott.

Kuhs, H. et al. (1989). The daily course of the symptomatology and the impaired time estimation in endogenous depression (melancholia). *Journal of Affective Disorders, 17,* 285–290.

Lehmann, H. (1967). Time and psychopathology. *Annals of the New York Academy of Sciences, 138,* 798–821.

Lewis, A. (1932). The experience of time in mental disorder. *Proceedings of the Royal Society of Medicine, 25,* 611–620.

Lopez-Ibor, J. J. (1972). Masked depressions. *British Journal of Psychiatry, 120,* 245–258.

Lyons, W. (1980). *Emotions.* Cambridge, England: Cambridge University Press.

Maier, S. F., & Seligman, M. E. P. (1976). Learned helplessness: Theory and evidence. *Journal of Experimental Psychology, 105,* 3–46.

Matthews, R. J., Weinman, M. K., & Mirabi, M. (1981). Physical symptoms of depression. *British Journal of Psychiatry, 139,* 293–296.

McGivern, R. F., & Berntson, G. G. (1980). Mediation of diurnal fluctuations in pain sensivity in the rat by food intake patterns: Reversal by naloxone. *Science, 210,* 210–211.

Melges, F. T., & Fougerousse, C. A. (1966). Time sense, emotions, and acute mental illness. *Journal of Psychiatric Research, 4,* 127–140.

Melzack, R., & Wall, P. (1982). *The challenge of pain.* Harmondsworth, England: Penguin Books.

Mezey, A. G., & Cohen, S. I. (1961). The effect of depressive illness on time judgement and time experience. *Journal of Neurology, Neurosurgery and Psychiatry, 24,* 269–270.

Middelhoff, H. D. (1967). Tagesrhythmische Schwankungen bei endogen Depressiven im symptomfreien Intervall und Wahrend der Phase. *Archive Psychiatrie Nervenkrank* 209, 315–339.

Miners, D. H., Healy, D., & Waterhouse, J. M. (in press). The attitudes & general health of student nurses before & immediately after their first eight weeks of night work. *Ergonomics.*

Paykel, E. S. (1985a). The clinical interview for depression: Development, reliability and validity. *Journal of Affective Disorders, 9,* 85–96.

Paykel, E. S. (1985b). Life events, social support and psychiatric disorders. In I. G. Sarason & B. R. Sarason (Eds.), *Social support: Theory, research and applications* (pp. 321–347). The Hague: Martinus Nijhiff.

Peselow, E. D., Robins, C., Block, P., Barouche, F., & Fieve, R. R. (1990). Dysfunctional attitudes in depressed patients before and after clinical treatment and in normal control subjects. *American Journal of Psychiatry, 147,* 439–444.

Pickar, D., Cohen, M. R., Naber, D., & Cohen, R. M. (1982). Clinical studies of endogenous opioid systems. *Biological Psychiatry, 17,* 1243–1276.

Puglisi-Allegra, S., Castellano, C., & Oliverio, A. (1982). Circadian variations in stress-induced analgesia. *Brain Research, 252,* 373–376.

Ramos-Brieva, J. A., Cordero-Villafafila, A., Ayuso-Mateos, J. L., Rios, B., Montejo, M. L., Rivera, A., Caballero, L., Ponce, C., & Canas, F. (1987). Distinct quality of depressed mood: An attempt to develop an objective measure. *Journal of Affective Disorders, 13,* 241–248.

Schneider, K. (1959). *Clinical psychopathology.* New York: Grune & Stratton.

Souetre, E., Salvati, E., Belugou, J.-L., Pringuey, D., Candito, M., Krebs, B., Ardison, J.-L., Darcourt, G. (1989). Circadian rhythms in depression and recovery: Evidence for blunted amplitude as the main chronobiological abnormality. *Psychiatric Research, 28,* 263–278.

Spitzer, R. L., Endicott, J., & Robins, E. (1978). *Research diagnostic criteria (RDC) for a selected group of functional disorders* (3rd ed.). New York: New York State Psychiatric Institute.

Stallone, F., Huba, G. J., Lawlor, W. G., Fieve, R. L. (1973). Longitudinal studies of diurnal variation in depression: A sample of 643 patient days. *British Journal of Psychiatry, 123,* 311–318.

Strauss, E. (1928). Das zeiterlebnis in der endogen depression und in der psychopathischen verstimmung. *Monatsschrift fur Psychiatrie und Neurologie, 68,* 640–656.

Teasdale, J. D. (1988a). Cognitive vulnerability to persistent depression. *Cognition and Emotion, 2,* 247–274.

Teasdale, J. D. (1988b, September). *Cognitive therapy for depression: The state of the art.* Paper presented at Behaviour Therapy World Congress, Edinburgh.

Tolle, R., & Goetze, V. (1987). On the daily rhythm of depressive symptomatology. *Psychopathology, 20,* 237–249.

Tsujimoto, T., Yamada, N., Shimoda, K., Hanada, K., Takahashi, S. (1990). Circadian rhythms in depression. *Journal of Affective Disorders, 18,* 199–210.

Tysk, L. (1984). Time perception and affective disorders. *Perceptual and Motor Skills, 58,* 455–464.

Waldmann, H. (1972). Die Tagesschwankung in der Depression als rhythmisches Phenomenon. [Diurnal variation in mood as a rhythmic phenomenon]. *Fortschritte Neurologie und Psychiatrie, 40,* 83–104.

Walsh, J. D. (1983). Antidepressants in chronic pain. *Clinical Neuropharmacology, 6,* 271–295.

Williams, J. M. G. (1985). Attributional formulation of depression as a diathesis-stress model: Metalsky et al reconsidered. *Journal of Personality and Social Psychology, 48,* 1–4.

Williams, J. M. G., Healy, D., Teasdale, J. D., White, W., & Paykel, E. S. (1990). Dysfunctional attitudes and vulnerability to persistent depression. *Psychological Medicine, 20,* 375–381.

Wyrick, R., & Wyrick, L. (1977). Time experience during depression. *Archives of General Psychiatry, 34,* 1441–1443.

CHAPTER 3

Loss of Interest

ERIC KLINGER

INTRODUCTION

Depression, a normal human affliction and in some forms the most common group of psychopathologies, is widely labeled as a state of "mood." Here the emphasis is on affect, whether feeling sad, empty, or very little at all. Nevertheless, there has been growing recognition that the most pivotal attributes of depression include less apparent features. It is also an affliction of beliefs and of motivation. Recent decades have seen a surge of research on cognitive factors in depression. The motivational aspects of depression have received considerably less attention. Indexes of standard reference works list few entries for the motivational features of depression, except perhaps in the form of fatigue. Yet, fundamental motivational deficits, often described as loss of interest, are a central feature of depression.

Integrative theories of psychological functioning have often before recognized the close links between affect and motivation. Accordingly, loss of interest or its equivalent in other terminology plays a critical role in a number of theories of depression. Rigorous research in this area, however, is substantially less advanced than in cognitive areas. Loss of interest is still commonly conceptualized and assessed ad hoc. Data relevant to it come under a variety of sometimes unlikely guises. This chapter will begin with an overview of conceptualization and assessment of diminished interest and will then examine its prominence in depression, relevant theories, supporting evidence, and implications.

CONCEPTUALIZATION AND ASSESSMENT

Variants of the Construct

The construct "loss of interest" takes a variety of conceptual forms that range from the pervasive to the particular. Considered in general, it means apathy toward nearly everything in the depressed individual's life. The decision function that implicitly governs our every activity seems in depression to have shifted. The positive value that the individual once awaited from, for example, friendly conversations, community activities, recreational pursuits, and occupational achievements, has dropped to the point that they no longer seem worth the trouble. Motivation for activities has shifted, if it survives at all, to the costs of not performing them.

The general apathy extends to the most basic sources of ordinary pleasure, and in these rather more concrete, more easily measurable forms it has earned a secure place in diagnostic checklists and investigations. Loss of appetite and of interest in sex, although not universal even in severe depression, are among the widely recognized symptoms of clinical depression. Somewhat more broadly, loss of interest may appear on checklists as social withdrawal or isolation.

It is hard to disentangle outward-looking interest from its inner base in affect. Therefore, blunted affect is often taken as a proxy for the diminished valuation of goals reflected in behavioral loss of interest. The external observer's label is often "flat affect." Patients complain of being unable to feel. Some theorists refer to "anhedonia," though its locus may be particular to blunted *positive* affect (e.g., Tellegen, 1985).

Assessment Approaches

Most investigations of depression assess loss of interest through an examiner's judgment of presence or absence. However, the operationalization may also take the form of clinician ratings, self-ratings, and self-report psychometric scales.

Perhaps the most thoroughly examined inventory aimed fairly squarely at interest and pleasure in activities is the Pleasant Events Schedule (PES; MacPhillamy & Lewinsohn, 1982), a 320-item list of common activities to which the respondent assigns ratings for frequency over the past 30 days and average amount of enjoyment. Its scores are correlated significantly and inversely with independent measures of depression. Inconsistent evidence from previous studies indicates that this relationship can probably not be attributed to depressed individuals' underestimation of the number or enjoyability of their pleasant events. PES scores have been validated successfully against peer ratings, observers' ratings, and subjects' concurrent records of activities engaged in during a subsequent time period. A companion inventory, the 320-item Unpleasant Events Schedule (Lewinsohn et al., 1985), is positively correlated with depression, to a degree independently of the PES.

Lewinsohn had intended the PES and UES to represent relatively objective measures of the positive and aversive reinforcements that respondents experience. However, they can also be interpreted as in part reflecting the activities in which respondents have chosen to engage. For example, the first several items of the PES are "Being in the country," "Wearing expensive or formal clothes," "Making contributions to religious, charitable, or other groups," and "Talking about sports" (MacPhillamy & Lewinsohn, 1982, p. 376). These are activities that people choose to engage in rather than events that befall them. The UES is less vulnerable to this interpretation, but even it contains a fair number of events that would sometimes be under respondents' control, such as "Being hungry or thirsty," "Coming home to a messy house," "Getting separated or divorced from my spouse," "Being alone," or "Performing in public" (Lewinsohn, Mermelstein, Alexander, & MacPhillamy, 1985, p. 486).

These scales therefore assess both reinforcements for behavior emitted and the respondents' decisions to emit it. From a substantive standpoint, the inverse correlation of the PES and the direct correlation of the UES with depression can be interpreted as indicating that depressed individuals lose interest in appetitive activities and positive affect but remain emotionally quite responsive to aversive events.

The Multidimensional Personality Questionnaire (MPQ; Tellegen, 1985) contains scores for Social Closeness and Achievement, which bear on interest in social and achievement goal striving; and it yields a Positive Emotionality (PEM) score, which presumably assesses the affective substrate of interest, as well as a Negative Emotionality (NEM) score. Similar scores are also obtainable with the Positive and Negative Affect Scale (PANAS; Watson, Clark, & Tellegen, 1988). Both MPQ PEM and PANAS Positive Affect correlate inversely with depression measures, and the respective negative scales correlate directly with depression and anxiety measures (Kroll-Mensing, 1992; Watson & Kendall, 1989). The MPQ scales have shown corresponding relationships with clinical diagnoses of depressive and anxiety disorders (Watson, Clark, & Carey, 1988).

CENTRALITY OF DIMINISHED INTEREST IN DEPRESSION

Diagnostic Criteria

Recent diagnostic criteria for depression have given loss of interest a prominent spot. Following an evolution via the Feighner criteria (Feighner et al., 1972), the Research Diagnostic Criteria (Spitzer, Endicott, & Robins, 1978) made loss of interest an alternative symptom to dysphoric mood in the pivotal first criterion for major depressive disorder. The *Diagnostic and Statistical Manual of Mental Disorders, Third Edition Revised* (DSM-III-R; American Psychiatric Association, 1987) places loss of interest second on its list of criteria for a depressive episode, following only "depressed mood" itself, in the form of "markedly diminished interest or pleasure in all, or almost all, activities most of the day, nearly every day," including general "apathy." The DSM-III-R lists "loss of interest or pleasure" and "lack of reactivity to usually pleasant stimuli" as the first two criteria for depressive disorder of a melancholic type. These placements accord with a number of empirical findings.

Correlations with Depression

Measures of diminished interest have been found significantly correlated with measures of mood and/or diagnostic classification. Using clinician ratings of depression in a large, mixed psychiatric sample, Beck (1967) found 92% of severely depressed patients suffered "loss of gratification" (as compared with 35% of nondepressed patients) and 86% suffered "loss of motivation" (as compared with 33% of the nondepressed). In the severely depressed group, the latter variable was exceeded only by "dejected mood" (88%) and "negative expectation" (87%). No variable exceeded the rate of gratification loss.

The PES is correlated significantly (coefficients in the .30s to .40s) with a number of psychometric measures of depressed mood, including the Beck Depression Inventory (BDI), Scale D of the Minnesota Multiphasic Personality Inventory (MMPI), and Radloff's Center for Epidemiological Studies-Depression Scale (CES-D; Lewinsohn et al., 1985). When PES items are scored for both frequency and enjoyability, differences in frequency but not enjoyability were related to depression levels assessed jointly by the MMPI and interview ratings (Lewinsohn & Amenson, 1978).

In a latent trait analysis of the BDI, Clark, Cavanaugh, and Gibbons (1983) found the most discriminating items to be those most associated with diminished interest: dissatisfaction and loss of social interest. This was true in a mixed sample of psychiatric patients and normals. These symptoms were also found to discriminate well in samples of medical (Clark et al., 1983) and alcoholic patients (Clark, Gibbons, Fawcett, Aagesen, & Sellers, 1985).

Scores from a scale to assess inner emptiness correlated at .69 with Costello–Comrey depression scores (Hazell, 1984). Finally, in a study of the burdens of living with a depressed individual (Coyne et al., 1987), the most significantly burdensome factor, in comparison with living with a nondepressed individual, was the other's lack of interest in social life. General lack of interest in things was another potent factor.

Besides the various investigations that show interindividual correlations between loss of interest in its various forms and depression, one (Hibbert, Teasdale, & Spencer, 1984) shows in*tra*individual covariation between them. This method is important because it avoids complications with individual differences in self-presentation, other personality variables, unreported life situations, and so on. It therefore serves as an important validation of the interindividual findings. Unfortunately, the data were all obtained by a single clinician's ratings based on individual repeated interviews. This may have introduced rater biases into the relationships obtained, although interrater reliabilities were quite high. Specifically, Hibbert et al. interviewed individual patients from 14 to 53 times and for each patient correlated the ratings obtained on each of the various rating scales per occasion with the ratings summed across scales for each of those occasions—that is, intrapatient item–total correlations. The scale "Inability to Feel," defined as reduced interest, had a mean correlation across occasions of .72 with the sum of all scales, which followed in magnitude only sadness, retardation, lassitude, and pessimism.

Prevalence in Depressed Samples

A number of investigations using no comparison groups report high prevalence of diminished interest among depressed patients. In a group of depressed adolescents assessed through semistructured interviews, the most common symptoms besides depressed mood were apathy/boredom (90%), loss of pleasure (83%), and loss of interest (77%) (Inamdar, Siomopoulos, Osborn, & Bianchi, 1979). Similarly, within a depressed group of children hospitalized for orthopaedic reasons, the most prevalent symptom, afflicting 87%, was a pervasive loss of interest (Kashani, Venzke, & Millar, 1981). Among 208 adult depressed patients, including day patients, outpatients, and inpatients, 66% were rated as having decreased appetite, a condition that was associated with "impaired work and interests" (Paykel, 1977).

Such findings appear to hold up cross-culturally. A comparison of depressed patients in Italy and Sweden shows that three quarters or more of the patients in both groups scored 3 or higher on the Zung Self-Rating Depression Scale items for loss of interest and dissatisfaction, loss of libido, and anhedonia, which were among the most elevated items (Perris et al., 1981). Factor analyses of symptoms in mostly depressed samples from Britain and Benin show impaired work and interests to be either the second or third highest loading variable on the first factor, following only depressed mood (London) or depressed mood and general somatic complaints (Benin) (Binitie, 1975).

Experimental Evidence

Cunningham (1988) induced elated, neutral, and depressed moods in college students using the Velten procedure. Immediately after rating their own moods, these students indicated their desire to engage in activities drawn from the PES. Those who had undergone the depression induction reported significantly less interest in social and leisure activities and in physically strenuous activities than either of the other groups. This finding is consistent with the position that depressed mood entails loss of interest in pleasurable activities.

Specificity of Diminished Interest to Depression

Although diminished interest and reduced pleasure seem to be among the most characteristic symptoms of depression, they are not specific to depression.

Precise comparisons with other psychopathologies are difficult because the relevant constructs used in research vary according to different disorders. Most particularly, loss of interest functions as a common construct in research on depression but seems rarely applied to research on other disorders such as schizophrenia, whereas the overlapping but nonidentical constructs of social withdrawal and emotional blunting or flatness are often applied to schizophrenia but less often to depression. Nevertheless, it is possible to make some general observations.

Blunted affect characterizes perhaps two thirds of schizophrenic patients (Berenbaum & Oltmanns, 1992). The two highest loading variables on a Negative Syndrome first factor obtained with factor analysis of schizophrenic symptoms were "emotional withdrawal" and "passive/apathetic social withdrawal" (Kay, 1991). However, the blunting affected facial reactions to both positive and negative stimuli on the part of outpatient schizophrenics, but chiefly to positive stimuli in outpatient depressive patients (Berenbaum & Oltmanns, 1992). This result supports the view of depression as centrally involving impaired positive affect (Tellegen, 1985).

A complication in comparisons between diagnostic groups is that schizophrenics (like anxiety-disordered patients) are also often intensely depressed. The BDI scores of schizophrenic outpatients in the study of Berenbaum and Oltmanns were nearly as elevated as those of the depressed sample, as were their scores on self-reported anhedonia (Berenbaum & Oltmanns, 1992).

There are differences in such findings depending on whether the measure is facial expression or self-report. Berenbaum and Oltmanns obtained nonsignificant differences between schizophrenics and depressives in self-reported reactions to positive and negative stimuli. Another investigation (Brown, Sweeney, & Schwartz, 1979), this time of inpatients, found significantly greater facial responsiveness by schizophrenics than by depressives to pleasurable experiences, but significantly higher self-ratings of pleasure by depressives than by schizophrenics.

Curiously, Arieti (1974), reflecting on 33 years of clinical experience, asserted that withdrawal had become much less common among schizophrenics over that time span. Insofar as his observation reflects general reality, it raises the question whether emotional and social withdrawal are inherent in schizophrenia or particular to specific cultural contexts.

THEORETICAL ACCOUNTS OF DIMINISHED INTEREST DURING DEPRESSION

The Current Concerns and Disengagement Framework

"Normal" reactive depression is fruitfully viewed in a broader context than it is usually accorded—the context of goal-striving, which accounts for almost all zoological activity. Normal depression may be regarded as a phase in a longer sequence of overcoming impediments to goal attainment, of resistance to relinquishing goals, and, when necessary, of disengaging from their pursuit.

Normal depression is the common reaction to any significant kind of loss. Some theorists have advanced other formulations, but the common denominator of normal depression-eliciting circumstances seems to be the perceived final failure to achieve or maintain something of importance (Hammen, 1988; Klinger, 1975, 1977, 1987), whether that is a job, a home, a personal relationship, or a child's transitional stuffed animal. Depression is ordinarily not the first response to thwarting but rather forms the latter part of a sequence that begins with invigoration of goal striving, moves gradually toward anger and possible aggression, and then continues through depression toward disengagement from the goal and emotional recovery. I have elsewhere (Klinger, 1975, 1977) brought together evidence in support of this *incentive-disengagement cycle* as an integrated entity.

Within this theoretical view, becoming committed to a goal sets in train changes in neural functioning (a *current concern*) that can be terminated by consummation of the goal or, in the face of insuperable obstacles, inhibited through a gradual process of disengagement from the goal. Thus, normal depression constitutes a regular and possibly indispensable phase in relinquishing goals. Although this model was constructed to represent normal reactive depression, including grief, it applies in varying degrees to clinical forms of depression as well.

Incentive-disengagement cycles have features that go well beyond subjective mood to include changes in activity levels, cognitions, and values. The value changes are highly relevant to loss of interest. During early phases of the cycle, the subjective value of a jeopardized incentive rises, a phenomenon described and labeled *reactance* by Brehm (1972). At the same time, the relative and probably absolute subjective values of other incentives decline. With progress into the depressed phase of the cycle, the goal that is slipping away absorbs the person to the neglect of other, now relatively less valued, incentives. These have now lost some of their "reinforcer effectiveness" (Costello, 1972) and hence their control over behavior. Generally the lost goal also eventually loses its exaggerated subjective value until perspective on it is restored. The mechanism for the declines in value is unclear, but the neurological basis for reduced value during major depression is becoming better understood and will be described in the next section.

Because depression is generally regarded as undesirable and maladaptive, its selection in the course of evolution as an apparently normal reaction to loss, failure, and defeat may seem puzzling. There are, however, a number of reasons to suppose that it promotes species survival (Klinger, 1975, 1977).

First of all, given that commitment to a goal sets in train persistent goal striving, there needs to be a mechanism to halt it when goals turn out to be unattainable or too costly—a stop mechanism. However, to avoid reinforcing the relinquishment of goals—and perhaps to counter the benefits of giving up, as in reduced effort and discomfort—such a stop mechanism needs to be aversive. Given that the attractiveness of goals is largely provided by their emotional pull—that is, their subjective value—a stop mechanism would benefit from diminishing the value of the blocked goal. That might be accomplished by gradually reducing the value of the lost goal by progressively inhibiting emotional reactions to its cues, but it might be accomplished more quickly and effectively by turning down responsiveness of appetitive systems across the board. These hypothetical properties of an effective stop mechanism are, of course, and not accidentally, the properties of normal reactive depression.

A second reason for the adaptiveness of depression may lie in population ecology. During periods of scarcity, whether of food or of mates, it is to the advantage of the species to eliminate the least well-equipped members of populations from the competition, thereby providing better nourishment and breeding opportunities for better equipped members. One way to promote such a system is to exact a biological price for failure. The pathogenic properties of depression (e.g., Denney, Stephenson, Penick, & Weller, 1988; Stone, Cox, Valdismarsdottir, Jandorf, & Neale, 1987) provide such a price by increasing depressed individuals' vulnerability to disease for a transitional period.

A third reason may arise out of the requirements of goal striving in a social species. With organisms designed to pursue their goals to consummation and to eliminate the competition if necessary, it is desirable to gear a stop mechanism to kick in before the point of intraspecies killing or mutual exhaustion (Price, 1972). Thus, depression may form an essential mechanism in social submission and in the formation of dominance hierarchies, as has been observed in vervet monkeys (Gartlan & Brain, 1968). The point of the mechanism is to limit competitive goal striving, a capitulation facilitated by loss of interest.

Neuroscientific Accounts

Depression may also fruitfully be viewed in the context of broad behavioral systems as these are becoming gradually defined in neuropsychology and neuropharmacology. There is increasing support for the proposition that behavior is governed by three such major systems (Gray, 1982; 1990): (a) a behavioral approach system (BAS), which is also called a "behavioral activation system" (Fowles, 1980) or "behavioral facilitation system" (BFS; Depue & Iacono, 1989); (b) a behavioral inhibition system (BIS); and (c) a fight–flight system (FFS).

In Gray's (1982) extensive formulation, the BAS underlies appetitive and active avoidance behavior and predation, and it responds to signals of reward and of nonpunishment; the BIS underlies behavioral inhibition, including passive avoidance, and responds to conditioned signals of punishment and nonreward, as well as novel and innate fear stimuli; and the FFS underlies unconditioned escape and aggression, and it responds to unconditioned signals of punishment and nonreward.

During the early stages of a stress experience, Gray (1982) associates the BIS with anxiety. With prolonged stress, to follow Gray's argument, the BIS continues to inhibit outputs from the BAS while gradually leading to a noradrenergic exhaustion in hypothalamic areas involved in defense and aggression. The ultimate overall effect is to reduce both BAS and FFS activity and hence to produce depression.

Thus in this formulation, both anxiety and depression are products of the same system at different stages of stress. The linkage of the BIS with both anxiety and depression has the virtue of accommodating considerable pharmacological data regarding effects of tricyclic antidepressants on panic and some other anxiety disorders, and it also helps to account for the frequent clinical comorbidity of anxiety and depression. Furthermore, inasmuch as the BAS is important to appetitive behavior, to the initiation of goal-related locomotor activity, and, presumably, to positive affect, some such model can explain depressives' loss of interest in—unresponsiveness to—the positive incentives associated with reward and pleasure.

Depue and Iacono (1989) indeed argue for impaired BAS functioning in bipolar depression (and BAS hyperactivity in hypomania and mania), but with a focus on the role of dopamine pathways. Given the involvement of BAS pathways in the initiation of locomotion, this model can account for motor retardation in bipolar depression. In view of BAS involvement in appetitive goal-striving, it also handily accounts for diminished interest is positively rewarding incentives.

This view fits nicely with other positions. It is consistent with the psychometrically based proposition that depression reflects impaired positive affect (Tellegen, 1985). It also suggests the substrate for the depression phase of incentive-disengagement cycles. What remains most in doubt is the nature of the mechanism responsible for switches from normal or manic mood to depression.

The proposition that BIS activity or exhaustion, as proposed by Gray, may affect BAS/dopamine function is supported by evidence that long-term tricyclic antidepressants affect relevant dopamine activity (Depue & Iacono, 1989). However, there is reason to doubt that the linkage that leads to depression reflects noradrenergic exhaustion. First, assuming that depression constitutes a continuum ranging from mild disappointment to melancholic depression, it is hard to attribute relatively quick, short-term effects on exhaustion. For example, receiving news of an incontestable rejection—from a school, job, or promotion for which one had applied, a journal to which one had submitted an article—generally leads to at least a mild depressive state, and it does so quickly and without a long preliminary period of unusual behavioral inhibition or avoidance behavior. Second, depression following frustrative excitement probably follows a course similar to (and possibly identical with) that observed in operant extinction (Klinger, 1975), which depends on numbers of trials more than on temporal duration or spacing. Third, an activity-box analogue of incentive disengagement in rats produced the predicted sinusoidal curve in activity levels (elevation followed by decline below baseline followed by recovery) even though the points on the curve were obtained following different nonrewarded runway trials some of which were separated in time by many hours, which ought to have permitted nonadrenergic recovery (Klinger, Barta, & Kemble, 1974). It therefore seems more likely that the switch into depression is normally triggered by a learned-inhibitory process rather than by noradrenergic exhaustion. Whether the latter contributes to clinical levels of depression is still an open question.

Insufficient Positive Reinforcement

Peter Lewinsohn and his colleagues have systematically pursued the operant view that depression results from receiving too little positive reinforcement. In this view, "depression is conceptualized as an extinction phenomen(on)" (Lewinsohn, 1974, p. 175). Extinction thus accounts for depressives' low levels of activity and apparent interest, which Lewinsohn saw as virtually the only common denominator of the various depressive disorders.

Subsequent work has shown that the instrument designed to assess positive reinforcements, the PES, does indeed correlate with depression levels (Lewinsohn & Graf, 1973; Lewinsohn et al., 1985; MacPhillamy & Lewinsohn, 1974, 1982). For a number of reasons, however, it can more readily be interpreted as reflecting loss of interest during depression than as assessing a causative lack of reinforcement. First, when correlations are lagged by a day, neither measure is better at predicting the other. Rather, they vary together. Second, instructing subjects to increase the number of positive experiences failed to raise subsequent mood; in fact, mood worsened slightly (Hammen & Glass, 1975). Third, the theory is unable to explain why extinction of some behaviors should make people less receptive to other incentives.

Lewinsohn explains depressives' low rates of reinforcements as resulting from impaired social skills. There is, indeed, ample evidence to indicate that interpersonal difficulties and lack of social support are antecedents as well as consequences of depression; but there is on balance little reason to believe that depressives suffer from premorbid attributional or other cognitive deficits (Barnett & Gotlib, 1988), and there appears to be no prospective evidence to indicate poorer premorbid social skills. Thus, the reinforcement theory of diminished interest is inconsistent with some of the data and displays little predictive power.

Deficits in Action Control: State Orientation

Kuhl (1981; Kuhl & Beckmann, in press) has proposed an individual-differences variable named *action control,* which runs from *state orientation* at one end to *action orientation* at the other. Action orientation refers to a tendency to move quickly from a given behavioral point to the next steps required by tasks, previous intentions, or personal best interests. State orientation, on the other hand, represents an individual's focus on savoring or ruminating about his or her current state or about the past rather than getting on with instrumental activity.

Kuhl (1985; Kuhl & Beckmann, in press) has devised an inventory, the Action Control Scale (ACS), to assess this variable, which is differentiated into (a) preoccupation with past events, especially aversive ones such as failure, (b) hesitation in decision making, and (c) volatility in interrupting pleasant activities to switch to something else. Research has shown this scale to be correlated with measures of depression and, possibly, to represent an antecedent of depression (Kammer, in press; Keller, Straub, & Wolfersdorfer, in press; Kuhl & Kazen-Saad, in press: cited in Kuhl, 1990). Experience-sampling work has also shown depressed mood to be correlated with thinking about the past, in contrast to anxious mood, which is correlated with thinking about the future (Kroll-Mensing, 1992).

The theory behind these relationships is that state orientation represents difficulty in letting go, whether of previous emotional experiences or of previously formed intentions, including those that warrant disengagement. Therefore, state-oriented individuals are slower to complete the disengagement process and hence prolong and deepen their depressions. Preoccupation with goals lost but not yet buried encumbers processing capacity and may help account for diminished interest in new opportunities for pleasure.

There is at least one experimental confirmation of this theory (Kuhl & Helle, 1986). Subjects in one condition were given an instruction to clean up a messy table and then instructed to defer that activity until after completion of other tasks. They were subsequently instructed to number the pages used in the tasks. Subjects in another condition were introduced to the messy table but not asked to clean it. Those with a diagnosis of depression significantly more often neglected to number pages after receiving the first instruction to clean the table than when they had received no such instruction. This was true regardless of the subjects' current BDI scores, thus suggesting that the lapses were not the side effects of current mood but may reflect a longer term vulnerability of depressed individuals. A nondepressed psychiatric control group and a student control group showed no such difference between conditions. On the other hand, BDI scores were related to the frequency of self-reported thoughts about the cleaning task and to reduced memory span following cleanup instructions. In Kuhl's and Helle's interpretation of these results, some disposition associated with having once been depressed causes overcommitment to one intention to interfere with execution of a subsequent intention.

Cognitive Perspectives

Hopelessness Theory

Hopelessness theory (Abramson, Metalsky, & Alloy, 1989) purports to derive demotivation as a symptom of depression. "Hope" may seem an emotional rather than a cognitive term, but within this theory "hopelessness . . . is an expectation" (Abramson et al., 1989, p. 359) that acts as a "proximal cause" of depression and demotivation.

As a theory of depression, hopelessness theory has undergone a two-decade-long odyssey, from its beginnings as learned helplessness (Seligman, 1974, 1975) through its cognitive reformulation (Abramson, Seligman, & Teasdale, 1978), which built on attributional concepts drawn from Kelley (1967) and Weiner (1974), to its most recent reformulation (Abramsom et al., 1989). It has engendered a torrent of valuable research and theoretical refinement. However, this research has tended to invalidate some of its own most distinctive propositions, especially lack of "controllability"—a rendering of helplessness—as the precipitator of depression. Apart from an important residue of findings regarding causal attributions and other cognitive peculiarities of depressed individuals, the theory has, in fact, come back to a more traditional stance. Indeed, its current version is essentially a reduced version of the incentive-disengagement theory of depression (Klinger, 1975, 1977, 1987; Klinger, Barta, & Maxeiner, 1980), with an important elaboration of the cognitions that moderate the impact of loss and failure.

This resemblance remains unacknowledged. The 1989 formulation dismisses "current concerns" theory in a footnote. The footnote, unfortunately, reveals a fundamental misunderstanding of the essence of current concerns, ignores the specifics of their applications to depression, and is uninformed by the developments in that theory since 1975. There are in fact numerous parallels.

1. The 1989 formulation of hopelessness theory addresses a "new subtype" of depression that seems indistinguishable from what has long been recognized as reactive depression, to which the 1975 presentation of incentive-disengagement theory of depression also explicitly devoted itself.

2. Hopelessness theory posits two elements of a "proximal sufficient cause of the symptoms of hopelessness depression" as "a negative outcome expectancy" and "a helplessness expectancy" (Abramson et al., 1989, p. 359). These do not seem substantially different from "unrelieved frustration" and "failure, loss, and disappointment (in the objective sense)" regarding a goal while "feeling helpless and hopeless" (Klinger, 1975, pp. 10–11). The 1975 formulation of incentive-disengagement furthermore recognized that "all

phases also presumably depend on cognitive factors" (Klinger, 1975, p. 14) and then listed some of them. Like incentive-disengagement theory, hopelessness theory views cognitive factors as moderators ("contributory causes") of the impact that negative life events have on mood.

3. Abramson et al. declare that "the possibility exists that once an individual becomes hopeless, some biological or psychological processes are triggered that need to run their course and do not dissipate as quickly as hopelessness" (1989, p. 363). This proposition is central to the incentive-disengagement theory and has been treated in considerable detail (Klinger, 1975, especially pp. 12–14; 1977, 1987).

4. They write that "in contrast to the traditional view, the hopelessness theory reorganizes the phenomena of depression into a hypothesized causal sequence" (Abramson et al., 1989, p. 365), which incentive-disengagement theory has done from the beginning.

What remains a unique and important contribution of hopelessness theory is embodied in its cognitive formulations. Abramson et al. cite a variety of recent and current evidence from student samples supporting a vulnerability to experience depression, especially perhaps longer durations of depression, as a result of attributional style. Even with respect to a cognitive diathesis, however, it has been necessary to retrench, in view of evidence that (a) many depressed individuals do not manifest the dysfunctional cognitions posited by hopelessness theory (Barnett & Gotlib, 1988; Hamilton & Abramson, 1983) and (b) those dysfunctional cognitions that do emerge vary and decline with improvement in mood, even without specific cognitive therapy (Hamilton & Abramson, 1983; Simons, Garfield, & Murphy, 1984). That is, "depressogenic" cognition is at least as much a correlate or consequence of mood as its cause. Abramson et al. handle this problem by declaring hopelessness depression to be a different subtype from "major depressive episode, with melancholia" or "endogenomorphic depressions," which have as their "core process" "impairment in the capacity to experience pleasure" rather than hopelessness (Abramson et al., 1989, p. 365).

This resolution also, however, runs into difficulty. As we have seen, diminished interest and anhedonia are closely related variables and are among the most central symptoms of depression. Indeed, Klerman, Weissman, Rounsaville, and Chevron (1984) consider "an inability to experience pleasure" as "almost universal among depressed patients" (p. 35). This would be an unlikely finding if a large portion of clinically depressed patients experienced hopelessness without anhedonia. Furthermore, again as indicated earlier, psychometric analyses have repeatedly shown low positive emotionality to be a specific attribute of depressed mood. These investigations have used college-student normal as well as psychiatric samples, the more depressed members of which should have included large proportions of reactive depression. Finally, with respect to endogenicity, it has been hard to find consistent differences between reactive and endogenous varieties of depressed patients in the role that negative life events play in instigating them (Free & Oei, 1989), which raises the question of why some should experience hopelessness and others anhedonia but few should experience both.

In any event, hopelessness theory appears not to venture an explanation for loss of pleasure, which is closely associated with diminished interest. It asserts that the latter, in the sense of diminished motivation, is a symptom of "hopelessness depression," but this conclusion is not rigorously derived from the theory. Perhaps Abramson et al. mean to imply some variant of Expectancy X Value Theory, such that reduced expectancy weakens the tendency to choose available incentives. This formulation would, however, leave out anhedonic reductions in the value term.

Other Cognitive Dysfunctions

Therapists since Ellis (1962) and Beck (1967) have postulated dysfunctional cognitions as the source of depression. Beck in particular explicitly discusses "loss of positive motivation" and attributes it to "an attitude of hopelessness underlying this symptom" (Beck, Rush, Shaw, & Emery, 1979, p. 183). There is no attempt at a more rigorous derivation of the symptom. However, Beck asserts that depressives' negative schemata distort their information processing so as to yield gloomier conclusions about themselves, the future, and the world. Presumably this formulation again implies an Expectancy X Value type of transformation that discourages choice and action.

More specifically, Pietromonaco and Rook (1987) have found specific evidence of heightened risk perception associated with depression. Using BDI scores in a college student sample to assess depression, the investigators asked subjects to rate the benefits and risks of hypothetical actions and the likelihood that they would take the actions indicated. Mildly depressed subjects rated benefits lower on average for some scenarios and risks higher for all scenarios. Their expressed likelihood of taking the actions was lower than for nondepressed subjects only in "sociability" scenarios. The amount of risk perceived was inversely correlated with the likelihood of taking the actions, and this relationship was significantly stronger for depressed than for nondepressed subjects. These relationships did not emerge when subjects were asked to imagine a friend as the actor rather than themselves in each scenario. The results suggest that depressed individuals assess self-referent risks differently than do nondepressed individuals and also weight them more heavily in their decision making. The effect would be to discourage especially social goal striving.

There were few differences with regard to ratings or weightings of the benefits of actions in these data. Hence, these results are unable to account for anhedonic effects. However, they suggest a basis for depressed individuals' rejection of the opportunities—especially the social opportunities—available to them.

CONCLUSIONS AND CLINICAL IMPLICATIONS

Loss of interest is a pervasive quality of depression, enough so as to qualify it as one of the most central symptoms. Evidence for this comes from clinical, psychometric, and experimental observations and seems reasonably consistent cross-culturally. Depression may not be the only class of disorder characterized by diminished interest, but it is more central to depression than to any other class of syndromes, such as schizophrenia.

Diminished interest in new incentives may be understood as a normal feature of incentive-disengagement cycles, which involve inhibition of the pursuit of blocked goals, an inhibition that appears to generalize temporarily to other goals as well. The likely psychological mechanisms for this diminished interest are reduced positive emotionality, which reduces the subjective value of incentives, and pessimistic formulation of expectancies, such as heightened perception and weighting of risks in decision making. Another possible factor may be impaired ability to let go of previous emotions and unfulfilled intentions and devote adequate attention to new opportunities for action. Whether these factors can account for diminished interest during depressions other than reactive ones is still unresolved. At a neural level, depression is likely to entail impairment of the dopaminergic behavioral activation system.

Some people deepen and protract their depressions beyond the normal requirements of incentive-disengagement, sometimes through dysfunctional beliefs about themselves and their relationships with other people. Loss of interest in others is presumably both an accompaniment of depression and a factor in retarding patients' efforts to restore sources of pleasure. Both interpersonal and cognitive therapy work in somewhat different ways on both the beliefs and the relationship difficulties that discourage such attempts; and both appear capable of helping depressed patients out of their depressions, without medication, if the depressions are not too extreme (Elkin et al., 1989; Hollon, Evans, & DeRubeis, 1988).

There is, in fact, widespread agreement on the desirability of encouraging depressed patients to become involved in new sources of potential pleasure as soon as practicable, especially social ones. For example, interpersonal therapy (Klerman et al., 1984) is directed among other things toward moving patients into new relationships. Abramson et al. (1989) point out the likelihood that experiences with success can reduce hopelessness. Lantz (1981) assigned a random half of his therapy patients to 2 hours per week of social-service volunteer activity over a 7-week period. At the end of that time, the volunteer group had made significantly greater improvement than the controls in depression scores.

Some patients may benefit from social skills training. The benefit, however, may reside in an improved general sense of efficacy rather than from the specific skills taught (Zeiss, Lewinsohn, & Munoz, 1979). Thus, social skills training may function toward some of the same ends as cognitive and interpersonal therapy in reshaping patients' decision functions.

ACKNOWLEDGMENTS

I thank Richard A. Depue and William G. Iacono for helpful comments on an earlier draft.

REFERENCES

Abramson, L. Y., Metalsky, G. I., & Alloy, L. B. (1989). Hopelessness depression: A theory-based subtype of depression. *Psychological Review, 96,* 358–372.

Abramson, L. Y., Seligman, M. E., & Teasdale, J. D. (1978). Learned helplessness in humans: Critique and reformulation. *Journal of Abnormal Psychology, 87,* 49–74.

American Psychiatric Association (1987). *Diagnostic and statistical manual of mental disorders (3rd ed.–rev.).* Washington, DC: Author.

Arieti, S. (1974). *Interpretation of schizophrenia* (2nd ed.). New York: Basic Books.

Barnett, P. A., & Gotlib, I. H. (1988). Psychosocial functioning and depression: Distinguishing among antecedents, concomitants, and consequences. *Psychological Bulletin, 104,* 97–126.

Beck, A. T. (1967). *Depression: Clinical, experimental, and theoretical aspects.* New York: Hoeber.

Beck, A. T., Rush, A. J., Shaw, B. E., & Emery, G. (1979). *Cognitive therapy of depression.* New York: Guilford.

Berenbaum, H., & Oltmanns, T. F. (1992). Emotional experience and expression in schizophrenia and depression. *Journal of Abnormal Psychology, 101,* 37–44.

Binitie, A. (1975). A factor-analytical study of depression across cultures (African and European). *British Journal of Psychiatry, 127,* 559–563.

Brehm, J. W. (1972). *Responses to loss of freedom: A theory of psychological reactance.* Morristown, NJ: General Learning Press.

Brown, S.-L., Sweeney, D. R., & Schwartz, G. E. (1979). Differences between self-reported and observed pleasure in depression and schizophrenia. *Journal of Nervous and Mental Disease, 167,* 410–415.

Clark, D. C., Cavanaugh, S. von A., & Gibbons, R. D. (1983). The core symptoms of depression in medical and psychiatric patients. *Journal of Nervous and Mental Disease, 171,* 705–713.

Clark, D. C., Gibbons, R. D., Fawcett, J., Aagesen, C. A., & Sellers, D. (1985). Unbiased criteria for severity of depression in alcoholic inpatients. *Journal of Nervous and Mental Disease, 173,* 482–487.

Costello, C. G. (1972). Depression: Loss of reinforcers or loss of reinforcer effectiveness? *Behavior Therapy, 3,* 240–247.

Coyne, J. C., Kessler, R. C., Tal, M., Turnbull, J., Wortman, C. B., & Greden, J. F. (1987). Living with a depressed person. *Journal of Consulting and Clinical Psychology, 55,* 347–352.

Cunningham, M. R. (1988). What do you do when you're happy or blue? Mood, expectancies, and behavioral interest. *Motivation and Emotion, 12,* 309–331.

Denney, D. R., Stephenson, L. A., Penick, E. C., & Weller, R. A. (1988). Lymphocyte subclasses and depression. *Journal of Abnormal Psychology, 97,* 499–502.

Depue, R. A., & Iacono, W. G. (1989). Neurobehavioral aspects of affective disorders. *Annual Review of Psychology, 40,* 457–492.

Elkin, I., Shea, T., Watkins, J. T., Imber, S. D., Sotsky, S. M., Collins, J. F., Glass, D. R., Pilkonis, P. A., Leber, W. R., Docherty, J. P., Fiester, S. J., & Parloff, M. B. (1989). National Institute of Mental Health treatment of depression collaborative research program. *Archives of General Psychiatry, 46,* 971–982.

Ellis, A. (1962). *Reason and emotion in psychotherapy.* New York: Lyle Stuart.

Feighner, J. P., Robins, E., Guze, S. B., Woodruff, R. A., Jr., Winokur, G., & Munoz, R. (1972). Diagnostic criteria for use in psychiatric research. *Archives of General Psychiatry,* 1972, *26,* 57–63.

Fowles, D. C. (1980). The three arousal model: Implications of Gray's two-factor learning theory for heart rate, electrodermal activity, and psychopathy. *Psychophysiology, 17,* 87–104.

Free, M. L., & Oei, T. P. S. (1989). Biological and psychological processes in the treatment and maintenance of depression. *Clinical Psychology Review, 9,* 653–688.

Gartlan, J. S., & Brain, C. K. (1968). Ecology and social variability in *Cercopithecus aethiops* and *C. mitis.* In P. C. Jay (Ed.), *Primates: Studies in adaptation and variability* (pp. 253–292). New York: Holt, Rinehart and Winston.

Gray, J. A. (1982). *The neuropsychology of anxiety.* New York: Oxford University Press.

Gray, J. A. (1990). Brain systems that mediate both emotion and cognition. *Cognition and Emotion, 4,* 269–288.

Hamilton, E. W., & Abramson, L. Y. (1983). Cognitive patterns and major depressive disorder: A longitudinal study in a hospital setting. *Journal of Abnormal Psychology, 92,* 173–184.

Hammen, C. (1988). Depression and cognition about personal stressful life events. In L. B. Alloy (Ed.), *Cognitive processes in depression.* New York: Guilford.

Hammen, C., & Glass, D. R. (1975). Depression, activity, and evaluation of reinforcement. *Journal of Abnormal Psychology, 84,* 718–721.

Hazell, C. G. (1984). A scale for measuring experienced levels of emptiness and existential concern. *Journal of Psychology, 117,* 177–182.

Hibbert, G. A., Teasdale, J. D., & Spencer, P. (1984). Covariation of depressive symptoms over time. *Psychological Medicine, 14,* 451–455.

Hollon, S. D., Evans, M. D., & DeRubeis, R. J. (1988). Preventing relapse following treatment for depression: the Cognitive Psychopharmacology Project. In T. M. Field, P. M. McCabe, & N. Scheiderman (Eds.), *Stress and coping across development* (pp. 227–243). Hillsdale, NJ: Erlbaum.

Inamdar, S., Siomopoulos, G., Osborn, M., & Bianchi, E. C. (1979). Phenomenology associated with depressed moods in adolescents. *American Journal of Psychiatry, 136,* 156–159.

Kammer, D. (in press). On depression and state orientation: A few empirical and theoretical remarks. In J. Kuhl & J. Beckmann (Eds.), *Volition and personality: Action versus state orientation.* Göttingen: Hogrefe.

Kashani, J. H., Venzke, R., & Millar, E. A. (1981). Depression in children admitted to hospital for orthopaedic procedures. *British Journal of Psychiatry, 138,* 21–25.

Kay, S. R. (1991). *Positive and negative syndromes in schizophrenia: Assessment and research.* New York: Brunner/Mazel.

Keller, F., Straub, R., & Wolfersdorfer, M. (in press). State orientation and depression. In J. Kuhl & J. Beckmann (Eds.), *Volition and personality: Action versus state orientation.* Göttingen: Hogrefe.

Kelley, H. H. (1967). Attribution theory in social psychology. In D. Levine (Ed.), *Nebraska Symposium on Motivation* (Vol. 15; pp. 192–238). Lincoln: University of Nebraska Press.

Klerman, G. L., Weissman, M. M., Rounsaville, B. J., & Chevron, E. S. (1984). *Interpersonal psychotherapy of depression.* New York: Basic Books.

Klinger, E. (1975). Consequences of commitment to and disengagement from incentives. *Psychological Review, 82,* 1–25.

Klinger, E. (1977). *Meaning and void: Inner Experience and the incentives in people's lives.* Minneapolis: University of Minnesota Press.

Klinger, E. (1987). Current concerns and disengagement from incentives. In F. Halisch & J. Kuhl (Eds.), *Motivation, intention and volition.* Berlin: Springer.

Klinger, E., Barta, S. G., & Kemble, E. D. (1974). Cyclic activity changes during extinction in rats: A potential model of depression. *Animal Learning and Behavior, 2,* 313–316.

Klinger, E., Barta, S. G., & Maxeiner, M. E. (1980). Motivational correlates of thought content frequency and commitment. *Journal of Personality and Social Psychology, 39,* 1222–1237.

Kroll-Mensing, D. (1992). *Differentiating anxiety and depression: An experience-sampling analysis.* Doctoral dissertation, University of Minnesota.

Kuhl, J. (1981). Motivational and functional helplessness: The moderating effect of state versus action orientation. *Journal of Personality and Social Psychology, 40,* 155–170.

Kuhl, J. (1985). Volitional mediators of cognition behavior consistency: Self-regulatory processes and action versus state orientation. In J. Kuhl & J. Beckmann (Eds.), *Action control: From cognition to behavior* (pp. 101–128). Berlin: Springer.

Kuhl, J. (1990). *Self-regulation: A new theory for old applications.* Paper presented at the International Congress on Applied Psychology, Kyoto, Japan.

Kuhl, J., & Beckmann, J. (in press). *Volition and personality: Action versus state orientation.* Göttingen: Hogrefe.

Kuhl, J., & Helle, P. (1986). Motivational and volitional determinants of depression: The degenerated-intention hypothesis. *Journal of Abnormal Psychology, 95,* 247–251.

Kuhl, J., & Kazen-Saad, M. (in press). Motivational and volitional aspects of depression. In J. Kuhl & J. Beckmann (Eds.), *Volition and personality: Action versus state orientation.* Göttingen: Hogrefe.

Lantz, J. E. (1981). Depression and social interest tasks. *Journal of Individual Psychology, 37,* 113–116.

Lewinsohn, P. M. (1974). A behavioral approach to depression. In R. J. Friedman & M. M. Katz (Eds.),*The psychology of depression: Contemporary theory and research* (pp. 157–178). Washington, DC: Winston.

Lewinsohn, P. M., & Amenson, C. S. (1978). Some relations between pleasant and unpleasant mood-related events and depression. *Journal of Abnormal Psychology, 87,* 644–654.

Lewinsohn, P. M., & Graf, M. (1973). Pleasant activities and depression. *Journal of Consulting and Clinical Psychology, 41,* 261–264.

Lewinsohn, P. M., Mermelstein, R. M., Alexander, C., & MacPhillamy, D. J. (1985). The Unpleasant Events Schedule: A scale for the measurement of aversive events. *Journal of Clinical Psychology, 41,* 483–498.

MacPhillamy, D. J., & Lewinsohn, P. M. (1974). Depression as a function of levels of desired and obtained pleasure. *Journal of Abnormal Psychology, 83,* 651–657.

MacPhillamy, D. J., & Lewinsohn, P. M. (1982). The Pleasant Events Schedule: Studies on reliability, validity, and scale intercorrelation. *Journal of Consulting and Clinical Psychology, 50,* 363–380.

Paykel, E. S. (1977). Depression and appetite. *Journal of Psychosomatic Research, 21,* 401–407.

Perris, C., Eisemann, M., Eriksson, U., Perris, H., Kemali, D., Amati, A., del Vecchio, M., & Vacca, L. (1981). Transcultural aspects of depressive symptomatology. *Psychiatria clinica, 14,* 69–80.

Pietromonaco, P., & Rook, K. S. (1987). Decision style in depression: The contribution of perceived risks versus benefits. *Journal of Personality and Social Psychology, 52,* 399–408.

Price, J. S. (1972). Genetic and phylogenetic aspects of mood variation. *International Journal of Mental Health, 1,* 124–144.

Simons, A. D., Garfield, S. L., & Murphy, G. E. (1984). The process of change in cognitive therapy and pharmacotherapy for depression. *Archives of General Psychiatry, 41,* 45–51.

Spitzer, R. L., Endicott, J., & Robins, E. (1978). Research diagnostic criteria: Rationale and reliability. *Archives of General Psychiatry, 35,* 773–782.

Stone, A. A., Cox, D. S., Valdimarsdottir, H., Jandorf, L., & Neale, J. M. (1987). Evidence that secretory IgA antibody is associated with daily mood. *Journal of Personality and Social Psychology, 52,* 988–993.

Tellegen, A. (1985). Structures of mood and personality and their relevance to assessing anxiety, with an emphasis on self-report. In A. H. Tuma & J. Maser (Eds.), *Anxiety and the anxiety disorders* (pp. 681–706). Hillsdale, NJ: Erlbaum.

Watson, D., Clark, L. A., & Carey, G. (1988). Positive and negative affectivity and their relation to anxiety and depressive disorders. *Journal of Abnormal Psychology, 97,* 346–353.

Watson, D., Clark, L. A., & Tellegen, A. (1988). Development and validation of brief measures of Positive and Negative Affect: The PANAS Scales. *Journal of Personality and Social Psychology, 54,* 1063–1070.

Watson, D., & Kendall, P. C. (1989). Understanding anxiety and depression: Their relation to negative and positive affective states. In P. C. Kendall & D. Watson (Eds)., *Anxiety and depression: Distinctive and overlapping features* (pp. 3–26). New York: Academic Press.

Weiner, B. (1974). *Achievement motivation and attribution theory.* Morristown, NJ: General Learning Press.

Zeiss, A. M., Lewinsohn, P. M., & Munoz, R. F. (1979). Nonspecific improvement effects in depression using interpersonal skills training, pleasant activity schedules, or cognitive training. *Journal of Consulting and Clinical Psychology, 47,* 427–439.

CHAPTER 4

Anhedonia

PAUL WILLNER

DEFINITION AND MEASUREMENT

The term *anhedonia* was coined by Ribot (1897) to denote a diminished ability to experience pleasure (in contrast with *analgesia,* a diminished ability to experience pain). Anhedonia was suggested by Klein (1974) to be the defining characteristic of a subtype of depression that he termed *endogenomorphic.* Klein hypothesized that anhedonia reflected a state of subsensitivity in the brain mechanisms of reward and showed how many other symptoms of depression, such as a negative information processing bias (Beck, 1967) or a lack of motivation, could flow naturally from this underlying disorder. Klein's view of thc primacy of anhedonia was influential in the formulation of the Research Diagnostic Criteria (RDC) for endogenous depression (Spitzer, Endicott, & Robins, 1978) and their further development in the DSM-III (*Diagnostic and Statistical Manual of Mental Disorders,* 3rd edition) system (American Psychiatric Association, 1980). Anhedonia ("pervasive loss of interest or pleasure") is one of the RDC core symptoms and is even more prominent in DSM-III: A DSM-III diagnosis of melancholia requires both "loss of pleasure in all or almost all activities" and "lack of reactivity to usually pleasurable stimuli," plus three further symptoms from a list of six.

A study of the construct validity of these two sets of diagnostic criteria identified two subsets of endogenous symptoms, one defined by anhedonia, and the other defined by vegetative symptoms (terminal insomnia and weight loss) (Young, Scheftner, Klerman, Andreasen, & Hirschfeld, 1986); while these two sets of symptoms can vary independently (Hibbert, Teasdale, & Spencer, 1984), vegetative symptoms are only rarely seen in nonanhedonic patients (Young et al., 1986). These results support the concept of anhedonia as a core symptom of melancholia. However, a more relaxed attitude has been adopted in DSM-III-R (American Psychiatric Association, 1987), which gives equal weight to all items in the diagnostic checklist, requiring simply the presence of five features from a list of nine for a diagnosis of melancholia, with no "core." It is clear from an account of the DSM-III-R decision-making process that anhedonia was demoted from its DSM-III pedestal because there were insufficient data at the time (1985) to support its retention, not because evidence had emerged to justify its removal (Zimmerman & Spitzer, 1989). In the light of evidence that pervasive anhedonia may be a central characteristic in depressions with reduced rapid eye movement (REM) sleep latency (Giles, Roffwarg, Schlesser, & Rush, 1986), which is a reliable biological marker of melancholia (Kupfer & Thase, 1983), the decision to downplay the diagnostic significance of anhedonia may have been mistaken. Because anhedonia is strongly associated with suicidal ideation (Robbins & Alessi, 1985; Oei, Verhoeven, Westenberg, Zwart, & van Ree, 1990) and highly predictive of successful suicide (Fawcett, 1988), this question is of more than theoretical significance.

A number of instruments have been developed for the measurement of anhedonia, including a scale derived from the Minnesota Multiple Personality Inventory (Watson, Klett, & Lorei, 1970), and a subscale of the Schedule for Assessment of Negative Symptoms (Andreasen, 1981). Two rather more substantial self-report instruments have been extensively validated and widely used: the Chapman Anhedonia Scale and the Fawcett-Clark Pleasure Scale. The Anhedonia scale, which consists of 87 true–false items, contains two subscales, giving measures of Physical Anhedonia (lack of pleasure in physical activities) and Social Anhedonia (lack of pleasure in social activities) (Chapman, Chapman, & Raulin, 1976); there is also a more recent revised version of the Social Anhedonia Scale (Mishlove & Chapman, 1985). The shorter Pleasure Scale lists 36 potentially pleasurable events on which subjects rate their imagined response on a 5-point scale from "no pleasure at all" to "extreme and lasting pleasure" (Fawcett, Clark, Scheftner, & Gibbons, 1983). Within a group of depressed patients, there was a significant negative correlation ($r = -.42$, $p < .001$) between scores on the Anhedonia and Pleasure Scales (Fawcett, Clark, Scheftner, & Gibbons, 1983). A version of the Pleasure Scale suitable for use with children has also been developed: Children high in anhedonia, independent of their diagnosis, had lower aspirations, higher expectations of negative outcomes, and a greater tendency to attribute negative outcomes to internal causes (Kazdin, 1988).

Curiously, there has been very little attempt at behavioral assessment of pleasure capacity or pleasure seeking. One exception is a pilot study of the extent to which psychiatric patients availed themselves of the opportunity to play a selection of computer games (Miller, 1987). In another study the facial expressions of subjects were observed while watching selected film clips and rated for the presence or absence of happiness or disgust. Neither emotion differed between subjects scoring high or low on the Chapman Physical Anhedonia Scale (Berenbaum, Snowhite, & Oltmanns, 1987). This finding is corroborated by a further study in which pleasure capacity was assessed using a 9-point observer rating scale in a small sample of depressed patients: Again, these behavioral ratings did not correlate with scores on the Fawcett–Clark Pleasure Scale (H. D'Hanaen, personal communication,

1991). Similarly, we found no correlation (r = .03) between scores on the Fawcett–Clark Pleasure Scale and ratings of the pleasantness of an orange drink in a group of student volunteers (n = 40) (Willner & Breeze, unpublished observations, 1991). This apparent lack of correlation between scores on the Fawcett–Clark and Chapman scales and behavioral responses to pleasurable stimuli is disconcerting and requires further investigation. In addition to resolving this issue, the development of behavioral methodologies for the study of anhedonia would facilitate a convergence between the study of reward processes in people and in animals. As the latter is an extremely active research area, the relative lack of interest in the behavioral assessment of hedonic responses is a significant oversight.

CLINICAL MANIFESTATIONS

Fawcett, Clark, Scheftner, and Gibbons (1983) reported that depressed patients' scores on the Pleasure Scale were significantly lower than those of control subjects and, additionally, were bimodally distributed between a small group (18%) of patients who were severely anhedonic and a larger group whose scores were within the normal range. Similar findings were reported in a subsequent study using a French translation of the Pleasure Scale (Hardy, Jouvent, Lancrenon, Roumengous, & Feline, 1986). However, these studies may seriously underestimate the extent of anhedonia in depressed patients. A recent study using a Dutch translation of the Fawcett–Clark Scale found very little overlap between patients and controls: In this study, patients were withdrawn from antidepressant medication for at least 1 week before testing (H. D'Hanaen, personal communication).

Within the depressed group, anhedonia was strongly correlated with scores on two other scales, Hopelessness (Beck et al., 1974) and Social Impairment (Weissman & Bothwell, 1976); these characteristics reliably distinguished anhedonic patients from depressed patients with Pleasure scores in the normal range (Fawcett, Clark, Scheftner, & Gibbons, 1983; Fawcett, Clark, Scheftner, & Hedeker, 1983). Anhedonia scores appear also to be correlated with Introversion scores on the Eysenck Personality Inventory (Eysenck & Eysenck, 1968), in both depressed (Fawcett, Clark, Scheftner, & Gibbons, 1983; Fawcett, Clark, Scheftner, & Hedeker, 1983) and normal populations (Peterson & Knudson, 1983). From one perspective, this is only to be expected. Gray (1970) has proposed that the introversion–extroversion dimension is derived from two underlying dimensions of susceptibility to rewards and susceptibility to punishments; introverts being oversensitive to punishments but undersensitive to rewards (i.e., hypohedonic). Some conditioning experiments support this reformulation: Introverts performed better than extroverts when punishments (e.g., disapproval) were used but performed worse than extroverts with reward (Gray, 1981; McCord & Wakefield, 1981).

A second group of apparently anhedonic patients suffer from the subtype of chronic mild depression known as dysthymia. The dysthymic personality has been characterized as passive, gloomy, self-derogatory, complaining, self-disciplining, brooding, and preoccupied with inadequacy and failure (Akiskal, 1983; Standage, 1979). Dysthymia can be considered as a chronic mild melancholia: In Klein's (1974) terminology, dysthymia is a form of endogenomorphic depression. Dysthymic patients share a number of the biological features of melancholia, such as shortened REM sleep latencies, and they have a high probability of developing melancholia (Akiskal, 1983). Although the Pleasure or Anhedonia Scales have not been applied to a dysthymic population, there is a strong presumption that they would display a diminished pleasure capacity. Indeed, in ICD-9 (International Classification of Diseases, 9th edition) anhedonia is listed as one of the symptoms of neurasthenia.

Perhaps surprisingly, considering the historical importance of anhedonia in the diagnosis of depression, prior to Klein's (1974) account of endogenomorphic depression, anhedonia was more commonly thought of as a symptom of schizophrenia; the theoretical lineage of this concept runs from Bleuler (1911/1950) and Kraepelin (1919) through Myerson (1923, 1946) to Rado (1956) and Meehl (1962). And in fact, the Chapman Anhedonia Scales were originally developed as part of a group of five "schizophrenia-proneness" scales (Mishlove & Chapman, 1985). Studies using the Chapman Scales to measure anhedonia in schizophrenic patients have given mixed results: some studies have found schizophrenics to be more anhedonic than controls, as predicted (Chapman, et al., 1976; Katanis, Iacono, & Beiser, 1990), whereas others have not (Fawcett, Clark, Scheftner, & Gibbons, 1983; Schuck, Leventhal, Rothstein, & Irizarry, 1984). These inconsistencies probably reflect heterogeneity within the schizophrenic patient population in the distribution of positive and negative symptoms (cf. Crow, 1980). A schizophrenic deficit syndrome has been defined, comprising only negative symptoms, which tend to be increasingly prominent in more chronic cases. Anhedonia is not one of the diagnostic criteria for the deficit syndrome. Nevertheless, patients with the deficit syndrome were significantly more anhedonic on the Chapman Anhedonia Scales than the majority of schizophrenic patients, who did not meet the criteria for the deficit syndrome; the two groups did not differ in their scores on the other three Chapman Scales (Kirkpatrick & Buchanan, 1990).

Other overlaps between melancholia and the negative symptoms of schizophrenia may provide clues to the neural substrates of anhedonia as a symptom of depression: A second DSM-III-R symptom of melancholia, retardation, is strongly associated with negative symptoms in schizophrenic patients (Kulhara et al., 1989); whereas other negative symptoms such as affective flattening and apathy are frequently observed in depression (Andreasen & Akiskal, 1983; Pogue-Guile & Harrow, 1984). Liddle (1987) has hypothesized that this "psychomotor poverty" syndrome may reflect a functional impairment of the dorsolateral prefrontal cortex. However, the prefrontal cortex is also implicated in depression; damage to this region of the dominant hemisphere tends to cause severe depressive reactions (Robinson & Szetela, 1981; Jeste, Lohr, & Goodwin, 1988). Brain imaging studies provide a further parallel between schizophrenia and depression. There has been considerable recent interest in the observation that the cerebral ventricles are enlarged in a subgroup of schizophrenic patients, characterized by predominantly negative symptoms (Crow, 1980). It is less well known that exactly the same pathology, of a similar magnitude, is seen in a similar proportion (around 20%) of depressed patients (Jeste et al., 1988). However, the relationship of ventricular enlargement to anhedonia is uncertain. Some studies of depressed patients have reported that ventricular enlargement is associated with "endogenous features," but others report an association with delusional symptoms (Jeste et al., 1988); the primary association may simply be with the severity of depression.

As noted earlier, the construction of the Chapman Anhedonia Scales was motivated by the concept of a schizophrenia-prone ("schizotypal") personality (Meehl, 1962). However, although the concept of schizotypy has attracted considerable attention, there have been very few prospective studies of whether anhedonia is actually predictive of later schizophrenic episodes (Watson, Kucala, & Jacobs, 1978), and while not entirely consistent (e.g., Mishlove & Chapman, 1985), studies in normal populations have tended to find that anhedonia and schizophrenia-like perceptual and cognitive dysfunctions vary independently (Chapman, Edell, & Chapman, 1980; Chapman, Chapman, & Miller, 1982; Venables, Wilkins, Mitchell, Raine, & Boules, 1990). Given the importance of anhedonia as a symptom of depression, the question must arise whether anhedonia might be a better predictor of depression. Evidence that anhedonia might be a preexisting personality trait among depression-prone (and schizophrenia-prone) individuals comes from a recent study showing that anhedonia scores were elevated not only among depressed (and schizophrenic) patients but also, to a lesser extent, in their nondepressed (and nonschizophrenic) first-degree relatives (Katsanis et al., 1990). The concept of anhedonia as a character trait of some depressed patients is supported by the observation that, relative to normally hedonic depressed patients, anhedonic patients remained significantly anhedonic at discharge and in a subsequent follow-up (Clark, Fawcett, Salazar-Gruesco, & Fawcett, 1984). However, in the only prospective study, low scores on the Pleasure Scale did not predict the onset of depression (Clark, Salazar-Gruesco, Grabler, & Fawcett, 1984). Thus, whether anhedonia is a personality trait of some depressed people or a characteristic of the depressed state is at present uncertain.

BRAIN MECHANISMS OF REWARD

Unlike most other symptoms of depression, anhedonia has an explicit behavioral conceptualization, in terms of subsensitivity to rewards (Klein, 1974; Meehl, 1975). This carries the major benefit that anhedonia can be studied in subhuman species, in which the underlying physiological mechanisms are open to experimental investigation.

The brain mechanisms of reward have been the subject of a substantial recent research effort, in which attention has focused increasingly on a pathway known as the mesolimbic dopamine (DA) system. This system originates in the ventral tegmental area (VTA) of the midbrain and projects forward through the basal forebrain in the medial forebrain bundle, to terminate in the ventral striatum and, in particular, the nucleus accumbens, with some fibers extending further forward to the prefrontal cortex (the mesocortical system). There is considerable evidence that this system plays a crucial role in the reward process, and this hypothesis provides a unified framework within which to interpret the effects of diverse sources of reward, including brain stimulation, drugs of abuse, natural reinforcers, and second-order (conditioned) reinforcers. Certainly, many loose ends, exceptions, and diversions remain, but a focus on the mesolimbic DA system provides considerable explanatory power (Liebman & Cooper, 1989; Willner & Scheel-Kruger, 1991; Wise, 1982, 1989).

Until recently, and since its discovery by Olds and Milner in 1954, intracranial self-stimulation (ICSS) has been the major paradigm used for the investigation of reward processes. In this procedure, electrical stimulation of the brain is used to reinforce behavior, typically, lever pressing. ICSS may be elicited from many parts of the brain, including most regions of the limbic system. Although early studies suggested that ICSS had unusual properties compared with natural rewards (for example, rapid extinction), it was later recognized that these properties derive from differences in the experimental procedures typically employed (such as the delay of reinforcement); when such extraneous factors are equated, ICSS appears comparable to a high-incentive natural reward presented under conditions of low drive (e.g., Gibson, Reid, Sakai, & Porter, 1965). These parallels, together with the observation that responding for ICSS performance is influenced by many of the factors that control responding for natural rewards, have justified the assumption that the ICSS electrode stimulates directly the neural substrates that are activated indirectly by natural rewards (Hoebel, 1976). A degree of caution, however, is required: Although people implanted with self-stimulation electrodes report a variety of pleasurable sensations, they also report other reasons for stimulating, such as curiosity (Atrens, 1984; Valenstein, 1973). Nevertheless, the commonality of anatomical substrate between ICSS and other types of reward supports the use of this procedure as an animal model of hedonic behavior (see also Koob, 1989; Wise, 1989).

The role of the mesolimbic DA system in ICSS is well established. ICSS electrodes located in the lateral hypothalamus or medial forebrain bundle (the classic ICSS sites) stimulate a descending fiber system whose terminals make synaptic contact with the DA cell bodies in the VTA (Bielajew & Shizgal, 1986) and activate the mesolimbic DA projection, as demonstrated by an increase in the metabolic activity of DA cells in the VTA (Porrino et al., 1984) and an increase in the release of DA in the nucleus accumbens (Phillips & Fibiger, 1989). Conversely, destruction of the DA innervation of the nucleus accumbens, or the administration of DA receptor antagonists, causes a profound decrease in sensitivity to ICSS that cannot be attributed to motor deficits (Phillips & Fibiger, 1989).

The mesolimbic system is also an important substrate for the rewarding properties of self-administered drugs. The evidence is particularly clear in the case of psychomotor stimulants: Again, the destruction of DA terminals in the nucleus accumbens or the administration of DA receptor antagonists can lead to the cessation of responding for drug self-administration (Koob & Goeders, 1989). The opposite effect, an increase in responding, is sometimes observed; this appears to be an attempt to compensate for loss of reward, and lesioned animals will rapidly cease responding if the work requirement is increased (Koob & Goeders, 1989). The actions of other drugs of abuse also involve the mesolimbic DA system, though here the evidence is more complex because some drugs appear to act beyond the DA system. In the case of opiates, for example, intracranial self-administration of morphine to the VTA is blocked by procedures that impair mesolimbic DA function, but these procedures spare morphine self-administration in the nucleus accumbens (Cooper, 1991).

The most important body of evidence, in relation to hedonic behavior in people, is that implicating the mesolimbic DA system in the effects of natural rewards. Behavior maintained by a wide variety of natural rewards, and under a wide variety of experimental conditions, is impaired by DA antagonist drugs (Bradshaw & Szabadi, 1989; Willner, Phillips, & Muscat, 1991). Consummatory responses are relatively resistant to DA receptor antagonists: for example, low doses of DA receptor antagonists can abolish the conditioned activity that precedes food delivery, without affecting consumption of the food when it is delivered (Salamone, 1991). Similarly, operant behavior maintained by frequent reinforcement is more resistant to suppression by DA receptor antagonists than behavior maintained by infrequent reinforcement (see Willner, 1991). Nevertheless, DA receptor antagonists do also impair consummatory responses and, as in the case of drug reward and ICSS, it can be demonstrated that motor impairments are not responsible. For example, DA receptor antagonists can decrease the preference for a favored reward in a choice test, without affecting the overall level of consumption (see Willner, Phillips, & Muscat, 1991). Furthermore, if very sweet rewards are used, DA receptor antagonists can, in some circumstances, cause a paradoxical increase in responding, similar to that observed with drug rewards. In general, the effects of DA receptor antagonists on sweet reward closely resemble those of a decrease in sweetness (see Willner, Phillips, & Muscat, 1991).

In people, the majority of pleasurable events involve higher order, conditioned reinforcers, rather than primary reinforcers such as food or water. It is therefore of particular significance that the mesolimbic DA system appears to be a crucial substrate for the acquisition and expression of conditioned reinforcement. A conditioned reinforcer is a previously neutral stimulus that controls behavior by virtue of having been paired with a primary reward. Amphetamine and other indirect DA agonists facilitate responding maintained by conditioned reinforcement, and these effects are abolished by lesions of DA terminals in the nucleus accumbens (see Cador et al., 1991). Conversely, DA antagonists have been found to impair conditioned reinforcement (Hoffman & Beninger, 1985). This effect has been studied primarily in the place preference paradigm. In this paradigm, rewards are administered in one of two distinctive environments. Following a series of conditioning trials, the animal is allowed to choose between the two environments in the absence of the primary reward, and the strength of the reward is assessed by measuring the time the animal spends in the reward-associated environment. This paradigm has been used extensively to study the rewarding properties of self-administered drugs and is also sensitive to natural reinforcers such as food or sucrose (Carr, Phillips, & Fibiger, 1989). Following DA antagonist treatment or the destruction of DA terminals in the nucleus accumbens, environments paired with rewarding drugs or with food do not support place preference conditioning (Carr et al., 1989).

In addition to acting as a substitute for the primary reinforcer, conditioned reinforcers also elicit active preparatory behaviors, and indeed, this is their major function (Wise, 1989). The preparatory phase of appetitive behavior is accompanied by a substantial increase in the release of DA in the nucleus accumbens (Phillips, Pfauss, & Blaha, 1991). Conversely, appetitive behavior is abolished by DA antagonists or by lesions of the mesolimbic system (Phillips et al., 1991). This impairment of the DA-dependent preparatory behavior elicited by conditioned reinforcers may be homologous to the symptom "loss of interest," which, along with anhedonia, is the second cardinal symptom of major depression.

ANIMAL MODELS OF ANHEDONIA

Animal models of depression provide a potentially productive means of investigating the brain mechanisms underlying anhedonia, and their relationship to the systems implicated in the normal response to hedonic events. Although many animal models of depression have been developed, however, only a small minority are concerned with responsiveness to rewards. The majority are directed toward peripheral aspects of depression, typically, psychomotor changes (cf. Willner, 1990, 1991; Willner, Sampson, Papp, Phillips, & Muscat, 1991). This is surprising, considering the extent of current research interest in the brain mechanisms of reward, and the significance of anhedonia within the clinical picture. Those animal models of depression that do attempt to model anhedonia vary somewhat in the methods of inducing subsensitivity to reward, and in the techniques used to detect it. Four such paradigms have been described, three of which use ICSS as their model of hedonic behavior.

One recent model is based on the observation that responding for ICSS in adult male rats was decreased by neonatal administration of the tricyclic antidepressant clomipramine (CMI), which also caused a number of other abnormalities, including decreases in sexual and aggressive behavior, and a shortening of REM sleep latency (Vogel, Neill, Hagler, & Kors, 1991a,b). This model is impressive for the range of symptoms displayed, though at present, the extent to which they can be reversed by antidepressants is uncertain, and the mechanisms by which neonatal CMI has adverse effects in mature animals are unknown. These studies raise the disconcerting possibility that a breast-fed infant could develop a susceptibility to melancholia by ingesting tricyclic antidepressants prescribed to the nursing mother for the relief of postpartum depression.

A second manipulation that has been reported to decrease responding for ICSS is withdrawal from chronic amphetamine treatment. In these studies, amphetamine was administered to rats for between 4 to 14 days, typically using several administrations each day, at increasing doses. Following withdrawal, the threshold for ICSS was elevated (Cassens, Actor, Kling, & Schildkrant, 1981; Leith & Barrett, 1976); after 2 weeks of amphetamine treatment, this effect lasted for at least 18 days (Leith & Barrett, 1976). The demonstration of an increase in ICSS threshold, rather than simply a decrease in response rate, rules out a trivial explanation of these effects in terms of a decrease in locomotor activity. There is an obvious parallel between the effects of stimulant withdrawal and the depressions that frequently follow the cessation of chronic stimulant use (Blum, 1976; Watson, Hartman, & Schildkraut, 1972), though in the animal model, the time course is rather more compressed. As in the neonatal CMI model, the neural mechanisms have not been established; in a single pharmacological study, normal responding was restored, following amphetamine withdrawal, by chronic treatment with imipramine or amitriptyline (Kokkinidis, Zacharko, & Predy, 1980).

The best known animal model of depression, learned helplessness, is based on the after effects of exposure to uncontrollable stress (usually electric shocks) (Seligman, 1975), which are comparable in many respects to symptoms of depression (Weiss et al., 1982) and are reversed with reasonable selectivity by subchronic (3–7 days) treatment with tricyclic or atypical antidepressants (Sherman, Saquitre, & Petty, 1982). The interpretation of the learned helplessness phenomenon has been the subject of considerable controversy, and there are numerous reviews of the validity of this procedure as an animal model of depression (see Willner, 1986, 1991).

The majority of studies within this tradition have investigated the effects of stress on aversively motivated behaviors. However, inescapable electric footshock has also been shown to decrease ICSS responding in mice; this effect is not seen following exposure to comparable escapable shock. Normal sensitivity to brain stimulation reward was restored by chronic, but not acute, treatment with antidepressant drugs, administered prophylactically or following exposure to inescapable shock. These studies have mainly used the rate of ICSS as the dependent variable, which is susceptible to a variety of nonspecific influences. However, an impairment of sensitivity to reward is indicated by the observation that the effects of inescapable shock are anatomically specific: ICSS elicited from the VTA (the origin of the mesolimbic DA projection), or from the nucleus accumbens or frontal cortex (two of its terminal fields), was suppressed by inescapable shock, but ICSS elicited from the substantia nigra (the origin of the nigrosriatal DA projection) was unaffected. Furthermore, within the VTA, ICSS from certain regions was affected by footshock, whereas comparable rates of ICSS elicited from other regions were not (Zacharko, Bowers, Kokkinidis, & Anisman, 1983; Zacharko, Bowers, & Anisman, 1984; Zacharko, Lalonde, Kasian, & Anisman, 1987; Zacharko & Anisman, 1991). The anatomical specificity of the aftereffects of inescapable shock probably reflects a similar specificity in its acute effects. Thus, shock and other stressors are known to increase DA release in the VTA and its projections in the nucleus accumbens and frontal cortex; by contrast, stress does not usually activate the nigrastriatal DA system (see Zacharko & Anisman, 1991).

Two observations regarding this model may contribute to an eventual understanding of the origins of anhedonia. One is that a prolonged decrease in ICSS responding was only found if the animals were tested for ICSS in the immediate aftermath of stress; otherwise, the effect dissipated rapidly (Zacharko et al., 1983). The second is that uncontrollable electric shock has variable behavioral effects (most of which are antidepressant-reversible) in different inbred mouse strains. To take an extreme example, in the C57BL/67 strain, exposure to inescapable shock severely impaired subsequent learning to escape shock but had no effect on ICSS responding, whereas the DBA/2J strain showed exactly the opposite pattern (Shanks & Anisman, 1988; Zacharko et al., 1987). These studies may provide a starting point for investigation of the physiological mechanisms underlying individual differences in responses to stress, and they may be of relevance to individual differences in patterns of depressive symptomatology.

The fourth anhedonia paradigm involves chronic sequential exposure to a variety of mild stressors, such as overnight illumination, tilting of the cage, periods of food or water deprivation, or changes of cagemates. Rats subjected chronically (1 to 4 weeks) to these low-grade stressors reduced their consumption of, and preference for, weak solutions of sucrose and saccharin. Stressed animals were also subsensitive to reward in the place conditioning paradigm: The normal preference for environments paired with food, sucrose solutions, or amphetamine was abolished or greatly attenuated in stressed animals. The impairment of sucrose consumption was restored to normal, during continued application of the stress schedule, by treatment with tricyclic antidepressants for 2 to 5 weeks (Willner, Towell, Sampson, Muscat, & Sophokleous, 1987; Willner, Sampson, Papp, Phillips, & Muscat, 1991; Sampson, Muscat, & Willner, 1991).

As in the uncontrollable shock–ICSS model, chronic mild stress has been found to have selective effects on DA transmission within the mesolimbic system. In an initial study, postmortem levels of DA and its metabolites were increased in the nucleus accumbens, but not in the caudate nucleus or septal area, following several weeks of exposure to chronic mild stress (Willner, Klimek, Golembiowska, & Muscat, 1991). Subsequent experiments used fast cyclic voltammetry to monitor DA release in vivo in response to electrical stimulation of the medial forebrain bundle; chronic stress increased DA release in the nucleus accumbens, but not in the caudate nucleus (Stamford et al., 1991). These effects are consistent with the evidence that DA release in the mesolimbic system is increased by acute stress (see Zacharko & Anisman, 1991) but inconsistent with the evidence that anhedonia results from a reduction in mesolimbic DA function. A resolution of this discrepancy lies in the further observation that, in addition to increasing DA release in the nucleus accumbens, chronic mild stress also decreases the sensitivity of postsynaptic DA receptors. This effect, which is probably explains why chronically stressed animals are anhedonic, may be secondary to a prolonged exposure to abnormally high DA levels (Willner, Klimek, Golembiowska, & Muscat, 1991; Papp, Muscat, & Willner, 1992).

Antidepressant drugs have traditionally been assumed to exert their clinical effects through an interaction with noradrenergic or serotonergic systems. However, after chronic administration, antidepressants have also been found to potentiate the psychomotor stimulant effects of DA agonists, administered either systemically or by direct injection into the nucleus accumbens (reviewed by Willner, Muscat, Papp, & Sampson, 1991); the biochemical basis of these effects was for some years obscure but has now been elucidated (Klimek & Maj, 1989). An increase in the sensitivity of DA receptors in the nucleus accumbens might be expected to counteract anhedonia, and recent studies have confirmed that this is indeed the mechanism by which tricyclic antidepressants normalize behavior in the chronic mild stress model. In these experiments, antidepressant treatment was initiated following the appearance of a reliable impairment of sucrose consumption (3–5 weeks), and continued for the remainder of the experiment (5–9 weeks). Following the recovery of performance in the antidepressant-treated stressed groups, the role of DA was assessed by administering a single injection of a low dose of a DA receptor antagonist prior to the sucrose test. DA antagonists had no effect on sucrose consumption in nonstressed animals or in stressed but untreated animals treated with tricyclic antidepressants. These results suggest that the anti-anhedonic action of antidepressants may result from increases in the sensitivity of postsynaptic DA receptors (Muscat, Sampson, & Willner, 1990; Sampson et al., 1991; Willner, Phillips, & Muscat, 1991).

It is important to emphasize that these data should not be overinterpreted. If they are of clinical relevance, it is in relation to a specific subset of symptoms: There is no suggestion that dopaminergic mechanisms are solely responsible for the many varieties of depressive symptomatology. This point is illustrated by studies using another model, which involves cooperative behavior between pairs of rats. Cooperative behavior deteriorates if the animals are housed singly, but may be restored by chronic antidepressant treatment. However, unlike hedonic reactivity, cooperative behavior does not appear to involve a dopaminergic substrate, and the action of imipramine in this model was reversed by the 5-HT antagonist metergoline (Willner et al., 1989); by contrast, metergoline did not reverse the action of imipramine in the chronic mild stress model (Muscat et al., 1990). Thus, imipramine reverses some symptoms displayed in animal models of depression by increasing transmission at DA synapses, but other symptoms are reversed by actions on the 5-HT system; and there is no reason to suppose that this represents an exhaustive analysis. The bottom line is that the role of DA in depression and in the clinical actions of antidepressants cries out for reevaluation (cf. Del Zompo, Boccheta, Bernardi, Burrai, & Corsini, 1989; Mayeux et al., 1986; Mouret, Lemoine, & Minuit, 1987; Mouret, LeMoin, Minuit, & Robelin, 1988).

ORIGINS OF ANHEDONIA

As noted earlier, the origins of anhedonia are uncertain. Some theorists (e.g., Meehl, 1975) consider that a diminished capacity of pleasure is a characterological trait ("hypohedonia"), which worsens at the onset of a depressive episode. This position is supported by several lines of evidence previously discussed. First, anhedonia, as measured by the Chapman Scales, was elevated in first-degree relatives of depressed patients (Katsanis et al., 1990) raising the possibility that there might be a genetic contribution to anhedonia. This suggestion receives support from studies showing that the suppression of ICSS responding by uncontrollable electric shock varied considerably between different inbred strains of mice (Zacharko & Anisman, 1991). Finally, studies showing decreased ICSS performance in mature animals that were administered CMI shortly after birth demonstrate that anhedonia can result from early experience (Vogel et al., 1991a); this model involves a specific neonatal drug experience, but presumably other types of early event could have similar consequences.

The intensification of a long-standing hypohedonia at the start of an episode of major depression carries some conviction as an account of the origin of anhedonia in dysthymic patients, who are at high risk to develop major depression (Akiskal, 1983). However, the role of preexisting hypohedonia is far less compelling in nondysthymic individuals. On the one hand, there is evidence of continuity between depressive and normal states. Anhedonia in depressed patients is associated with dysfunctional attitudes characteristic of depression (Fawcett, Clark, Scheftner, & Gibbons, 1983; Fawcett, Clark, Scheftner, & Hedeker, 1983); similarly, undepressed subjects scoring low on the Pleasure Scale also have dysfunctional attitudes, including higher expectations of negative outcomes (Kazdin, 1988) and a tendency to blame themselves, rather than external factors, for undesirable events (Kazdin, 1988). Nevertheless, there is at present no reliable evidence that low pleasure capacity in a normal individual places that person at risk for depression, let alone melancholia. The only prospective study to ask this question directly found that low scores on the Pleasure Scale did not predict the onset of depression (Clark, Salazar-Gruesco, Grabler, & Fawcett, 1984).

Even if it could be shown that a state of hypohedonia always precedes a melancholic episode (and this at present seems rather unlikely), it would still be necessary to explain the intensification of this predisposition into full-blown anhedonia. Some theorists have suggested ways in which the loss of significant sources of reinforcement could lead to the devaluation of related reinforcers (Costello, 1972; Klinger, 1975), but these hypotheses have received little investigation. In the absence of relevant clinical studies, it comes as something of a shock to discover that in animal models, anhedonia is readily and reliably induced by relatively mild stressors (Willner, Muscat, Papp, & Sampson, 1991; Willner, Sampson, Papp, Phillips, & Muscat, 1991; Zacharko & Anisman, 1991). These observations must serve as one starting point for future investigations of the origins of anhedonia in the clinic, but their implications are at present far from clear.

Depressed patients find stressful events more painful than nondepressed subjects (Schless, Schwartz, Goetz, & Mendels, 1974; Lewinsohn & Tarkington, 1979; Hammen & Cochran, 1981); and one study has reported that this effect was specific to melancholic patients (Willner, Wilkes, & Orwin, 1990). Thus, anhedonia could result from an increase in perceived stress, as distinct from, or in addition to, an increase in the objective frequency or severity of stressors. Only prospective studies (which have not yet been carried out) will establish whether changes in the perception of stress precede the onset of depression. However, the tendency to perceive stressors as more intense is probably part of the more general negtive information processing bias that typifies depressive thinking (Beck, 1967); and while the concept of a depressed cognitive style is well established, the evidence that depressive thinking precedes the onset of a depressive episode is rather weak (see e.g., Golin, Sweeney, & Schaeffer, 1981; Hammen, Adrian, & Hiroto, 1988; Lewinsohn, Steinmetz, Larson, & Franklin, 1981; Manly, McMahon, Bradley, & Davidson, 1982).

An alternative is that both depressive thinking and/or anhedonia might be secondary to depressed mood. There is good evidence from studies using mood induction procedures in normal volunteers that the onset of depressed mood does cause a negative information processing bias (Goodwin & Williams, 1982). Significantly, the induction of a depressed mood not only accentuates the negative but also reduces pleasure capacity, as assessed by ratings of the enjoyability of pleasant activities (Carson & Adams, 1980). We have recently observed that the induction of a depressed or an elated mood by the Velten (1968) procedure caused corresponding changes in hedonic responses to taste stimuli (Willner, Netherton, & Breeze, unpublished observations, 1991).

To summarize, there is evidence that anhedonia may precede the onset of depression in some individuals; that stress may play a role in the onset or intensification of anhedonia; and that anhedonia may be secondary to depressed mood. The relative contribution of these factors and the extent of their explanatory power, particularly in relation to the difference between anhedonic and normally hedonic depressions, are questions that remain to be answered.

STATUS AND PROSPECTS

This review has highlighted a number of issues that require and deserve further investigation. First, there is an urgent need for more studies of how depressed patients actually respond in potentially pleasurable situations, and for the development of reliable standardized instruments for behavioral assessment of anhedonia. Work to date suggests that anhedonia as measured by the Chapman Anhedonia Scales and the Fawcett–Clark Pleasure Capacity Scale may not predict hedonic behavior. It will be of great importance to clarify this relationship and, if possible, resolve the apparent discrepancy between subjective and objective assessments: If it cannot be resolved, it will be essential to establish whether rating scales or behavioral assessment methods have greater clinical relevance.

Research using experimental animals has established the mesolimbic dopamine system as a major substrate for hedonic behavior, and this raises a further series of issues. Dopaminergic mechanisms have not featured prominently in most accounts of the neurobiology of depression (see Willner, 1985); yet evidence has been reviewed that dopaminergic mechanisms are responsible not only for anhedonic behavor in animal models but also for the reversal of anhedonia by antidepressant drugs. Some of the techniques used in the animal studies could be readily implemented in a clinical context. For example, in the chronic mild stress model, the administration of single low doses of DA receptor antagonists reinstate anhedonia following successful chronic antidepressant treatment. An attempt to replicate this finding in recovered patients would provide a rapid means of evaluating both the role of DA in human anhedonia and the relevance of the animal data.

The origins of anhedonia constitute another area of relative ignorance that probably will only be illuminated by prospective longitudinal studies of hedonic attitudes and behavior in relation to the onset of depression. It will be necessary also to evaluate the temporal relationships between changes in hedonic measures on the one hand and changes in perceptions of stress and cognitive styles on the other. This is a particularly challenging research agenda. However, it is fully justified by the pivotal position of anhedonia as a prominent clinical manifestation, a powerful theoretical construct, and a unique bridge to the neurobiology of depression.

ACKNOWLEDGMENTS

I am grateful to the editor and to Dr. H. D'Hanaen for their perceptive comments on an earlier draft of this chapter. Experiments from the author's laboratory were partly supported by the Medical Research Council of Great Britain.

REFERENCES

Akiskal, H. S. (1983). Dysthymic disorder: Psychopathology of proposed chronic depressive subtypes. *American Journal of Psychiatry 140,* 11–20.

American Psychiatric Association. (1980). *Diagnostic and statistical manual of psychiatric disorders* (DSM-III, 3rd ed.). Washington DC: Author.

American Psychiatric Association. (1987). *Diagnostic and statistical manual of psychiatric disorders* (DSM-III-R; 3rd ed.-rev.). Washington DC.: Author.

Andreasen, N. C. (1981). The Scale for the Assessment of Negative Symptoms. Iowa City: University of Iowa Press.

Andreasen, N. C., & Akiskal, H. S. (1983). The specifity of Bleulerian and Schneiderian symptoms: A critical reevaluation. *Psychiatric Clinics of North America, 6,* 41–54.

Atrens, D. M. (1984). Self-stimulation and psychotropic drugs: A methodological and conceptual critique. In N. S. Bond (Ed.), *Animal models in psychopathology* (pp. 227–256). Sydney, Australia: Academic Press.

Beck, A. T. (1967). *Depression: Clinical, experimental and therapeutic aspects.* New York: Harper & Row.

Beck. A. T., Weissman, A., Leste, A., & Trexler, L. (1974). The measurement of pessimism: The Hopelessness Scale. *Journal of Consulting and Clinical Psychology, 42,* 861–865.

Berenbaum, H., Snowhite, R., & Oltmanns, T. F. (1987). Anhedonia and emotional responses to affect evoking stimuli. *Psychological Medicine, 17,* 677–684.

Bielajew, C., & Schizgal, P. (1986). Evidence implicating descending fibres in self-stimulation of the medial forebrain bundle. *Journal of Neuroscience, 6,* 919–929.

Bleuler, E. (1950). *Dementia praecox, or the group of schizophrenias.* New York: International Universities Press. Original work published 1911.

Blum, K. (1976). Depressive states induced by drugs of abuse: Clinical evidence, theoretical mechanisms and proposed treatment. *Journal of Psychedelic Drugs,* 8, 235–262.

Bradshaw, C. M., & Szabadi, E. (1989). Central neurotransmitter systems and the control of operant behavior by "natural" positive reinforcers. In J. M. Liebman & S. J. Cooper (Eds.), *The neuropharmacological basis of reward* (pp. 320–376). Oxford: Oxford University Press.

Cador, M., Robbins, T. W., Everitt, B. J., Simon, J., LeMoal, M., & Stinus, L. (1991). Limbic-striatal interactions in reward-related processes: Modulation by the dopaminergic system. In P. Willner, & J. Scheel-Kruger (Eds.), *The mesolimbic dopamine system: From motivation to action* (pp. 225–250). Chichester: Wiley.

Carr, G. D., Fibiger, H. C., & Phillips, A. G. (1989). Conditioned place preference as a measure of drug reward. In J. M. Liebman & S. J. Cooper (Eds.), *The neuropharmacological basis of reward* (pp. 264–319). Oxford: Oxford University Press.

Carson, T. C., & Adams, H. E. (1980). Activity valence as a function of mood change. *Journal of Abnormal Psychology, 89,* 368–377.

Cassens, G. P., Actor, C., Kling, M., & Schildkraut, J. J. (1981). Amphetamine withdrawal affects threshold of intracranial self-stimulation. *Psychopharmacology, 73,* 318–322.

Chapman, L. J., Chapman, J. P., & Miller, E. N. (1982). Reliabilities and intercorrelations of eight measures of proneness to psychosis. *Journal of Consulting and Clinical Psychology, 50,* 187–195.

Chapman, L. J., Chapman, J. P., & Raulin, M. (1976). Scales for physical and social anhedonia. *Journal of Abnormal Psychology, 85,* 374–382.

Chapman, L. J., Edell, W. S., & Chapman, J. P. (1980). Physical anhedonia, perceptual aberration and psychosis proneness. *Schizophrenia Bulletin, 6,* 639–653.

Clark, D. C., Fawcett, J., Salazar-Gruesco, E., & Fawcett, E. (1984). Seven-month clinical outcome of anhedonic and normally hedonic depressed inpatients. *American Journal of Psychiatry, 141,* 1216–1220.

Clark, D. C., Salazar-Gruesco, E., Grabler, P., & Fawcett, J. (1984). Predictors of depression during the first six months of internship. *American Journal of Psychiatry, 141,* 1095–1098.

Cooper, S. J. (1991). Interactions between endogenous opioids and dopamine: Implications for reward and aversion. In P. Willner & J. Scheel-Kruger (Eds.), *The mesolimbic dopamine system: From motivation to action* (pp. 331–366). Chichester: Wiley.

Costello, C. G. (1972). Depression: Loss of reinforcement or loss of reinforcer effectiveness? *Behavior Therapy, 3,* 240–247.

Crow, T. J. (1980). Molecular pathology of schizophrenia: More than one disease process? *British Medical Journal, 280,* 66–68.

Del Zompo, M., Boccheta, A., Bernardi, F., Burrai, C., & Corsini, G. U. (1989). Clinical evidence for a role of dopaminergic systems in depressive syndromes. In G. L. Gessa & G. Serra (Eds.), *Dopamine and mental depression: Advances in the biosciences* (Vol. 77; pp. 177–184). New York: Pergamon.

Eysenck, H. J., & Eysenck, S. B. G. (1968). *Manual for the Eysenck Personality Inventory.* San Diego: Educational and Industrial Testing Services.

Fawcett, J. (1988). Predictors of early suicide: Identification and appropriate intervention. *Journal of Clinical Psychiatry,* (Suppl.) *49*(10), 7–8.

Fawcett, J., Clark, D. C., Scheftner, W. A., & Gibbons, R. D. (1983). Assessing anhedonia in psychiatric patients. The pleasure scale. *Archives of General Psychiatry, 40,* 79–84.

Fawcett, J., Clark, D. C., Scheftner, W. A., & Hedeker, D. (1983). Assessing differences between anhedonic and normally hedonic depressive states. *American Journal of Psychiatry, 140,* 1027–1030.

Gibson, W. E., Reid, L. D., Sakai, M., & Porter, P. B. (1965). Intracranial reinforcement compared with sugar-water reinforcement. *Science, 148,* 1357–1358.

Giles, D. E., Roffwarg, H. P., Schlesser, M. A., & Rush, A. J. (1986). Which endogenous depressive symptoms relate to REM latency reduction? *Biological Psychiatry, 21,* 473–482.

Golin, S., Sweeney, P. D., & Schaeffer, D. E. (1981). The causality of causal attributions in depression: A cross-lagged panel correlational analysis. *Journal of Abnormal Psychology, 90,* 14–22.

Goodwin, A. M., & Williams, J. M. G. (1982). Mood-induction research: Its implications for clinical depression. *Behavioral Research and Therapy, 20,* 373–382.

Gray, J. A. (1970). The psychophysiological basis of introversion-extraversion. *Behavioral Research and Therapy, 8,* 249–266.

Gray, J. A. (1981). A critique of Eysenck's theory of personality. In H. J. Eysenck (Ed.), *A model for personality* (pp. 246–276). New York: Springer.

Hammen, C. L., & Cochran, S. D. (1981). Cognitive correlates of life stress and depression in college students. *Journal of Abnormal Psychology, 90,* 23–27.

Hammen, H., Adrian, C., & Hiroto, D. (1988). A longitudinal test of the attributional vulnerability model in children at risk for depression. *British Journal of Clinical Psychology, 27,* 37–46.

Hardy, P., Jouvent, R., Lancrenon, S., Roumengous, V., & Feline, A. (1986). L'echelle de plaisir-deplaisir. Utilisation dans l'evaluation de la maladie depressive. *L'Encephale, 12,* 149–154.

Hibbert, G. A., Teasdale, J. D., & Spencer, P. (1984). Covariation of depressive symptoms over time. *Psychological Medicine, 14,* 451–455.

Hoebel, B. G. (1976). Brain stimulation reward and aversion in relation to behavior. In A. Wauquier & E. Rolls (Eds.), *Brain stimulation reward* (pp. 331–372). New York: Elsevier.

Hoffman, D. C., & Beninger, R. J. (1985). The effects of pimozide on the establishment of conditioned reinforcement as a function of the amount of conditioning. *Psychopharmacology, 87,* 454–460.

Jeste, D. V., Lohr, J. B., & Goodwin, F. K. (1988). Neuroanatomical studies of major affective disorders: A review and suggestions for further research. *British Journal of Psychiatry, 153,* 444–459.

Katsanis, J., Iacono, W. G., & Beiser, M. (1990). Anhedonia and preceptual aberration in first-episode psychotic patients and their relatives. *Journal of Abnormal Psychology, 99,* 202–206.

Kazdin, A. E. (1988). Evaluation of the pleasure scale in the assessment of anhedonia in children. *Journal of the American Academy of Child and Adolescent Psychiatry, 28,* 364–372.

Kirkpatrick, B., & Buchanan, R. W. (1990). Anhedonia and the deficit syndrome of schizophrenia. *Psychiatry Research, 31,* 25–30.

Klein, D. F. (1974). Endogenomorphic depression: A conceptual and terminological revision. *Archives of General Psychiatry, 31,* 447–454.

Klimek, V., & Maj, J. (1989). Repeated administration of antidepressant drugs enhanced agonist affinity for mesolimbic D-2 receptors. *Journal of Pharmacy and Pharmacology, 41,* 555–558.

Klinger, E. (1975). Consequences of commitment to and disengagement from incentives. *Psychological Reviews, 82,* 1–24.

Kokkinidis, L., Zacharko, R. M., & Predy, P. A. (1980). Post-amphetamine depression of self-stimulation responding from the substantia nigra: Reversal by tricyclic antidepressants. *Pharmacology Biochemistry and Behavior, 13,* 379–383.

Koob, G. F. (1989). Anhedonia as an animal model of depression. In G. F. Koob, C. L. Ehlers, & D. J. Kupfer (Eds.), *Animal models of depression* (pp. 162–183). Boston: Birkhauser.

Koob, G. F., & Goeders, N. E. (1989). Neuroanatomical substrates of drug self-administration. In J. M. Liebman & S. J. Cooper (Eds.), *The neuropharmacological basis of reward* (pp. 214–263). Oxford: Oxford University Press.

Kraepelin, E. (1919). *Dementia praecox.* Edinburgh: Livingstone.

Kulhara, P., Avasthi, A., Chadda, R., Chandiramani, K., Mattoo, S. K., Kota, S. K., & Joseph, S. (1989). Negative and depressive symptoms in schizphrenia. *British Journal of Psychiatry, 154,* 207–211.

Kupfer, D. J., & Thase, M. E. (1983). The use of the sleep laboratory in the diagnosis of affective disorders. *Psychiatric Clinics of North America, 6,* 3–25.

Leith, N. J., & Barrett, R. J. (1976). Amphetamine and the reward system: Evidence for tolerance and post-drug depression. *Psychopharmacology, 46,* 19–25.

Lewinsohn, P. M., Steinmetz, J. L., Larson, D. W., & Franklin, J. (1981). Depression-related cognitions: Antecedent or consequence? *Journal of Abnormal Psychology, 90,* 213–219.

Lewinsohn, P. M., & Tarkington, J. (1979). Studies on the measurement of unpleasant events and relations with depression. *Applied Psychological Measurement, 3,* 83–101.

Liddle, P. F. (1987). Schizophrenic syndromes, cognitive performance and neurological dysfunction. *Psychological Medicine, 17,* 49–57.

Liebman, J. M., & Cooper, S. J. (Eds.), (1989). *The neuropharmacological basis of reward.* Oxford: Oxford University Press.

Manly, P. C., McMahon, R. J., Bradley, C. F., & Davidson, P. O. (1982). Depressive attributional style and depression following childbirth. *Journal of Abnormal Psychology, 91,* 245–254.

Mayeux, R., Stern, Y., Williams, J. B., Cote, L., Frantz, A., & Dyrenfurth, I. (1986). Clinical and biochemical features of depression in Parkinson's disease. *American Journal of Psychiatry, 143,* 756–759.

McCord, P. R., & Wakefield, J. A. (1981). Arithmetic achievement as a function of introversion-extraversion and teacher-presented reward and punishment. *Personality and Individual Differences, 2,* 145–152.

Meehl, P. E. (1962). Schizotaxia, schizotypy, schizophrenia. *American Psychologist, 17,* 827–838.

Meehl, P. E. (1975). Hedonic capacity: Some source conjectures. *Bulletin of the Meninger Clinic, 39,* 295–307.

Miller, R. E. (1987). Method to study anhedonia in hospitalized psychiatric patients. *Journal of Abnormal Psychology, 96,* 41–45.

Mishlove, M., & Chapman, L. J. (1985). Social anhedonia in the prediction of psychosis proneness. *Journal of Abnormal Psychology, 94,* 384–396.

Mouret, J., LeMoine, P., & Minuit, M. (1987). Marqueurs polygraphiques, cliniques et therapeutiques des depressions dopamino-dependantes (DDD). *Comptes Rendus de l'Academie de Science, Paris,* 305, Serie III, 301–306.

Mouret, J., LeMoine, P., Minuit, M. & Robelin, N. (1988). La L-tyrosine guerit, immediatement et a long terme, les depressions dopamino-dependantes (DDD). Etude clinique et polygraphique. *Comptes Rendus de l'Academie de Science, Paris,* 306, Serie III, 93–98.

Muscat, R., Sampson, D., & Willner, P. (1990). Dopaminergic mechanism of imipramine action in an animal model of depression. *Biological Psychiatry, 28,* 223–230.

Myerson, A. (1923). Anhedonia. *American Journal of Psychiatry, 2,* 87–1013.

Myerson, A. (1946). The constitutional anhedonic personality. *American Journal of Psychiatry, 102,* 774–449.

Nelson, J. C. (1987). The use of antipsychotic drugs in the treatment of depression. In J. Zohar, R. H. Belmaker (Eds.), *Treating resistant depression* (pp. 131–146). New York: PMA Publishing Corp.

Oei, T. I., Verhoeven, W. M. A., Westenberg, H. G. M., Zwart, F. M., & van Ree, J. M. (1990). Anhedonia, suicide ideation and dexamethasone nonsuppression in depressed patients. *Journal of Psychiatric Research, 24,* 25–35.

Olds, J., & Milner, P. (1954). Positive reinforcement produced by electrical stimulation of septal area and other regions of rat brain. *Journal of Comparative and Physiological Psychology, 47,* 419–427.

Papp, M., Muscat, R., & Willner, P. (1992). Subsensitivity to rewarding and locomotor stimulant effects of a dopamine agonist in an animal model of depression. *Psychopharmacology,* in press.

Papp, M., Willner, P., & Muscat, R. (1991). An animal model of anhedonia: Attenuation of sucrose consumption and place preference conditioning by chronic unpredictable mild stress. *Psychopharmacology, 104,* 255–259.

Peterson, C. A., & Knudson, R. M. (1983). Anhedonia; A construct validation approach. *Journal of Personality Assessment, 47,* 539–551.

Phillips, A. G., & Fibiger, H. C. (1989). Neuroanatomical bases of intracranial self-stimulation: Untangling the Gordian knot. In J. M. Liebman & S. J. Cooper (Eds.), *The neuropharmacological basis of reward* (pp. 66–105). Oxford: Oxford University Press.

Phillips, A. G., Pfauss, J. G., & Blaha, C. D. (1991). Dopamine and motivated behavior: Insights provided by in vivo analyses. In P. Willner & J. Scheel-Kruger (Eds.), *The mesolimbic dopamine system: From motivation to action* (pp. 199–224). Chichester, England: Wiley.

Pogue-Geile, M. F., & Harrow, M. (1984). Negative and positive symptoms in schizophrenia and depression: A follow-up. *Schizophrenia Bulletin, 10,* 371–387.

Porrino, L. J., Esposito, R. U., Seeger, T. F., Crane, A. M., Pert, A., & Sokoloff, L. (1984). Metabolic mapping of the brain during rewarding self-stimulation. *Science, 224,* 306–309.

Rado, S. (1956). *Psychoanalysis of behavior. Collected papers.* New York: Grune & Stratton.

Ribot, T. (1897). *The psychology of the emotions.* London: W. Scott.

Robbins, D. R., & Alessi, N. E. (1985). Depressive symptoms and suicidal behaviour in adolescents. *American Journal of Psychiatry, 142,* 588–592.

Robinson, R. G., & Szetela, B. (1981). Mood changes following left hemisphere brain injury. *Annals of Neurology, 9,* 447–453.

Salamone, J. (1991). *Behavioral pharmacology of dopamine systems: A new synthesis.* In P. Willner & J. Scheel-Kruger (Eds.), *The mesolimbic dopamine system: From motivation to action* (pp. 509–613). Chichester: Wiley.

Sampson, D., Muscat, R., & Willner, P. (1991). Reversal of antidepressant action by dopamine antagonists in an animal model of depression. *Psychopharmacology, 104,* 491–495.

Schless, A. P., Schwartz, L., Goetz, C., & Mendels, J. (1974). How depressives view the significance of life events. *British Journal of Psychiatry, 125,* 406–410.

Schuck, J., Leventhal, D., Rothstein, H., & Irizarry, V. (1984). Physical anhedonia and schizophrenia. *Journal of Abnormal Psychology, 93,* 342–344.

Seligman, M. E. P. (1975). *Helplessness: On depression, development and death.* San Francisco: Freeman.

Shanks, N., & Anisman, H. (1988). Stressor-provoked behavioral changes in six strains of mice. *Behavioral Neuroscience, 102,* 894–905.

Sherman, A. D., Saquitne, J. L., & Petty, F. (1982). Specificity of the learned helplessness model of depression. *Pharmacology Biochemistry and Behavior, 16,* 449–454.

Spitzer, R. L., Endicott, J., & Robins, E. (1978). Research diagnostic criteria: Rationale and reliability. *Archives of General Psychiatry, 355,* 773–782.

Stamford, J. A., Muscat, R., O'Connor, J. J., Patel, J., Trout, S. J., Wieczorek, W. J., Zruk, Z. L., & Willner, P. (1991). Subsensitivity to reward following chronic mild stress is associated with increased release of mesolimbic dopamine. *Psychopharmacology, 105,* 275–282.

Standage, K. F. (1979). The use of Schneider's typology for the diagnosis of personality disorder: An examination of reliability. *British Journal of Psychiatry, 135,* 238–242.

Valenstein, E. S. (1973). *Brain control: A critical examination of brain stimulation and psychosurgery.* New York: Wiley.

Velten, E. (1968). A laboratory task for induction of mood states. *Behavior Research and Therapy, 6,* 473–482.

Venables, P. H., Wilkins, S., Mitchell, D. A., Raine, A., & Bailes, K. (1990). A scale for the measurement of schizotypy. *Personality and Individual Differences, 11,* 481–495.

Vogel, G. W., Neill, D., Hagler, M., & Kors, D. (1991a). Decreased intracranial self-stimulation in a new animal model of endogenous depression. *Neuroscience and Biobehavioral Reviews, 14,* 65–68.

Vogel, G. W., Neill, D., Hagler, M., & Kors, D. (1991b). A new animal model of endogenous depression: A summary of present findings. *Neuroscience and Biobehavioral Reviews, 14,* 65–68.

Watson, R., Hartman, E., & Schildkraut, J. J. (1972). Amphetamine withdrawal: Affective state, sleep patterns and MHPG excretion. *American Journal of Psychiatry, 129,* 263–269.

Watson, C. G., Klett, W. G., & Lorei, T. W. (1970). Toward an operational definition of anhedonia. *Psychological Reports, 26,* 371–376.

Watson, C. G., Kucala, T., & Jacobs, L. (1978). The prediction of outcome from anhedonia and process-reactive scales. *Journal of Clinical Psychology, 34,* 889–892.

Weiss, J. M., Bailey, W. H., Goodman, P. A., Hoffman, L. J., Ambrose, M. J., Salman, S., & Charry, J. M. (1982). A model for the neurochemical study of depression. In M. Y. Spiegelstein & A. Levy (Eds.), *Behavioral models and the analysis of drug action* (pp. 195–223). Amsterdam: Elsevier.

Weissman, M. M., & Bothwell, S. (1976). Assessment of social adjustment by patient self-report. *Archives of General Psychiatry, 33,* 1111–1115.

Willner, P. (1985). *Depression: A Psychiological Synthesis.* New York: Wiley.

Willner, P. (1986). Validating criteria for animal models of human mental disorders: Learned helplessness as a paradigm case. *Progress in Neuropsychopharmacology and Biological Psychiatry, 10,* 677–690.

Willner, P. (1990). Animal models of depression: An overview. *Pharmacology & Therapeutics, 45,* 425–455.

Willner, P. (1991). Animal models as simulations of depression. *Trends in Pharmacological Sciences, 12,* 131–136.

Willner, P., & Scheel-Kruger, J. (Eds.) (1991). *The mesolimbic dopamine system: From motivation to action.* Chichester: Wiley.

Willner, P., Klimek, V., Golembiowska, K., & Muscat, R. (1991). Changes in mesolimbic dopamine may explain stress-induced anhedonia. *Psychobiology, 19,* 79–84.

Willner, P., Muscat, R., Papp, M., & Sampson, D. (1991). Dopamine, depression and antidepressant drugs. In P. Willner, & J. Scheel-Kruger (Eds.), *The mesolimbic dopamine system: From motivation to action* (pp. 387–410). Chichester: Wiley.

Willner, P., Phillips, G., & Muscat, R. (1991). Suppression of rewarded behaviour by neuroleptic drugs: Can't or won't, and why? In P. Willner & J. Scheel-Kruger (Eds.), *The mesolimbic dopamine system: From motivation to action* (pp. 251–271). Chichester: Wiley.

Willner, P., Sampson, D., Papp, M., Phillips, G., & Muscat, R. (1991). Animal models of anhedonia. In P. Soubrie (Ed.), *Animal models of psychiatric disorders: Vol. 3 Anxiety, depression and mania* (pp. 71–99). Basel: Karger.

Willner, P., Sampson, D., Phillips, G., Fichera, R., Foxlow, P., & Muscat, R. (1989). Effects of isolated housing and chronic antidepressant treatment on cooperative social behaviour in rats. *Behavioural Pharmacology, 1,* 85–90.

Willner, P., Towell, A., Sampson, D., Muscat, R., & Sophokleous, S. (1987). Reduction of sucrose preference by chronic mild stress and its restoration by a tricyclic antidepressant. *Psychopharmacology, 93,* 358–364.

Willner, P., Wilkes, M., & Orwin, O. (1990). Attributional style and perceived stress in endogenous and reactive depression. *Journal of Affective Disorders, 18,* 281–287.

Wise, R. A. (1982). Neuroleptics and operant behaviour: The anhedonia hypothesis. *Behavioral and Brain Sciences, 5,* 39–87.

Wise, R. A. (1989). The brain and reward. In J. M. Liebman & S. J. Cooper (Eds.), *The neuropharmacological basis of reward* (pp. 377–424). Oxford: Oxford University Press.

Young, M. A., Scheftner, W. A., Klerman, G. L., Andreasen, N. C., & Hirschfeld, R. M. A. (1986). The endogenous sub-type of depression: A study of its internal construct validity. *British Journal of Psychiatry, 148,* 257–267.

Zacharko, R. M., & Anisman, H. (1991). Stressor-provoked alterations of intracranial self-stimulation in the mesocortiolimbic dopamine system: An animal model of depression. In P. Willner & J. Scheel-Kruger (Eds.), *The mesolimbic dopamine system: From motivation to action* (pp. 411–442). Chichester: Wiley.

Zacharko, R. M., Bowers, W. J., & Anismam, H. (1984). Responding for brain stimulation: Stress and desmethylimipramine. *Progress in Neuro-Psychopharmacology and biological Psychiatry, 8,* 601–606.

Zacharko, R. M., Bowers, W. J., Kokkinidis, L., & Anisman, H. (1983). Region specific reductions of intracranial self-stimulation after uncontrollable stress: Possible effects on reward processes. *Behavioral Brain Research, 9,* 129–141.

Zacharko, R. M., Lalonde, G. T., Kasian, M., & Anisman, H. (1987). Strain specific effects of inescapable shock on intracranial self-stimulation from the nucleus accumbens. *Brain Research, 426,* 164–168.

Zimmerman, M., & Spitzer, R. L. (1989). Melancholia: From DSM-III to DSM-III-R. *American Journal of Psychiatry, 146,* 20–28.

CHAPTER 5

Social Dysfunction

LISA A. FELDMAN and IAN H. GOTLIB

INTRODUCTION

Over the past two decades, researchers have increasingly recognized the importance of social functioning in the depressive disorders. Indeed, not only is there a growing body of literature examining social aspects of depression, but in the recent multi-site National Institutes of Mental Health (NIMH) Collaborative Treatment of Depression Project (cf. Elkin et al., 1989), one of the major interventions being assessed was Interpersonal Psychotherapy for Depression (IPT; Klerman, Weissman, Rounsaville, & Chevron, 1984). IPT is based on the assumptions that depression can result from difficulties in interpersonal relationships, and that social dysfunction constitutes an important symptom of this disorder. Consequently, IPT attempts to improve interpersonal functioning in depressed patients by focusing on how the individuals are coping with current interpersonal stressors. A number of other therapies have also been developed for the treatment of depression that focus on interpersonal functioning, such as social skills training (Becker, Heimberg, & Bellack, 1987), inpatient family intervention (Clarkin et al., 1986), interpersonal systems therapy (Gotlib & Colby, 1987), and marital therapy for depression (Beach, Sandeen, & O'Leary, 1990).

Despite this increasing interest in the role played by social factors associated with depression, social dysfunction is not an explicit defining characteristic of this disorder. Indeed, virtually all the criteria necessary for a diagnosis of Major Depressive Episode are intrapsychic (e.g., depressed mood, sleep disturbance, weight loss, concentration difficulties), rather than interpersonal, in nature. Nevertheless, not only do major theoretical formulations of depressive disorders emphasize the importance of interpersonal functioning in the etiology and maintenance of this disorder, empirical studies also have demonstrated consistently that depression is associated with difficulties in social functioning. The primary purpose of this chapter is to review the results of empirical investigations that are relevant to the role of social dysfunction in depression. In addition, we will attempt to provide a theoretical framework within which to understand these data.

We begin this chapter by reviewing the empirical investigations that have assessed the social functioning of depressed persons. To establish the empirical association between depression and social dysfunction, we examine research assessing the social networks of depressed persons and the social support available to depressed individuals. We then examine the social behavior of depressed persons in interactions with others. As noted earlier, unlike other symptoms of depression that are primarily intrapsychic, social dysfunction is interpersonal. To understand this symptom more fully, we next present the results of investigations of others' reactions to depressed people, and present a systemic framework within which to understand the symptom. In the final sections of this chapter, we discuss the possible nature of the relation between social dysfunction and depression, and we suggest directions for future research in this area.

THE SOCIAL FUNCTIONING OF DEPRESSED PERSONS

To begin a discussion on the role of social dysfunction as a symptom of depression, we must first determine if, in fact, social dysfunction is associated with depression. In this section, we provide evidence that both global and specific assessments suggest that depressed individuals experience greater social difficulties than do their nondepressed counterparts.

Social Networks

The results of a number of studies are consistent in suggesting that, compared with nondepressed controls, clinically depressed persons report having smaller and less supportive social networks, as well as less frequent contact with individuals in their social networks. In both self-report and interview studies, depressed persons nominate fewer social intimates, report having fewer friends, experience fewer contacts outside their immediate families, and report having less integrated social networks than have nondepressed persons (e.g., Billings & Moos, 1984; Brim, Witcoff, & Wetzel, 1982; Gotlib & Lee, 1989; Henderson, Byrne, & Duncan-Jones, 1981; Youngren & Lewinsohn, 1980). In fact, depressed individuals report interacting less frequently with their primary attachment figures than do nondepressed controls (Brugha et al., 1982).

Not only do depressed people report having smaller social networks and less contact with others than do nondepressed people, but there are also significant differences in the quality of relationships reported by depressed and nondepressed persons. For example, depressed individuals report being uncomfortable in interactions with others, often perceiving these interactions as unhelpful, or even as unpleasant or negative (Brim et al., 1982; Brugha et al., 1982; Henderson et al., 1981; Youngren & Lewinsohn, 1980). Furthermore, depressed people, particularly depressed women, experience their interpersonal contacts to be less supportive than do nondepressed controls (Belsher & Costello, 1991; Billings, Cronkite, & Moos, 1983). Indeed, Gotlib and Lee (1989) found that depressed women rated the quality of their significant relationships more poorly than did nondepressed women, and reported that there were arguments in their families over a greater number of issues than was the case for nondepressed controls.

It is important to note that these findings do not appear to be due to negatively distorted perceptions associated with depression (cf. Beck, Rush, Shaw, & Emery, 1979; Gotlib, 1983). There is evidence to suggest that the depressed people's characterizations of their social networks do not merely reflect transient mood-related perceptions. Studies in which the social functioning of depressed subjects was assessed first when they were depressed and again when they were no longer symptomatic have provided evidence that the way in which depressed people characterize their social world is not the result of a reporting bias. For example, depressed individuals reported having restricted social networks both while they were in depressive episode and again 1 year later when they were nonsymptomatic (Billings & Moos, 1985a, b; Gotlib & Lee, 1989). At both assessment times, depressed subjects reported having fewer friends and fewer close relationships than did nondepressed controls. In addition, depressed persons' reports of restricted social networks have been corroborated by nondepressed family members (Billings et al., 1983). Indeed, one of the "risk factors for nonremission" identified by Billings and Moos (1985b) was few close social relationships at intake.

It appears, then, that depression is consistently and veridically associated with social dysfunction on a global level as measured by the number of social contacts. The reduced size of the social networks that characterize the depressed person's interpersonal world likely results in a reduction of social support. Another broad indicator of social dysfunction as a symptom of depression, then, is the amount of social support that characterizes a social network. A number of investigators have examined the relationship between social support and depression and have found that, like other general measures of social dysfunction, decreased social support is not only a symptom of depression, but may be meaningfully associated with the development and maintenance of this disorder as well (see Barnett & Gotlib, 1988, for a more detailed review of this literature).

Several researchers have demonstrated that perceptions of low social support antedate the onset of depression (e.g., Cutrona, 1984; Monroe, Imhoff, Wise, & Harris, 1983), suggesting that low social support leads to depression. Other theorists have argued that this unidirectional relation between low social support and depression is too simple, contending that low social support leads to depression by increasing people's vulnerability to the debilitating effects of stressful life events. In a number of studies, low social support has been found to be most strongly associated with subsequent depression when it occurs in the presence of stressful life events (e.g., Costello, 1982; Cutrona & Troutman, 1986; Monroe, Bromet, Connell, & Steiner, 1986). Indeed, both the lack of a supportive intimate relationship and the presence of negative, conflictual relationships have been identified as important risk factors for depression, especially when individuals were experiencing major stressors in their lives (e.g., Brown & Harris, 1978; Pagel, Erdly, & Becker, 1987; Weissman, 1987). Social resources seem to help individuals cope more effectively with stress, resulting in a reduced incidence of depressed mood. Consistent with this formulation, research suggests that support is associated with the use of effective coping strategies, such as problem-focused coping, that are less related to the development of depressive symptoms (Billings et al., 1983; Holahan & Moos, 1991).

In addition to the reduction in network size, the quality of interactions with network members can also lead to decreased social support. A number of investigators have suggested that "social support" should not be conceptualized simply as low levels of supportiveness in relationships; rather, it can also include the presence of negativity in relationships. In fact, the negative features of social relationships appear to be more strongly related to measures of perceived support and to the presence of psychological symptoms than do the positive features (e.g., Coyne & Bolger, 1990; Pagel, Erdly, & Becker, 1987). It is the negative, conflictual features of intimate relationships that appear to be highly related to the development of depression, whereas the degree of positivity was not (Pagel et al., 1987; Weissman, 1987).

In sum, ample research indicates that broad measures of social functioning suggest a meaningful association between social dysfunction and depression. The social networks of depressed people are smaller and less supportive than are those of their nondepressed counterparts. The reason for these differences in social networks between depressed and nondepressed persons, however, is not clear. One reasonable explanation for the greater negativity in the social networks of depressed persons is that when people begin to become depressed, they behave in ways that lead to problematic interpersonal relationships and to a loss of social support, which in turn exacerbates the depression. In the following section, we describe the results of research examining the social behavior of depressed persons in interactions with strangers, friends, and family members.

Social Behavior

Behavioral or interpersonal theories of depression posit that depressed people receive little reinforcement from others in their social environments, in large part because they behave in aversive ways toward others around them. Much of the research examining the social behavior of depressed persons has been guided by Lewinsohn's formulation (e.g., Lewinsohn, 1974; Lewinsohn, Youngren, & Grosscup, 1979) that depressed individuals experience a reduced rate of positive reinforcement from others because of deficits in their social skills. Libet and Lewinsohn (1973) defined social skills as ". . . the complex ability both to emit behaviors which are positively or negatively reinforced, and not to emit behaviors which are punished or extinguished by others" (p. 304). An individual is considered to be socially skillful to the extent that he or she elicits positive (and avoids negative) consequences from the social environment. Lewinsohn postulated that, because of insufficient positive reinforcement, depressed persons find it difficult to initiate or maintain instrumental behavior. Consequently, they become increasingly passive and inactive. This lack of rewarding interchanges with the environment is also assumed to result in the subjective experience of dysphoria. The results of research that has been conducted to examine this formulation suggest that depressed individuals do, indeed, demonstrate difficulties in their social behavior.

Depressed Persons with Strangers

A number of investigations have assessed the interpersonal behavior of depressed persons in interactions with strangers, both in dyads and in groups. The results of these studies indicate that, compared with nondepressed controls, depressed individuals are less socially skilled in a number of ways (see Table 5.1). For example, when engaging in conversation, depressed individuals

TABLE 5.1. Summary of Social Behaviors of Depressed Persons

Relationship	Behaviors	Content
With strangers	Little smiling	Self-focused
	Little eye contact	Negatively toned, with themes of self-devaluation and helplessness
	Slow and monotonous speech	High proportion of self-disclosure
	Long response latencies	
	Inappropriately timed responses	
With spouses	Disruptions	Few positive comments
	Negative emotional outbursts	Many negative comments
	Incongruity between verbal and nonverbal behaviors	
With children	Infrequent gazing at infants	Less structure and discipline
	Less activity, playing, and speaking	Disapproving and critical statements, shouting
	Not contingently responsive, or long response latencies	Actively negative, angry, and intrusive
	Little reciprocal interaction and affectionate contact with infants	Few positive and confirming statements
	Flattened affect	Difficulty resolving conflicts, avoid confrontation

smile less frequently than do nondepressed individuals (Gotlib, 1982; Gotlib & Robinson, 1982). Persons who are depressed tend to make less eye contact with those with whom they are interacting (Gotlib, 1982); they speak more slowly and more monotonously (Gotlib & Robinson, 1982; Libet & Lewinsohn, 1973; Youngren & Lewinsohn, 1980). Depressed individuals also take longer to respond to others in a conversation and offer more inappropriately timed responses (Gotlib & Robinson, 1982; Jacobson & Anderson, 1982; Libet & Lewinsohn, 1973).

Depressed individuals are also differentiated from their nondepressed counterparts with respect to the content of conversations with strangers. Specifically, depressed persons make more self-focused and negatively toned comments than do nondepressed individuals (Blumberg & Hokanson, 1983; Gotlib & Robinson, 1982; Jacobson & Anderson, 1982). Depressed individuals also tend to engage in higher levels of self-disclosure (Cane & Gotlib, 1985). The content of the conversations of depressed persons also center more frequently on themes of self-devaluation and helplessness (Blumberg & Hokanson, 1983; Jacobson & Anderson, 1982).

Given these differences in both conversation behavior and content, with few exceptions (e.g., Gotlib & Meltzer, 1987; Youngren & Lewinsohn, 1980), the interpersonal behaviors of depressed persons are judged both by the depressed person and by others to be less socially competent than are those of nondepressed individuals (e.g., Dykman, Horowitz, Abramson, & Usher, 1991; Gotlib, 1982; Lewinsohn, Mischel, Chaplin, & Barton, 1980).

It is clear from the results of these studies that the interpersonal behaviors exhibited by depressed persons in interactions with strangers are significantly more problematic than are those demonstrated by nondepressed individuals. Given that meaningful social relationships seem to be affected by depression to a greater extent than are superficial relationships with strangers, we might expect to find that depressed people exhibit even more pronounced social skill deficits in their close relationships. A number of investigators have examined the behaviors of depressed persons with respect to more intimate relationships. The results of this body of research indicate that, in interactions both with their spouses and with their children, the interpersonal behavior of depressed persons is often negative, and at times can be characterized as overtly hostile and aggressive.

Depressed Persons with Spouses

The social skill deficits of depressed individuals appear to be most pronounced in interactions with their spouses (cf. Gotlib & Hooley, 1988). For example, depressed people tend to be less verbally productive with their spouse than with strangers (Hinchliffe, Hooper, & Roberts, 1978). In addition, whereas the marital interactions of depressed patients are characterized by interruptions and pauses (Hinchliffe et al., 1978), this is less true of their interactions with strangers.

A number of investigators have compared the marital interactions of couples with a depressed spouse with those of nondepressed couples. The results of these studies are consistent in reporting that the interactions of depressed persons and their spouses are associated with more negative verbal and nonverbal behaviors (e.g., Hautzinger, Linden, & Hoffman, 1982; Kahn, Coyne, & Margolin, 1985; Ruscher & Gotlib, 1988). For example, marital interactions of couples in which one partner is depressed are characterized by high levels of disruption, negative emotional outbursts, and incongruity between verbal messages and nonverbal behaviors (Hinchliffe et al., 1978), such that depressed individuals emit a greater number of behaviors in which the nonverbal communication is more negative than is the accompanying verbal message (Ruscher & Gotlib, 1988). When interacting with a spouse, depressed individuals have been found to emit a lower proportion of positive verbal behavior and a greater proportion of negative verbal behavior than do nondepressed individuals (Ruscher & Gotlib, 1988). Moreover, data reported by Kowalik and Gotlib (1987) indicate that this pattern of negative behavior on the part of depressed individuals may be deliberate; depressed persons in this study coded their communications to their spouses as more intentionally negative and less positive than did nondepressed couples. In addition, other findings suggest that depressed individuals are often openly aggressive when interacting with their spouses (Biglan et al., 1985). There is some evidence, however, that marital distress, rather than depression per se, may be responsible for the negative interaction patterns frequently observed in depressed couples (e.g., Ruscher & Gotlib, 1988; Schmaling & Jacobson, 1990).

The results of these studies make clear that the marital relationships of depressed persons are characterized by negative social behaviors, tension, and hostility. Although the degree of negativity present in the interactions of depressed women and their children does not appear to be as intense as that characterizing the marital relationships (cf. Gotlib & Whiffen, 1991), a number of investigators have nevertheless found depressed women to be withdrawn and/or overtly negative in interactions with their children (Bettes, 1988; Field, Healy, Goldstein, & Guthertz, 1990; see Gotlib & Lee, 1990; Hammen, 1991).

Depressed Persons with Children

Much of the research examining the overt behavior of depressed mothers in interactions with their children has been conducted with depressed mothers and their infants. Livingood, Daen, and Smith (1983), for example, found that depressed mothers gaze less often at their infants than do nondepressed women and seem to be less ready to interact with their infants; the two groups did not differ, however, with respect to contact and stimulation. The results of studies conducted by Field and her colleagues (Field, 1984; Field et al., 1985; Field et al., 1990) similarly indicate that, compared with their nonsymptomatic counterparts, depressed mothers are less active, less playful, and less contingently responsive in face-to-face interactions with their 3- to

6-month-old infants. Bettes (1988) reported that symptomatic mothers were delayed in speech directed toward their infants. In fact, Bettes emphasized that the mean response delay of the depressed women in her study was sufficiently long to suggest disengagement from the child. Finally, Fleming, Ruble, Flett, and Shaul (1988) found that, compared with nondepressed mothers, women with postpartum depression showed less reciprocal vocalization and affectionate contact with their infants.

Although these studies indicate that depression interferes with responsiveness of mothers toward their infants, the results of other studies raise more serious concerns in suggesting that some depressed mothers may be explicitly negative in interactions with their infants. Lyons-Ruth, Zoll, Connell, and Grunebaum (1986), for example, reported that relatively depressed low-income mothers displayed covert hostility and flattened affect with their 1-year-old babies. Similarly, Cohn, Matias, Tronick, Connell, and Lyons-Ruth (1986); Cohn, Campbell, Matias, and Hopkins (1990); and Field et al. (1990) also reported that depressed mothers displayed angry, negative, and intrusive behaviors toward their babies.

Fewer observational studies have been conducted with toddler-age offspring of depressed women. Radke-Yarrow, Cummings, Kuczynski, and Chapman (1985); Breznitz and Sherman (1987); and Kochanska, Kuczynski, Radke-Yarrow, and Welsh (1987) all observed the same sample of 1- to 4-year-old children interacting with their unipolar or bipolar mothers. The results of these investigations indicated that more children of women with affective disorders, compared with those of normal mothers, displayed insecure attachment. Mothers of insecurely attached children also showed less positive and more negative affect toward them (Radke-Yarrow et al., 1985). Mothers with affective disorders spoke less to their 2- to 3-year-old children and responded more slowly to their children's speech than did nondepressed control mothers (Breznitz & Sherman, 1987). Depressed mothers were also less successful than were normal mothers in resolving conflict situations, commonly avoiding confrontation with their children (Kochanska et al., 1987). Finally, two other studies have been reported examining independent samples of depressed mothers and their young children. Goodman and Brumley (1990) found that, compared with normal controls, depressed mothers were less responsive to their children and used less structure and discipline. Similarly, Mills, Puckering, Pound, and Cox (1985) observed depressed community women in England and their 2- to 3-year-old toddlers. Using a concept similar to "responsiveness," Mills et al. (1985) found that the depressed women were less responsive and reciprocal in their interactions than were nondepressed women. In fact, the children with the greatest levels of behavior problems were those of mothers with the lowest proportions of reciprocated interactions.

Finally, a small number of investigations have been conducted examining the behavior of depressed or dysphoric mothers with their older children. Panaccione and Wahler (1986) observed relatively dysphoric mothers interacting with their preschoolers. Level of maternal depression was associated with mothers' negative interactions with the child, often involving disapproval and shouting. Webster-Stratton and Hammond (1988) observed mothers of 3- to 8-year-old clinic-referred children. Women with elevated self-report depression scores in this study directed more critical statements toward their children than did nondepressed mothers. Hammen and her colleagues conducted systematic observations of a conflict discussion task involving diagnosed unipolar depressed women and their children, and similar pairs from bipolar, medically ill, and normal families. Gordon et al. (1989), for example, found unipolar depressed women to be the most negative and critical, the least positive and confirming and, replicating Kochanska et al.'s (1987) results, to have the most difficulty sustaining a focus on resolving a conflict. Interestingly, Anderson and Hammen (1991) subsequently examined a subset of sibling pairs in which one had a psychiatric diagnosis and the other did not. Examination of the mother–child interactions of these pairs indicated that the more symptomatic siblings had significantly more negative interactions with the mother. Thus, the mothers interacted more negatively only with those children who had problems, suggesting that depressed mothers may not be invariably dysfunctional in their parenting behaviors. Echoing behavioral differences cited earlier in the interactions of depressed persons with spouses and with strangers, depressed mothers may have difficulties with their difficult children but may interact more positively with their well-functioning children.

In sum, compared with nondepressed individuals, depressed persons exhibit behaviors that are characterized as socially dysfunctional both when interacting with strangers and with intimates. Whereas depressed persons exhibit social skill deficits in their interactions with strangers, their interactions with their partners and their children are more apt to be characterized by hostility and anger. Theories formulated by Coyne (1976b) and Coates and Wortman (1980) suggest that such behavior exhibited by depressed individuals elicits negative responses from others with whom they interact, and that these reactions are largely responsible for maintaining the depressive affect. In this sense, the responses of others to depressed persons are an integral part of the perceptual world of the depressed, and may contribute to and exacerbate the dysfunctional social behavior that depressed people emit. A review of the social dysfunction associated with depression, therefore, would be incomplete without at least a brief overview of the way in which others react to depressed people during social interactions.

The Response of Others

Two theories have focused on the responses of others to depressed persons in prolonging the course of the disorder. Coyne (1976b) contended that depression is a response to disruptions in the social field of the individual. Specifically,

Coyne suggested that depression is maintained by the negative responses of significant others to the depressive's symptomatic behavior. Coyne maintained that depressed individuals create a negative social environment by engaging others in such a manner that support is lost, or at best, ambiguous (both supportive and hostile) reactions are elicited. Coyne postulated a sequence of behavior that begins with the depressed person's initial demonstration of depressive symptoms, typically in response to stress. Individuals in the depressed person's social environment respond immediately to these depressive symptoms with genuine concern and support. The depressive's behaviors gradually become demands for support, however, that are expressed with increasing frequency. Consequently, the depressive's behavior becomes aversive and elicits feelings of resentment and anger from other family members. At the same time, however, the depressed person's obvious distress also elicits feelings of guilt that inhibit the open expression of this hostility. In an attempt to reduce both their guilt and anger, family members respond to the depressed person not only with veiled hostility, but with false reassurance and support. Being aware of, and feeling rejected by, these discrepant or incongruous messages, the depressed person becomes more symptomatic in an attempt to gain support, thus making it even more aversive for others to interact with him or her. This "deviation-amplifying" process continues to the point where people either withdraw from interactions with the depressive, or have the person withdrawn through hospitalization.

Coates and Wortman (1980) offered a similar formulation of the etiology of depression but placed greater emphasis on the social comparison processes of depressed persons and the attempts made by others in the social environment to control directly the depressive's display of aversive symptoms. As in Coyne's (1976b) model, Coates and Wortman suggested that others initially react sympathetically to the depressed person and try to ameliorate the negative feelings through encouragement and distraction. These initial attempts at controlling the depressed person, however, may leave the individual feeling worse, doubting the appropriateness of his/her feelings and reactions. Over time, others in the depressive's social environment become increasingly annoyed and frustrated with the depressive displays, and their initially supportive responses become more disjointed and ambiguous. The depressed person begins to emit more symptoms to regain the lost support. As others' attempts to control the depressive's behavior become more overt and insistent, the depressed person is left feeling inadequate, isolated, and rejected. Thus, both Coyne and Coates and Wortman implicate the negative reactions of others in the maintenance of depression.

Research examining the responses of others to depressed individuals has focused on two basic questions: Do interactions with depressed people cause their interaction partners to experience negative mood; and do interaction partners of depressed people reject opportunities to interact with them in future? With respect to the first question, there has been equivocal support for the notion that the behavior of depressed individuals can induce negative affect in others. The majority of findings do suggest that interactions with depressed people seem to leave those around them feeling more negative. People have been found to report experiencing negative affect, particularly depression and hostility, after having a phone conversation with depressed outpatients (Coyne, 1976a), after reading transcripts describing a depressed person (Gotlib & Beatty, 1985; Hammen & Peters, 1977), after listening to audiotaped interviews with depressed inpatients (Boswell & Murray, 1981), and after engaging in dyadic interactions with individuals exhibiting depressive symptoms (Strack & Coyne, 1983). A number of studies have failed to replicate these findings, however (e.g., Belsher & Costello, 1991; Gotlib & Robinson, 1982; King & Heller, 1984; McNiel, Arkowitz, & Pritchard, 1987), calling into question the robustness of this phenomenon as a general reaction of others to depressed persons.

The results of studies addressing the second question concerning whether or not people reject opportunities for further interaction with depressed individuals have also been mixed. Studies in this domain typically assess rejection by asking subjects to report their willingness to engage in future interaction with their depressed partners. Whereas some studies have reported that individuals who interacted with a depressed patient were less willing to interact with their partners in the future (e.g., Boswell & Murray, 1981; Coyne, 1976a; Gotlib & Beatty, 1985; Hammen & Peters, 1977; Strack & Coyne, 1983), other investigations have failed to obtain this pattern of results (e.g., Gotlib & Robinson, 1982; King & Heller, 1984; McNiel et al., 1987).

According to Coyne's (1976b) formulation, individuals interacting with depressed persons continue to react positively on an overt level but reject the person covertly. Presumably, such rejection may be communicated to the depressed person through behavioral cues during social interactions. In fact, interesting findings reported by Gotlib and Robinson (1982) support this hypothesis. Gotlib and Robinson found that although subjects who interacted with depressed individuals did not report more rejection of their partners than did subjects who interacted with nondepressed persons, they did emit a greater number of negative verbal and nonverbal behaviors during their interactions. Once again, however, whereas some studies have replicated this finding (e.g., Yarkin, Harvey, & Bloxom, 1981), others have not (e.g., McNiel et al., 1987).

The studies discussed above have typically involved interactions of depressed people with strangers. While such interactions provide valuable information about the interactional theory of depression, we might expect that the negative quality of interactions may be especially pronounced within a close relationship in which the other cannot leave the social arena (cf. Burchill & Stiles, 1988). Indeed, research conducted on the interactions of depressed individuals with roommates, friends, and spouses indicates that depressed persons are rejected and devalued by those in their social network.

Both behavioral and attitude questionnaire data suggest that depressed college students are less accepted and less valued by their roommates than are nondepressed students. Roommates of depressed college students have been found to like their roommates less and to reject their roommates more than did roommates of nondepressed subjects (Burchill & Stiles, 1988). Indeed, roommates of individuals exhibiting "chronic" depressive symptoms have been found to display a progressive increase in their reports of their own levels of depression (Howes, Hokanson, & Loewenstein, 1985). Interestingly, and attesting to the likely reciprocal nature of this association, Hokanson, Hummer, and Butler (1991) recently reported that the depressed persons also perceived high levels of hostility and low levels of friendliness in their roommates.

Similar results have been reported by investigators examining the interactions of depressed individuals with their best friends. Rosenblatt and Greenberg (1991), for example, found that although the best friends of subjects who were exhibiting depressive symptoms were not more depressed or liked their friend less than did the best friends of subjects who were not depressed, they nevertheless reported feeling significantly more depressed. Belsher and Costello (1991) examined the interactions of depressed women and their nominated confidants and found that the speech of both the depressed women and their confidants were characterized by an elevated number of negative statements concerning the self and their situations.

Similar results have been obtained in studies examining the marital interactions of depressed persons. The results of these investigations indicate that spouses of depressed persons report negative mood and exhibit behaviors reflecting rejection of their spouses. For example, spouses of depressed partners have been found to report feeling more depressed, hostile, and critical following interactions with their depressed partners (e.g., Gotlib & Whiffen, 1989). They have also been found to argue with their spouses more often (Hautzinger et al., 1982), to be more negative in their communications with their spouses (e.g., Kowalik & Gotlib, 1987; McCabe & Gotlib, 1991; Ruscher & Gotlib, 1988), and to be more critical of their spouses (e.g., Hooley, 1986; Hops et al., 1987; Krantz & Moos, 1987).

Overall, the results of this research suggest that depressed individuals can engender negative mood and rejection in those with whom they interact, although the robustness of this mood-induction phenomenon is equivocal. Moreover, the negative reactions from others appear to be more compelling in the significant relationships of depressed people than in their superficial relationships. An important question arising from these investigations is whether the induction of negative mood plays a major role in the sequence of events that lead to interpersonal rejection. Although most research has not addressed this question explicitly, the existing evidence does not support this position (Gurtman, 1986). For example, Gotlib and Robinson (1982) found that those interacting with depressed persons displayed behavioral rejection in the absence of any reported negative mood induction. Similarly, Boswell and Murray (1981) found only small correlations between self-ratings of negative mood and rejection (see also Strack & Coyne, 1983). Finally, Belsher and Costello (1991) found that although confidants of depressed persons exhibited more negative speech in interactions than did confidants of depressed persons, they did not indicate more negative affect following the interactions.

PROCESSES UNDERLYING SOCIAL DYSFUNCTION IN DEPRESSION

Thus far, we have presented theories and research suggesting that depressed people experience social isolation and dysfunction. They exhibit deficits in social skills when interacting with strangers, friends, spouses, and children, and their behaviors often lead to ambivalence and rejection from those in their social environment. The bulk of this research, however, is cross-sectional in design, essentially examining social concomitants of depression. Thus, although the results of this body of research clearly indicate that depressed persons are less socially skillful and elicit more negative interpersonal responses from others than their nondepressed counterparts, the nature of the relation between depression and social dysfunction is not clear. The results of these studies indicate that social dysfunction may be a concomitant of depression; the theories that we reviewed earlier, however, postulate that social dysfunction plays a more important and more complex role in the development and maintenance of this disorder. In the final sections of this chapter, we offer a framework for understanding the relation between social dysfunction and depression, and we discuss the processes that might underlie this association. In presenting this framework, we will suggest that social dysfunction in depressed persons reflects the operation and interaction of a number of variables. In an effort to understand the social dysfunction and interpersonal behaviors of depressed persons, we will discuss the roles of the early childhood experiences of depressed individuals and their cognitive functioning.

The Role of Early Experiences, Cognitions, and the Reactions of Depressed Individuals

A number of factors must be considered in attempting to understand the nature of the association between interpersonal difficulties and depression. The framework that we will describe in this section places particular importance on the early experiences of depressed adults and their cognitive functioning in determining their responses to others during social interactions. Essentially, we will suggest that the adverse early environments experienced by some individuals have a number of important consequences for their subsequent functioning. Through these early experiences, individuals develop low self-esteem, negative self-schemata, and dependent personality characteristics. They also develop a style of cognitive functioning that leaves them more aware of, and more sensitive to, negative aspects of their environment. Finally, these adverse early experiences leave the individuals at increased risk for developing depressive symptoms in response to stressors. Their displays of depressive symptoms elicit mixed responses from others in their social spheres. Because of their increased vigilance to negative aspects of their environment and their elevated dependency needs, depressed persons focus on the negative aspects of others' responses to the relative exclusion of more positive responses. Their sensitivity to these negative responses leaves depressed persons feeling rejected and angry, and this in turn inhibits more adaptive interpersonal behavior. These negative feelings then become stronger in further interpersonal interactions and exacerbate the aversive exchanges, leading ultimately to rejection on the part of significant others and social withdrawal on the part of the depressed person. The following paragraphs present a more detailed presentation of this framework.

Childhood Experiences and Vulnerability to Depression

Psychoanalytic theorists have emphasized the importance of early childhood experiences and the quality of the mother–child relationship in the first year of life as vulnerability factors for subsequent depression. In one of the earliest psychoanalytic formulations of depression, Abraham (1911/1985) theorized that individuals who are vulnerable to depression experience a marked ambivalence toward other people, with positive and negative feelings alternating and reciprocally blocking expression of the other. Abraham, and later Freud (1917/1961), postulated that this ambivalent form of interpersonal relating has its origins in problematic object-relationships during childhood, typically involving the young child and his or her mother. Bowlby (1978, 1981) similarly emphasized the importance of early attachment experiences in predisposing an individual to later development of depression. Bowlby believed that all people are vulnerable to impaired interpersonal relations and social dysfunction if they do not develop strong attachment bonds early in their lives. Bowlby suggested that if attachment bonds are disrupted, either through actual separation or emotional unresponsiveness or inaccessibility, individuals may become vulnerable to depression.

Interestingly, the results of a growing number of investigations suggest that the childhood experiences of depressed individuals are often characterized by disturbed parenting, typically brought about through experiences of rejection and deprivation (cf. Blatt, Wein, Chevron, & Quinlan, 1979). Indeed, research findings indicate rather consistently that the early experiences of depressed individuals are marked by parental rejection, abuse, inattention, and/or family discord (cf. Gerlsma, Emmelkamp, & Arrindell, 1990). Raskin, Boothe, Reating, Schulterbrandt, and Odle (1971), for example, found that depressed patients rated their parents more negatively than did matched nondepressed controls. Patients perceived their parents as having been less positively involved in their children's activities, less affectionate, and more controlling. Lamont and Gottlieb (1975) found that depressed individuals rated their mothers as less positively involved and more guilt inducing than did nondepressed controls. Abrahams and Whitlock (1969) and Jacobson, Fasman, and DiMascio (1975) both found that depressed patients reported greater parental rejection and less parental affection during childhood than did normal controls.

The results of several studies suggest that such negative perceptions are not merely a distortion of mood-related recall by depressed individuals (Brewin, Andrews, & Gotlib, in press). Gotlib, Mount, Cordy, and Whiffen (1988) found that the negative perceptions of early parenting were stable over a 3-year period. Similarly, Gotlib, Whiffen, Wallace, and Mount (1991) found that perceptions of early parenting obtained from nondepressed women during pregnancy were a significant predictor of the subsequent onset of postpartum depression. From a different perspective, insecurely attached children whose parental relationships were characterized as relatively intolerant and emotionally negative have been found to develop negative self-worth and depression as early as the fifth grade (Rubin & Mills, 1988).

The experience of an adverse early environment has implications for the personality development of depressed adults. Indeed, psychoanalytic theories of object relations and theories of social-cognitive development both suggest that children's relationships with their parents are critical in the development of working models of the self and relationships with others (cf. Gotlib & Hammen, 1992; Westen, 1991). It is likely that the early aversive childhood experiences of some depressed individuals led to the development of both self-schemas that are characterized by low self-worth and expectations of interpersonal negativity and rejection. According to both psychodynamic and social-cognitive theories of the self, such negative cognitive/affective structures may leave individuals with chronically low self-esteem, persistent interpersonal problems, and at risk for developing the social dysfunction symptom of depression when faced with life stressors. Indeed, developmentally acquired traits, such as interpersonal dependency and labile self-esteem, have been identified as being characteristic of the personalities of people who are prone to depression (cf. Barnett & Gotlib, 1988; Hirschfeld, Klerman, Clayton, & Keller, 1983). Vulnerable individuals are hypothesized to depend primarily on the love and attention of others for the maintenance of their fragile self-esteem. When these extreme dependency needs are frustrated, the resulting threat to self-worth is defended against by increasing demands for support, or by denying interpersonal dependency and developing obsessive, perfectionistic tendencies. Thus, these two traits, dependency and perfectionism, are thought to share a common etiology related to low self-esteem.

Depressive Cognitive Functioning and the Response to Others

It appears, then, that adverse early experiences may indeed serve as a vulnerability factor by lowering self-esteem, which in turn leads to increased interpersonal dependency and impaired development of effective coping strategies. When these vulnerable individuals are confronted with a stressful event, particularly an interpersonal stressor, they are likely to respond by displaying symptoms of dysphoria, or mild depression. Once an individual begins to become depressed, both interpersonal and intrapsychic factors may converge to leave the individual with problematic social relationships (cf. Gotlib & Colby, 1987). The interpersonal factors involve the nature and quality of the responses from others in the depressive's social environment. As we have demonstrated earlier, depressed individuals exhibit social behavior that others find aversive. Initially, others may respond with sympathy and support, but ultimately they respond with negativity and rejection.

The important intrapsychic factors involve the activation of dysfunctional cognitive structures or processes. Consistent with the psychoanalytic positions discussed earlier, the early parental rejection and deprivation that characterizes the childhood experiences of depressed individuals leads to the development of interpersonal cognitive/affective structures and personality characteristics that leave these individuals vulnerable to feeling rejected in interpersonal interactions. Thus, although others might respond to depressed persons with a combination of both positive and negative behaviors, these vulnerability factors lead depressed persons to attend more closely and to be more sensitive to the negative aspects of their environment (cf. Gotlib & Cane, 1987; Gotlib & McCabe, in press; Lewinsohn, Lobitz, & Wilson, 1973).

Given that their self-schemas are typically characterized by low self-esteem (cf. Segal, 1988), depressed persons may be inclined to attribute the negativity of the interactions to a characterological aspect of themselves (Abramson, Seligman, & Teasdale, 1978), thereby leading to even lower self-esteem. In this context, it is not surprising that depressed persons have been found to perceive their interactions with others to be negative and unhelpful (e.g., Gotlib & Lee, 1989; Henderson et al., 1981; Rosenblatt & Greenberg, 1991), to evaluate themselves negatively in interpersonal interactions (e.g., Hokanson, Loewenstein, Hedeen, & Howes, 1986; Youngren & Lewinsohn, 1980), and to be distrustful of others (Hokanson et al., 1986). In addition to reacting negatively to the aversive feedback that they are perceiving in their social environment, depressed individuals may also anticipate negativity from those in their close social network. Indeed, depressed individuals have been found to anticipate correctly more rejection from their partners (Strack & Coyne, 1983).

This focus on negative aspects of their social environment leads depressed persons to become increasingly more depressed and, as a result, to display more severe symptomatic behaviors, including dysfunctional social behaviors.

Others, in turn, may become more negative and rejecting and may begin to avoid interactions with the depressed individuals. Moreover, the negative affect and rejection that depressed individuals anticipate and perceive in others may activate memories of early parental rejection (cf. Beck, 1967). This activation likely leaves depressed persons feeling even more frustrated and helpless at being unable to alter their situation, and may lead to feelings and behaviors of anger, betrayal, and hostility toward their social partners. Ultimately, such reactions may lead depressed persons to withdraw from others.

Social Withdrawal

It may be instructive at this point to consider in more detail the construct of social withdrawal in depression. We have argued that depressed individuals' anticipation of negativity and rejection from others, combined with their increased sensitivity to such information, may lead them to withdraw from others in an attempt to avoid further insult. In fact, many depressed individuals report avoiding interactions with others that they believe will make them feel worse (Rippere, 1980). In some investigations, depressed persons have been found to reject others with whom they interact (Strack & Coyne, 1983). Interestingly, consistent with our emphasis on the importance of the early experiences of depressed persons, social withdrawal has been found to be characteristic of children who are insecurely attached to their parents, who engage in negative thoughts about themselves, who exhibit poor social skills, and who later go on to develop feelings of loneliness and depression (Rubin & Mills, 1991). It is possible, therefore, that social withdrawal is learned early in childhood by individuals who are at elevated risk for subsequent depression. Indeed, it is possible that social withdrawal increases the risk for subsequent depression in already vulnerable individuals.

Additional scenarios can also be imagined to explain why the depressed person might withdraw from others. For example, significant others often encourage depressed persons to stop emitting depressive symptoms (Coyne, 1976b), and it is possible that the depressed individuals experience this as criticism, and consequently feel inadequate and rejected. They then withdraw from others to avoid further negative evaluation. This encouragement may also leave depressed individuals doubting the sincerity of the support that others offer, resulting in feelings of distrust and betrayal. It is also possible that depressed individuals use others with whom they interact as social comparison objects, only to find them threatening as social partners because they leave the depressed individuals feeling inadequate (Rosenblatt & Greenberg, 1988). This hypothesis is supported indirectly by the results of studies suggesting that individuals with depressive symptoms do not experience as much negative affect when they interact with a depressed target as they do when they interact with a nondepressed target (Rosenblatt & Greenberg, 1991).

Withdrawal behavior on the part of depressed individuals may represent an attempt to cope with the stress of negative social interactions. Recently,

Repetti (1991) conceptualized social withdrawal as an emotion-focused coping strategy to situational stressors that involves decreased emotional responsivity to others. Our review of the literature suggests that depressed individuals are often faced with negative social interactions that they find stressful, that they tend to engage in emotion-focused coping, and that they may have developed a tendency in childhood to withdraw from social situations. Interestingly, the social withdrawal of depressed persons is consistent with recent theories suggesting that depressed persons are more self-focused than are their nondepressed counterparts (e.g., Ingram, 1990; Lewinsohn, Hoberman, Teri, & Hautzinger, 1985; Pyszczynski & Greenberg, 1987). Indeed, a shift in attention away from others and toward the self may be an important component not only of social withdrawal but of most emotion-focused coping strategies as well.

Although withdrawal may represent a coping strategy of depressed persons, it is apparent from the stress and coping literature that negative interpersonal consequences may result from the use of social withdrawal in this context. Specifically, the long-term use of social withdrawal as a way to deal with chronic stressors may lead ultimately to more aversive interpersonal relationships. In addition, a repeated pattern of social withdrawal in response to stress may also reduce the size of an individual's social network (cf. Repetti, 1991). Paradoxically, increased negativity in interpersonal relationships and decreased social network size may prove particularly problematic for depressed individuals if they choose to cope with interpersonal stress by withdrawing from others, because these consequences will simply compound the original interpersonal stress.

Finally, it is important to understand the role of social withdrawal in the context of the increased interpersonal dependency that characterizes the relationships of depressed people. As we noted earlier, depressed persons have been found to be more interpersonally dependent than nondepressed controls. This is true even when they are no longer symptomatic (e.g., Pilowsky & Katsikitis, 1983; Reich, Noyes, Hirschfeld, Coryell, & O'Gorman, 1987). The elevated interpersonal dependency of depressed individuals may exacerbate the impact of the negative responses from significant others, causing depressed persons to withdraw relatively quickly following negative interactions. It is possible to imagine a pattern of social behaviors whereby the intimate relationships of the depressed may be characterized by both dependency and withdrawal. Initially, depressed people may engage in proximity-seeking behavior, only to anticipate, sense, and react angrily to negative interactions with a significant other. They may avoid or withdraw from the significant other at this point, feeling rejected or disparaged. But as the depressed person begins to feel the need for emotional support or comfort, he or she may approach again. It is even possible that depressed individuals may approach and, in anticipation of rejection, withdraw before significant others have the chance to respond, resulting in ambivalent messages and the frustration of others with whom they interact.

CONCLUDING COMMENTS

In this chapter, we have examined the social functioning of depressed persons. There is little question that depressed individuals exhibit behaviors in social situations that differ from those emitted by nondepressed persons. It is also clear that others respond to these behaviors negatively, although the precise reasons for these responses are not well understood. Indeed, it will be important in future research to attempt to examine the processes underlying social dysfunction in depression and to analyze in temporal terms the interpersonal interactions of depressed persons. As noted earlier, to gain a better understanding of the patterns of social interactions associated with depression, it will also be important for researchers to examine social withdrawal in the context of the elevated interpersonal dependency of depressed people.

We also noted that the negativity and hostility associated with depression appears to be more marked in intimate relationships than in interactions with strangers. In this context, it may prove instructive in future research to examine how interpersonal expectancies of rejection and the resulting hostility affect the formation of new relationships, that is, as strangers are becoming intimates. For example, we can speculate that when entering a new relationship, depressed people may proceed more quickly than do nondepressed persons through the stages of friendship formation, in an attempt to gain a new supportive contact. Perhaps through increased self-disclosure or other proximity-seeking behavior, the depressed person may come to think of relative strangers as closer social contacts and thereby expect interactions that are more characteristic of significant others. In contrast, the new social contacts may not approach the depressed person with the same proximity-seeking behavior. Not only may depressed persons readily interpret this caution as rejection, but their high expectations will leave them feeling disparaged and more rejected when the interactions are not as intimate as they expect.

Finally, we must point out that it is not clear that deficits in social functioning are specific to depression, rather than being a characteristic of psychopathology in general. In fact, recent research findings suggest that social dysfunction is not unique to depression. The results of studies that have included nondepressed psychiatric patients as subjects indicate that the deficits in social functioning associated with depression are also often related to more general psychological distress. These studies suggest that, like depressed persons, individuals exhibiting other types of psychopathology perceive themselves to have small and fragmented networks (cf. Kessler, Price,

& Wortman, 1985) and experience negativity and hostility in interactions with the members of their social networks (e.g., Markowitz, Weissman, Ouellette, Lish, & Klerman, 1989). Furthermore, nondepressed psychiatric patients have been found to exhibit interpersonal skill deficits similar to those demonstrated by depressed persons (e.g., Gotlib, 1982; Youngren & Lewinsohn, 1980); they have also been found to induce negative affect and rejection in others (e.g., Boswell & Murray, 1981; Gurtman & Froh, 1990). Thus, the social behaviors and attributes that have been found to be associated with depression appear to be a characteristic of psychopathology in general rather than a specific feature of depression.

The fact that social variables do not distinguish depressed individuals from people with other types of psychological disturbance does not mean that social dysfunction has no theoretical value in relation to depression. Indeed, several other aspects of depressive functioning have also been found to be associated with other forms of psychopathology (cf. Hollon, Kendall, & Lumry, 1986) but remain useful nonetheless in studying depression. It may be the case that what is uniquely related to depression is not the conditions of depressed persons' social environments per se, but rather the reactions they have to their social world. In this chapter, we have conceptualized the social variables that characterize the person's social world as stressors to which they must react. Depressed persons may be particularly reactive to their own social skills deficits and to the negativity they perceive from others, not only because the responses they perceive are in fact negative, but also because their cognitive systems lead them to be more sensitive than are nondepressed persons to negative information (cf. Lewinsohn et al., 1973). It is possible, therefore, that this cognitive predisposition to be sensitive and reactive to negative environmental information distinguishes depressed persons from individuals with other forms of psychopathology who experience the same social stressors. Although this formulation is given support by the finding that depressed patients are more vulnerable to family tension and hostile statements made by family members than are schizophrenics (Vaughn & Leff, 1976), further research is required to examine this formulation more explicitly. The results of investigations aimed at identifying aspects of social dysfunction that are specific to depression, both topographically and with respect to underlying processes, may also have implications for improving diagnostic criteria in this disorder. It is our hope that this chapter will contribute to this endeavor.

ACKNOWLEDGMENTS

Preparation of this chapter was facilitated by Grant 6606-3465-51 from Health and Welfare Canada and by an Ontario Mental Health Foundation Senior Research Fellowship to Ian H. Gotlib.

REFERENCES

Abraham, K. (1985). Notes on the psychoanalytic investigation and treatment of manic-depressive insanity and allied conditions. In J. C. Coyne (Ed.), *Essential papers on depression.* New York: New York University Press. (Original work published 1911.)

Abrahams, M. J., & Whitlock, F. A. (1969). Childhood experience and depression. *British Journal of Psychiatry, 115,* 883–888.

Abramson, L. Y., Seligman, M. E. P., & Teasdale, J. (1978). Learned helplessness in humans: Critique and reformulation. *Journal of Abnormal Psychology, 87,* 49–74.

Anderson, C. A., & Hammen, C. (1991). *Psychosocial functioning in children at risk for depression: Longitudinal follow-up.* Manuscript under review.

Barnett, P. A., & Gotlib, I. H. (1988). Psychosocial functioning and depression: Distinguishing among antecedents, concomitants, and consequences. *Psychological Bulletin, 104,* 97–126.

Beach, S. R. H., Sandeen, E. E., & O'Leary, K. D. (1990). *Depression in marriage.* New York: Guilford.

Beck, A. T. (1967). *Depression: Clinical, experimental, and theoretical aspects.* New York: Harper & Row.

Beck, A. T., Rush, A. J., Shaw, B. F., & Emery, G. (1979). *Cognitive therapy of depression.* New York: Guilford.

Becker, R. E., Heimberg, R. G., & Bellack, A. S. (1987). *Social skills training treatment for depression.* New York: Pergamon.

Belsher, G., & Costello, C. G. (1991). Do confidants of depressed women provide less social support than confidants of nondepressed women? *Journal of Abnormal Psychology, 100,* 516–525.

Bettes, B. A. (1988). Maternal depression and motherese: Temporal and intonational features. *Child Development, 59,* 1089–1096.

Biglan, A., Hops, H., Sherman, L., Friedman, L. S., Arthur, J., & Osteen, V. (1985). Problem-solving interactions of depressed women and their husbands. *Behavior Therapy, 16,* 431–451.

Billings, A. G., Cronkite, R. C., & Moos, R. H. (1983). Social-environmental factors in unipolar depression: Comparisons of depressed patients and nondepressed controls. *Journal of Abnormal Psychology, 92,* 119–133.

Billings, A. G., & Moos, R. H. (1984). Coping, stress, and social resources among adults with unipolar depression. *Journals of Personality and Social Psychology, 46,* 877–891.

Billings, A. G., & Moos, R. H. (1985a). Life stressors and social resources affect posttreatment outcomes among depressed patients. *Journal of Abnormal Psychology, 94,* 140–153.

Billings, A. G., & Moos, R. H. (1985b). Psychosocial processes of remission in unipolar depression: Comparing depressed patients with matched community controls. *Journal of Consulting and Clinical Psychology, 53,* 314–325.

Blatt, S. J., Wein, S. J., Chevron, E., & Quinlan, D. M. (1979). Parental representations and depression in normal young adults. *Journal of Abnormal Psychology, 88,* 388–397.

Blumberg, S. R., & Hokanson, J. E. (1983). The effects of another person's response style on interpersonal behavior in depression. *Journal of Abnormal Psychology, 92,* 196–209.

Boswell, P. C., & Murray, E. J. (1981). Depression, schizophrenia, and social attraction. *Journal of Consulting and Clinical Psychology, 49,* 641–647.

Bowlby, J. (1978). *Attachment and loss. Vol. 2: Separation: Anxiety and anger.* Harmondsworth, Middx.: Penguin.

Bowlby, J. (1981). *Attachment and loss: Vol. 3. Loss: Sadness and depression.* Harmondsworth, Middx.: Penguin.

Brewin, C. R., Andrews, B., & Gotlib, I. H. (in press). Psychopathology and early experience: A reappraisal of retrospective reports. *Psychological Bulletin.*

Breznitz, Z., & Sherman, T. (1987). Speech patterning of natural discourse of well and depressed mothers and their young children. *Child Development, 58,* 395–400.

Brim, J. A., Witcoff, C., & Wetzel, R. D. (1982). Social network characteristics of hospitalized depressed patients. *Psychological Reports, 50,* 423–433.

Brown, G. W., & Harris, T. (1978). *Social origins of depression.* New York: Free Press.

Brugha, T., Conroy, R., Walsh, N., Delaney, W., O'Hanlon, J., Dondero, E., Daly, L., Hickey, N., & Bourke, G. (1982). Social networks, attachments and support in minor affective disorders: A replication. *British Journal of Psychiatry, 141,* 249–255.

Burchill, S. A. L., & Stiles, W. B. (1988). Interactions of depressed college students with their roommates: Not necessarily negative. *Journal of Personality and Social Psychology, 55,* 410–419.

Cane, D. B., & Gotlib, I. H. (1985). Implicit conceptualizations of depression: Implications for an interactional perspective. *Social Cognition, 3,* 341–368.

Clarkin, J. F., Spencer, H. H., Lestelle, V., Peyser, J., DeMane, N., Haas, G. L., & Glick, I. D. (1986). *IFI for affective disorder: A manual of inpatient family intervention.* Unpublished manuscript, Cornell University Medical College.

Coates, D., & Wortman, C. B. (1980). Depression maintenance and interpersonal control. In A. Baum & J. E. Singer (Eds.), *Advances in environmental psychology: Vol. 2. Applications of personal control* (pp. 149–182). Hillsdale, NJ: Erlbaum.

Cohn, J. F., Campbell, S. B., Matias, R., & Hopkins, J. (1990). Face-to-face interactions of postpartum depressed and nondepressed mother–infant pairs at 2 months. *Developmental Psychology, 23,* 583–592.

Cohn, J. F., Matias, R., Tronick, E., Connell, D., & Lyons-Ruth, K. (1986). Face-to-face interactions of depressed mothers and their infants. In E. Tronick & T. Field (Eds.), *Maternal depression and infant disturbance.* (*New Directions for Child Development, 34,* pp. 31–46). San Francisco: Jossey-Bass.

Costello, C. G. (1982). Social factors associated with depression: A retrospective community study. *Psychological Medicine, 12,* 329–339.

Coyne, J. C. (1976a). Depression and the response of others. *Journal of Abnormal Psychology, 85,* 186–193.

Coyne, J. C. (1976b). Toward an interactional description of depression. *Psychiatry, 39,* 28–40.

Coyne, J. C., & Bolger, N. (1990). Doing without social support as an explanatory concept. *Journal of Social & Clinical Psychology, 9,* 148–58.

Cutrona, C. E. (1984). Social support and stress in the transition to parenthood. *Journal of Abnormal Psychology, 93,* 378–390.

Cutrona, C. E., & Troutman, B. R. (1986). Social support, infant temperament, and parenting self-efficacy: A mediational model of postpartum depression. *Child Development, 57,* 1507–1518.

Dykman, B. M., Horowitz, L. M., Abramson, L. Y., & Usher, M. (1991). Schematic and situational determinants of depressed and nondepressed students' interpretation of feedback. *Journal of Abnormal Psychology, 100,* 45–55.

Elkin, I., Shea, M. T., Watkins, J. T., Imber, S. D., Sotsky, S. M., Collins, J. F., Glass, D. R., Pilkonis, P. A., Leber, W. R., Docherty, J. P., Fiester, S. J., & Parloff, M. B. (1989). National Institute of Mental Health Treatment of Depression Collaborative Research Program: General effectiveness of treatments. *Archives of General Psychiatry, 46,* 971–983.

Field, T. (1984). Early interactions between infants and their postpartum depressed mothers. *Infant Behavior and Development, 7,* 517–522.

Field, T., Healy, B., Goldstein, S., & Guthertz, M. (1990). Behavior-state matching and synchrony in mother–infant interactions of nondepressed versus depressed dyads. *Developmental Psychology, 26,* 7–14.

Field, T., Sandberg, D., Garcia, R., Vega-Lahr, N., Goldstein, S., & Guy, L. (1985). Pregnancy problems, postpartum depression and early mother–infant interactions. *Developmental Psychology, 21,* 1152–1156.

Fleming, A., Ruble, D., Flett, G., & Shaul, D. (1988). Postpartum adjustment in first-time mothers: Relations between mood, maternal attitudes, and mother–infant interactions. *Developmental Psychology, 24,* 71–81.

Freud, S. (1961). Mourning and melancholia. In J. Strachey (Ed. and Trans.), *The standard edition of the complete psychological works of Sigmund Freud* (Vol. 14). London: Hogarth Press. (Original work published 1917.)

Gerlsma, C., Emmelkamp, P. M. G., & Arrindell, W. A. (1990). Anxiety, depression, and perception of early parenting: A meta-analysis. *Clinical Psychology Review, 10,* 251–277.

Goodman, S. H., & Brumley, H. E. (1990). Schizophrenic and depressed mothers: Relational deficits in parenting. *Developmental Psychology, 26,* 31–39.

Gordon, D., Burge, D., Hammen, C., Adrian, C., Jaenicke, C., & Hiroto, D. (1989). Observations of interactions of depressed women with their children. *American Journal of Psychiatry, 146,* 50–55.

Gotlib, I. H. (1982). Self-reinforcement and depression in interpersonal interaction: The role of performance level. *Journal of Abnormal Psychology, 91,* 3–13.

Gotlib, I. H. (1983). Perception and recall of interpersonal feedback: Negative bias in depression. *Cognitive Therapy and Research, 7,* 399–412.

Gotlib, I. H., & Beatty, M. E. (1985). Negative responses to depression: The role of attributional style. *Cognitive Therapy of Research, 9,* 91–103.

Gotlib, I. H., & Cane, D. B. (1987). Construct accessibility and clinical depression: A longitudinal approach. *Journal of Abnormal Psychology, 96,* 199–204.

Gotlib, I. H., & Colby, C. A. (1987). *Treatment of depression: An interpersonal systems approach.* New York: Pergamon Press.

Gotlib, I. H., & Hammen, C. L. (1992). *Psychological aspects of depression: Toward a cognitive-interpersonal integration.* Chichester, England: Wiley.

Gotlib, I. H., & Hooley, J. M. (1988). Depression and marital distress: Current status and future directions. In S. Duck (Ed.), *Handbook of personal relationships* (pp. 543–570). Chichester, England: Wiley.

Gotlib, I. H., & Lee, C. M. (1989). The social functioning of depressed patients: A longitudinal assessment. *Journal of Social and Clinical Psychology, 8,* 223–237.

Gotlib, I. H., & Lee, C. M. (1990). Children of depressed mothers: A review and directions for future research. In C. D. McCann & N. S. Endler (Eds.), *Depression: New directions in theory, research, and practice* (pp. 187–208). Toronto: Wall & Thompson.

Gotlib, I. H., & McCabe, S. B. (1992). An information-processing approach to the study of cognitive functioning in depression. In E. F. Walker, B. A. Cornblatt, & R. H. Dworkin (Eds.), *Progress in experimental personality and psychopathology research, Vol. 1.5* (pp. 131–161). New York: Springer.

Gotlib, I. H., & Meltzer, S. J. (1987). Depression and the perception of social skill in dyadic interaction. *Cognitive Therapy and Research, 11,* 41–53.

Gotlib, I. H., Mount, J. H., Cordy, N. I., & Whiffen, V. E. (1988). Depressed mood and perceptions of early parenting: A longitudinal investigation. *British Journal of Psychiatry, 152,* 24–27.

Gotlib, I. H., & Robinson, L. A. (1982). Responses to depressed individuals: Discrepancies between self-report and observer-rated behavior. *Journal of Abnormal Psychology, 91,* 231–240.

Gotlib, I. H., & Whiffen, V. E. (1989). Depression and marital functioning: An examination of specificity and gender differences. *Journal of Abnormal Psychology, 98,* 23–30.

Gotlib, I. H., & Whiffen, V. E. (1991). The interpersonal context of depression: Implications for theory and research. In W. H. Jones & D. Perlman (Eds.), *Advances in Personal Relationship* (Vol. 3; pp. 177–206). Greenwich: JAI Press.

Gotlib, I. H., Whiffen, V. E., Wallace, P. M., & Mount, J. H. (1991). A prospective investigation of postpartum depression: Factors involved in onset and recovery. *Journal of Abnormal Psychology, 100,* 122–132.

Gurtman, M. B. (1986). Depression and the response of others: Reevaluating the reevaluation. *Journal of Abnormal Psychology, 965,* 99–101.

Gurtman, M. B., & Froh, A. (1990, August). *Comparison of the interpersonal impact of depression and social anxiety.* Paper presented at the annual meeting of the American Psychological Association, Boston.

Hammen, C. L. (1991). *Depression runs in families: The social context of risk and resilience in children of depressed women.* New York: Springer-Verlag.

Hammen, C. L., & Peters, S. D. (1977). Differential responses to male and female depressive relations. *Journal of Consulting and Clinical Psychology, 45,* 994–1001.

Hautzinger, M., Linden, M., & Hoffman, N. (1982). Distressed couples with and without a depressed partner: An analysis of their verbal interaction. *Journal of Behaviour Therapy and Experimental Psychology, 13,* 307–314.

Henderson, A. S., Byrne, D. G., & Duncan-Jones, P. (1981). *Neurosis and the social environment.* Sydney, Australia: Academic Press.

Hinchliffe, M., Hooper, D., & Roberts, F. J. (1978). *The melancholy marriage.* New York: Wiley.

Hirschfeld, R. M. A., Klerman, G. L., Clayton, P. J., & Keller, M. B. (1983). Personality and depression: Empirical findings. *Archives of General Psychiatry, 40,* 993–998.

Hokanson, J. E., Hummer, J. T., & Butler, A. C. (1991). Interpersonal perceptions by depressed college students. *Cognitive Therapy and Research, 15,* 443–457.

Hokanson, J. E., Loewenstein, D. A., Hedeen, C., & Howes, M. J. (1986). Dysphoric college students and roommates: A study of social behaviors over a three-month period. *Personality and Social Psychology Bulletin, 12,* 311–324.

Holahan, C. J., & Moos, R. H. (1991). Life stressors, resistance factors, and improved psychological functioning: An extension of the stress resistance paradigm. *Journal of Personality and Social Psychology, 58,* 909–917.

Hollon, S. D., Kendall, P. C., & Lumry, A. (1986). Specificity of depressotypic cognitions in clinical depression. *Journal of Abnormal Psychology, 95,* 52–59.

Hooley, J. M. (1986). Expressed emotion and depression: Interactions between patients and high- versus low-expressed-emotion spouses. *Journal of Abnormal Psychology, 95,* 237–246.

Hops, H., Biglan, A., Sherman, L., Arthur, J., Friedman, L., & Osteen, V. (1987). Home observations of family interactions of depressed women. *Journal of Consulting and Clinical Psychology, 55,* 341–346.

Howes, M. J., Hokanson, J. E., & Loewenstein, D. A. (1985). Induction of depressive affect after prolonged exposure to a mildly depressed individual. *Journal of Personality and Social Psychology, 49,* 1110–1113.

Ingram, R. (1990). Self-focused attention in clinical disorders: Review and a conceptual model. *Psychological Bulletin, 107,* 156–176.

Jacobson, N. S., & Anderson, E. (1982). Interpersonal skills deficits and depression in college students: A sequential analysis of the timing of self-disclosures. *Behavior Therapy, 13,* 271–282.

Jacobson, S., Fasman, J., & DiMascio, A. (1975). Deprivation in the childhood of depressed women. *The Journal of Nervous and Mental Disease, 160,* 5–3.

Kahn, J., Coyne, J. C., & Margolin, G. (1985). Depression and marital disagreement: The social construction of despair. *Journal of Social and Personal Relationships, 2,* 447–461.

Kessler, R. C., Price, R. H., & Wortman, C. B. (1985). Social factors in psychopathology: Stress, social support, and coping processes. *Annual Review of Psychology, 36,* 531–572.

King, D. A., & Heller, K. (1984). Depression and the response of others: A reevaluation. *Journal of Abnormal Psychology, 93,* 477–480.

Klerman, G. L., Weissman, M. M., Rounsaville, B. J., & Chevron, E. (1984). *Interpersonal psychotherapy of depression.* New York: Basic Books.

Kochanska, G., Kuczynski, L., Radke-Yarrow, M., & Welsh, J. D. (1987). Resolutions of control episodes between well and affectively ill mothers and their young children. *Journal of Abnormal Child Psychology, 15,* 441–456.

Kowalik, D. L., & Gotlib, I. H. (1987). Depression and marital interaction: Concordance between intent and perception of communication. *Journal of Abnormal Psychology, 96,* 127–134.

Krantz, S. E., & Moos, R. H. (1987). Functioning and life context among spouses of remitted and nonremitted depressed patients. *Journal of Consulting and Clinical Psychology, 55,* 353–360.

Lamont, J., & Gottlieb, H. (1975). Convergent recall of parental behaviors in depressed students of different racial groups. *Journal of Clinical Psychology, 31,* 9–11.

Lewinsohn, P. M. (1974). A behavioral approach to depression. In R. J. Friedman & M. M. Katz (Eds.),*The psychology of depression: Contemporary theory and research* (pp. 157–185). New York: Wiley.

Lewinsohn, P. M., Hoberman, H., Teri, L., & Hautzinger, M. (1985). An integrative theory of depression. In S. Reiss & R. Bootzin (Eds.), *Theoretical issues in behavior therapy* (pp. 331–359). New York: Academic Press.

Lewinsohn, P. M., Lobitz, W. C., & Wilson, S. (1973). "Sensitivity" of depressed individuals to aversive stimuli. *Journal of Abnormal Psychology, 81,* 259–263.

Lewinsohn, P. M., Mischel, W., Chaplin, C., & Barton, R. (1980). Social competence and depression: The role of illusory self-perceptions. *Journal of Abnormal Psychology, 89,* 203–217.

Lewinsohn, P. M., Youngren, M. A., & Grosscup, S. J. (1979). Reinforcement and depression. In R. A. Depue (Ed.), *The psychobiology of the depressive disorders: Implications for the effects of stress* (pp. 291–315). New York: Academic Press.

Libet, J., & Lewinsohn, P. M. (1973). The concept of social skill with special reference to the behavior of depressed persons. *Journal of Consulting and Clinical Psychology, 40,* 304–312.

Livingood, A. B., Daen, P., & Smith, B. D. (1983). The depressed mother as a source of stimulation for her infant. *Journal of Clinical Psychology, 39,* 369–375.

Lyons-Ruth, K., Zoll, D., Connell, D., & Grunebaum, H. U. (1986). The depressed mother and her one-year-old infant: Environment, interaction, attachment, and infant development. In E. Tronick & T. Field (Eds.), *Maternal depression and infant disturbance* (*New Directions for Child Development, 34,* pp. 31–46). San Francisco: Jossey-Bass.

Markowitz, J. S., Weissman, M. M., Ouellette, R., Lish, J. D., & Klerman, G. L. (1989). Quality of life in panic disorder. *Archives of General Psychiatry, 46,* 984–992.

McCabe, S. B., & Gotlib, I. H. (1991). *Interactions of couples with and without a depressed spouse: Self-report and observations of problem-solving situations.* Manuscript under review.

McNiel, D. E., Arkowitz, H. S., & Pritchard, B. E. (1987). The response of others to face-to-face interaction with depressed patients. *Journal of Abnormal Psychology, 96,* 341–344.

Mills, M., Puckering, C., Pound, A., & Cox, A. (1985). What is it about depressed mothers that influences their children's functioning? In J. E. Stevenson (Ed.), *Recent research in developmental psychopathology* (pp. 11–17). Oxford, England: Pergamon.

Monroe, S. M., Bromet, E. J., Connell, M. M., & Steiner, S. C. (1986). Social support, life events, and depressive symptoms: A 1-year prospective study. *Journal of Consulting and Clinical Psychology, 54,* 424–431.

Monroe, S. M., Imhoff, D. F., Wise, B. D., & Harris, J. E. (1983). Prediction of psychological symptoms under high risk psychosocial circumstances: Life events, social support and symptom specificity. *Journal of Abnormal Psychology, 92,* 338–350.

Pagel, M. D., Erdly, W. W., & Becker, J. (1987). Social networks: We get by with (and in spite of) a little help from our friends. *Journal of Personality and Social Psychology, 53,* 793–804.

Panaccione, V. F., & Wahler, R. G. (1986). Child behavior, maternal depression, and social coercion as factors in the quality of child care. *Journal of Abnormal Child Psychology, 14,* 263–278.

Pilowsky, I., & Katsikitis, M. (1983). Depressive illness and dependency. *Acta Psychiatrica Scandinavica, 66,* 11–14.

Pyszczynski, T., & Greenberg, J. (1987). Self-regulatory perseveration and the depressive self-focusing style: A self-awareness theory of reactive depression. *Psychological Bulletin, 102,* 122–138.

Radke-Yarrow, M., Cummings, E. M., Kuczynski, L., & Chapman, M. (1985). Patterns of attachment in two- and three-year olds in normal families and families with parental depression. *Child Development, 56,* 884–893.

Raskin, A., Boothe, H. H., Reating, N. A., Schulterbrandt, J. G., & Odle, D. (1971). Factor analyses of normal and depressed patients' memories of parental behavior. *Psychological Reports, 29,* 871–879.

Reich, J., Noyes, R., Hirschfeld, R., Coryell, W., & O'Gorman, T. (1987). State and personality in depressed and panic patients. *American Journal of Psychiatry, 144,* 181–187.

Repetti, R. L. (1991). *Social withdrawal as a short-term coping response to daily stressors.* Unpublished manuscript.

Rippere, V. (1980). What makes depressed people feel worse? *Behaviour Research and Therapy, 18,* 87–97.

Rosenblatt, A., & Greenberg, J. (1988). Depression and interpersonal attraction: The role of perceived similarity. *Journal of Personality and Social Psychology, 55,* 112–119.

Rosenblatt, A., & Greenberg, J. (1991). Examining the world of the depressed: Do depressed people prefer others who are depressed? *Journal of Personality and Social Psychology, 60,* 620–9.

Rubin, K. H., & Mills, R. S. L. (1988). The many faces of social isolation in childhood. *Journal of Consulting and Clinical Psychology, 56,* 916–924.

Rubin, K. H., & Mills, R. S. L. (1991). Conceptualizing developmental pathways to internalizing disorders in childhood. *Canadian Journal of Behavioural Science, 23,* 300–317.

Ruscher, S. M., & Gotlib, I. H. (1988). Marital interaction patterns of couples with and without a depressed partner. *Behavior Therapy, 19,* 455–470.

Schmaling, K. B., & Jacobson, N. S. (1990). Marital interaction and depression. *Journal of Abnormal Psychology, 99,* 229–236.

Segal, Z. V. (1988). Appraisal of the self-schema construct in cognitive models of depression. *Psychological Bulletin, 103,* 147–162.

Strack, S., & Coyne, J. C. (1983). Social confirmation of dysphoria: Shared and private reactions to depression. *Journal of Personality and Social Psychology, 44,* 798–806.

Vaughn, C. E., & Leff, J. P. (1976). The influence of family and social factors on the course of psychiatric illness: A comparison of schizophrenic and depressed neurotic patients. *British Journal of Psychiatry, 129,* 125–137.

Webster-Stratton, C., & Hammond, M. (1988). Maternal depression and its relationship to life stress, perceptions of child behavior problems, parenting behaviors, and child conduct problems. *Journal of Abnormal Child Psychology, 16*(3), 299–315.

Weissman, M. M. (1987). Advances in psychiatric epidemiology: Rates and risks for depression. *American Journal of Public Health, 77,* 445–451.

Westen, D. (1991). Cognitive-behavioral interventions in the psychoanalytic psychotherapy of borderline personality disorders. *Clinical Psychology Review, 11,* 211–230.

Yarkin, K., Harvey, J. L., & Bloxom, B. M. (1981). Cognitive sets, attribution, and social interaction. *Journal of Personality and Social Psychology, 41,* 243–252.

Youngren, M. A., & Lewinsohn, P. M. (1980). The functional relationship between depression and problematic behavior. *Journal of Abnormal Psychology, 89,* 333–341.

CHAPTER 6

Problems of Memory and Concentration

FRASER N. WATTS

INTRODUCTION

Classical psychiatric accounts of the presentation of clinical depression emphasize the prominence of subjective complaints, including complaints of diminished intellectual powers. For example, Slater and Roth (1969) describe "an uncomfortable realisation of diminishing quickness of thought and action; of difficulty with customarily easy mental activities. . . ." (p. 207). In part, such problems are regarded as a facet of retardation. In describing the symptoms of retardation in depression, they comment, "The power of imagination fails; ideas and images lose their vividness; memory does not respond promptly to attempts at recollection. . . ." However, this does not necessarily imply objective intellectual loss. On the contrary, they comment that "intelligence and memory are unimpaired in depressive states, insofar as they are accessible to testing. Severe retardation may stimulate stupidity or even dementia; but the moment the patient becomes accessible his faculties are found to be intact. Consciousness remains lucid, even in states of stupor and over-mastering retardation" (p. 210).

SUBJECTIVE REPORTS

Concentration Problems

The literature is unanimous about the fact that depressed patients *report* impaired memory and concentration. Watts and Sharrock (1985) have provided one of the more detailed studies of the subjective complaints of concentration problems in depressed patients. They studied a sample of 31 patients in whom the diagnosis of depressive disorder was confirmed by the Levine–Pilowsky Depression Questionnaire (Pilowsky & Boulton, 1970), which has been shown to be a sensitive indicator of major depressive disorder (Carr & Smith, 1985). Patients rated on a four-point scale the extent to which their concentration had been affected by depression on a series of everyday tasks. The percentages reporting that concentration was either "impossible" or "affected a lot" were 71% for watching television, 68% for reading, 65% for household jobs, 45% for having conversations, and 42% for shopping. When asked how much distress their concentration problems caused them, 35% of the patients reported them as causing "a very great deal" of distress, and 51% reported that the problem prevented them from doing what they would like to do "a very great deal." When patients were asked whether their problems were due to depression/anxiety *or* to losing their mental powers, a surprisingly high percentage (29%) said the latter. Consistent with this, 35% said that they did not expect their concentration to return to normal when they were better.

Complaints of concentration problems in reading and watching television were themselves highly correlated. Also, it was noteworthy that both were significantly correlated with severity of depression, endogeneity of depression, and state anxiety. In contrast, reported concentration problems with conversation, work/jobs, and shopping showed no significant correlations with mood variables. Complaints of concentration problems in reading and watching television were also the only ones to show significant correlations with a more "on-line" concentration task in which patients were asked to read silently from a prose passage for 10 minutes and to signal each time they lost concentration. Finally, reported problems of concentration in reading and watching television were the only ones to show correlations with an objective memory task.

These are sufficient indications that it may be particularly useful in clinical interviews to ask about concentration in reading and watching television. However, it is not clear exactly *why* this is a particularly helpful indicator, whether it represents something about the nature of these tasks, or about their central place in modern life. Perceived problems with reading were explored in more detail by asking patients, at the end of the passage, to report problems relating to processing of *words* (focusing on them and grasping their meaning) and of *sentences* (grasping their meaning and connecting them up) and in *remembering* earlier material. There was a hierarchical relationship between these three levels of problem, in that the lower level problems were found less commonly and only in patients who had higher level ones. Reports of problems with sentences and with remembering earlier material showed good correlations with mood variables and other reports of concentration difficulties, though problems with words generally did not.

Memory Problems

Reports of concentration problems are paralleled by reports of poor memory in depression. However, a series of studies have suggested that depression is associated more strongly with memory complaints than with an objective impairment in memory performance. It so happens, however, that a majority of these studies have focused on depressed elderly subjects, and it is possible that the relationship between subjective and objective aspects of memory impairment is different in young and old depressed subjects.

It may be helpful to highlight the key findings from some of the studies that have emphasized the subjective nature of depressive memory problems. Generally, complaints of memory problems have been found to be more closely related to mood state than to objective memory performance. Kahn, Zarit, Hilbert, and Niederehe (1975) studied subjects aged 50 or over with varying degrees of depression and found that memory complaints were correlated with level of depression, whereas memory performance was not. In contrast, neuropsychological tests such as a mental status questionnaire predicted memory performance but were not related to memory complaint. Similarly, West, Boatwright, and Schleser (1984) studied subjects 65 years or older and found that measures of depression were associated with self assessment of memory skills but not with memory performance. Scogin (1985) studied subjects 60 years or older and found that depressed subjects showed a lower level of correlation between self-reported memory performance and objective memory performance than did nondepressed subjects. A related paper by Scogin, Storandt, and Lott (1985) showed that memory training had a beneficial effect on memory performance but not on memory complaints or level of depression.

O'Hara, Hinrichs, Kohout, Wallace, and Lemke (1986), studying elderly subjects, found that depression symptom level (though not diagnosis of depression) was associated with memory complaints, whereas neither was associated with objective memory performance. Williams, Little, Scates, and Blockman (1987) studying subjects 40 years or older found that a depressed group complained of greater problems in memory performance than a nondepressed group but that the two groups did not differ in objective performance. O'Connor, Pollitt, Roth, Brook, and Reiss (1990) in a survey of subjects of 75 years or older found that depression was associated with indecisiveness and impaired concentration. However, objective evidence of memory impairment was patchy, with depressed subjects performing significantly worse than normals on only two out of seven tasks (recall of information from the distant past and recall of a name and address).

Two papers have explicitly examined age trends. Chandler and Gerndt (1988), looking at memory complaints in psychiatric patients, found an overall trend for there to be more memory complaints in subjects over 60 than those under 60. However, this increased frequency of memory complaints in older subjects was found principally in those who were depressed; among those who were not depressed, elderly subjects actually showed fewer memory complaints than younger subjects. No overall difference was found in objective memory performance between subjects with and without memory complaints. Niederehe and Yoder (1989) also studied depression in both younger and older subjects but did not find similar age-related trends, though the memory complaints of depressed subjects were found to differ from those of the normal elderly in being much more general and global. The reported memory problems of depressed subjects were found to focus particularly on recent rather than remote memory. However, depression was not related to basic metamemory knowledge or to expectations about the effect of aging on memory.

As shown in this series of studies, it is relatively easy to demonstrate that depressed subjects complain about memory performance but much more difficult to demonstrate objective impairment of memory. However, it would be premature to conclude that there is *no* objective impairment of memory in depression. As the remainder of this chapter will indicate, a great deal of evidence now demonstrates objective impairments of memory in depression. The question therefore is why so many of these studies that have looked at both subjective and objective issues of memory performance have failed to demonstrate an objective deficit. The reasons no doubt differ from one study to another. However, several possible explanations suggest themselves.

As already noted, it may also be significant that many of the studies that have demonstrated subjective, but not objective, memory impairments have used elderly subjects. The relationship between subjective and objective memory problems in depressed elderly subjects may have distinctive features. In the first place, the memory deficits associated with depression are probably not dissimilar from those found in the normal elderly. There may therefore be particular problems in demonstrating objective memory problems associated with depression in a population many of whom are already showing comparable problems due to aging. Though failures to demonstrate objective memory impairment associated with depression have not been confined to studies using elderly subjects, a disproportionate number appear to have involved a comparison of elderly depressives with normal elderly (e.g., Hart, Kwentus, Taylor, & Harkins, 1987; Kendrick & Post, 1967; Miller & Lewis, 1977; Whitehead, 1973).

There are also indications in the Chandler and Gerndt (1988) study that subjective memory complaints may be a particular feature of elderly depressives, though the study of Niederehe and Yoder (1989) does not support this view. It remains a matter that requires further investigation. In general, the relationship between subjective reports on memory and objective test performance has been problematic (see Morris, 1984). There are many possible reasons for this. One is that subjects with mild-to-moderate memory problems are able to raise their level to perform normally on a relatively short-term objective test. However, problems may nevertheless arise in the round-the-clock, everyday memory performance that is assessed by self-evaluations of memory.

The severity of the depression studied is also relevant. Among nonclinical subjects, college students, for example, it is by no means uncommon to fail to find an association between depression and poor memory performance.

Subclinical individual differences in depression probably represent a relatively weak mood manipulation for the purpose of studying performance deficits (Ellis, 1985). Also, the correlational methods used in a number of the preceding studies are also statistically less powerful than the comparison of two clearly contrasting groups of depressed and nondepressed subjects. Another relevant factor is the nature of the memory task studied. Brief tasks of relatively low reliability, or which are relatively undemanding of processing resources, are also less likely to show effects of depression (Ellis, 1985).

OBJECTIVE TESTS OF MEMORY

Types of Study

Evidence for poor memory performance in depressed subjects comes mainly from three kinds of controlled study. Each raises different methodological problems or questions of interpretation. Together, however, the evidence forms an impressive case. No attempt will be made at this stage to provide a comprehensive overview, because many studies are better dealt with in relation to questions about the qualitative nature of the memory deficit. There are helpful reviews by McAllister (1981), Johnson and Magaro (1987), and Ellis and Ashbrook (1989).

The first kind of controlled study compares depressed patients with normal controls. The main methodological problem here is to ensure that the two groups are comparable on other relevant factors apart from depression. A number of earlier studies, and even some recent ones (e.g., Golinkoff & Sweeney, 1989), have failed to take any steps to "match" depressed and normal control subjects on general intelligence or educational levels. Unfortunately, such studies are of little value.

An early and influential comparison of memory performance in depressed patients and matched normal controls was that of Cronholm and Ottosson (1961). The control groups consisted of surgical patients, and careful steps were taken to ensure matching. Three specially devised memory tests were used, examining memory for word pairs, for simple figures, and for personal data about fictitious people. Both immediate and delayed (3-hour) testing were used. Significant differences between groups were found on all three tests on both occasions of testing. The study was substantially replicated by Sternberg and Jarvik (1976).

A second kind of controlled study has used depressed patients as their own controls, comparing their memory performance when ill with performance when recovered. (E.g., Stromgren, Christensen, & Fromholt, 1976; Stromgren, 1977). While such evidence corroborates the overall picture of poor memory performance being associated with depression, the possibility remains that, to some degree, the improved performance observed at the second testing may be due to practice effects or to statistical regression toward the mean of an initially below-average group.

Third, there have been studies using induction of depressed mood, in which the work of Ellis, (e.g., Leight & Ellis, 1981; Ellis, Thomas, McFarland, & Lane, 1985; Ellis, Thomas, & Rodriguez, 1984) has been influential. Such mood-induction studies have been well reviewed by Ellis and Ashbrook (1989). The strength of such studies is that they demonstrate more clearly than any others the causal direction of the effect of depressed mood on memory performance. They also do not carry the risk of confounding variables such as institutionalization that may be present in patient studies. However, the problem remains of how close a correspondence in memory performance there is between depressed patients and normal subjects with induced depressed mood (Hertel & Rude, 1991a).

Memory Deficit or Just Poor Performance on Memory Tests?

Even if the evidence that depressed patients perform poorly on memory tests is accepted, it does not necessarily mean that depressed patients are impaired in their ability to remember. They may do poorly on memory tests for other reasons. It may be, for example, that depressed patients can access memories but tend not to produce them in memory tests. There are two reasons this might happen.

One is that depressed patients are often retarded, and this may interfere with their verbal productivity in memory tests. Evidence from qualitative analyses of errors in serial learning is consistent with this poverty of output hypothesis. Both Henry, Weingartner, and Murphy (1973) and Whitehead (1973) have shown that the errors associated with depression are often those of omission. For example, Whitehead found, in a serial learning task, that depression was associated with an increased rate of omission errors but a reduced rate of transposition errors. This would be consistent with the hypothesis that the poor memory performance of depressed patients on recall tasks is due to the poverty of their output.

The other possibility is that depressed patients lack confidence; this may also result in their producing fewer memories than they are potentially able to access. This latter view has been advocated by Johnson and Magaro (1987):

> . . . Response bias has been demonstrated in depression such that a conservative response bias may modulate performance and account for the apparent memory deficit. It appears that depressed patients may have the correct answer stored in memory but, because of an overly cautious response strategy, may be unwilling to tell it to the experimenter. This is not a thought disorder or deficient memory structure but simply a decision to respond at a particular level of confidence. The choice to respond conservatively may be due to the pathology itself, that is, not wishing to display the confusion inherent in the pathology. (p. 32)

Such evidence as is available generally argues against a hypothesis that memory performance is impaired in depression because of retardation or poor productivity. The most direct approach is to use a forced recall paradigm. Leight and Ellis (1981) testing normal subjects in whom a depressed mood has been induced, rather than depressed patients, found that use of a forced recall paradigm did not prevent them demonstrating that depressed mood lowered memory performance. Another approach is to vary the amount of productivity required in the memory test and to see whether this affects the apparent depressive memory deficit. If the deficit is due to poor productivity, it should be greater in free recall than in paradigms that require more minimal responses. Watts and Sharrock (1987) compared free recall for a passage of prose with a cued recall paradigm in which subjects simply had to answer a series of questions with answers of one word or, at most, a short phrase. The difference in memory performance for a depressed and a matched control group was actually somewhat more reliable for cued than for free recall.

If the apparent depressive memory deficit were due to poor productivity, depressed patients would not be expected to be impaired on recognition tests. In fact, a series of studies have found that depression is associated with poor performance on recognition memory tasks (Dunbar & Lishman, 1984; Miller & Lewis, 1977; Silberman, Weingartner, Laraia, Byrnes & Post, 1983; Watts, Morris & MacLeod, 1987; Niederehe & Camp, 1985; Golinkoff & Sweeney, 1989; Wolfe, Granholm, Butters, Saunders, & Janowsky, 1987). Admittedly, depressed patients seem to show a less marked deficit on recognition than on free recall, even when the tests and other psychometric properties are matched in difficulty (Calev & Erwin, 1985). This could be seen as consistent with the hypothesis that the poor memory performance of depressed patients is in part due to problems of response productivity on recall tests. However, that recognition memory is impaired at all seems to indicate this is not the whole of the problem.

Conservative Response Style?

The more interesting aspect of recognition memory results in depression is that it permits the most sensitive test of the hypothesis that poor performance is due to a conservative response style. If depressed patients have a conservative response style, reduced rates of hits *and* false alarms would be expected. Alternatively, if signal detection analyses are used, depression would be expected to lead to an effect on β (an index of the severity or laxness of the criterion subjects use) rather than d' (an index of their ability to discriminate material correctly in tests of recognition). Unfortunately, the available recognition memory studies are conflicting from this point of view. Some studies have produced a pattern of recognition memory results consistent with the hypothesis of a cautious response strategy. Others have produced a pattern of results indicating impaired memory sensitivity. The two most satisfactory studies indicating that depressives show cautious response criteria are those of Miller and Lewis (1977) and Dunbar and Lishman (1984). (The Dunbar and Lishman study included both neutral and hedonically toned words, but it is the former that are of concern for the time being.) Both studies found that depression was associated with lower levels of both hits and false alarms. When signal detection analyses were carried out, these studies found that depressed subjects differed from controls in β but not d'. The failure to find an effect of depression on d' in the Dunbar and Lishman study has to be interpreted cautiously as the controls did little better than chance, so the failure to find a difference between groups may have been due to a floor effect.

One further study (Larner, 1977) deserves mention because it is quoted by Johnson and Magaro (1987) as providing at least nonsignificant support for depression being associated with cautious response criteria. However, this appears to represent a misinterpretation of the study. In fact, the depressed subjects were more cautious than a group of demented patients but showed no differences from controls (physically ill patients) on either discriminability or bias. In contrast, another study (Silberman et al., 1983) found that depression affected hits but not false alarms. This must also be treated with caution, however, as there was no check that the depressed and control groups were matched on intelligence or educational level, so the group differences obtained may not have been due to depression at all. The recognition results of Wolfe et al. (1987) appear to indicate that unipolar depressed patients may have had a relatively *lax* response criterion in relation to control subjects. Certainly, depression was associated with increased false positives but decreased false negatives. However, results for hits and misses are not reported separately, which makes the pattern of results difficult to interpret.

More satisfactory evidence that depression is associated with reduced memory sensitivity rather than the change in criteria is provided by Watts et al. (1987). To guard against problems of lack of statistical power, the researchers used a relatively substantial (n = 36) group of quite severely depressed patients. The control subjects were matched on vocabulary scores. Three consecutive lists were used, each consisting of 20 concrete nouns, with recognition memory for each being tested before the next was presented. Two methods of presentation were used. Some subjects simply received visual presentations of words; others were required to vocalize the word as they saw it. The vocalization condition was included partly to check that any memory deficit in depression held up even with a procedure that ensured at least a minimal level of attention to the word. In both conditions, depressed subjects showed fewer hits than control subjects. In the silent condition, depression was also associated with reduced false alarms. However, intriguingly, in the vocalization condition, depression had the reverse effect on false alarms, with the depressed group now showing more. The analysis of the false alarms data showed a significant interaction between conditions and groups. When a signal detection analysis was applied to the data, d' showed a main effect of depression with no other terms approaching significance. In the analysis of β, no terms at all approached significance.

The unexpected effects of presentation procedure on response bias invite a reconsideration of the earlier literature. Most studies, such as Miller and Lewis (1977) and Dunbar and Lishman (1984), had not required any response from subjects at presentation. The findings of Watts et al. under the "silent" condition parallelled these in that depression was found to be associated with a reduced rate of both hits and false alarms. However, hints can be found in other studies that requiring a response from subjects at presentation modifies this effect of depression on false alarms. Silberman et al. (1983) had required subjects to rate the emotionality of words and found that depression reduced hits, but not false alarms. Also Zuroff, Colussy, and Wielgus (1983), in a study using emotionally toned words, had used a self-description task at presentation and found that depression was associated with increased false alarms (significantly for negative words, nonsignificantly for positive words). It can be suggested tentatively that the main effect of vocalization in depressed subjects was on confidence. When depressives vocalized words at presentation, they may have approached the recognition task with more confidence, using less conservative response criteria, and therefore showed more false alarms. However, the effect of vocalization in controls may be primarily on discriminability, with vocalization simply reducing mistakes in the recognition task. Needless to say, this post hoc interpretation of an unpredicted effect must be treated cautiously.

The important fact is that there are conditions under which depression is associated with a reduced level of hits without reduced false alarms. It would therefore be a mistake to interpret the effect of depression on hits as being attributable in general to cautious response criteria. If reduced hits in depression were the result of cautious response criteria, it would be found only where reduced false alarms were also found. In the overall analysis of the data from the study of Watts et al., depression had a highly significant effect on d' but not on β.

Memory for Hedonically Toned Words

There has been an extensive series of studies on memory in depression using hedonically toned material, examining the hypothesis that depressed subjects show enhanced recall for negative material and poor recall for positive material. This literature has been reviewed elsewhere (e.g., Blaney, 1986; Bower, 1987; Ellis & Ashbrook, 1989; Johnson & Magaro, 1987; Singer & Salovey, 1988; Ucros, 1989; Dalgleish & Watts, 1990), and it will be considered here only insofar as it bears on the hypothesis that there is an impairment of memory in depression.

First, it is important to consider the implications of depressed patients characteristically showing memory for negative material that is at least as good as that of normal controls, and often better. This makes the memory deficit in depression an unusual memory disorder. In neuropsychological amnesias, patients often vary in the extent of the deficit depending on the kind of task and the kind of material used. However, there is probably no example of neuropsychological patients performing a memory task *better* than do normals. It is clear from this that depressed patients have no absolute incapacity for memory.

The general assumption would be something such as the following (e.g., Ellis & Ashbrook, 1989), that cognitive resources are adequately allocated to the coding and retrieval of negative information, with the result that memory for it is good. However, for whatever reason, the resources allocated to the processing of other kinds of material is inadequate.

STAGE MODELS OF ATTENTION AND MEMORY

A good deal of older information processing research has been conceived within a "stage" model of cognitive processing. Thus, for example, memory tasks might be classified as "immediate," "short-term," or "long-term," depending on the time scale of the tasks involved. Tasks classified in this way undoubtedly do involve differences in the cognitive processes required. Thus, for example, relatively long-term memory tasks require increasing degrees of encoding and rehearsal. However, the cognitive processes required do not map onto such a classification of memory tasks in any exact way. This is the principal reason stage models attract less interest now than they used to. However, a significant body of data on cognitive deficits in depression has been conceived within a stage framework and still makes a useful contribution to knowledge.

At a number of points, however, we are unfortunately dependent on only one or two studies, which may not have been replicated. The conclusions that can be drawn are therefore somewhat uncertain.

Vigilance and Filtering

To begin with studies of vigilance and filtering, Byrne (1976) demonstrated deficits in depressed patients on the vigilance task. Interestingly, different patterns of deficits were found for psychotic and neurotic depressives, though caution needs to be exercised because the results have not been replicated (Byrne, 1977).

Psychotic depressives were hypothesized to be underaroused. Consistent with this, they showed a pattern of vigilance performance with a low level of correct detections and marked deterioration over time. In contrast, neurotic depressives, who were hypothesized to be overaroused, were affected less in their vigilance performance, and their errors mostly took the form of false positives.

There is also evidence that depressives are poor at attentional tasks with opportunities for filtering, that is, where relevant stimuli can be distinguished from irrelevant ones on the basis of a clear physical cue. An example would be an experiment in which subjects listen to a list of digits, some of which are in a male, and others in a female voice. In such experiments that provide opportunities for filtering, performance is generally improved by telling subjects which digits they will be required to recall *before* rather than *after* they are presented. Most subjects show this effect, though depressives do not (Hemsley & Zawada, 1976).

Stimulus Identification and Sensory Memory

The time course of stimulus identification can be investigated in a paradigm in which the presented stimulus is followed after a variable interval by a masking stimulus. Very short interstimulus intervals produce backward masking. Both depressives and normals have been found to benefit from extensions of the ISI from 60 to 120 ms. However, only depressed subjects benefited from a further extension from 120 to 300 ms (Sprock, Braff, Saccuzzo, & Alkinson, 1983). This can be interpreted as showing that depressives take longer to form a representation of a stimulus. However, their stimulus *registration* appeared to be normal; generally speaking, it is *encoding* rather than registration that is affected by masking stimuli.

Colby and Gotlib (1988) have reported a study of sensory memory that comes to somewhat parallel conclusions. Using an array of 64 characters, they compared deficits in reporting part or the whole of the array. Generally, partial report can be taken to reflect sensory store processes, while whole report is assumed to reflect short-term memory (Sperling, 1960). Depressed and control showed no difference in partial recall. However, they did show a difference in recall of the whole array, which became more pronounced over successive trials, reflecting increased interference or fatigue effects in the depressed subjects. The experiment also varied the delay before the array appeared and before recall was required. However, these did not interact with depression.

Delay effects, were, however, found in the same sample of depressed subjects in a digit span task. No group differences were found with immediate (1 second) delay. However, depressives were significantly worse when there was a delay of 20 or 30 seconds. Colby and Gotlib (1988) considered two explanations for this delay effect. One is that delayed recall is more effortful. Explanations in terms of cognitive effort will be discussed later in this chapter. The other is that delay involves greater rehearsal, and the capacity for rehearsal may well be impaired in depression. Berndt and Berndt (1980) found, consistent with this explanation, that when rehearsal on a Brown–Peterson task was prevented by requiring subjects to count backward, control subjects performed as poorly as depressed subjects. Also consistent with this suggestion that rehearsal processes are a significant factor in the depressive memory deficit is the finding of Cohen, Weingartner, Smallerberg, Pickar, and Murphy (1982) that depressed patients were impaired only in the delayed recall of sets of trigrans. Another relevant finding is that of Henry et al. (1973), who found that patients performed less well on a serial learning task on days when they were depressed than on days when they were not. However, the difference emerged only from the second trial onward, not on the first trial. They suggested that the problem is with encoding the material in a way that facilitates transfer from short-term to long-term memory.

Additive Factors

A systematic approach to the analysis of task performance, based on a stage model of information processing, is the "additive factors" approach developed by Sternberg (1969), though the assumptions on which this approach is based have not gone unchallenged (Sanders, 1983). One of the stages in Sternberg's model is the "memory comparison stage" (i.e., scanning and retrieval), and this has been the focus of a number of studies of depressed subjects. Performance on memory comparison tasks can be further subdivided into indices of speed of scanning, and performance on nonscanning stages (encoding, binary decision, and response output). Most studies (Glass, Uhlenhuth, Hastl, Matuzas, & Fischman, 1981; Hilbert, Niederehe, & Kahn, 1976; Koh & Wolpert, 1983) have found no association between depression and slow scanning performance. However, a more recent study by Brand and Jolles (1987) was able to demonstrate slower scanning in depressed subjects. They suggest that this may have been due to their employment of newly developed versions of the memory comparison task that were shorter and designed to be more acceptable in the clinic. There is more support for depression being associated with impaired performance on the nonscanning aspects of memory comparison tasks (e.g., Glass et al., 1981; Brand & Jolles, 1987). Glass et al. comment that depressed patients normally adopt a conservative response strategy in which they maintain accuracy at the expense of speed. Brand and Jolles found evidence that depression was associated with a less efficient search strategy involving greater reliance on control as opposed to automatic processing.

Encoding and Retrieval

Studies using induced depressed mood, rather than clinical depression, provide a valuable way of investigating the relative contributions of depressed mood at learning and recall on memory performance. The most relevant data is that reported by Leight and Ellis (1981; experiment 2). The data suggest that subjects who were depressed at learning but not at recall performed less well on recall of letter sequences than those who were depressed at recall but not at learning (though the paper does not include a statistical test of exactly this comparison). It was possible to demonstrate a significant effect of mood at learning, regardless of mood and recall; there was also significant effect of mood at recall regardless of mood at learning. It is thus clear that mood at both occasions is relevant. However, the effect of mood on learning achieved a higher degree of statistical reliability. Though effects of depression on retrieval are probably less powerful than on encoding, Ellis, Thomas, McFarland, and Lane (1985) have confirmed that they are demonstrable.

PROCESSING RESOURCES AND COGNITIVE EFFORT

An alternative theoretical approach to the memory deficit of depressed patients is in terms of processing resources theory (Ellis & Ashbrook, 1989). The model assumes that the processing resources of depressed subjects are depleted, largely because resources are devoted to depressive thoughts. Further, it is assumed that the more depressed subjects are, the more processing resources will be depleted, and the poorer will be their performance on memory tasks. Within this framework, Ellis and Ashbrook have suggested that the reason the memory performance of mildly depressed subjects such as college students is often not found to be significantly impaired is that they are less depressed than clinical samples or subject in mood induction studies and thus have their processing resources relatively intact.

Next, the theory assumes that the extent to which depressed subjects show impaired performance on a task depends on how demanding it is of processing resources. Tasks that are relatively demanding of processing resources, or cognitive "effort," are more likely to be impaired in depressed subjects. On the other hand, undemanding tasks may well be performed as adequately by depressed subjects as by controls.

Evidence for Processing Recovery Theory

Ellis et al. (1984) presented evidence to support this theory that deserves to be summarized. The first experiment made use of the fact that normal subjects recall words better when they are embedded in an elaborated sentence than a simple "base" sentence because it requires cognitive "effort," that is, the allocation of processing resources. (A base sentence might be "The hungry child opened the door," whereas the elaborated sentence would include a phrase consistent with the target adjective, such as "The hungry child opened the door of the refrigerator.") Depressed patients are hypothesized not to have the additional resources needed to process an elaborated sentence. The prediction, which was confirmed, was therefore that depressed patients would not show the same advantage of having a word embedded in an elaborated rather than just a base sentence. The second experiment was based on the assumption that incidental recall of semantic information is better if a semantic orienting task is given. The semantic orienting task was rating the word for pleasantness–unpleasantness, whereas the control orienting task was to count the number of *e*'s. Again it would be assumed that semantic processing requires cognitive effort, which depressed subjects would not be expected to be able to make. As predicted, subjects in depressed mood showed less improvement as a result of semantic orienting instruction. In the third experiment, sentences were presented with a missing word, and subjects had to select a word from two possible alternatives to complete the sentence. In the low-effort condition, the selection was obvious; in the high-effort condition, it was more difficult. Again, it was predicted and found that whereas normal subjects did better in the high-effort condition, depressed subjects did not. All three of these experiments used subjects with induced depressed mood rather than depressed patients.

The assumption underlying the second of these experiments, that semantic processing requires more cognitive effort than nonsemantic, makes a link to another seminal paper by Weingartner, Cohen, Murphy, Martello, and Gerdt (1981), which reported a series of studies on depressed patients. In one of these, subjects were required to produce an acoustic associate to some words and semantic associate to others. Normal subjects showed better recall of semantically processed words, though this advantage was not found for depressed patients. Actually, there is a possibility that this result may have been due to a floor effect, but taken in conjunction with the results of Ellis et al., it is reasonable to conclude that depressed subjects do not show the normal advantage of semantic processing on recall.

Another experiment of Weingartner et al. (1981) compared recall for lists of words drawn from a variety of different semantic categories according to whether or not words drawn from the same category were clustered together at presentation. Depressed and control subjects differed little in their recall of words presented in clustered form, but depressed subjects were at a disadvantage in recall of unclustered lists, presumably a more effortful task. An incidental finding from this study was that control subjects were more likely to recall words in clustered form even when they were unclustered at presentation, something that has also been found by Koh, Kayton, and Berry (1973), Russell and Beekhuis (1976), and Calev and Erwin (1985).

Two other experiments have also compared memory for word lists differing in structure. Levy and Maxwell (1968) compared word lists differing in their degree of approximation to text. (At one extreme would be a normal sentence; at the other would be a random series of words. An example of intermediate approximation to text would be, "They saw the play Saturday and sat down beside him.") Watts, Dalgleish, Bourke, and Healy (1990) used lists differing both in approximation to text and also, like Weingartner, in the extent to which words from the same semantic category were clustered together. Unfortunately, these experiments have failed to produce a consistent picture. Though Weingartner found, as might be predicted from resource theory, that relatively structured, "clustered" lists showed less depressive memory deficit, Levy and Maxwell found that depressives benefited *less* than normals from increasing approximation to text. There was thus a more marked difference in memory between depressed and control subjects for the more highly structured lists. However, Watts et al. (1990) found that it was with lists of medium approximation text that the difference between groups was greatest. With medium structure, depressed subjects performed little better than with low structure, whereas control subjects performed almost as well with medium structure as with high structure.

Channon, Baker, and Robertson (in press) have results based on memory for word lists that are consistent with this view. The clearest difference between depressed and control subjects was for word lists in which words from different semantic categories were presented in random order. Differences were less marked both for lists in which words were clustered at presentation and for lists in which the words were semantically unrelated. Again, the intermediate level of structure seemed to show the most marked effect of depression.

It is plausible that with very unstructured material, the additional processing resources that control subjects have available should be of relatively little benefit because there is no implicit structure in the material to which processing resources can usefully be deployed to process. On the other hand, as resource theory would predict, with highly structured materials, little processing resources are needed for processing. However, it seems that the threshold of increasing structure at which performance improves is lower for control subjects than for depressed patients. The results of Watts et al. (1990) for lists varying in the extent of clustering by semantic categories differed from those of Weingartner et al. (1981) in that the trend was for differences between groups to become less marked with increasing structure. The reasons for the discrepant results of Weingartner et al. and Watts et al. are not entirely clear. However, they at least indicate the need for caution in drawing conclusions from both experiments.

The subsequent development of the theoretical ideas of Weingartner's group has brought them even closer to those of Ellis. For example, Roy-Byrne, Weingartner, Bierer, Thompson, and Post (1986) claimed that "cognitive impairments in depression are most evident in situations or tasks that require effort, particularly sustained effort." Two experiments were reported in support of this proposition, comparing effortful and automatic tasks. One criterion of an automatic task is that it is relatively unaffected by circumstances and individual differences. In contrast, effortful tasks are held to require more attention and performance on them is more variable (Hasher & Zachs, 1979).

In the first, depressed patients were presented with pairs of nouns and asked to make a comparative judgment about the items of each pair. The effortful task was free recall of the words presented. In contrast, as a test of more automatic processing, word pairs were presented and subjects were asked to recall which judgment they had made about them. Depressed patients were impaired on the effortful tasks, but not on the automatic task. In a second similar experiment, subjects were presented with a list of categorically similar words in which some words were repeated. During presentation, they were asked to raise their right hands when they heard a word repeated. The effortful task was free recall of the words. In contrast, automatic processing was tested by asking subjects to recognize which words had been presented twice. Again, subjects were impaired on the effortful task but not on the automatic one. Similarly, Golinkoff and Sweeney (1989) showed that paired associate learning, an effortful task, was impaired in depression whereas frequency judgments, an automatic task, were not. Subsequently, Calev, Nigal, and Chazan (1989) have extended these ideas about automatic and effortful processing to a word production task. They predicted and found that depressed subjects were more impaired with the effortful task of producing words belonging to a semantic category than the more automatic task of producing words beginning with a common letter.

Ellis and Ashbrook (1989) have observed that experiments using relatively structured materials such as sentences or passages of prose are less likely to show memory deficits associated with depression than are lists of unconnected words. Of course, it would generally be assumed that processing of lists of unconnected words is more effortful than processing of prose, though this is advanced more as an interpretation of apparently discrepant results from different experiments than as a conclusion from a single experiment using different kinds of material.

Watts and Cooper (1989) were able to demonstrate that depression was associated with poor recall for a prose passage, "Circle Island." Though reports of deficits in prose recall with depression are relatively rare, the subjects were rather severely depressed and the passage is a complicated one. Attention focused specifically on an internal comparison of units of the story that differed in how central they were to its gist. Control subjects showed the normal effect for "high gist" units to be better recalled than "low gist" units. However, depressed subjects did not show this. When a nonstructural variable, the imageability of units, was examined, controls and depressed subjects were found to show comparable benefits from imageability on recall. The failure to show preferential recall of units central to the gist of the story suggests that depressed subjects may not have been processing the passage in a way that led them to discern its overall structure and to identify the place of individual unit within that structure.

No subsequent work has so far been done to test the generalizability of this finding. However, if it were the case that depressed patients have a relatively general deficit in identifying which material is important to remember and giving priority to it, this could have serious implications for their everyday functioning. They might be more handicapped by their memory problems than would be suggested by the sheer quantitative diminution in the amount of material they were able to remember.

Recent work by Ellis (1991) has examined the effect of induced depressed mood. Effects of mood were found when stories were presented for subjects to read but not when they were presented auditorially. (This is at variance with the findings of Watts and Cooper (1989) where *clinical* depression was shown to affect recall of a story even when it was auditorially presented. However, the most interesting aspect of Ellis's findings relates to the presentation of a title at the start of a story. Generally, the omission of a title makes recall more difficult because more work needs to be done to structure the material. Depressed subjects were at a particular disadvantage when the title was omitted. Equally, they were also at a relative disadvantage when a different story had been presented immediately previously. These findings are consistent with the view that depressed patients do not have the resources to structure prose materials adequately, especially under conditions where this is relatively difficult to do.

Appraisal of Processing Resources Theory

The processing resources theory of Ellis and Ashbrook (1989) has made a valuable contribution in bringing order to the field, and has received an encouraging degree of empirical support. However, it remains desirable that the key results supporting the theory should be replicated, and especially that those (e.g., Ellis et al., 1984) carried out with normal subjects with induced depressed mood should be replicated with depressed patients.

Greater attention is also needed to the methodological problems that always attend the demonstration of any differential deficits (Chapman & Chapman, 1973; Watts, 1989). Where a memory deficit is found with one task and not another, there is always the possibility that this could be due to the psychometric properties of the two tasks (e.g., differences in difficulty, discriminating powers, etc.) rather than to the qualitative differences between the two tasks on which theoretical interpretations often prefer to focus. Relatively few of the experiments in the field so far have attended to this methodological issue (though see Calev & Erwin, 1985; Calev, Korin, Shapira, Kugelmass, & Lerer, 1986; Watts & Cooper, 1989). The methodological problems raised by testing for differential deficits are not easily handled. Chapman and Chapman (1973) advocate creating tasks matched on psychometric properties. This is usually possible, but often it has to be achieved at the cost of introducing a difference between conditions (e.g., list length) besides the intended subject of study. Because of this, there often remains an ambiguity in the interpretation of results even where matched tasks have been created (Watts, 1989).

There is also a need for processing resources theory to achieve greater specificity. Ellis (1990) has commented that resource allocation theory "is completely open as to where the depressed mood states have their effect." There is a stage in the development of a field at which a relatively open theory of this kind is helpful. However, it ultimately becomes necessary, if our understanding is to advance, to formulate a more specific theoretical interpretation of the memory deficit associated with depression. It is also desirable, at the appropriate stage, to formulate a theory which, through being more specific, is more open to refutation. One of the uncomfortable features of processing resources theories, in whatever context, is that they are difficult to test directly, and the currently available paradigms from which inferences about processing resources are made are often capable of alternative explanations (Navon, 1984).

One of the specific issues about which processing resources theory has so far been open is whether (a) the processing resources that depressed subjects have available are depleted, perhaps because they are partly taken up with depressive ruminations, or (b) potentially available resources are not appropriately deployed to the task in hand. To focus this issue, it may be helpful to compare the cognitive deficits associated with depression and anxiety. Eysenck and Calvo (in press) have advanced a capacity theory of the effects of anxiety. In parallel with the assumption that Ellis makes for depression, Eysenck assumes that part of the capacity of anxious subjects is taken up by extra-task processing (e.g., worry). However, Eysenck assumes that the potential adverse effects of this on performance may be compensated for by *increased* effort, whereas Ellis and Ashbrook (1989) assume that in depression fewer processing resources are available *and* fewer resources are deployed to the task in hand. Eysenck's theory for anxiety leads him to locate the primary effect of anxiety on "effectiveness," that is, the ratio of performance to effort.

Eysenck (1982; 1992) has assembled a variety of evidence consistent with the hypothesis that anxiety is associated with increased effort and that therefore anxious subjects have fewer undeployed processing resources. These include (a) the findings from dual task studies that secondary tasks, which are not the main focus of effort, are affected by anxiety more severely than primary ones, which are the central focus of effort (e.g., Hamilton, 1983); (b) studies using self-report indices of subjective effort (e.g., Dornic, 1977, cited by Eysenck, 1982); (c) the fact that ego-involving instructions have less beneficial effect on anxious subjects than controls (e.g., Nicholson, 1958); and (d) the fact that anxiety is often associated with *better* performance than controls on *easy* tasks. Hockey (1986) has put forward a similar theory of the effects of stress on performance in terms of increased effort to preserve levels of performance in the short term, even though there may be longer term physiological costs.

Through the relevant experiments do not appear to have been carried out, it seems most unlikely that depression is associated with a similar expenditure of cognitive effort to compensate for reduced processing resources. The more plausible conclusion is that there are two parallel phenomena in depression: (a) fewer processing resources are available because some are taken up with depressive cognitions, and (b) even such processing resources as are available are not effectively deployed on the task in hand. Research directed to the question of the deployment of available resources in depression would lend greater specificity to processing resources theory.

Strategies

Hertel and Hardin (1990) have raised important conceptual issues concerning the extent to which depressed patients employ appropriate cognitive strategies. They make the important suggestion that the performance of depressed patients is likely to be most impaired with tasks where the use of appropriate strategies is not well controlled by the task itself. This can be compared, on the one hand, with situations in which subjects are *directed* to use appropriate cognitive strategies that might be expected to bring the performance of depressed patients up to the standard of controls and, on the other hand, with situations where the nature of the task is concealed and so where neither depressed nor control subjects are likely to use appropriate strategies. The suggestion that depressed patients may not employ cognitive strategies that control subjects employ spontaneously is close to the hypothesis that depressed patients do not deploy available cognitive resources, though it makes that hypothesis more specific and open to experimental tests.

Hertel and Hardin report a cleverly designed series of experiments to test their ideas. As would be expected, depressed and control subjects did not differ on a test of "unaware memory" in which neither group of subjects would be expected to use cognitive strategies. In contrast, in a subsequent experiment, differences were obtained in recognition memory according to mood state. There was also evidence that the provision of directions guiding subjects to appropriate strategies improved the performance of subjects with naturally occurring depression, though it was less helpful in subjects with induced depressed mood.

Effects of Depressive Thoughts

Another assumption of processing resources theory that invites more specific investigation concerns the proposition that processing resources are taken up by task-irrelevant, depressive thoughts. It is a central assumption of current cognitive models of depression that depressed patients are adversely affected by negative automatic thoughts. These have been extensively studied by questionnaire methods (e.g., Harrell & Ryon, 1983), but there have been surprisingly few attempts to study automatic thoughts directly with on-line report during task performance. Using induced depressed mood, however, Ellis, Seibert, and Herbert (1990) have shown that depression is associated with a higher percentage of thoughts that were rated as unfavorable. Subsequently, Seibert and Ellis (1991) were able to demonstrate that task-irrelevant thoughts were higher in both sad and happy students and that there was a negative relationship between irrelevant thoughts and performance on memory tasks. A strong mood state of either kind can apparently distract from the task in hand, a happy mood state as much as a sad one.

Despite the relative lack of directly relevant research, especially on clinical depression, there is probably little doubt that depression is associated with negative task-irrelevant thoughts, and that these contribute to the poor cognitive performance of depressed patients. The hypothesis would be that negative thoughts function as a secondary task in impairing performance on the primary task. In support of this, Krames and McDonald (1985) have shown that the cognitive performance of normal subjects given a secondary task is like that of depressed subjects without one.

Despite the plausibility of this view, there are grounds for doubting how important a factor negative task-irrelevant thoughts are in producing impaired cognitive performance in depression. The parallel argument for how intrusive thoughts in anxiety produce impaired performance has often failed to receive support from a correlation between task performance and the frequency of intrusive thoughts (e.g., Galassi, Frierson, & Siegal, 1984). It seems that the subjective meaning attached to task-irrelevant thoughts may be more significant than their frequency.

One of the few directly relevant studies on depressed patients is that of Watts, MacLeod, and Morris (1988a). Phenomenologically, a distinction can be made between two different kind of lapses of concentration in depressed patients: (a) "mind wandering" (i.e., task-irrelevant) thoughts, and (b) "blanking" (i.e., where patients neither concentrate on the task nor think about anything else). Though mind wandering is the most widespread form of lapse of concentration in depressed patients, blanking is by no means uncommon. For example, it occurs more frequently than disruption of concentration due to external distraction (Watts & Sharrock, 1985). Moreover, Watts, MacLeod, and Morris (1988a) reported correlational evidence suggesting that the relative contribution of mind wandering and blanking to poor task performance depends on the kind of task patients have to perform. Memory for prose under ordinary processing conditions was correlated negatively with mind wandering but not with blanking. In contrast, memory for prose under more effortful conditions (i.e., forming visual images) showed the reverse pattern of a negative correlation with blanking but not with mind wandering; the same was true of correlations with the "Tower of London" planning task. (This is a task in which three colored beads are presented on three rods, and subjects have to go from the pattern in which the beads are presented to one shown on a card in as few moves as possible.)

The implication seems to be that task-irrelevant thoughts contribute to poor performance of some tasks, but it should not necessarily be assumed that this is the key factor on all tasks. The phenomenological distinction between mind wandering and blanking may correspond to the theoretical distinction between processing resources being depleted by allocation to task-irrelevant operations and, on the other hand, available cognitive resources simply not being deployed to the task in hand.

REMEDIAL STRATEGIES

This last experiment of Hertel and Hardin introduces the important subject of remedial strategies that can improve the performance of depressed subjects. So far, there has been very little relevant work. Though Hertel and Hardin have found that the performance of depressed subjects can be improved by directing subjects to use appropriate strategies on concealed tasks, it is not clear that this would have any general clinical applicability. First, the tasks with which depressed patients have difficulty are generally ones that are already clearly identified by them *as tasks.* Second, strategies of the kind subjects were directed to use by Hertel and Hardin would be highly specific to a particular task; no general benefits in task performance would be expected. Occasionally, however, there may be tasks that are highly salient for specific patients who are not spontaneously using the appropriate cognitive strategies. It may then be beneficial and appropriate to direct patients to the use of the appropriate strategy.

There is a further question as to which kinds of strategies *are* appropriate. A distinction can be made between (a) strategies of a kind that depressed subjects specifically tend not to employ or tend not to benefit from and (b) those that operate normally in depression. For example, "semantic" processing may come into the first category. It is consistent with this that Weingartner et al. (1981) found that depressed patients did not benefit as controls did from semantic processing strategies. On the other hand, some strategies appear to work perfectly normally in depressed patients. For example, Watts and Cooper (1989) found that the correlation between the imageability of a unit of a prose passage and its recall was normal in depressives. High imageability units were better recalled in both depressives and controls. The question of clinical tactics that arises is whether it is better to try to find ways of restoring artificially the cognitive strategies with which depressed patients have particular difficulty (e.g., semantic processing), or to guide them to make additional compensatory use of strategies that appear to be operating normally. Watts, MacLeod, and Morris (1988b) reported a study of the latter kind. Subjects were given an auditory presentation of three comparable prose passages. In one condition, subjects used their ordinary processing strategies. In the others, they were (a) trained to form visual images as they listened to the passage or (b) trained in prior relaxation as a control condition. Use of imagery produced a significant improvement in memory performance.

If there is any merit in the idea discussed in the previous section that depression affects the allocation of resources, benefits could also be expected from remedial strategies that focus subjects' attention on the task in hand. Pursuing this idea, Hertel and Rude (1991b) compared "focused" and "unfocused" versions of a task in which subjects had to make judgments about how well a specified word fitted into a sentence frame. In the focused condition, the word appeared only briefly before being replaced by the sentence. Subjects had to report their judgment as soon as the sentence went off the screen. In the unfocused condition, both were on the screen concurrently and subjects would report their judgment at any time. The deficit that depressed patients showed in the unfocused condition disappeared in the focused condition.

The relatively small amount of attention that has so far been paid to remedial cognitive strategies in depressed patients might be justified on the argument that other treatments are available for producing a general improvement in mood state, and when this occurs, cognitive performance will improve as a secondary consequence. In many cases, this may well be so. However, it is at least plausible that there are tasks of sufficient everyday importance that poor performance of them is a factor in maintaining a depressed mood state. Remedial cognitive strategies to improve performance on these may contribute to an improvement in mood state. From general clinical observations, there is little doubt that inability to perform important everyday tasks is a source of frustration. Also, on general rehabilitation principles, it would be expected that improved functioning would contribute to an alleviation of patients' general condition.

It is much more speculative what role impairments in cognitive function may play in the onset of depression. There is a tendency among depression theorists to fasten on the aspects of depression in which they are most interested, whether these be the biological aspects, negative thoughts, or depressed mood, and to claim that these are "primary." In fact, in depression as with most psychological disorders, the different facets of the condition are so systemically intertwined that it is relatively implausible that any one facet of the condition will really be primary (Watts, 1989), and convincing evidence for such claims is seldom forthcoming. Therefore, it would be rash to suggest that problems of concentration, attention, and memory are primary in the onset of depression. However, they may be less exclusively secondary than is often supposed. Thus, Healy and Williams (1988) have suggested that aberrant physiological functioning, of which poor cognitive performance would be an index, leads, via attributional processes, to dysphoria. Clinically, there seem to be at least some cases of depression where patients describe deteriorating cognitive performance as their first warning of oncoming depression. It is a symptom of depression that may warrant more attention from clinicians than it has so far received.

REFERENCES

Berndt, D. J., & Berndt, S. M. (1980). Relationship of mild depression to psychological deficit in college students. *Journal of Clinical Psychology, 36,* 868–874.

Blaney, P. H. (1986). Affect and memory: A review. *Psychological Bulletin, 99,* 229–246.

Bower, G. H. (1987). Commentary on mood and memory. *Behaviour Research and Therapy, 25,* 443–455.

Brand, N., & Jolles, J. (1987). Information processing in depression and anxiety. *Psychological Medicine, 17,* 145–153.

Byrne, D. G. (1976). Vigilance on arousal in depressive states. *British Journal of Clinical Psychology, 15,* 167–174.

Byrne, D. G. (1977). Affect and vigilance performance in depressive illness. *Journal of Psychiatric Research, 13,* 185–191.

Calev, A., & Erwin, P. G. (1985). Recall and recognition in depressive: use of matched task. *British Journal of Clinical Psychology, 24,* 127–128.

Calev, A., Korin, Y., Shapira, B., Kugelmass, S., & Lerer, B. (1986). Verbal and nonverbal recall by depressed and euthymic affective patients. *Psychological Medicine, 16,* 789–794.

Calev, A., Nigal, D., & Chazan, S. (1989). Retrieval from semantic memory using meaningful and meaningless constructs by depressed, stable bipolar and manic patients. *British Journal of Clinical Psychology, 28,* 67–73.

Carr, V., & Smith, J. (1985). Assessment of depression by questionnaire compared to DSM-III diagnosis. *Journal of Affective Disorders, 8,* 167–170.

Chandler, J. D., & Gerndt, J. (1988). Memory complaints and memory deficits in young and old psychiatric inpatients. *Journal of Geriatric Psychiatry and Neurology, 1,* 84–88.

Channon, S., Baker, J. E., & Robertson, M. M. (in press). Effects of structure and clustering on recall and recognition memory in clinical depression. *Journal of Abnormal Psychology.*

Chapman, L. J., & Chapman, J. P. (1973). Problems in the measurement of cognitive deficit. *Psychological Bulletin,* 380–385.

Cohen, R. M., Weingartner, H., Smallerberg, S. A., Pickar, D., & Murphy, D. L. (1982). Effort and cognition in depression. *Archives of General Psychiatry, 39,* 593–597.

Colby, C. A., & Gotlib, I. H. (1988). Memory deficits in depression. *Cognitive Therapy and Research, 12,* 611–627.

Cronholm, B., & Ottosson, J. O. (1961). The experience of memory function after electroconvulsive therapy. *British Journal of Psychiatry, 109,* 251–258.

Dalgleish, T., & Watts, F. N. (1990). Biases of attention and memory in disorders of anxiety and depression. *Clinical Psychology Review, 10,* 589–604.

Dornic, S. (1977). *Mental load, effort and individual differences.* Reports of the Department of Psychology, University of Stockholm, No. 509.

Dunbar, G. C., & Lishman, W. A. (1984). Depression, recognition-memory and hedonic tone: A signal detection analysis. *British Journal of Psychiatry, 144,* 376–382.

Ellis, H. C. (1985). On the importance of mood intensity and encoding demands in memory: Commentary on Hasher, Rose, Zacks, Sanft and Doren. *Journal of Experimental Psychology General, 114,* 392–395.

Ellis, H. C. (1990). Depressive deficits in memory: Processing initiative and resource allocation. *Journal of Experimental Psychology General, 119,* 60–62.

Ellis, H. C. (1991, April 11–13). Mood, memories, and cognition: Data, theory, and applications. Invited keynote address to the annual meeting of the Southwestern Psychological Association, New Orleans.

Ellis, H. C., & Ashbrook, P. W. (1989). The "state" of mood and memory research: A selective review. Special Issue: Mood and memory: Theory, research and applications. *Journal of Social Behaviour and Personality, 4,* 1–21.

Ellis, H. C., Seibert, P. S., & Herbert, B. J. (1990). Mood state effects on thought listing. *Bulletin of the Psychonomic Society, 28,* 147–150.

Ellis, H. C., Thomas, R. L., McFarland, A. D., & Lane, J. W. (1985). Emotional mood states and retrieval in episodic memory. *Journal of Experimental Psychology Learning, Memory and Cognition, 11* 363–370.

Ellis, H. C., Thomas, R. L., & Rodriguez, I. A. (1984). Emotional mood states and memory: Elaborative encoding, semantics processing, and cognitive effort. *Journal of Experimental Psychology Learning, Memory and Cognition, 10,* 470–482.

Eysenck, M. W. (1982). *Attention and arousal: Cognition and performance.* Berlin: Springer-Verlag.

Eysenck, M. W. (1992). *Anxiety: The cognitive perspective.* Hove: Erlbaum.

Eysenck, M. W., & Calvo, M. G. (in press). Anxiety and performance: The processing efficiency theory. *Cognition and Emotion.*

Galassi, J. P., Frierson, H. T., Jr., & Siegal, R. G. (1984). Cognitions, test anxiety, and test performance: A closer look. *Journal of Consultant and Clinical Psychology, 51,* 292–293.

Glass, R. M., Uhlenhuth, E. H., Hastl, F. W., Matuzas, W., & Fischman, M. W. (1981). Cognitive dysfunction and imipramine in outpatient depressives. *Archives of General Psychiatry, 38,* 1048–1051.

Golinkoff, M., & Sweeney, J. A. (1989). Cognitive impairments in depression. *Journal of Affective Disorders, 17,* 105–112.

Hamilton, V. (1983). *The cognitive structures and processes of human motivation and personality.* Chichester: Wiley.

Harrell, H., & Ryon, N. B. (1983). Cognitive-behavioural assessment of depression: Clinical validation of the Automatic Thoughts Questionnaire. *Journal of Consulting and Clinical Psychology, 51,* 721–725.

Hart, R., Kwentus, A., Taylor, R., & Harkins, S. W. (1987). Rate of forgetting in dementia and depression. *Journal of Consulting and Clinical Psychology, 55,* 101–105.

Hasher, L., & Zachs, R. T. (1979). Automatic and effortful processes in memory. *Journal of Experimental Psychology, 108,* 365–388.

Healy, D., & Williams, J. M. (1988). Dysrhythmia, dysphoria and depression: The interaction of learned helplessness and circadian dysrhythmia in the pathogenesis of depression. *Psychological Bulletin, 103,* 163–178.

Hemsley, D. R., & Zawada, S. L. (1976). "Filtering" and the cognitive deficit in schizophrenia. *British Journal of Psychiatry, 128,* 456–461.

Henry, G. M., Weingartner, H., & Murphy, D. L. (1973). Influence of affective states and psychoactive drugs on verbal learning and memory. *American Journal of Psychiatry, 130,* 966–971.

Hertel, P. T., & Hardin, T. S. (1990). Remembering with and without awareness in a depressed mood: Evidence of deficits in initiative. *Journal of Experimental Psychology: General, 199,* 45–59.

Hertel, P. T., & Rude, S. S. (1991a). Recalling in a state of natural or experimental depression. *Cognitive Therapy and Research, 15,* 103–127.

Hertel, P. T., & Rude, S. S. (1991b). Depressive deficits in memory: Focusing attention improves subsequent recall. *Journal of Experimental Psychology: General, 120,* 301–309.

Hilbert, N. M., Niederehe, G., & Kahn, R. L. (1976). Accuracy and speed of memory in depressed and organic aged. *Educational Gerontology, 1,* 131–146.

Hockey, G. R. J. (1986). A state control theory of adaptation to stress and individual differences in stress management. In A. W. K. Gaillard & M. G. H. Coles (Eds.), *Energetics and human information processing* (pp. 285–298). Dordrecht Nijhoff.

Johnson, M. H., & Magaro, P. A. (1987). Effects of mood and severity on memory processes in depression and mania. *Psychological Bulletin, 101,* 28–40.

Kahn, R. L., Zarit, S. H., Hilbert, N. M., & Niederehe, G. (1975). Memory complaint and impairment in the aged: The effect of depression and altered brain function. *Archives of General Psychiatry, 32,* 1569–1573.

Kendrick, D. C., & Post, F. (1967). Differences in cognitive status between healthy, psychiatrically ill and diffusely brain-damaged elderly subjects. *Journal of Psychiatry, 113,* 75–81.

Koh, S. D., Kayton, L., & Berry, R. (1973). Mnemonic organization in young nonpsychotic schizophrenics. *Journal of Abnormal Psychology, 81,* 299–310.

Koh, S. D., & Wolpert, E. A. (1983). Memory scanning and retrieval in affective disorders. *Psychiatry Research, 8,* 289–297.

Krames, L., & McDonald, M. R. (1985). Distraction and depressive cognition. *Cognitive Therapy and Research, 9,* 561–573.

Larner, S. (1977). Encoding in senile dementia and elderly depressives: A preliminary study. *British Journal of Social and Clinical Psychology, 16,* 379–390.

Leight, K. A., & Ellis, H. S. (1981). Emotional mood states, strategies and state-dependency in memory. *Journal of Verbal Learning and Verbal Behaviour, 20,* 251–266.

Levy, R., & Maxwell, A. E. (1968). The effect of verbal context on the recall of schizophrenics and other psychiatric patients. *British Journal of Psychiatry, 114,* 311–316.

McAllister, T. W. (1981). Cognitive functioning in the affective disorders. *Comprehensive Psychiatry, 22,* 572–586.

Miller, E., & Lewis, P. (1977). Recognition memory in elderly patients with depression and dementia. *Journal of Abnormal Psychology, 86,* 84–86.

Morris, P. E. (1984). The validity of subjective reports on memory. In J. E. Harnis & P. E. Morris (Eds.), *Everyday memory: Actions and absent-mindedness* (pp. 153–172). London: Academic Press.

Navon, D. (1984). Resources—A theoretical soup stone? *Psychological Review, 91,* 216–234.

Nicholson, W. M. (1958). The influence of anxiety upon learning: Interference or drive increment. *Journal of Personality, 26,* 303–319.

Niederehe, G., & Camp, C. (1985). Signal detection analysis of recognition memory in depressed elderly. *Experimental Ageing Research, 11,* 207–213.

Niederehe, G., & Yoder, C. (1989). Metamemory perceptions in depressions of young and older adults. *Journal of Nervous and Mental Disease, 177,* 4–14.

O'Connor, D. W., Pollitt, P. A., Roth, M., Brook, P. B., & Reiss, B. B. (1990). Memory complaints and impairment in normal, depressed, and demented elderly persons identified in a community survey. *Archives of General Psychiatry, 47,* 224–227.

O'Hara, M. W., Hinrichs, J. V., Kohout, F. J., Wallace, R. B., & Lemke, J. H. (1986). Memory complaint and memory performance in the depressed elderly. *Psychology and Aging, 1,* 208–214.

Pilowsky, I., & Boulton, D. M. (1970). Development of a questionnaire-based decision rule for classifying depressed patients. *British Journal of Psychiatry, 116,* 647–650.

Roy-Byrne, P. J., Weingartner, H., Bierer, L. M., Thompson, K., & Post, R. M. (1986). Effortful and automatic cognitive processes in depression. *Archives of General Psychiatry, 43,* 265–267.

Russell, P. N., & Beekhuis, M. E. (1976). Organization in memory: A comparison of psychotics and normals. *Journal of Abnormal Psychology, 85,* 527–534.

Sanders, A. F. (1983). Towards a model of stress and human performance. *Acta Psychologica, 53,* 61–97.

Scogin, F. (1985). Memory complaints and memory performance: The relationship reexamined. Special Issue: Aging and mental health. *Journal of Applied Gerontology, 4,* 79–89.

Scogin, F., Storandt, M., & Lott, L. (1985). Memory skills training, memory complaints, and depression in older adults. *Journal of Gerontology, 40,* 562–568.

Seibert, P. S., & Ellis, H. C. (1991). Irrelevant thoughts, emotional mood states and cognitive task performance. *Memory and Cognition, 19,* 507–513.

Silberman, E. K., Weingartner, H., Laraia, M., Byrnes, S., & Post, R. M. (1983). Processing of emotional properties of stimuli by depressed and normal subjects. *Journal of Nervous and Mental Diseases, 171,* 10–14.

Singer, J. A., & Salovey, P. (1988). Mood and memory: Evaluating the network theory of affect. *Clinical Psychology Review, 8,* 211–251.

Slater, E., & Roth, M. (Eds.). (1969). *Clinical Psychiatry.* London: Baillière, Tindall & Cassell.

Sperling, G. (1960). The information available in brief visual presentations. *Psychological Monographs, 74* (Whole No. 498), 1–29.

Sprock, J., Braff, D. L., Saccuzzo, D. P., & Alkinson, J. H. (1983). The relationship of depression and thought disorder in pain patients. *British Journal of Medical Psychology, 56,* 351–360.

Sternberg, D. E., & Jarvik, M. E. (1976). Memory functions in depression. *Archives of General Psychiatry, 33,* 219–224.

Sternberg, S. (1969). The discovery of processing stages: Extensions of Donder's method. *Acta Psychologia, 30,* 276–315.

Stromgren, L. S. (1977). The influence of depression on memory. *Acta Psychiatrica Scandinavica, 56,* 109–128.

Stromgren, L. S., Christensen, A. L., & Fromholt, P. (1976). The effects of unilateral brief-interval ECT on memory. *Acta Psychiatrica Scandinavica, 54,* 336–346.

Ucros, C. G. (1989). Mood state-dependent memory: A meta-analysis. *Cognition and Emotion, 3,* 139–169.

Watts, F. N. (1989). Experimental abnormal psychology. In G. Parry and F. N. Watts (Eds.). *Behavioural and Mental Health Research: A Handbook of Skills and Methods.* (pp. 139–161). Hove: Lawrence Erlbaum.

Watts, F. N., & Cooper, Z. (1989). The effects of depression on structural aspects of the recall of prose. *Journal of Abnormal Psychology, 98,* 150–153.

Watts, F. N., Dalgleish, T., Bourke, P., & Healy, D. (1990). Memory deficit in clinical depression: Processing resources and the structure of materials. *Psychological Medicine, 20,* 345–349.

Watts, F. N., MacLeod, A. K., & Morris, L. (1988a). Associations between phenomenal and objective aspects of concentration problems in depressed patients. *British Journal of Psychology, 79,* 241–250.

Watts, F. N., MacLeod, A. K., & Morris, L. (1988b). A remedial strategy for memory and concentration problems in depressed patients. *Cognitive Therapy and Research, 12,* 185–193.

Watts, F. N., Morris, L., & MacLeod, A. K. (1987). Recognition memory in depression. *Journal of Abnormal Psychology, 96,* 273–275.

Watts, F. N., & Sharrock, R. (1985). Description and measurement of concentration problems in depressed patients. *Psychological Medicine, 15,* 317–326.

Watts, F. N., & Sharrock, R. (1987). Cued recall in depression. *British Journal of Clinical Psychology, 26,* 149–150.

Weingartner, H., Cohen, R. M., Murphy, D. L., Martello, J., & Gerdt, C. (1981). Cognitive processes in depression. *Archives of General Psychiatry, 38,* 42–47.

West, R. L., Boatwright, L. K., & Schleser, R. (1984). The link between memory performance, self-assessment, and affective status. *Experimental Aging Research, 10,* 197–200.

Whitehead, A. (1973). Verbal learning and memory in elderly depressives. *British Journal of Psychiatry, 123,* 203–208.

Williams, J. M., Little, M. M., Scates, S., & Blockman, N. (1987). Memory complaints and abilities among depressed older adults. *Journal of Consulting and Clinical Psychology, 55,* 595–598.

Wolfe, J., Granholm, E., Butters, N., Saunders, E., & Janowsky, D. (1987). Verbal memory deficits associated with major affective disorders: A comparison of unipolar and bipolar patients. *Journal of Affective Disorders, 13,* 83–92.

Zuroff, D. C., Colussy, S. A., & Wielgus, M. S. (1983). Selective memory and depression: A cautionary note concerning response bias. *Cognitive Therapy & Research, 7,* 223–232.

CHAPTER 7

Self-Esteem

CHRISTINE Z. BERNET, RICK E. INGRAM, and BRENDA R. JOHNSON

INTRODUCTION

Lowered self-esteem is a widely recognized feature of depression. Indeed, self-esteem deficits are so thoroughly established by empirical studies (see Sacco & Beck, 1985) that decreased self-esteem is considered a symptom of depression by the dominant psychological disorder classification system in use in North America. The Diagnostic and Statistical Manual of Mental Disorders (DSM-III-R; American Psychiatric Association, 1987), for instance, includes feelings of worthlessness as a diagnostic criterion for depression and notes that "the sense of worthlessness varies from feelings of inadequacy to completely unrealistic negative evaluations of one's worth. The person may reproach himself or herself for minor failings that are exaggerated and search for environmental cues confirming the negative self-evaluation" (p. 219). Whether self-esteem is a symptom of depression or is instead implicated in the causal sequence of the disorder, however, is unclear; some theorists argue that self-esteem is a major cause of depression while others view it as a symptom arising from the process of depression.

Given the predominance of self-esteem deficits observed in depression, along with the lack of clarity regarding the causal versus consequential nature of this process, the purpose of this chapter is to examine several aspects of this construct within depression. In particular, we start with a brief overview of self-esteem that examines both historical and developmental perspectives on self-esteem. Building on these perspectives, we then review several of the major theories and research studies that have examined whether self-esteem is a causal factor in depression or is a symptom of the disorder. Finally, we propose a model that attempts to describe the functioning of self-esteem deficits in depression from both a causal and a symptom standpoint.

HISTORICAL AND DEVELOPMENTAL PERSPECTIVES ON SELF-ESTEEM

In a thorough review of self-esteem theory and measurement, Wells and Marwell (1976) have outlined the historical course of this construct. In providing a brief overview of self-esteem concepts, we follow the evolutionary course they have charted. Wells and Marwell (1976) note that William James was the first to discuss the self-esteem construct, followed by the psychodynamic theorists Freud, Adler, Horney, and Sullivan, and then subsequently by humanistic theorists such as Maslow and Rogers. Following the humanistic theorists, the field of experimental social psychology contributed significantly to the conceptualization and assessment of self-esteem (Deaux, 1972; Silverman, Ford, & Morganti, 1966). Although social psychological researchers continue to explore basic self-esteem issues, clinical processes are the focus of much of the contemporary work in self-esteem, particularly as the self-esteem construct relates to depression.

James (1890) viewed self-esteem as an evaluative process; he argued that self-esteem, at its simplest, could be measured as the ratio of a person's successes to his or her pretensions. Pretensions are viewed as goals, purposes, or aims, whereas successes constitute the perception of the attainment of those goals. As people attain more of their pretensions, the ratio grows larger and self-esteem becomes correspondingly stronger. Pretensions also add a vulnerability component to self-esteem in that these are the areas where the individual is proposed to be most competent. If he or she comes up short in the perception of goal-attainment, or in comparison with others in the same pretension arena, self-esteem suffers. A realization of shortcomings in an area that was not important to the individual, however, would not result in a devaluation of personal worth.

In contrast to James, Freud (1917/1986) viewed lowered self-esteem as a key factor that distinguishes mourning from depression or melancholia; in mourning the world looks bleak, whereas in depression the soul looks bleak. More specifically according to Freud, depression is an emotional state resulting from the actual or perceived loss of a desired object or person. During the course of the depressed state, the individual vulnerable to melancholia becomes angry toward the lost object but believes that this is unacceptable. This unacceptability leads the person to assume the lost object's faults and turns inward the anger caused by the loss of the object. This turning inward of anger and consequent self-blame adversely affects the person's self-esteem. Low self-esteem is therefore a defining feature of depression according to Freud.

Although humanistic psychologists such as Rogers and Maslow also theorized about self-esteem, the first empirical work on the self-esteem construct was begun by experimental social psychologists. In particular, several social-psychological researchers began to examine self-esteem as it applied to the idea of "persuasibility," that is, how various levels of self-esteem affected the individual's susceptibility to persuasion (Silverman et al., 1966). They also began to examine different types of self-esteem such as chronic or "traitlike" self-esteem versus a more transitory or "state" level of self-esteem (Wells & Marwell, 1976). Following the notion of state self-esteem, many researchers began to study, in controlled experiments, the effects of manipulating levels of self-esteem (e.g., Deaux, 1972).

Working during the same period, Rosenberg's (1979) focus differed from the other experimental psychologists in that he relied on a more unified theoretical base (Wells & Marwell, 1976). Rosenberg, like James, viewed self-esteem as the evaluative portion of the self-concept that allows the individual to hold a positive or negative orientation toward himself or herself (Rosenberg, 1979). In Rosenberg's view, the drive to preserve self-esteem is a primary motive in human striving. In contrast to both James and Freud, though, his theoretical basis was more sociological and developmental. For instance, his work in the area of self-esteem concentrated on differences between racial groups and differences in self-esteem at different stages of development, notably adolescence. Rosenberg's work contributed significantly to the early empirical examinations of the construct of self-esteem (Wells & Marwell, 1976).

Developmental Aspects of Self-Esteem

To provide a context for conceptualizing the relationship between depression and self-esteem, we believe it is helpful to trace the developmental antecedents of self-esteem. Many would agree that the rudiments of self-esteem originate in infancy. According to Fenichel (1945), for example, "the first supply of satisfaction from the external world, the supply of nourishment, is simultaneously the first regulator of self-esteem" (p. 40). Moreover, because the infant's needs can only be met by others, self-esteem is strongly mediated by interpersonal relating. In discussing such interpersonal mediation, Blanck and Blanck (1974) have noted that self-esteem emerges through the infant's "internalization of parental affection combined with favorable experiences of success in mastery" (p. 345).

Interpersonal influences on self-esteem can be conceptualized in terms of attachment theory, and indeed, findings suggest that self-esteem is mediated in infancy and childhood by a history of secure attachments (e.g., Egeland & Sroufe, 1981; Waters, Noyes, Vaughn, & Ricks, 1985). Not only are securely attached children rated higher in self-esteem, they are also identified as more self-confident, curious, and persistent in problem solving. Conversely, children who demonstrate an insecure or more avoidant pattern of attachment evidence greater degrees of depression and self-esteem deficits (Sameroff & Emde, 1989).

Drawing from a number of theoretical orientations, Becker (1979) has succinctly outlined how developmental difficulties in interpersonal relating can lead to impaired self-esteem which, in turn, may predispose some individuals to depression. Becker (1979) describes self-esteem as "a cognitive-affective product of self-evaluation processes" (p. 319) that initially stems from the infant's pattern of attachment to important caregivers. Drawing from Bowlby's (1977) work, Becker notes that when the infant's attachment to the parent is not secure, it hampers the ability to individuate and seek gratification from sources other than the parent. The child's impaired ability to satisfy important needs results in the experience of frustration and anxiety. Becker speculates that when the child is unable to express this frustration, it further erodes self-esteem and increases vulnerability to depression. This researcher has also applied an element of Beck's (1967) cognitive triad, the negative view of the self, to suggest how negative cognitive biases can maintain and exacerbate the low self-esteem engendered by early childhood experience. That is, the selective filtering of experience in a negative manner continues to assail the individual's already poor self-esteem.

A Working View of Self-Esteem

The thread that appears to bind all definitions of self-esteem is its evaluative aspect. For example, Becker (1979) views self-esteem as a cognitive-affective product of the self-evaluative processes, whereas James saw self-esteem as an evaluation of how effectively people perceive they have met their goals. Rosenberg (1979) viewed it as a negative evaluation of the self, as did Freud. Likewise, Steffenhagen (1990) has woven a very elaborate model of self-esteem but at the core of his model is the evaluation an individual makes regarding personal attainment of goals. According to Steffenhagen (1990), lowered self-esteem can result from failing to reach realistic goals or from setting unattainable goals.

Combining these theoretical notions along with existing developmental perspectives, it seems reasonable to assume that we begin to form aspects of the self and self-esteem from the moment we are able to perceive ourselves as separate from our caregivers. The formation of self-esteem undoubtedly continues past childhood, however, as people process new information regarding achievements, successes, disappointments, and failures. Given the variety of areas in life where people believe it important to demonstrate competence, self-esteem levels can vary across a variety of different life domains. Thus, self-esteem is multifaceted in the sense that people can have areas of their lives in which they feel competent and their self-esteem is correspondingly high, whereas in other areas they may feel inferior and suffer low self-esteem.

Despite self-esteem differences across a variety of areas, we suggest that individuals also have a core level of self-esteem based on an overall evaluation of an individual's self and the resulting affective response to this evaluation. Core self-esteem develops from the earliest interactions with significant others and guides much of the momentary fluctuations observed in daily self-esteem levels. We will discuss in greater depth the implications of core self-esteem in the section where we propose a model of the relationship between self-esteem and depression.

SELF-ESTEEM IN DEPRESSION

Self-esteem deficits are a widely observed feature of depression. As with any feature of depression, self-esteem may be casual or consequential (see Barnett & Gotlib, 1988; Hollon, DeRubeis, & Evans, 1987). Hypothesizing lowered self-esteem as either causal or consequential in depression has significant ramifications for investigations of depression. In postulating that it is causal, theorists must decide whether they consider it to be a sufficient cause, a necessary cause, or one part of a series of events that precipitates depression. Alternatively, when self-esteem deficits are conceptualized as one of a constellation of symptoms of depression, the thrust of basic theory and research changes; investigators need to assess whether factors precipitating depression also result in lowered self-esteem. Thus, the focus of research that assumes a consequential role for self-esteem in depression must examine the symptoms that arise with depression.

Extant theory and research have tended to emphasize self-esteem in depression from either an etiological (causal) or symptom (consequential) standpoint. In this section, we will examine some of the recent literature that has approached this issue from the etiological or the symptom view. We will not attempt to be comprehensive in covering all the literature on self-esteem but will instead focus on theory and data that appear particularly pertinent to questions concerning the role of self-esteem in depression. Although various investigators have tended to approach self-esteem as either a causal agent or as a consequence of depression, our impression is that this represents a matter of emphasis rather than a clear-cut distinction. That is, we assume that most investigators, while emphasizing one view or the other, would acknowledge that self-esteem processes may serve both a causal and a consequential role.

A widely known depression theory that incorporates self-esteem deficits is the reformulated learned helplessness model (Abramson, Seligman, & Teasdale, 1978). To address the inadequacies of Seligman's original learned helplessness model, Abramson et al. (1978) offered a theoretical reformulation of this model that relied heavily on attributional theory (cf. Weiner, 1979). Among the inadequacies noted by Abramson et al. (1978) was the original theory's inability to account for lowered self-esteem as a symptom of depression. Postulating an attributional account of depression allows for the explication of self-esteem deficits in depression; lowered self-esteem is a symptom that results from attributions for negative events that are internal, stable, and global. More specifically, attributing the cause of negative events to the self (an internal attribution) leads to lower self-esteem. Thus, the locus of control dimension of the various attributional possibilities causes the self-esteem symptoms of depression.

The revised learned helplessness theory of depression has itself been subsequently revised (Abramson, Alloy, & Metalsky, 1988, 1990; Abramson, Metalsky, & Alloy, 1989). This revision specifies a hopelessness depression that is a model of what Abramson et al. (1988) refer to as "negative cognition depression." Negative cognition depression also encompasses Beck's model and suggests that a specific subtype of depression is caused by dysfunctional thinking patterns in response to negative life events. The hopelessness theory of depression retains the emphasis on attributional patterns as causal agents of negative cognition depression and specifically proposes that these attributional patterns cause lowered self-esteem as a symptom of depression. Interestingly, although Abramson et al. (1988) group both hopelessness and Beck's model under the category of negative cognition depression, they draw a distinction for self-esteem as a symptom of depression. Specifically, they suggest that because Beck proposes a negative cognitive triad, with negative views of the self (negative self-esteem) as a causal factor of depression, it would be a tautology for Beck's model to suggest that self-esteem can also be a symptom. Abramson et al. (1988) thus explicitly exclude self-esteem as a causal factor in their model of depression.

Brewin and Furnham (1986) have also proposed a modification to the traditional attributional model of depression. They suggest that other cognitive variables are likely to be involved in the maintenance of self-esteem. They termed these variables *preattributional* because, although attributions are at least partially based on them, they do not constitute causal material. These variables constitute the extent to which the individual evaluates success or failure in relation to the performance of others. They propose that the individual bases self-evaluations on *consistency* (how often similar events happen to the individual) and *consensus* (the possibility that the event is more likely to happen to the self than another). They hypothesize that the influence of consistency and consensus judgments on self-esteem and depression is mediated by causal attributions.

To examine the influence of consistency and consensus information on attributions, Brewin and Furnham (1986) assessed the preattributional judgments made for hypothetical positive and negative outcomes. For subjects with similar levels of self-esteem at the beginning of the experiment, higher levels of self-esteem were associated with internal attributions for positive events, and lower self-esteem levels were associated with internal attributions for negative events. Interestingly, the researchers also found that self-esteem and depression correlated substantially with internal attributes of both positive and negative events but that consensus and consistency judgments were associated with depression for negative but not positive events. It would thus appear that these two preattributional judgments impact significantly on the level of self-esteem in depression (at least in the realm of attributions for negative events) although it is still not possible to judge causality from these data.

In an attempt to determine which factors are predictive of depression (including self-esteem), several researchers have reported prospective studies based on relatively large samples. For instance, Lewinsohn, Steinmetz, Larson, and Franklin (1981) assessed subjects over a period of 1 year and examined depression, expectancy of positive and negative events, irrational beliefs, attributions for success and failure, and self-esteem. Subjects were assessed at the beginning of the study and after 1 year. Three hypotheses were examined: (1) the *antecedent hypothesis,* following from cognitive theorists' assumptions that people who become depressed have depressive cognitive styles before the onset of depression, (2) the *scar hypothesis,* in which individuals who were once depressed should be left with detectable depressive cognitions, and (3) the *consequent hypothesis,* which suggests that depressive cognitions arise as a result of depression. Lewinsohn et al. (1981) concluded that the data supported the consequent hypothesis. Of particular relevance to the present discussion, individuals who were depressed at the end of the study had significantly lower self-esteem at that time but not at the beginning of the study. Although some investigators may raise methodological questions concerning various aspects of this study, the data reported by Lewinsohn et al. (1981) do clearly favor low self-esteem as a symptom of depression rather than as a causal factor.

Although self-esteem was not found in the Lewinsohn et al. (1981) study to predict depression, in a subsequent model Lewinsohn, Hoberman, Teri, and Hautzinger (1985) have proposed a multifactorial model of depression that addresses self-esteem. They propose that the behavioral, emotional, somatic, and interpersonal symptoms of depression arise consequent to increased self-awareness. This increased focus on the self leads to self-criticism and negative expectancies that, in turn, increase dysphoric mood. They note, however, that a preexisting state of low self-esteem exacerbates dysphoric mood. That is, self-esteem is seen as a vulnerability factor that interacts with other variables to produce a depressive episode. Conversely, a preexisting high level of self-esteem is seen as a variable that helps ameliorate the depressive episode.

In a series of recent articles relevant to the issue of self-esteem, Brown and his associates (Brown, Andrews, Bifulco, & Veiel, 1990; Brown, Bifulco, & Andrews, 1990a, 1990b; Brown, Bifulco, Veiel, & Andrews, 1990) have reported follow-up findings from a longitudinal study (Brown, Craig, & Harris, 1985) originally designed to examine the roles of social support and self-esteem in the onset and maintenance of depression. In these more recent papers, self-esteem was examined as both a predictor and as a causal factor in depression.

Brown et al. (1990a) noted that in attempting to predict the onset of depression, self-esteem measures have met with inconsistent results (e.g.,

Brown et al., 1986; Lewinsohn et al., 1981). To attempt to understand these discrepancies, factor analysis was applied to 10 scales selected to assess various dimensions of self-esteem. From this analysis, two independent scales, the negative evaluation of self (NES) and positive evaluation of self (PES), were identified as distinct entities. In terms of ability to predict, only the NES was associated with the onset of depression, and then only after the occurrence of severe life events or difficulties. Scores on the PES did not predict depression. From these data, Brown et al. (1990a) suggest that negative and positive aspects of self-esteem should be considered independently in studies examining the relationship between self-esteem and depression.

In a related study, Brown and associates (1990b) examined the manner in which social factors (i.e., early inadequate parenting and negative and positive elements in close relationships) impact self-esteem. Through path analysis, they developed a model suggesting that early inadequate parenting predicts negative elements in current close relationships. They found that those with inadequate parenting and negative elements in close relationships were five times more likely to have low self-esteem, and correspondingly more depression.

Low self-esteem, while perhaps not the sole etiological factor in depression, may play an important role in setting the stage on which negative life events can interact to produce a depressive episode. It could be argued that the findings of Brown, Andrews, Bifulco, and Veiel (1990) demonstrate that low self-esteem, rather than being a causal factor in depression, serves as a mechanism by which a negative self-schema is chronically activated. This keeps the threshold for depression more easily accessed by negative life events to the extent that even trivial events are likely to push the individual over into a depressive episode. An analogy could be drawn between depression and the common cold. Although being overly tired does not cause a cold, it does make a person's immune system less able to ward off cold-causing viruses. Similarly, low self-esteem may make a person less able to defend against daily events that continually activate a low-threshold negative self-schema in such a way that he or she makes more and more frequent negative evaluations until reaching the point of depression.

As is evident from the foregoing discussion, neither existing theories nor data are clear on whether self-esteem constitutes an etiological factor in depression or is instead more properly considered a symptom. For example, Abramson et al. (1978, 1989) clearly view lowered self-esteem as a symptom, whereas Beck (1987) and Lewinsohn et al. (1985) tend to emphasize lowered self-esteem as a causal factor. On the other hand, data reported by Lewinsohn et al. (1981) are unable to support self-esteem as a causal factor, but research by Brown et al. (1990) suggests that negative self-esteem in the context of stressful life events may indeed play a role in precipitating depression. Based on this literature, we propose that self-esteem deficits may constitute both a symptom and a cause of depression.

A MODEL OF SELF-ESTEEM IN DEPRESSION

Following from theory and data that have examined self-esteem in depressive disorders, we will outline a model that attempts to explicate both causal and consequential facets of self-esteem within depression. In doing so, we will rely on previous theory and research on both the causal and symptomatic aspects of self-esteem in particular, and on depression theory and research in general. Figure 7.1 illustrates this model of self-esteem in depression. As can be seen from this illustration, the model is composed of an initiating loss-related event that leads to a set of cognitive, behavioral, and affective responses.

Of particular relevance for issues of self-esteem are the cognitive responses; one cognitive response is an evaluative process whereby the individual attempts to make sense of the event circumstances and their effects. At this point, individual differences serve an important mediating role in determining the various outcomes of this evaluative process, leading in a general fashion to either a benign evaluation or a negative evaluation. A benign evaluation produces little or no lowering of self-esteem during the depression while a negative evaluation produces self-esteem deficits.

In conceptualizing this framework, we make no attempt to present a comprehensive model of depression but instead focus on several key elements of depression as they pertain to self-esteem. Thus, at each point in this model a substantial body of theory and research is pertinent to depression, but not necessarily to self-esteem. For example, life events have been the focus of considerable research in depression, as have the affective consequences of these events. In a similar fashion, the idea that disruptions in life lead to a self-evaluative process is the topic of ample theory and research that would be essential to discuss in detail for a comprehensive model of depression. Likewise, there are numerous theories and studies on various individual difference variables that may moderate or mediate depression. Given our goal, we will touch on these areas only as they are necessary to present a basic

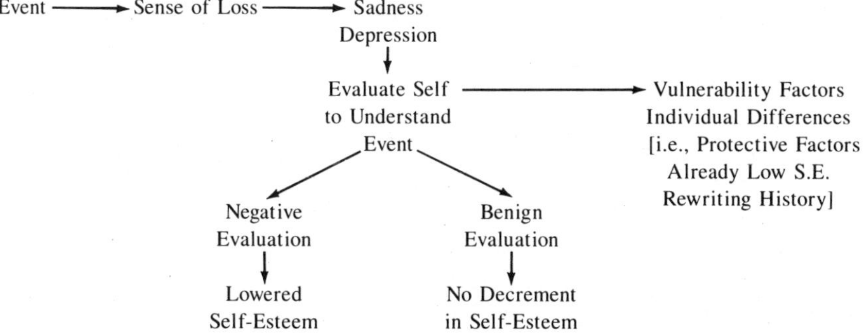

Figure 7.1. Model of the relationship between self-esteem and depression.

framework for the model we suggest. The major thrust of this conceptualization, however, is on self-esteem.

Event/Sense of Loss/Sadness-Depression/Evaluation

The idea that negative life events involving loss are key precipitants to depression has a long history in psychological theory and research (ranging from Freud to Brown). Although some events seem to be nearly universally interpreted as a loss (such as the loss of a loved one) and will lead to depressive states regardless of vulnerability or protective factors, individual difference variables may strongly influence the interpretation of events that are less clear-cut. For instance, Robins (1990) suggests that individuals can be categorized according to whether they exhibit sociotropic or autonomous personality styles. Sociotropic individuals are more likely to interpret negative events of an interpersonal nature as losses, and hence as a threat to their self-esteem, than are autonomous people. Autonomous people, on the other hand, are thought more likely to interpret achievement-related negative events as a loss and thus as a threat to their self-esteem. Regardless of these or other more idiosyncratic styles, it seems clear that events that are interpreted as a significant loss to the person will elicit a variety of reactions.

These reactions include affective, behavioral, and cognitive responses. Affectively, the person experiences sad mood and a variety of physiological manifestations. On a behavioral level, decreases in activity are frequently engendered, although sometimes agitation and an increase in activity are seen. Affective and behavioral response domains are important, however, we are primarily concerned here with cognitive responses to the negative event. Cognitive symptoms of depression are common and may include characteristics such as decreased concentration, pessimism, hopelessness, and recurrent thoughts of death. Another type of cognitive reaction is ruminations (Ingram, 1984; Nolen-Hoeksema, 1991; Teasdale, 1983) or self-focused attention (Ingram, 1990).

Although the content of such ruminations may encompass a wide range of phenomena, a critically important aspect of ruminations is their evaluative nature; people try to make some sense out of what is happening to their lives. Such evaluations are not only self-evaluative but are also other-evaluative, in that people examine not only themselves but also the circumstances surrounding the event that has affected them. These evaluative mechanisms are critical for effective self-regulation in the face of personal disruptions. That is, before people can adjust their responses to a situation, there must be some type of evaluation of the situation ("situation" here includes both self and other evaluation).

Given that reflection on oneself and the event is critical for self-regulatory functioning, it is tempting to speculate that such evaluative processes evidence evolutionary significance. That is, self-regulation provides for new learning and/or for decision-making strategies that may regain the lost object (or a suitable replacement). From an evolutionary standpoint, this process would have considerable adaptive significance for the propagation of the species (assuming that emotional bonds were/are helpful for producing, nurturing, and protecting children) and would thus benefit from selection pressures. Likewise, such processes have contemporary adaptive value because they provide for the same self-regulatory functions that permit new learning and the regaining of lost objects essential to the conception of self-worth.

INTRAPERSONAL FACTORS MEDIATING EVENT-RELATED EVALUATION

The factors mediating a loss-related event and the end result of depression and self-esteem symptoms are numerous. As a general rule, such factors can be broken down into protective and vulnerability factors, with protective factors mediating against increased depressive responses (and lowered self-esteem) and vulnerability factors serving to worsen the depression and self-esteem.

Vulnerability Factors

In terms of symptomatic self-esteem in depression, we argue that the key individual difference variable is core level of self-esteem. Earlier, we reviewed developmental literature suggesting that the core level of self-esteem originates from the individual's earliest interactions with significant others. As children develop and grow, life experiences and further interactions with significant others continue to mold core self-esteem. It seems unlikely, however, that this molding process continues indefinitely; at some point the basic structure of self-esteem appears to become solidified.

Although we have suggested that core self-esteem is relatively fixed by adulthood, moment-to-moment levels of self-esteem appear quite fluid; people report different levels of self-esteem on different occasions and in different situations. We view core self-esteem as a traitlike structure in a trait-by-state-by-situation framework (see Kendall, 1978). This framework suggests that the ultimate expression of any cognition, affect, or behavior is a convergent function of individuals' traits, current state, and the situations they encounter. In the case of self-esteem, people's experience of self-esteem at any given instance will be determined by core self-esteem, their current state (e.g., a bad mood), and the situations in which they find themselves (e.g., just learning that tenure has been denied). Although this framework suggests that all three elements are important for current estimates of self-esteem, the notion of a self-esteem core suggests that this core will exert a significant influence on current self-esteem. Thus, for example, a person with inadequate core self-esteem may not experience particularly high momentary self-esteem (or only fleetingly high self-esteem) even when success in an important area has been achieved. Conversely, people with high core self-esteem will not experience significantly lowered self-esteem even after failing to attain success.

The notion of core self-esteem (even as a moderator) would seem to imply that momentary levels of self-esteem should always be a direct reflection of core self-esteem; for example, if an individual has low core self-esteem, daily levels of self-esteem should be similarly low. Although we suggest that core self-esteem is indeed an important moderator of daily self-esteem, other factors mitigate against a direct relationship between core self-esteem and momentary self-esteem levels. For instance, individuals with low core self-esteem can build up a reservoir of competencies and abilities in particular areas that allow them to function successfully in everyday life (and feel good), even if their core self-esteem makes them vulnerable to depression and corresponding symptomatic self-esteem symptoms when negative events occur.

Core self-esteem, then, remains latent until activated by triggering events. This notion is highly similar to current conceptualizations of negative self-schema processes in depression. Although some investigators have suggested that because self-schemas were proposed to be traitlike structures and should thus always be observable (see Coyne & Gotlib, 1983), recent clarifications and refinement of the theoretical construct focus on the present but latent character of depressogenic structures (Beck, 1987; Segal & Shaw, 1986). Thus, although these structures are present in individuals who are vulnerable to depression, they should not be observable in the nondisordered state because they are inactive.

This notion is consistent with several current perspectives within social-cognition theory and research. For example, a number of cognitive and social-cognitive researchers have cautioned that it would be a mistake to conclude that a self-schema is a monolithic, static structure (e.g., Markus & Nurius, 1986). People have a diversity of self-representations available that cannot all be operative at the same time. Such a diathesis–stress conceptualization suggests that some individuals have self-representations available that interact with life events to initiate the processes that bring about disorder. Segal and Shaw (1986), for instance, have argued that some individuals have a predisposition (or diathesis) in which certain "stressors precipitate a pattern of negatively biased, self-referent information processing that initiates the first cycle in the downward spin of depression. . . . this predisposition consists of the operation of latent but reactive cognitive structures that are activated by events interpreted as personally significant" (p. 674).

The key to understanding depressogenic schema functioning from such a diathesis–stress perspective then is to study the activation processes of negative self-referent cognitive structures. Miranda and Persons (1988), Teasdale and Dent (1987), and Ingram (1991) have all reported efforts to assess cognitive processing tendencies in individuals who are vulnerable to depression but who are not currently in a depressed state. The critical aspect of this research is to prime the resurgence of negative cognitive schemas by inducing a negative mood state. What these investigators have generally found is that current mood is related to negative cognitive processing patterns *only* in people who are vulnerable to depression.

In a similar fashion, because the cognitive structures responsible for core self-esteem are latent throughout most of daily functioning, individuals with poor core self-esteem should ordinarily be able to function well without consistent intrusions of poor self-esteem. We suggest, however, that when negative events occur, they elicit this self-esteem core and state levels of self-esteem decrease. If depression is precipitated by these negative events, then a self-esteem decrement will become a symptom of the disorder. Such symptomatic self-esteem decrements should partially serve to perpetuate the disorder; as individuals feel acute negative affect about themselves, their motivation to engage in functional instrumental behaviors that may help alleviate the disorder will be negatively affected.

Although this characterization of core self-esteem as a latent process may appear to suggest that it is empirically unmeasurable, there are potentially several ways to assess this variable. For example, if our ideas are correct, it should be possible to obtain an index of core self-esteem by determining baseline level of situational self-esteem across time and various circumstances. Thus, if followed over time and situations, people with low (or vulnerable) core self-esteem should have more instances where they indicate feeling bad about themselves and should therefore have a lower average self-esteem baseline. Conversely, people with more adequate core self-esteem should have fewer instances where they feel bad and should have higher average baseline self-esteem. The experimental methods used by Miranda and Persons, Teasdale, and Ingram to access negative self-schemas in currently nondepressed people should also be applicable to measurement questions concerning low core self-esteem. That is, core self-esteem should become apparent when individuals are experimentally primed (usually by a mood induction).

In summary then, core self-esteem is seen as a critically important individual difference variable that will moderate the degree to which low self-esteem is observed as a symptom of depression. As loss-related events occur, individuals with a poor core self-esteem will appraise situations and themselves in a negative fashion, and decreased self-esteem will be the end result. Alternatively, peole with adequate core self-esteem are suggested to be less likely to make such negative appraisals. For these people, even though some self-esteem decrements may be seen, all other things being equal, self-esteem decrements will not be serious and will thus not be considered a symptom of the disorder.

Protective Factors

We suggest that vulnerability factors interact with protective factors to determine the eventual level of self-esteem observed in the depression. People can protect self-esteem through a variety of maneuvers. For instance, data have shown that males evidence a tendency to avoid self-focusing in negative situations (Ingram, Cruet, Johnson, & Wisnicki, 1988). We earlier suggested that rumination, or self-focused attention, is the process by which self-evaluation is achieved. We presume that adequate attention must be paid to the self in order for the individual to access his or her core level of self-esteem. A logical consequence of this introspective avoidance may be a behavioral acting out, with no apparent decrease in self-esteem. Such acting out is more frequently observed in males and, indeed, has been suggested by some to be a "male" expression of depression. At a more psychopathological level, this behavior may be seen in antisocial individuals, who are perhaps paradoxically quite self-focused on their own needs and desires but who lack introspection. The quick and impulsive acting out of these individuals precludes the time and cognitive processing necessary to assess their "true" selves and, correspondingly, to assess their feelings (core self-esteem).

To the extent that individuals activate these protective factors, self-appraisal in situations that evoke sadness and depression will be more benign. In line with the model we have offered, such benign evaluations should not result in self-esteem decrements in depression and thus lowered self-esteem should not be seen as a prominent symptom of depression.

Psychopathology, of course, is not the only way that individuals protect against self-esteem assaults in the face of negative events. In a classic article entitled "The Totalitarian Ego: Fabrication and Revision of Personal History," Greenwald (1980) reviewed evidence suggesting that, through processes such as selective attention, when negative events occur, people have a tendency to revise their personal history to protect themselves psychologically; they rewrite their experiences to make themselves feel better. Greenwald labeled this behavior totalitarian because of the psychological similarity to totalitarian societies that maintain control through information manipulation; for example they literally rewrite the history books to suit their views. Although this behavior is seen as totalitarian, we emphasize here that this is not psychopathological; normal people engage in these processes to protect their self-esteem. To the extent that they are able to do this, self-evaluations should be benign and self-esteem decrements should not accompany depression.

People also develop areas of competencies in their lives that can help make their self-evaluations benign in the face of negative events. As we already have noted, people with low core self-esteem are capable of building a store of competencies, talents, and abilities that can also help compensate for the effects of negative events. This idea is strongly reminiscent of Adler's 1929 classic approach to personality. Adler suggested that individuals with particular deficits strive to build areas of strength and superiority that compensate for these deficits. In much the same fashion, at least some individuals with low core self-esteem may strive to build areas of competencies to compensate for poor feelings about themselves. In the case of depression, these competencies may help protect the self. Thus, for example, people who face a loss in one area of life may focus their energies and talents on other areas of their lives. Directing energies toward these areas protects core self-esteem, and the evaluation of the self should be more benign. In several respects, this idea is similar to the notion that cognitive therapists may treat depression by assisting their clients in constructing compensatory schemas to effectively deal with negative life events (Hollon & Beck, 1986; Ingram & Hollon, 1986).

Although building compensatory strategies can be highly adaptive in warding off low self-esteem as a result of negative events, in some cases these strategies may be maladaptive. For instance, several researchers have suggested that at the heart of the Type A individual's competitiveness, extreme drive, and desire to accomplish more and more is poor core self-esteem (see Smith, 1986). These strategies may be effective in avoiding dealing with feelings about the self and perhaps for avoiding depression, but they may take a toll in other areas of life, both physically and interpersonally.

In sum, we have mentioned several protective factors here, but undoubtedly a number of potentially protective factors function to increase the probability of benign self-evaluations. Whatever the list of these protective factors, the idea we wish to emphasize is the interactive effect of these factors with vulnerabilities. The pattern of vulnerabilities and protective factors an individual possesses will thus play a significant role in determining the outcome of self-evaluations.

Situational Factors

Although we have focused considerable attention on intrapersonal factors in the evaluation of the self, situational factors will also play an important part; the person's actual responsibility for what happened to bring about the sadness-evoking event will influence the evaluation. Hence, if an individual bears clear-cut responsibility for the loss, then it will be difficult to escape an internal attribution and the subsequent loss of self-esteem that will ensue in the depression. In noting the important role of situational factors, however, it is not possible to discuss specific factors because there is no way to catalog the actual responsibility for the causes of loss-evoking life events. These are highly individualized and will vary as a function of scores of various elements.

Cognitive clinical researchers (see Ingram, 1986) tend to focus heavily on the intrapersonal mechanisms that determine various cognitive, affective, and behavioral outcomes. Indeed in this chapter, we have focused heavily on these as well; certainly core self-esteem is as intrapersonal as possible. Nevertheless, data can overwhelm even biased cognitive processing mechanisms and make certain conclusions inescapable. Although we recognize the importance of the real data in many cases of depression and self-esteem deficits, many causes of loss-related events may be ambiguous. To the degree that they are unclear, they permit cognitive processing mechanisms to fill in the gaps with data that are consistent with them, either protecting people or making them vulnerable.

SUMMARY

Lowered self-esteem can be an important and significant symptom in depression, but as with most symptoms of depression, it is not always observed. To begin to shed light on this particular symptom of depression, we have briefly outlined both the origins of the conceptualization of the self-esteem construct as well as some of the data describing the developmental antecedents of self-esteem. We next reviewed theoretical and empirical literature examining the role of self-esteem in depression, particularly literature that has focused on self-esteem as a cause versus as a symptom. Finally, we have suggested a model that outlines a potential route by which self-esteem may be causally related to depression; the model also shows how it may become a symptom of depression.

The model suggests that events which evoke an appraisal of meaningful loss to people lead to cognitive, affective, and behavioral responses. In determining whether self-esteem deficits will be a symptom of depression, a critically important element of cognitive responses is a self-evaluation. As people seek to understand the loss, they will evaluate themselves in response to the loss. Vulnerability, as well as protective and situational factors, interact to determine whether the outcome of the evaluation will be benign toward the self, with little resulting loss of self-esteem seen accompanying the depression, or will be negative, with a corresponding loss of self-esteem in the depression. The most important individual vulnerability factor is the person's core level of self-esteem. Although this may be less of an influence in the course of daily life, negative events will activate this core into ascendancy and will worsen the outcome of the evaluation for those people with poor core self-esteem. Likewise, protective factors mitigate the impact of poor self-esteem.

This framework is consistent with extant data and theory on the role of self-esteem in depression, but we acknowledge that it is simply a first approximation of ways to think about how these variables fit together. Nevertheless, we hope that this framework will serve as a heuristic to researchers interested in empirically examining the role of self-esteem in depression or in refining and proposing alternative models.

REFERENCES

Abramson, L. Y., Alloy, L. B., & Metalsky, G. I. (1988). The cognitive diathesis–stress theories of depression: Toward an adequate evaluation of the theories' validities. In L. B. Alloy (Ed.), *Cognitive processes in depression* (pp. 3–30). New York: Guilford.

Abramson, L. Y., Alloy, L. B., & Metalsky, G. I. (1990). Hopelessness depression: An empirical search for a theory-based subtype. In R. E. Ingram (Ed.), *Contemporary psychological approaches to depression* (pp. 3–30). New York: Plenum.

Abramson, L. Y., Metalsky, G. I., & Alloy, L. B. (1989). Hopelessness depression: A theory based subtype of depression. *Psychological Review, 96,* 358–372.

Abramson, L. Y., Seligman, M. E. P., & Teasdale, J. D. (1978). Learned helplessness in humans: Critique and reformulation. *Journal of Abnormal Psychology, 87,* 40–47.

Adler, A. (1929). *The science of living.* New York: Greenberg.

American Psychiatric Association (1987). *Diagnostic and statistical manual for mental disorders.* (DSM-III-R; third ed. rev.). Washington, DC: Author.

Barnett, P. A., & Gotlib, I. H. (1988). Psychosocial functioning in depression: Distinguishing among antecedents, concomitants, and consequences. *Psychological Bulletin, 104,* 97–126.

Beck, A. T. (1967). *Cognitive therapy and the emotional disorders.* New York: International University Press.

Beck, A. T. (1987). Cognitive models of depression. *Journal of Cognitive Psychotherapy: An International Quarterly, 1,* 5–37.

Becker, J. (1979). Vulnerable self-esteem as a predisposing factor in depressive disorders. In R. A. Depue (Ed.), *The psychobiology of the depressive disorders: Implications for the effects of stress* (pp. 317–334). New York: Academic Press.

Blanck, G., & Blanck, R. (1974). *Ego psychology: Theory and practice.* New York: Columbia University Press.

Bowlby, J. (1977). *Attachment and Loss.* New York: Basic Books.

Brewin, C. R., and Furnam, A. (1986). Attributional versus preattributional variables in self-esteem and depression: A comparison and test of learned helplessness theory. *Journal of Personality and Social Psychology, 50,* 1013–1020.

Brown, G. W., Andrews, B., Bifulco, A., & Veiel, H. (1990). Self-esteem and depression: I. Measurement issues and prediction of onset. *Social Psychiatry and Psychiatric Epidemiology, 25,* 200–209.

Brown, G. W., Andrews, B., Harris, T. O., Adler, Z., & Bridge, L. (1986). Social support, self-esteem and depression. *Psychological Medicine, 16,* 813–831.

Brown, G. W., Bifulco, A., & Andrews, B. (1990a). Self-esteem and depression: III. Aetiological issues. *Social Psychiatry and Psychiatric Epidemiology, 25,* 235–243.

Brown, G. W., Bifulco, A., & Andrews, B. (1990b). Self-esteem and depression: IV. Effects of course and recovery. *Social Psychiatry and Psychiatric Epidemiology, 25,* 244–249.

Brown, G. W., Bifulco, A., Veiel, H. O. F., & Andrews, B. (1990). Self-esteem and depression: II. Social correlates of self-esteem. *Social Psychiatry and Psychiatric Epidemiology, 25,* 225–234.

Brown, G. W., Craig, T. K., & Harris, T. O. (1985). Depression: Disease or distress? Some epidemiological considerations. *British Journal of Psychiatry. 147,* 612–622.

Coyne, J. C., & Gotlib, I. H. (1983). The role of cognition in depression: A critical appraisal. *Psychological Bulletin, 94,* 472–505.

Deaux, K. (1972). Anticipatory attitude change: A direct test of the self-esteem hypothesis. *Journal of Experimental and Social Psychology, 8,* 143–155.

Egeland, B., & Sroufe, L. A. (1981). Developmental sequelae of maltreatment in infancy. *New Directions for Child Development, 11,* 77–92.

Fenichel, O. (1945). *The psychoanalytic theory of neurosis.* New York: Norton.

Freud, S. (1986). Mourning and melancholia. In J. Coyne (Ed.), *Essential papers on depression* (pp. 48–63) New York: New York University Press. (Original work published 1917).

Greenwald, A. G. (1980). The totalitarian ego. *American Psychologist, 35,* 603–618.

Hollon, S. D., & Beck, A. T. (1986). Research on cognitive therapies. In S. L. Garfield & A. E. Bergen (Eds.) *Handbook of Psychotherapy and Behavior Change* (pp. 443–482, 3rd Edition). New York: Wiley.

Hollon, S. D., DeRubeis, R. J., & Evans, M. D. (1987). Causal mediation of change in treatment for depression: Discriminating between nonspecificity and noncausality. *Psychological Bulletin, 102,* 139–149.

Ingram, R. E. (1984). Toward an information-processing analysis of depression. *Cognitive Therapy and Research, 8,* 443–478.

Ingram, R. E. (1986). *Information Processing Approaches to Clinical Psychology.* Orlando: Academic Press.

Ingram, R. E. (1990). Self-focused attention in clinical disorders: Review and a conceptual model. *Psychological Bulletin, 107,* 156–176.

Ingram, R. E. (1991). *Cognitive constructs, information processing and depression.* Invited Address at the meeting of the American Psychological Association, San Francisco.

Ingram, R. E., Cruet, D., Johnson, B., & Wisnicki, K. S. (1988). Self-focused attention, gender, gender role, and vulnerability to negative affect. *Journal of Personality and Social Psychology, 55,* 967–978.

Ingram, R. E., & Hollon, S. D. (1986). Cognitive therapy of depression from an information processing perspective. In R. E. Ingram (Ed.), *Information processing approaches to clinical psychology* (pp. 259–281). Orlando: Academic Press.

James, W. (1890). *Principles of psychology,* (Vol. 1). New York: Henry Holt.

Kendall, P. C. (1978). Anxiety: States, traits—situations? *Journal of Consulting and Clinical Psychology, 46,* 280–287.

Lewinsohn, P. M., Hoberman, H., Teri, L., & Hautzinger, M. (1985). An integrative theory of depression. In S. Reiss & R. R. Bootzin (Eds.), *Theoretical issues in behavior therapy* (pp. 331–359). New York: Academic Press.

Lewinsohn, P. M., Steinmetz, J. L., Larson, D. W., & Franklin, J. (1981). Depression-related cognitions: Antecedent or consequence? *Journal of Abnormal Psychology, 90,* 213–219.

Markus, H., & Nurius, P. (1986). Possible selves. *American Psychologist, 41,* 954–969.

Miranda, J., & Persons, J. B. (1988). Dysfunctional attitudes are mood-state dependent. *Journal of Abnormal Psychology, 97,* 76–79.

Nolen-Hoeksema, S. (1991). Responses to depression and their effects on the duration of depressive episodes. *Journal of Abnormal Psychology, 100,* 569–582.

Robins, C. J. (1990). Congruence of personality and life events in depression. *Journal of Abnormal Psychology, 99,* 393–397.

Rosenberg, M. (1979). *Conceiving the Self.* New York: Basic Books.

Sacco, W. P., & Beck, A. T. (1985). Cognitive therapy of depression. In E. W. Beckham & W. R. Leber (Eds.), *Handbook of depression: Treatment, assessment, and research* (pp. 3–38). Homewood, IL: Dorsey.

Sameroff, A. J., & Emde, R. N. (1989). *Relationship Disturbances in Early Childhood: A Developmental Approach.* New York: Basic Books.

Segal, Z. V., & Shaw, B. F. (1986). Cognition in depression: A reappraisal of Coyne & Gotlib's critique. *Cognitive Therapy and Research, 10,* 671–694.

Silverman, I., Ford, L., & Morganti, J. (1966). Inter-related effects of social desirability, sex, self-esteem, and simplexity of argument on persuasibility. *Journal of Personality, 34,* 555–56.

Smith, T. W. (1986). Type A behavior and cardiovascular disease: An information processing approach. In R. E. Ingram (Ed.), *Information Processing Approaches to Clinical Psychology.* Orlando: Academic Press.

Steffenhagen, R. A. (1990). *Self-esteem therapy.* New York: Praeger.

Teasdale, J. D. (1983). Negative thinking in depression: Cause, effect, or reciprocal relationship? *Advances in Behaviour Research and Therapy, 5,* 3–25.

Teasdale, J. D., & Dent, J. (1987). Cognitive vulnerability to depression: An investigation of two hypotheses. *British Journal of Clinical Psychology, 26,* 113–126.

Waters, E., Noyes, E., Vaughn, B., & Ricks, M. (1985). Q-sort definitions of social competence and self-esteem: Discriminant validity of related constructs in theory and data. *Developmental Psychology, 21,* 508–522.

Weiner, B. (1979). A theory of motivation for some classroom experiences. *Journal of Eductional Psychology. 71*(1), 3–25.

Wells, L. E., & Marwell, G. (1976). *Self-esteem: Its conceptualization and measurement.* London: Sage.

CHAPTER 8

Shame and Guilt

JUNE P. TANGNEY

INTRODUCTION

In the past two decades, much of the theoretical and empirical literature on depression has focused on cognitive factors that predispose individuals to depressive disorders. This focus on cognitive aspects of depression has come at the expense of relevant affective factors. Nonetheless, there is a history of at least passing interest in "depressotypic" affective characteristics—among them, shame and guilt.

Shame and guilt have been cited in connection with a number of psychological disorders, including depression. The clinical and empirical literature, however, is inconsistent regarding the specific links between psychological symptoms and these moral affects. Theories vary in the functional role assigned to shame and guilt. Some theories conceptualize these negative emotions as symptoms associated with psychological problems. Other theoretical perspectives regard the disposition to experience shame and/or guilt as a significant vulnerability factor relevant to the development of subsequent psychological disorders. In addition, many psychologists have either failed to make a clear distinction between the experiences of shame and guilt or have adopted theoretical perspectives that focus on one emotion to the exclusion of the other. Thus, in much of the literature, the distinction between shame and guilt is lost.

In this chapter, I will describe the key phenomenological differences between shame and guilt and I will review the extant theoretical and empirical literature relating shame and guilt to depression. I will then describe results from several independent studies bearing on the relationship of shame and guilt to depression. Study 1 demonstrates that the *states* of shame, guilt, and depression represent distinct phenomenological experiences. Studies 2 and 3,

Portions of this chapter (including Table 2) were adapted from "Proneness to Shame, Proneness to Guilt, and Psychopathology" by J. P. Tangney, P. Wagner, and R. Gramzow (1992), *Journal of Abnormal Psychology, 103*, 469–478.

however, indicate that a *dispositional* tendency to experience shame, but not guilt, is an important correlate of depressive symptomotology, above and beyond that accounted for by attributional style. Although the issue of causality remains an open question, these results suggest that a consideration of shame-related issues may be useful in the treatment of depression.

PHENOMENOLOGICAL DIFFERENCES BETWEEN SHAME AND GUILT

Although the terms *shame* and *guilt* are often used interchangeably, a growing theoretical and empirical literature underlines important differences in the phenomenology of these two emotions (DeRivera, 1977; Erikson, 1950; Lewis, 1971; Lindsay-Hartz, 1984; Tangney, 1989; Weiner, 1985; Wicker, Payne, & Morgan, 1983).

In differentiating between shame and guilt, Lewis (1971) focused on the role of the self—with guilt involving the self's negative evaluation of specific behaviors, and shame involving the self's negative evaluation of the entire self. This is not simply a distinction in terms of attributions, however. Lewis describes a complex and contrasting interplay of cognitive, affective, and motivational features associated with shame and guilt experiences.

A number of phenomenological studies employing a range of methods lend strong support for Lewis's distinction between shame and guilt experiences (e.g., Lindsay-Hartz, 1984; Tangney, 1989 [summarized later in this chapter]; Wicker et al., 1983). Guilt is an affective state associated with a focus on *specific behaviors* that often involve harm to someone or something. Thus guilt involves the individual's perception of having done something "bad." Because of its focus on specific and presumably controllable behaviors, the guilt experience is uncomfortable, but not debilitating. That is, the self remains "able." Not surprisingly, phenomenological reports indicate that guilt's consequent motivation and behavior tend to be oriented toward reparative action.

Shame, on the other hand, is a much more global, painful, and devastating experience in which the *self,* not just behavior, is painfully scrutinized and negatively evaluated. This global, negative affect is often accompanied by a sense of shrinking and being small, and by a sense of worthlessness and powerlessness. Shame also involves a sense of exposure. In introducing the notion of an "internalized other," Lewis (1971) extended the definition of shame beyond an affective reaction to public disapproval. But there is typically the imagery of an explicit or implicit disapproving other. Even when alone, the disapproving self imagines how the self (as disapproved object) might look to another. Thus, it is not surprising that the shamed person often wants to hide from others—to sink into the floor and disappear.

THEORETICAL PERSPECTIVES ON SHAME AND GUILT IN DEPRESSION

Until recently, the theoretical and clinical literature has generally cited feelings of guilt, but not shame, in connection with depression. The *Diagnostic and Statistical Manual of Mental Disorders* (DSM-III-R American Psychiatric Association, 1987), for example, includes "excessive or inappropriate guilt" as one of the likely symptoms of a Major Depressive Episode (p. 222).

The focus on guilt as a component of depression dates back to the early writings of Freud (1917/1957, 1923/1961, 1933/1964), who suggested that guilt is a key feature of melancholia. In Freud's view, guilt arises when forbidden wishes or deeds conflict with superego standards. As a result, the superego retaliates with self-punitive responses that often lead to depressive symptoms. The link between guilt and psychopathology is quite clearly delineated in Freudian theory because of its close association with the interrelationship of id, ego, and superego. Freud, however, was much less systematic in his treatment of shame. By 1905, he had developed a fairly circumscribed view of shame as largely a reaction formation against sexually exhibitionistic impulses (Freud, 1905/1953). Recently, a number of theorists have suggested that Freud's relative neglect of shame may have been due to his focus on a conflict-defense model of psychological functioning and to his failure to distinguish between ego and self (Lewis, 1987a; Miller, 1985; Morrison, 1989). Morrison (1989), for example, has suggested that Freud might have further elaborated on the nature and implications of shame had he pursued the concepts of ego-ideal, narcissism, and self-regard (so central to shame) in greater depth. Instead, Freud's work subsequent to *On Narcissism: An Introduction* (1914/1957) focused to a much greater extent on guilt-inducing Oedipal issues and a structural theory that emphasized intrapsychic conflict among ego, id, and superego (with little regard for the more self-relevant ego-ideal). In any event, Lewis (1971) has argued that in developing a theory that focused almost exclusively on guilt, Freud may have mislabeled his patients' shame experiences as guilt experiences. And, in fact, Freud's description of some of the key symptoms associated with depression bear a striking resemblance to the shame experience. In *Mourning and Melancholia,* for example, Freud (1917/1957) described "an extraordinary diminution in self-regard," and a presentation of the self as "worthless, incapable of any achievement" as important features of melancholia.

The ambiguity introduced by a failure to distinguish between shame and guilt is evident, as well, in contemporary writings on depression. In Blatt's (1974) description of introjective depression, he also emphasized the role of guilt. But a closer reading of the phenomenology of introjective depression suggests that shame, not guilt, may be central to this type of depression. Blatt stated that introjective depression involves "feelings of being unworthy, unlovable . . . of having failed to live up to expectations, . . . a constant self-scrutiny and evaluation . . . and extensive demands for perfection" (p. 117). This description bears a close resemblance to many of the phenomenological aspects of shame described by Lewis (1971) and Lindsay-Hartz (1984).

Helen Block Lewis (1971) is one of the few psychologists who has presented an integrated theoretical account of the differential roles of shame and guilt in psychopathology. Drawing on her earlier work with Witkin (Witkin et al., 1954; Witkin, Lewis, & Weil, 1968), Lewis (1971) hypothesized that individual differences in cognitive style (i.e., field-dependence vs. field-independence) lead to contrasting modes of superego functioning (i.e., shame-proneness and guilt-proneness), and together these cognitive and affective styles set the stage for differential symptom formation. The global, less differentiated self of the field-dependent individual is particularly vulnerable to the global, less differentiated experience of shame—and ultimately then to the global experience of depression. In contrast, the more clearly differentiated self of the field-independent individual is particularly vulnerable to the experience of guilt (which requires a differentiation between self and behavior)—and also to obsessive and paranoid symptoms involving vigilance of the "field," separate from the self.

Lewis (1987b) and Hoblitzelle (1987) have noted some conceptual parallels between this view and current cognitive models of depression (e.g., Abramson, Seligman, & Teasdale, 1978; Beck, 1983). As described earlier, Lewis's (1971) phenomenological descriptions of shame and guilt include distinctions along affective, cognitive, and motivational dimensions. In fact, the cognitive components of shame and guilt can be reconceptualized in attributional terms. To the extent that guilt involves a focus on some specific behavior, the guilt experience is likely to involve internal, specific, and fairly unstable attributions. Shame, on the other hand, involves a focus on the global self that is presumably relatively enduring. Thus, the shame experience is likely to involve internal, stable, and global attributions or, in Janoff-Bulman's (1979) terms, characterological self-blame. An extensive empirical literature now links depression to a tendency to make internal, stable, and global attributions for negative events (for a review, see Robins, 1988). In this regard, the attributional literature is consistent with Lewis's notion that there may be a special link between depression and proneness to shame, but not guilt.

Finally, Self-Discrepancy Theory (Higgins, 1987) provides additional support for the notion that shame and guilt are differentially related to depression. Higgins's theory focuses on discrepancies between an individual's current self-perception (the actual self) and various "self-guides" that he or she aspires to. Four key self-guides are (1) the "ideal self" that an individual wishes ideally to possess (the ideal/own self); (2) the "ideal self" that some significant other wishes the individual would ideally possess (the ideal/other self); (3) the "ought self" that an individual believes he or she ought to possess (the ought/own self); and (4) the "ought self" that some significant other believes the individual should possess (the ought/other self). Dejection-related emotions, including depression, are hypothesized to arise from discrepancies between the actual self and the ideal selves. And shame, in particular, is thought to derive from discrepancies between the actual self and the ideal/other self. In contrast, agitation-related emotions, including anxiety, are hypothesized to arise from discrepancies between the actual self and the ought selves. And guilt is thought to derive from discrepancies between the actual self and the ought/own self. Thus, Self-Discrepancy Theory predicts that shame and guilt are associated with discrepancies involving different self-guides. Similar self-discrepancies are implicated in shame and depression.

In sum, guilt is often cited as a component of depression, but many psychologists use the term guilt quite broadly to encompass both shame and guilt experiences. A closer reading of the theoretical and clinical literature suggests that the tendency to experience shame about the entire self may be more central to depressive disorders than the tendency to experience guilt about specific behaviors.

EMPIRICAL STUDIES LINKING SHAME AND GUILT TO DEPRESSION

Although there is a rather rich theoretical literature pertaining to shame and guilt and depression, relatively little research has been conducted in this area. One factor that has impeded the empirical study of shame and guilt, in general, has to do with problems in the measurement of these constructs. Prior to the publication of Lewis's (1971) landmark *Shame and Guilt in Neurosis,* researchers largely failed to make a distinction between shame and guilt. Shame was ignored as a construct of interest in its own right. Rather, guilt scales were constructed that typically assessed both shame and guilt experiences (e.g., Buss & Durkee, 1957; Mosher, 1966). Thus, studies employing these earlier measures are of little use in distinguishing between the psychological correlates of guilt versus shame.

More recently, researchers have begun to develop measures that differentiate these affective experiences. Drawing on a qualitative analysis of clients' descriptions of their earliest memories, Smith (1972) reported that severely depressed patients evidenced more shame than guilt themes in such recollections. This finding, however, failed to replicate in a subsequent similar study by Crouppen (1977), and Hoblitzelle (1987) has raised concerns regarding the validity of the Early Memories Test as an index of shame-proneness and guilt-proneness. Using an entirely different methodology, a number of researchers have turned to more "objective" paper-and-pencil measures of shame and guilt. Harder and Lewis (1986) developed the Personal Feelings Questionnaire, a brief self-report measure of proneness to shame and proneness to guilt. In a sample of undergraduates, they found that both shame-proneness and guilt-proneness were associated with depression, anxiety, hostility, and low self-esteem. Using a more extended adjective checklist, Hoblitzelle (1987) reported a link between depression and shame-proneness in two independent studies. The relationship between depression and guilt-proneness, however, was less consistent across the two studies, perhaps owing to problems with Hoblitzelle's guilt scale (see following section).

MEASUREMENT CONSIDERATIONS AND AN OVERVIEW OF THE CURRENT STUDIES

Over the past several years, we have conducted a series of studies to explore the relation of shame and guilt to various aspects of psychological and social adjustment. One problem we have struggled with concerns the measurement of shame and guilt. As indicated earlier, most of the previous studies that have attempted to differentiate between shame and guilt have relied on adjective checklists. There are potential difficulties, however, with the use of adjective checklists, particularly for assessing guilt (Tangney, 1990). The crux of the problem is the structure of the adjective checklist task. Hoblitzelle's (1987) Revised Shame-Guilt Scale (RSGS), for example, consists of a series of negatively valenced adjectives (e.g., wicked, disgraced, unethical, inappropriate). Respondents are asked to rate the degree to which these adjectives describe them*selves*. Thus, although the adjectives may vary subtly in terms of shame and guilt, such adjective checklists essentially pose respondents with a shamelike task. Respondents are asked to make global ratings *about the self* (or, in the case of the Personal Feelings Questionnaire, global ratings of the self's general affective experience), rather than ratings of affective responses to circumscribed *behaviors* embedded in local contexts. Thus, the structure of such global adjective checklists seems more appropriate to the assessment of shame.

In lieu of adjective checklists, we have adopted several methods that are more amenable to the assessment of both shame and guilt. The first study reported here focused on the *states* of shame and guilt. We asked college students to describe personal shame, guilt, and depression experiences, and to rate these experiences along a number of theoretically derived dimensions. These ratings were then compared to examine the degree to which the phenomenology of real-life depressive episodes is similar to, or different from, everyday experiences of shame and guilt.

Studies 2 and 3 (reported in greater detail in Tangney, Wagner, & Gramzow, 1992) focused on the traits or *dispositions*—proneness to shame and proneness to guilt. In Studies 2 and 3, we employed the Self-Conscious Affect and Attribution Inventory (SCAAI), a scenario-based measure of affective style, to examine the degree to which shame-proneness and guilt-proneness differentially relate to depressive symptomotology. In Study 3, we also used the Test of Self-Conscious Affect (TOSCA), a revised version of the SCAAI constructed from subject-generated scenarios and responses.

In contract to the global adjective checklists used in previous studies, the scenario-based SCAAI and TOSCA measures provide a means of assessing shame and guilt with reference to specific behaviors or events. Participants are asked to imagine themselves in a series of common everyday situations and then to rate their likelihood of responding in a number of manners. The responses associated with each scenario include brief phenomenological descriptions of shame and guilt experiences. Thus, the structure of the SCAAI and TOSCA measures provides a more theoretically consistent method for assessing both shame and guilt, compared with the shamelike task posed by adjective checklists.

STUDY 1. SIMILARITIES AND DIFFERENCES BETWEEN THE STATES OF SHAME, GUILT, AND DEPRESSION

Our primary purpose in initially designing this study was to assess phenomenological differences between the states of shame and guilt. In addition, we were interested in the degree to which the experiences of shame and guilt differed from the experience of depression. A third component of the study concerned phenomenological aspects of pride. The pride data, however, are less relevant to the current chapter and so will not be presented here.

Participants were 65 undergraduate college students who received credit toward a psychology course requirement in return for participation. Students ranged in age from 17 to 64 years (M = 22), and the majority (74%) were female. Participants were asked to describe anonymously, in writing, personal shame, guilt, pride, and depression experiences. The order of emotional experiences (shame, guilt, pride, and depression) was randomized across subjects. Following each description, participants rated their situation/experience along 22 dimensions using a 7-point scale. These dimensions were selected based on a review of the case study observations of Lewis (1971) and Lindsay-Hartz (1984).

The mean ratings of participant-generated shame, guilt, and depression experiences are presented in Table 8.1. First, regarding the difference between shame and guilt, the results provide strong support for the distinction suggested by Lewis (1971) and Lindsay-Hartz (1984). Shame and guilt differed in the predicted direction for 17 of the 22 dimensions; the observed differences were statistically significant for 11 of those 17 dimensions.

Participant ratings indicated that shame is significantly more painful and more difficult to describe than the experience of guilt. Shame is more likely to be accompanied by a sense of being inferior and physically small. Participants felt they had less control in situations involving shame than in situations involving guilt. And consistent with the painful nature of shame, time was reported to move more slowly in shame than in guilt experiences.

There were also differences in the ways in which participants conceptualized their interpersonal relationships. When feeling shame, participants were more likely to feel observed by others, and they were also more concerned with others' opinions of the self, rather than with their own self-perception. Not surprisingly, shame, more than guilt, was related to a desire to hide from others. And when shamed, participants felt more isolated—less like they belonged—than when experiencing guilt.

Two dimensions yielded reliable differences counter to Lewis's (1971) distinction. In the shame experience, participants were *more* likely to feel they had violated a moral standard and were more likely to wish they had acted differently. These findings may be due to the greater pain associated with shame. The latter dimension was designed to assess the degree to which participants wished to change their *actions.* In rating this dimension, however, participants may have focused not on the question of actions but rather on whether they wished something about the situation to be *different.* Regarding the violation of moral standards, it is possible that serious violations of moral standards are more likely to result in a shameful focus on the individual's character, whereas relatively minor violations allow the individual to focus on his or her behavior apart from the self. In addition, because shame is more painful than guilt, respondents may have retrospectively interpreted the shame-eliciting transgression as more severe.

In sum, participants' ratings of shame and guilt experiences differed along the majority of dimensions postulated by Lewis (1971) and Lindsay-Hartz (1984), a pattern of findings that is quite striking because participants described and rated unique personal shame and guilt experiences that spanned a wide range of situations and contexts. These results replicate the findings of an earlier investigation by Wicker et al. (1983). Wicker et al. found similar, though in some cases less consistent, support for Lewis's (1971) distinction between shame and guilt. The common theme that emerges from both studies is that shame and guilt are distinct experiences that lead to quite different social perceptions and motivations.

In what ways is the experience of depression similar to or different from the experience of shame and guilt? As noted earlier, although "guilt" is often cited as a symptom of depression, clinical and theoretical accounts of depression typically include reference to experiences akin to shame. The results in Table 8.1, however, indicate that whereas depression shares a number of features with both shame and guilt, the experience of depression is distinct from each of these moral emotions.

Shame differed from depression on 8 of the 22 dimensions. Participants reported that their depression experiences lasted longer than their shame experiences. Shame was more likely than depression to involve a sense of exposure and a focus on what other people thought of the self. In shame,

TABLE 8.1. Adults' Phenomenological Ratings of Personal Depression, Shame, and Guilt Experiences

Dimension	Depression	Shame	Guilt	F-value
Felt bad during experience	5.57[g] (0.67)	5.41 (0.84)	4.95[a] (1.28)	6.13**
Writing situation was difficult	3.16 (1.96)	3.79 (2.13)	3.31[a] (1.81)	2.25
The emotion had a sudden onset	4.67 (2.08)	4.94 (2.12)	4.44 (2.02)	1.04
Time moved quickly	2.40[g] (1.59)	2.61 (1.84)	3.42[a] (1.90)	8.82***
The emotion lasted a short time	1.18[s,g] (1.33)	2.46 (1.70)	2.81 (1.76)	8.81***
Felt people were looking at me	3.95[s] (2.22)	5.30 (1.83)	4.22[a] (2.02)	11.17***
Focused on what I thought of myself (vs. others' opinions)	4.40[s] (2.11)	3.11 (2.23)	4.02[a] (2.30)	6.03**
Felt isolated from others	5.32[g] (1.89)	5.19 (1.70)	4.22[a] (1.84)	8.98***
Felt physically smaller	4.87 (1.58)	5.26 (1.57)	4.77[a] (1.48)	1.99
Felt inferior to others	4.11[g] (1.23)	4.43 (1.36)	3.65[a] (1.52)	7.24**
Desire to hide	5.27[s] (1.98)	5.86 (1.37)	4.89[a] (1.74)	11.74***
Wanted to admit what I'd done	3.61[s] (1.62)	2.66 (1.78)	3.08[a] (2.00)	5.69**
Desire to make amends	4.10[g] (1.91)	4.68 (2.21)	5.11 (1.79)	4.81*
Felt I had violated a moral standard	2.89[s,g] (2.01)	4.87 (2.21)	4.18[b] (2.29)	14.89***
Wished I had acted differently	4.41[s,g] (2.10)	5.90 (1.72)	5.33[b] (2.23)	8.78***
Felt responsible for what happened	3.90[s,g] (2.08)	6.00 (1.65)	5.84 (1.54)	23.67***
Felt in control of the situation	1.98[g] (1.21)	2.48 (1.67)	3.46[a] (2.18)	11.47***
Physical changes (sweating, blushing)	4.84 (2.07)	4.87 (1.95)	4.48 (2.20)	0.86
Viewed my *actions* (vs. self) as bad	3.85 (1.93)	4.70 (2.12)	4.46 (2.13)	2.97
Knew the reasoning behind my actions	4.87 (1.91)	4.40 (2.30)	4.68 (2.22)	1.05
My feelings (vs. thoughts) were important	5.20 (1.79)	4.70 (1.85)	4.62 (1.72)	2.46
Memory of event was more visual (vs. auditory)	2.90 (1.96)	2.73 (1.90)	2.87 (1.79)	0.15

Note. $N = 61$–63. Items were rated on a 1–7 scale. [s,g] indicate dimensions on which depression differed from shame or guilt at least at the .05 level (two-tailed tests).

[a]Indicates dimensions on which shame and guilt differed consistent with a priori hypotheses, at least at the .05 level.

[b]Indicates dimensions on which shame and guilt differed beyond chance, but in direction opposite from a priori hypothesis.

$^{*}p < .05$.
$^{**}p < .01$.
$^{***}p < .001$.

respondents reported a greater desire to hide from others, and they were less inclined to admit what they'd done. And not surprisingly, there appeared to be a stronger focus on an eliciting behavior or event in connection with shame than in connection with depression. When experiencing shame, participants were more likely to wish they had acted differently, to feel they had violated a moral standard, and to feel responsible for what had happened.

At the same time, there were some notable similarities between shame and depression experiences. For example, participant ratings of personal shame and depression episodes were roughly equivalent in terms of the degree of discomfort or dysphoria involved, the sense of isolation from others, and feelings of inferiority.

Guilt differed from depression on 10 of the 22 dimensions. Participants reported that their depression experiences involved greater discomfort and dysphoria than their guilt experiences. Depression episodes tended to last longer and time itself seemed to move more slowly, compared with guilt experiences. Depression also involved a greater sense of isolation from others, and a deeper sense of inferiority. As with shame, there appeared to be a stronger focus on an eliciting behavior or event in connection with guilt compared with depression. When experiencing guilt, participants were more likely to want to make amends, to wish they had acted differently, to feel they had violated a moral standard, and to feel responsible for what had happened. Finally, the guilt experience involved substantially greater feelings of control than depression.

As with shame, guilt differed from depression on some, but by no means all, dimensions. For example, participant ratings of personal guilt and depression episodes were roughly equivalent in terms of the desire to hide or to admit what had been done. And neither experience involved the imagery of exposure or the focus on others' opinions of the self.

In sum, Study 1 focused on the *states* of shame, guilt, and depression. Although there were some similarities among these experiences, the general pattern of results indicated that specific experiences of shame and guilt are distinct from the experience of depression. The question remains, however, whether a dispositional tendency to experience shame and/or guilt is associated with depressive symptomotology.

STUDIES 2 AND 3. THE RELATION OF SHAME-PRONENESS AND GUILT-PRONENESS TO DEPRESSIVE SYMPTOMOTOLOGY

Studies 2 and 3 (reported in greater detail in Tangney, Wagner, & Gramzow, 1992) focused on the personality traits or *dispositions*—proneness to shame and proneness to guilt. For better or worse, most people experience shame and guilt at various points in their lives. That is, each of us has the capacity to experience both emotions. But it appears that some people are more prone to one than the other. The clinical observations of Helen Block Lewis (1971), among others, indicate that when faced with negative situations, some people are consistently more biased toward responding with shame, while others are more likely to respond with guilt.

Are shame-prone or guilt-prone individuals also prone to depression? We examined this question in Studies 2 and 3. In addition, because shame-proneness and guilt-proneness theoretically share cognitive features in common with explanatory style, we also explored the relationship of shame-proneness and guilt-proneness to attributional style. And we evaluated the degree to which these affective style variables contribute to our understanding of depression above and beyond that accounted for by purely attributional factors.

Participants in Study 2 were 245 undergraduates who received credit toward a course requirement in return for their participation. Students ranged in age from 18 to 55 (M = 21.1). Most were female (71%), and the majority were white (77%).

Participants in Study 3 were 234 undergraduates who received credit toward a course requirement in return for their participation. The students ranged in age from 17 to 35 (M = 19.5). Again, most were female (72%), and the majority were white (83%).

The findings reported here were drawn from two larger investigations of the personality and adjustment correlates of proneness to shame and guilt. Participants anonymously completed a number of questionnaires including the Beck Depression Inventory (BDI; Beck, 1972), the Attributional Style Questionnaire (ASQ; Peterson, Semmel, von Baeyer, Abramson, Metalsky, & Seligman, 1982), and the Symptom Checklist 90 (SCL-90; Derogatis, Lipman, & Covi, 1973).

To assess proneness to shame and proneness to guilt, participants in both studies completed the Self-Conscious Affect and Attribution Inventory (SCAAI; Tangney, Burggraf, Hamme, & Domingos, 1988). The SCAAI is a paper-and-pencil measure comprising 13 brief scenarios that college students are likely to encounter in daily life. The 10 negative scenarios are followed, in random order, by responses indicating Shame, Guilt, Externalization, and Detachment/Unconcern. Three positive scenarios are followed by responses indicating Shame, Guilt, Externalization, Alpha Pride (pride in self), and Beta Pride (pride in behavior). The measure is not forced-choice in nature. Subjects rate, on a 5-point scale, their likelihood of responding in each of the manners indicated. Relevant items are summed across scenarios to create indices of Shame, Guilt, Externalization, Detachment/Unconcern, Alpha Pride, and Beta Pride.

Several studies provide support for the reliability and construct validity of the central scales of the SCAAI (Tangney, 1990, 1991; Tangney et al., 1988). Shame, Guilt, Externalization, and Detachment/Unconcern scales demonstrated satisfactory reliability, as indicated by analyses of their internal consistency and test–retest stability. Regarding validity, across several independent studies, shame has been consistently linked to low self-esteem, a tendency to externalize blame, a seething, bitter, resentful kind of anger, an impaired capacity for empathy, and dysfunctional family relationships (Burggraf & Tangney, 1989; Hamme, 1991; Tangney, 1991; Tangney, Wagner, Fletcher, & Gramzow, 1992). Guilt, on the other hand, has been consistently positively related to interpersonal empathy, and negatively related to externalization of blame, a detached/unconcerned attitude toward negative interpersonal events, resentment toward others, and a hostile sense of humor, particularly when considering the unique variance in guilt (independent of shame) (Gessner & Tangney, 1990; Tangney, 1990, 1991; Tangney, Wagner, Fletcher, & Gramzow, 1992).

Participants in Study 3 also completed the Test of Self-Conscious Affect (TOSCA; Tangney, Wagner, & Gramzow, 1989), which was modeled after the SCAAI. The TOSCA also consists of a series of brief scenarios (10 negative and 5 positive) and associated responses, yielding indices of Shame, Guilt, Externalization, Detachment/Unconcern, Alpha Pride, and Beta Pride. This entirely new set of scenarios was drawn from written accounts of personal shame, guilt, and pride experiences provided by a sample of several hundred college students and noncollege adults. The new responses were drawn from a much larger pool of affective, cognitive, and behavioral responses provided by a second sample of noncollege adults. The TOSCA has several advantages over the original SCAAI. First, the items were "subject-generated" rather than "experimenter-generated," enhancing the ecological validity of the measure. Second, the items are appropriate for adults of all ages, not specifically college students. Third, in terms of reliability and validity, our preliminary analyses indicate that the TOSCA is equivalent to, and in some respects more psychometrically sound than, the SCAAI.

SHAME-PRONENESS, GUILT-PRONENESS, AND DEPRESSION

The correlations of proneness to shame and proneness to guilt with Beck depression and SCL-90 depression scores are shown in Table 8.2. In both studies, the tendency to experience shame across a range of situations was strongly related to depression. In contrast, guilt-proneness was only moderately related to depression, and the part correlational analyses indicate that these moderate correlations are entirely due to the variance shared by shame and guilt.

We generally find a substantial positive correlation between our shame and guilt measures that is likely due to two distinct factors. First, as indicated in Study 1, the shame and guilt share a number of phenomenological features. For example, both are painful emotions that arise from the individual's perception the he or she has violated standards of one sort or another.

TABLE 8.2. Relationship of Shame-Proneness and Guilt-Proneness to Indices of Depression

		Bivariate Correlations		Part Correlations	
		Shame	Guilt	Shame Residuals	Guilt Residuals
SCL-90 Depression	Study 2–SCAAI	.32***	.24***	.23***	.10
	Study 3–SCAAI	.41***[a]	.22***	.36***[b]	−.05
	Study 3–TOSCA	.43***[a]	.15*	.41***[b]	−.06
Beck Depression	Study 2–SCAAI	.34***[a]	.15*	.31***[b]	−.01
	Study 3–SCAAI	.47***[a]	.24***	.41***[b]	−.07
	Study 3–TOSCA	.51***[a]	.19**	.47***[b]	−.05

Note. Reprinted with permission from the American Psychological Association. These results originally appeared in a more detailed report of the psychopathological correlates of shame and guilt (Tangney, Wagner, & Gramzow, 1992).

Study 2 *Ns* range, 242–243. Study 3 *ns* range, 222–225 and 227–230 for analyses involving the SCAAI and TOSCA, respectively.

[a]*T*-tests for dependent correlations indicate that the shame correlation is significantly higher than the guilt correlation at least at the .05 level.

[b]*T*-tests for independent correlations indicate that the shame part correlation is significantly higher than the guilt part correlation at least at the .05 level.

*$p < .05$.
**$p < .01$.
***$p < .001$.

Second, as noted by Lewis (1971), shame and guilt can be experienced simultaneously in connection with a given event. In other words, an individual can feel both shame and guilt subsequent to some misdeed, failure, or transgression. To further refine our analyses, we typically conduct part correlations, where shame is factored out from guilt and vice versa, in order to examine the correlates of the unique variance in shame and guilt, respectively.

In the current studies, both indices of depression were positively and significantly related to shame residuals. In contrast, the measures of depression were negligibly related to guilt residuals.[1]

[1]One question that arises when interpreting null results involving part correlational analyses is whether there remains in the residual variable any meaningful variance beyond measurement error—that is, whether in partialing out the variance shared with shame, we have effectively partialed out all of guilt's reliable and valid variance. Results involving measures of other constructs, however, indicate that this is not the case. In previous studies employing the SCAAI and in the current Study 3 employing the SCAAI and the TOSCA, guilt residuals (the unique variance in guilt) have shown consistent positive correlations with interpersonal empathy (Tangney, 1991), and consistent negative correlations with externalization of blame, resentment toward others, a hostile/aggressive sense of humor, and a detached/unconcerned attitude in response to negative events (Gessner & Tangney, 1990; Tangney, 1990; Tangney, Wagner, Fletcher, & Gramzow, 1992). Thus, the negligible correlations between indices of depression and guilt residuals are not simply due to a restriction of valid variance in the residual guilt variables.

DOES A CONSIDERATION OF SHAME AND GUILT OFFER SOMETHING NEW, BEYOND ATTRIBUTIONAL STYLE?

Much of the current literature focuses on cognitive factors associated with depression. A question that arises when considering shame and guilt is whether these constructs (or measures of these constructs) simply reflect individual differences in explanatory style. As noted earlier, the cognitive components of shame and guilt can be conceptualized in attributional terms. Shame—in its focus on the entire self—involves internal, stable, and global attributions, whereas guilt—in its focus on specific behaviors—involves internal, specific, and presumably unstable attributions. Given the correlation between shame and depression, it seemed important to examine whether these findings are simply a reflection of participants' attributional style. If so, a consideration of shame and guilt may be largely superfluous to our understanding of depressive disorders.

Participants in both studies completed the Attributional Style Questionnaire (ASQ; Peterson et al., 1982), in addition to the measures of shame, guilt, and depression. Our findings clearly indicated that shame-proneness is linked to a depressogenic attributional style. Proneness to shame (and the unique variance in shame) was positively correlated with the tendency to make internal, stable, and global attributions for negative events, and negatively correlated with internal, stable, and (to a lesser extent) global attributions for positive events.

In contrast, the correlations of guilt with attributional style variables did not show the expected pattern of results (e.g., proneness to guilt was not consistently associated with internal, unstable, and specific attributions for negative events). Rather, when considering the bivariate correlations, guilt was positively associated with global attributions for negative events in both studies, as well as with internal attributions for negative events in Study 3, and the part correlations revealed that these associations were entirely due to the shared variance with shame.

In both studies, then, shame-proneness but not guilt-proneness was clearly related to a depressogenic attributional style. Does a consideration of self-conscious affective style contribute to our understanding of depression, above and beyond that accounted for by attributional style? To answer this question, we conducted a series of hierarchical regression analyses predicting Beck and SCL-90 depression scores from attributional style and affective style variables. In doing so, we forced in attributional style dimensions first, to provide the most conservative test of the predictive utility of shame-proneness and guilt-proneness.

In both studies, attributional style accounted for a significant portion of the variance in depression (for the BDI, 9% and 13% in Studies 2 and 3, respectively; for SCL-90 Depression, 7% and 14% in Studies 2 and 3, respectively).

In each case, however, when shame-proneness and guilt-proneness were forced into the regression equations after attributional style variables, the change in R^2 was substantial. When predicting BDI scores, SCAAI shame and guilt accounted for an additional 8% and 12% of the variance in depression in Studies 2 and 3, respectively. In Study 3, TOSCA shame and guilt accounted for an additional 15% of the variance in BDI depression. When predicting SCL-90 Depression scores, SCAAI shame and guilt accounted for an additional 9% of the variance in depression in both Studies 2 and 3. In Study 3, TOSCA shame and guilt accounted for an additional 10% of the variance in SCL-90 Depression. In all cases, the change in R^2 was almost entirely due to individual differences in shame-proneness. Guilt-proneness emerged as a significant predictor of depression only in the Study 2 analysis involving the SCL-90.

These findings clearly indicate that the link between shame and depression is not solely due to attributional style. In fact, by including the affective component of shame (e.g., once attributional factors were controlled for) the proportion of variance predicted in depression was essentially doubled.

SUMMARY AND CONCLUSIONS

To summarize, although "guilt" is often cited as a component of depression, theoretical and clinical descriptions of depression typically include reference to shamelike experiences. Do people tend to blur the distinction between shame and depression? Do they simply use these terms interchangeably? Our findings from Study 1 indicate that the states of shame, guilt, and depression are indeed distinct phenomenological experiences. Participant ratings of personal shame, guilt, and depression episodes differed significantly along a number of dimensions. In other words, when people say they are depressed, they are not simply reporting a shame or guilt experience, and vice versa. Rather, the link between shame and depression is at the dispositional level. Results from Studies 2 and 3 indicate that individuals who are prone to experience shame are also prone to depression. Across two independent studies—each employing two measures of depression, and the second employing two different measures of shame—proneness to shame was consistently related to depressive symptomotology. Further, although shame-proneness was clearly related to a depressogenic attributional style, our findings indicate that the link between shame and depression is not solely due to attributional factors. Shame-proneness accounted for a substantial portion of variance in depression, above and beyond that accounted for by attributional style.

A question remains concerning the causal nature of the link between proneness to shame and depression. Does the tendency to experience shame place people at risk for depressive disorders? Or is shame more simply a symptom or by-product of depression? As noted earlier, the extant clinical and theoretical literature is rather unclear in this regard. Because the studies reported here were correlational in nature (the SCAAI, BDI, and SCL-90 were administered in a single session; in Study 3, the TOSCA was administered approximately 1 week earlier), our results cannot directly address the question of causality. It seems likely, however, that the observed link between shame and depression is due to a range of factors, and that the paths of influence are bidirectional.

On one hand, a tendency to experience shame in response to a diversity of day-to-day situations may contribute to the development of psychological problems in general. Shame is a devastatingly painful emotion that can overwhelm and cripple the self, at least temporarily. Both Lewis (1971) and Miller (1985) have described the debilitating nature of shame in their clinical case studies. Clients in the midst of the shame experience, for example, become uncharacteristically inarticulate, their capacity to process information is apparently diminished, and their ability to place self-relevant negative events in perspective is markedly impaired. To the extent that shame-prone individuals experience repeated disruptions in adaptive self-functioning, such individuals may be vulnerable to a range of psychological problems. In fact, our analyses of the other SCL-90 scales indicate that shame-proneness is linked to a wide range of psychological symptoms—not solely depression (Tangney, Wagner, & Gramzow, 1992).

In addition, several features of shame may contribute more specifically to the development of depressive symptoms. In particular, a chronic tendency to experience shame may lead to feelings of hopelessness, which has also been implicated in the development of depression. Abramson, Metalsky, and Alloy (1989) have cited internal, stable, and global attributions for negative events and associated inferred negative characteristics about the self (each components of the shame experience) as key causes of hopelessness and hopelessness depression. To the extent that shame entails a fairly sweeping negative response to the global self, repeated shame experiences may engender a sense of hopelessness—particularly vis-á-vis the possibility of changing a global, enduring, reprehensible self.

By the same token, depression very likely sets the stage for subsequent episodes of shame. Even moderate levels of depression can impair an individual's ability to effectively tackle life's tasks and challenges. The recognition of failures and shortcomings, real or imagined, may engender or intensify further bouts of shame.

Further research is needed to help clarify the functional relationship between shame and depression. Prospective studies utilizing latent variable modeling procedures would be particularly helpful in this regard. In addition, it will be important to replicate these findings in a clinical sample. The studies reported here were conducted with university undergraduates, and although considerable variance was observed in the indices of depression, the possibility remains that a different pattern of results would emerge when studying the shame and guilt correlates of depression in a clinical population. In particular, the nature of guilt itself may be qualitatively different in the clinical range. In fact, the guilt portrayed in much of the clinical literature is typically an insoluble guilt—that is, the patient sees no means for making reparation, apart from rather extreme forms of self-punishment—and it is typically a guilt fused with shame. The shame-free guilt assessed in the current studies, on the other hand, is more likely to afford a range of adaptive resolutions. In most instances, the individual can confess, apologize, or make amends for the bad thing that was done—and then move on to the business of everyday life.

With these caveats in mind, the results of our studies underline the importance of considering shame in our conceptualization and treatment of a number of psychological problems, including depression. Empirical studies of both children and adults indicate that proneness to the ugly feeling of shame is associated with a range of psychological symptoms (Burggraf & Tangney, 1990; Tangney, Wagner, Burggraf, Gramzow, & Fletcher, 1991; Tangney, Wagner, & Gramzow, 1992). In a number of respects, we may be able to enhance our treatment of depression and other psychological disorders by recognizing and developing a deeper understanding of shame in our clients.

ACKNOWLEDGMENTS

This research was supported by Grant No. IR15HD25506 from the National Institute for Child Health and Human Development and by a Faculty Research Grant from George Mason University. I wish to thank Carey Fletcher, Elly Bordeaux, Joe Constantin, Laura Flicker, Richard Gramzow, William Harman, Donna Marschall, James Maxfield, Jule Morig, Yvette Nageotte, Gary Russell, Provie Rydstrom, Gordon Shaw, Chris Smart, and Patricia Wagner for their assistance with the larger studies from which this report was drawn.

REFERENCES

Abramson, L. Y., Metalsky, G. I., & Alloy, L. B., (1989). Hopelessness depression: A theory-based subtype of depression. *Psychological Review, 96,* 358–372.

Abramson, L. Y., Seligman, M. E. P., & Teasdale, J. (1978). Learned helplessness in humans: Critique and reformulation. *Journal of Abnormal Psychology, 87,* 49–74.

American Psychiatric Association. (1987). *Diagnostic and statistical manual of mental disorders* (3rd ed.-rev.). Washington, DC: Author.

Beck, A. T. (1972). Measuring depression: The depression inventory. In T. A. Williams, M. M. Katz, & J. A. Shields (Eds.), *Recent advances in the psychobiology of the depressive illnesses* (pp. 299–302). Washington, DC: Government Printing Office.

Beck, A. T. (1983). Cognitive therapy of depression: New perspectives. In P. Clayton & J. Barrett (Eds.), *Treatment of depression: Old controversies and new approaches* (pp. 265–290). New York: Raven Press.

Blatt, S. (1974). Levels of object representation in anaclitic and introjective depression. *Psychoanalytic Study of the Child, 29,* 107–157.

Burggraf, S. A., & Tangney, J. P. (1989, June). *Proneness to shame, proneness to guilt, and self-concept.* Poster presented at the meetings of the American Psychological Society, Alexandria, VA.

Burggraf, S. A., & Tangney, J. P. (1990, June). *Shame-proneness, guilt-proneness, and attributional style related to children's depression.* Poster presented at the meetings of the American Psychological Society, Dallas.

Buss, A. H., & Durkee, A. (1957). An inventory for assessing different kinds of hostility in clinical situations. *Journal of Consulting Psychology, 21,* 343–348.

Crouppen, G. A. (1977). Field dependence-independence in depressive and "normal" males as an indicator of relative proneness to shame or guilt and ego-functioning. *Dissertation Abstracts International, 37,* 4669B–4607B. (University Microfilms No. 77-6292)

DeRivera, J. (1977). A structural theory of emotion. *Psychological Issues, 10.*

Derogatis, L. R., Lipman, R. S., & Covi, L. (1973). SCL-90: An outpatient psychiatric ratings scale—Preliminary report. *Psychopharmacology Bulletin, 9,* 13–28.

Erikson, E. H. (1950). *Childhood and society.* New York: W. W. Norton.

Freud, S. (1953). Three essays on the theory of sexuality. In J. Strachey (Ed. and Trans.), *The standard edition of the complete psychological works of Sigmund Freud* (Vol. 7, pp. 153–243). London: Hogarth Press. (Original work published 1905)

Freud, S. (1957). Mourning and melancholia. In J. Strachey (Ed. and Trans.), *The standard edition of the complete psychological works of Sigmund Freud* (Vol. 14, pp. 243–258). London: Hogarth Press. (Original work published 1917)

Freud, S. (1957). On narcissism: An introduction. In J. Strachey (Ed. and Trans.), *The standard edition of the complete psychological works of Sigmund Freud* (Vol. 14, pp. 73–102). London: Hogarth Press. (Original work published 1914)

Freud, S. (1961). The id and the ego. In J. Strachey (Ed. and Trans.), *The standard edition of the complete psychological works of Sigmund Freud* (Vol. 19, pp. 12–66). London: Hogarth Press. (Original work published 1923)

Freud, S. (1964). Dissection of the personality. In J. Strachey (Ed. and Trans.), *The standard edition of the complete psychological works of Sigmund Freud* (Vol. 22, pp. 57–81). London: Hogarth Press. (Original work published 1933)

Gessner, T. L., & Tangney, J. P. (1990, March). *Personality and adjustment correlates of wit and witticism.* Poster presented at the meeting of the Eastern Psychological Association, Philadelphia.

Hamme, H. (1991). *Family correlates of proneness to shame and proneness to guilt.* Unpublished dissertation, Bryn Mawr College.

Harder, D. W., & Lewis, S. J. (1986). The assessment of shame and guilt. In J. N. Butcher & C. D. Spielberger (Eds.), *Advances in personality assessment* (Vol. 6, pp. 89–114). Hillsdale, NJ: Erlbaum.

Higgins, E. T. (1987). Self-discrepancy: A theory relating self and affect. *Psychological Review, 94,* 319–340.

Hoblitzelle, W. (1987). Attempts to measure and differentiate shame and guilt: The relation between shame and depression. In H. B. Lewis (Ed.), *The role of shame in symptom formation* (pp. 207–235). Hillsdale, NJ: Erlbaum.

Janoff-Bulman, R. (1979). Characterological versus behavioral self-blame: Inquiries into depression and rape. *Journal of Personality and Social Psychology, 37,* 1798–1809.

Lewis, H. B. (1971). *Shame and guilt in neurosis.* New York: International Universities Press.

Lewis, H. B. (1987a). Introduction: Shame—The "sleeper" in psychopathology. In H. B. Lewis (Ed.), *The role of shame in symptom formation* (pp. 1–28). Hillsdale, NJ: Erlbaum.

Lewis, H. B. (1987b). The role of shame in depression over the life span. In H. B. Lewis (Ed.), *The role of shame in symptom formation* (pp. 29–50). Hillsdale, NJ: Erlbaum.

Lindsay-Hartz, J. (1984). Contrasting experiences of shame and guilt. *American Behavioral Scientist, 27,* 689–704.

Miller, S. (1985). *The shame experience.* Hillsdale, NJ: Erlbaum Press.

Morrison, A. P. (1989). *Shame: The underside of narcissism.* Hillsdale, NJ: Analytic Press.

Mosher, D. L. (1966). The development and multitrait-multimethod matrix analysis of three measures of three aspects of guilt. *Journal of Consulting and Clinical Psychology, 30,* 25–29.

Peterson, C., Semmel, A., von Baeyer, C., Abramson, L. Y., Metalsky, G. I., & Seligman, M. E. P. (1982). The Attributional Style Questionnaire. *Cognitive Therapy and Research, 6,* 287–299.

Robins, C. J. (1988). Attributions and depression: Why is the literature so inconsistent? *Journal of Personality and Social Psychology, 54,* 880-889.

Smith, R. L. (1972). The relative proneness to shame or guilt as an indicator of defensive style. *Dissertation Abstracts International, 33,* 2823B. (University Microfilms No. 72-3258)

Tangney, J. P. (1989, August). *A quantitative assessment of phenomenological differences between shame and guilt.* Poster presented at the meeting of the American Psychological Association, New Orleans.

Tangney, J. P. (1990). Assessing individual differences in proneness to shame and guilt: Development of the Self-Conscious Affect and Attribution Inventory. *Journal of Personality and Social Psychology, 59,* 102–111.

Tangney, J. P. (1991). Moral affect: The good, the bad, and the ugly. *Journal of Personality and Social Psychology, 61,* 598–607.

Tangney, J. P., Burggraf, S. A., Hamme, H., & Domingos, B. (1988, March). *Assessing individual differences in proneness to shame and guilt: The Self-Conscious Affect and Attribution Inventory.* Poster presented at the meeting of the Eastern Psychological Association, Buffalo, NY.

Tangney, J. P., Wagner, P. E., Burggraf, S. A., Gramzow, R., & Fletcher, C. (1991, June). *Children's shame-proneness, but not guilt-proneness, is related to emotional and behavioral maladjustment.* Poster presented at the meetings of the American Psychological Society, Washington, DC.

Tangney, J. P., Wagner, P., Fletcher, C., & Gramzow, R. (1992). Shamed into anger? The relation of shame and guilt to anger and self-reported aggression. *Journal of Personality and Social Psychology, 62,* 669–675.

Tangney, J. P., Wagner, P., & Gramzow, R. (1989). *The Test of Self-Conscious Affect.* Fairfax, VA: George Mason University.

Tangney, J. P., Wagner, P., & Gramzow, R. (1992). Proneness to shame, proneness to guilt, and psychopathology. *Journal of Abnormal Psychology. 103,* 469–478.

Weiner, B. (1985). An attributional theory of achievement motivation and emotion. *Psychological Review, 92,* 548–573.

Wicker, F. W., Payne, G. C., & Morgan, R. D. (1983). Participant descriptions of guilt and shame. *Motivation and Emotion, 7,* 25–39.

Witkin, H. A., Lewis, H. B., Hertzman, M., Machover, K., Meissner, P., & Wapner, S. (1954). *Personality through perception.* New York: Harper & Brothers.

Witkin, H. A., Lewis, H. B., & Weil, E. (1968). Affective reactions and patient-therapist interaction among more differentiated and less differentiated patients early in therapy. *Journal of Nervous and Mental Disorders, 146,* 193–208.

CHAPTER 9

Hopelessness

LYN Y. ABRAMSON, GERALD I. METALSKY, and LAUREN B. ALLOY

INTRODUCTION

In 1989, we presented the hopelessness theory of depression (Abramson, Metalsky, & Alloy, 1989), a revision of the 1978 reformulated theory of helplessness and depression (Abramson, Seligman, & Teasdale, 1978). The hopelessness theory has its roots in Seligman's (1975) laboratory studies of the effects of uncontrollable aversive events on animals. The theory evolved as we attempted to apply concepts derived from experimental work on learned helplessness to human depression. Complementing clinical and taxonometric approaches, the hopelessness theory represents a *theory-based* approach to the classification of a subset of depressive disorders that is *process-oriented* rather than symptom-oriented (see also Seligman, 1978). In essence, the hopelessness theory postulates the existence in nature of an as yet unidentified subtype of depression, *hopelessness depression.* In this chapter, we examine the current status of hopelessness depression. Does it exist in nature and conform to its theoretical description?

THEORETICAL DESCRIPTION OF HOPELESSNESS DEPRESSION

Cause

In contrast to symptom-based approaches to the classification of the depressive disorders (see Kendell, 1968), *cause* figures prominently in the definition of hopelessness depression. Few would disagree that, when possible,

The authors of this chapter have focused their discussion on a theory that postulates the existence of a subtype of depression, namely, "hopelessness depression," rather than on the phenomenon of hopelessness itself. However, the nature of hopelessness and its relationship to the symptoms of depression, that is, whether hopelessness is best viewed as a proximal cause of a subtype of depression or as a symptom of depression, has been thoroughly discussed in the chapter.

classification of psychopathologies by etiology in addition to other factors is more desirable than classification by symptoms alone because the former generally has more direct implications for cure and prevention than the latter (McLemore & Benjamin, 1979; Skinner, 1981). Overall, the hopelessness theory specifies a chain of distal and proximal contributory causes hypothesized to culminate in a proximal sufficient cause of the symptoms of hopelessness depression.

A Proximal Sufficient Cause of the Symptoms of Hopelessness Depression: Hopelessness

According to the theory, a proximal sufficient cause of the symptoms of hopelessness depression is the individual's expectation that highly desired outcomes will not occur or that highly aversive outcomes will occur and that no response in his or her repertoire will change the likelihood of occurrence of these outcomes. Abramson et al. (1989) viewed this theory as a "hopelessness" theory because the common language term *hopelessness* captures the core elements of the proximal sufficient cause featured in the theory: negative expectations about the occurrence of highly valued outcomes (a negative outcome expectancy) and expectations of helplessness about changing the likelihood of occurrence of these outcomes (a helplessness expectancy). Throughout the chapter, we use the term hopelessness to refer to this proximal sufficient cause. Abramson et al. used the phrase *generalized hopelessness* to describe a person's exhibition of negative outcome–helplessness expectancy about many areas of life. In contrast, *circumscribed pessimism* occurs when the individual exhibits the negative outcome–helplessness expectancy about only a limited domain. They suggested that cases of generalized hopelessness should produce severe symptoms of hopelessness depression, whereas circumscribed pessimism is likely to be associated with fewer and/or less severe symptoms.

According to the theory, hopelessness is a proximal sufficient, but not a necessary, cause of depressive symptoms. The theory therefore explicitly recognizes that depression may be a heterogeneous disorder and that other factors such as genetic vulnerability, neurotransmitter aberrations, and loss of interest in reinforcers also may cause depressive symptoms. Thus, the hopelessness theory presents an etiological account of one hypothesized subtype of depression, hopelessness depression.

It is useful to compare the hopelessness theory with its evolutionary precursor, Seligman's (1975) original helplessness theory, with respect to proximal sufficient cause. Seligman's original statement is best characterized as a helplessness theory because it featured the expectation that the individual cannot control outcomes (regardless of their hedonic valence or likelihood of occurrence) as a proximal sufficient cause of depressive symptoms. In contrast, not all cases of perceived lack of control are predicted to lead to depressive symptoms according to the hopelessness theory. For example, whereas Seligman emphasized the concept of "golden girl depression" (depression caused by not having control over events but obtaining everything you desire), golden girls should not become depressed according to the hopelessness theory. Although the golden girl has an expectation of no control (helplessness expectancy), she does not have a negative expectation about the occurrence of highly valued outcomes (negative outcome expectancy). She is helpless but not hopeless. Thus, although helplessness is a necessary component of hopelessness, it is not sufficient to produce hopelessness (i.e., hopelessness is a subset of helplessness).

A Hypothesized Causal Pathway to the Symptoms of Hopelessness Depression

How does a person become hopeless? As can be seen in Figure 9.1., the hypothesized causal chain begins with the perceived occurrence of *negative life events (or nonoccurrence of positive life events).*[1] Negative events serve as "occasion setters" for people to become hopeless. At least three types of inference that people make about negative events modulate whether they become hopeless in the face of these events: (a) Inferences about why the event occurred (i.e., inferred cause or causal attribution); (b) Inferences about consequences that might result from the occurrence of the event (i.e., inferred consequences); and (c) Inferences about themselves given that the event happened to them (i.e., inferred characteristics about the self).

Proximal Contributory Causes

INFERRED STABLE, GLOBAL CAUSES OF PARTICULAR NEGATIVE LIFE EVENTS AND A HIGH DEGREE OF IMPORTANCE ATTACHED TO THESE EVENTS. The causal inferences people make for negative events and the degree of importance they attach to these events are important factors contributing to whether or not they develop hopelessness. People are more likely to develop relatively generalized hopelessness when they attribute negative life events to stable (i.e., enduring) and global (i.e., likely to affect many outcomes) causes and view them as important than when they attribute these events to unstable, specific causes and view them as unimportant.

What influences the kinds of causal inferences people make? People's causal attributions for events are, in part, a function of the situational information they confront (Kelley, 1967; McArthur, 1972). People tend to attribute an event to the factor or factors with which it covaries. According to this view, an individual will make internal, stable, and global attributions for an event (e.g., being beaten by a husband) when confronted with situational information suggesting that the event is low in consensus (e.g., other women are not beaten by this man), high in consistency (e.g., the woman is frequently beaten by this man), and low in distinctiveness (e.g., the woman is put down by many other people as well; Kelley, 1967; Metalsky & Abramson, 1981). Thus, informational cues make

[1]For the sake of brevity, we will use the phrase *negative life events* to refer to both the occurrence of negative life events and the nonoccurrence of positive life events.

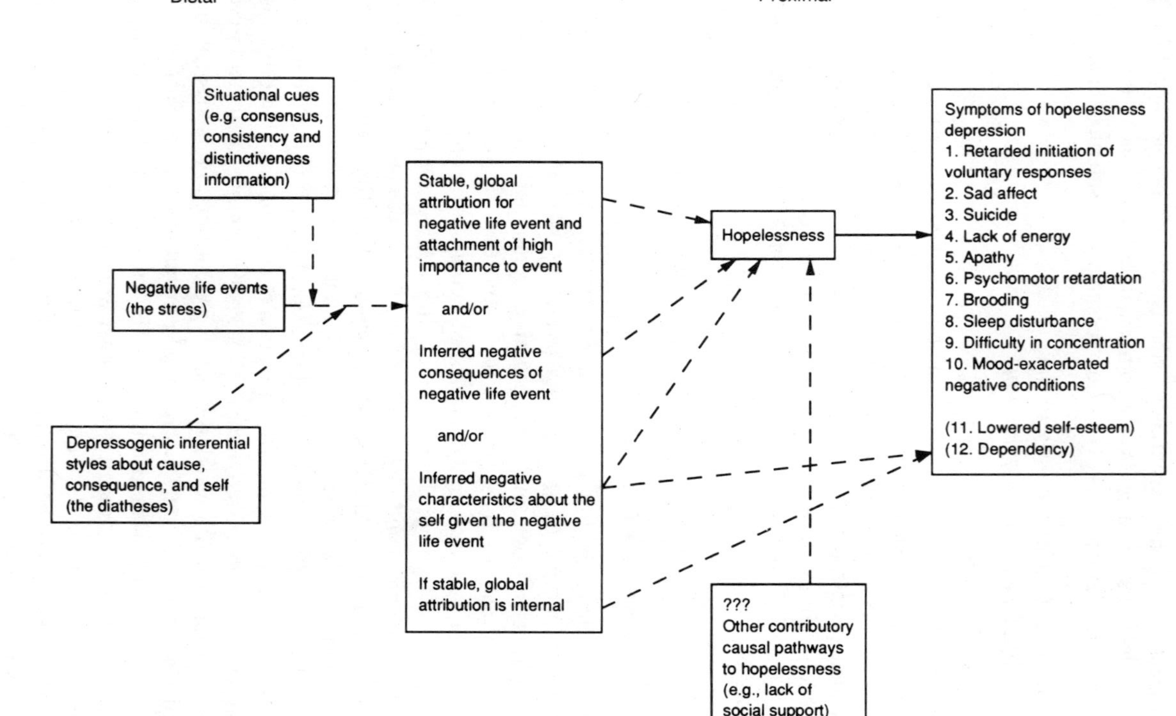

Figure 9.1. Causal chain specified in the Hopelessness Theory of Depression. (Arrows with solid lines indicate sufficient causes. Arrows with broken lines indicate contributory causes.)

some causal inferences for particular life events more plausible than others and some not plausible at all (see also Hammen & Mayol, 1982). Social psychologists have suggested a number of additional factors that also may guide the causal attribution process, including expectations for success and failure, motivation to protect or enhance self-esteem, focus of attention, salience of a potential causal factor, and self-presentational concerns, to name a few. Later, we discuss a more distal cause, cognitive style, that is also hypothesized to influence the causal inferences that people make.

INFERRED NEGATIVE CONSEQUENCES OF PARTICULAR NEGATIVE LIFE EVENTS. Hammen and her colleagues (e.g., Gong-Guy & Hammen, 1980; Hammen & Cochran, 1981; Hammen & de Mayo, 1982) have argued that the inferred consequences of negative events, independently of causal inferences for these events, may modulate the likelihood that people will become depressed when confronted with a negative life event. For example, a student may attribute his low scores on the Graduate Record Examination (GRE) to distracting noises in the testing room (an unstable, specific attribution) but infer that a consequence of his poor performance on the GRE is that he never will be admitted to a graduate program in mathematics, his preferred career choice. Abramson et al. (1989) suggested that inferred negative consequences moderate the relationship between negative life events and the symptoms of hopelessness depression by affecting the likelihood of becoming hopeless. Following the same logic as for causal attributions, inferred negative consequences should be particularly likely to lead to hopelessness when the negative consequence is viewed as important, not remediable, unlikely to change, and as affecting many areas of life. When the negative consequence is seen as affecting only a limited sphere of life, relatively circumscribed pessimism rather than generalized hopelessness should result.

INFERRED NEGATIVE CHARACTERISTICS ABOUT THE SELF AS A RESULT OF NEGATIVE LIFE EVENTS. In addition to inferred consequences of negative events, Abramson et al. (1989) suggested that inferred characteristics about the self, given these events, also may modulate the likelihood of formation of hopelessness. Inferred characteristics about the self are those inferences a person draws about his or her own worth, abilities, personality, desirability, and so on, as a result of the occurrence of a particular negative life event. Such a concept appears central in Beck's (1967) description of cognitive processes and depression. For example, Beck (1976, pp. 99–100) reported the case of a depressed suicidal woman who, after a breach in her relationship with her lover, said, "I am worthless." When the therapist asked why she believed she was worthless, she replied, "If I don't have love, I am worthless." Again, following the same logic as for causal attributions, inferred negative characteristics about the self should be particularly likely to lead to hopelessness when the person believes that the negative characteristic is not remediable or likely to change and that possession of it will preclude the attainment of important outcomes in many areas of life. When the negative characteristic is seen as precluding the attainment of outcomes in only a very limited sphere of life, relatively circumscribed pessimism rather than generalized hopelessness should result. Given negative events, inferred characteristics about the self may not be independent of causal attributions for these events, but it is useful to conceptualize and operationalize them as distinct.

For any given negative life event, the three kinds of inferences (cause, consequence, and self-characteristics) may not contribute equally to the likelihood that a person will become hopeless. For example, a young girl's inferences about the negative consequences of her mother's death, rather than about its cause or immediate implications for her view of herself, may be most important in determining whether or not she becomes hopeless.

Distal Contributory Causes: Cognitive Styles

Individual differences may exist in people's characteristic tendencies to make "depressogenic" inferences when confronted with a negative life event. We refer to these patterns of inference as *cognitive styles.* For example, as a complement to social psychologists' work on the situational determinants of causal attributions, Abramson et al. (1978) suggested a more distal factor that also may influence the content of people's causal inferences for a particular event: individual differences in *attributional style* (see also Ickes & Layden, 1978). Some individuals may exhibit a general tendency to attribute negative events to stable, global factors and to view these events as very important, whereas other individuals may not. We use the phrase *hypothesized depressogenic attributional style* to refer to this tendency.

Individuals who exhibit the hypothesized depressogenic attributional style should be more likely than individuals who do not to attribute any particular negative event to a stable, global cause and view the event as very important, thereby incrementing the likelihood of becoming hopeless. However, in the presence of positive life events or in the absence of negative life events, people exhibiting the hypothesized depressogenic attributional style should be no more likely to develop hopelessness than people not exhibiting this attributional style. This aspect of the theory is conceptualized usefully as a *diathesis–stress component* (Metalsky, Abramson, Seligman, Semmel, & Peterson, 1982). That is, the hypothesized depressogenic attributional style (the diathesis) is a distal contributory cause of the symptoms of hopelessness depression that operates in the presence, but not in the absence, of negative life events (the stress).

The logic of the diathesis–stress component implies that a depressogenic attributional style in a particular content domain (e.g., for interpersonal-related events) provides *specific vulnerability* (cf. Beck, 1967) to the symptoms of hopelessness depression when an individual is confronted with negative life events in that same content domain (e.g., social rejection). This specific vulnerability hypothesis requires a match between the content areas of an individual's depressogenic attributional style and the negative life events he or she encounters for the attributional diathesis–stress interaction to predict future symptoms of hopelessness depression (cf. Alloy, Clements, & Kolden, 1985; Alloy, Hartlage, & Abramson, 1988; Alloy, Kayne, Romer, & Crocker, 1992; Anderson & Arnoult, 1985; Anderson, Horowitz, & French, 1983; Hammen, Marks, Mayol, & de Mayo, 1985; Metalsky, Halberstadt, & Abramson, 1987).

As with causal inferences, individual differences may exist in the general tendency to infer negative consequences and negative characteristics about the self given the occurrence of negative life events. It is not known whether such cognitive styles are independent of the hypothesized depressogenic attributional style. Abramson et al. (1989) suggested these two additional cognitive styles also are diatheses that operate in the presence, but not in the absence, of negative life events according to the specific vulnerability hypothesis. Abramson et al. referred to these three negative styles as *cognitive diatheses.* Beck's (Weissman & Beck, 1979) concept of dysfunctional attitudes and Ellis's (1977) concept of irrational beliefs appear to overlap, in part, with these cognitive diatheses.

Cognitive styles probably are best conceptualized as continua, with some people exhibiting more negative styles than others. Similarly, it may be more appropriate to speak of a continuum of negativity of life events. The continuum view suggests a *titration* model (cf. Zubin & Spring, 1977) of the diathesis–stress component. That is, the less negative a person's cognitive style, the more negative an event must be to interact with that style and contribute to the formation of symptoms. Thus, although many cases of hopelessness depression will occur among cognitively vulnerable people when they are confronted with negative events, people who do not exhibit the cognitive diatheses also may develop hopelessness depression when they are confronted with events that engender hopelessness in many or most people (e.g., a person who is put in a concentration camp and repeatedly told by the guards that the only way to leave the camp is as a corpse). In a related vein, it is likely that major negative life events are not required to initiate the series of inferences hypothesized to culminate in the symptoms of hopelessness depression. Instead, the occurrence of minor events, chronic stressors, or even daily hassles also may trigger the hypothesized depressogenic inferences among cognitively vulnerable people.

In addition to the preceding cognitive factors, interpersonal (e.g., lack of social support; Brown & Harris, 1978), developmental (e.g., death of mother during the child's early years; Brown & Harris, 1978), and even genetic factors also may modulate the likelihood that a person will develop hopelessness (see Tiger, 1979, for an intriguing discussion of genetic and biological factors in the development of hope and hopelessness).

Symptoms

Hopelessness depression should be characterized by a number of symptoms including retarded initiation of voluntary responses, sad affect, suicide attempts and ideation, lack of energy, apathy, psychomotor retardation, brooding, sleep disturbance, difficulty in concentration, mood-exacerbated negative cognitions, and perhaps low self-esteem and/or dependency. The symptom of retarded initiation of voluntary responses derives from the helplessness expectancy component of hopelessness. If a person expects that nothing he or she does matters, why try? The incentive for emitting active instrumental responses decreases (Alloy, 1982; Bolles, 1972). Sadness derives from the negative outcome expectancy component of hopelessness and is a likely consequence of the expectation that the future is bleak.

The rationale for the other hypothesized symptoms also follows from the theory. Because hopelessness is a key factor in suicide attempts and suicidal ideation (Beck, Kovacs, & Weissman, 1975; Kazdin, French, Unis, Esveldt-Dawson, & Sherick, 1983; Minkoff, Bergman, Beck & Beck, 1973; Petrie & Chamberlain, 1983), suicide attempts and suicidal ideation are likely symptoms of hopelessness depression. If lack of energy, apathy, and psychomotor retardation are, in part, concomitants of a severe decrease in the motivation to initiate voluntary responses (see Beck, 1967), then they should be symptoms of hopelessness depression. Abramson et al. (1989) hypothesized that to the extent that people brood about the highly desired outcomes they feel hopeless to attain, sleep disturbance (e.g., initial insomnia) and difficulty in concentration will be important symptoms of hopelessness depression. Based on work showing that mood affects cognition (e.g., Bower, 1981), Abramson et al. (1989) predicted that as individuals suffering from hopelessness depression become increasingly sad, their cognitions will become even more negative.

Although not necessarily symptoms of hopelessness depression, low self-esteem and/or dependency sometimes will accompany the other hypothesized symptoms. Lowered self-esteem will be a symptom of hopelessness depression when the event that triggered the episode was attributed to an internal, stable, global cause as opposed to any type of external cause or to an internal, unstable, specific cause. In addition, lowered self-esteem should occur in cases of hopelessness depression when people have inferred negative characteristics about themselves that they view as important to their general self-concept and not remediable or likely to change. Finally, dependency frequently may co-occur with lowered self-esteem because the conditions that give rise to lowered self-esteem will leave the person feeling inferior to others and thereby increase the likelihood that he or she may become excessively dependent on them (Brewin & Furnham, 1987).

In general, circumscribed pessimism may not be associated with the full syndrome of the symptoms of hopelessness depression. Circumscribed pessimism is likely to produce fewer and/or less severe symptoms than generalized hopelessness. Whereas the motivational deficit should occur in cases of circumscribed pessimism, sadness may be less intense or even absent. Similarly, people with circumscribed pessimism should be less likely to commit suicide or exhibit the other hypothesized symptoms of hopelessness depression. Thus, circumscribed pessimism should lead to an identifiable behavioral syndrome, but this syndrome should be characterized primarily by a motivational deficit in the relevant domain.

Course

In considering the course of a disorder, the concepts of *maintenance, recovery, relapse, and recurrence* need to be distinguished (Klerman, 1978). Maintenance refers to the duration of a given episode of a disorder, and recovery refers to its remission. Relapse is a return of clinically significant symptoms within a relatively short period following remission, whereas recurrence is the onset of a new episode following a prolonged interval of remission.

Insofar as hopelessness is viewed as a proximal sufficient cause of the symptoms of hopelessness depression, the maintenance, or duration, of an episode of hopelessness depression should be influenced by how long this expectation is present. The more stable a person's attribution for a negative life event, the longer the person will be hopeless and, consequently, symptomatic. As a corollary, the maintenance of hopelessness should be influenced not only by the stability of the attribution for the event that triggered the given episode but also by the stability of attributions for newly occurring negative life events (see Brown & Harris, 1978; Lloyd, Zisook, Click, & Jaffe, 1981). Maintenance also may be influenced by the consequences the individual infers from being depressed, as well as by the attribution he or she makes for the depression itself (Nolen-Hoeksema, 1991). Similarly, maintenance may be influenced by the characteristics that the depressed individual infers about himself or herself. More generally, any factor that influences the duration of hopelessness should, in turn, influence the maintenance or chronicity of the symptoms of hopelessness depression. These predictors of the duration of a given episode of hopelessness depression follow directly from the logic of the hopelessness theory. In addition, the possibility exists that once an individual becomes hopeless, some biological or psychological processes are triggered that need to run their course and do not dissipate as quickly as hopelessness. Such factors might maintain a hopelessness depression after hopelessness remits. Similarly, other factors such as lack of social support also may influence the duration of an episode of hopelessness depression after hopelessness remits.

Needles and Abramson (1990) proposed a model of recovery from hopelessness depression that highlights positive events. They suggested that positive events provide the occasion for people suffering from hopelessness depression to become "hopeful." Analogously to the logic of the diathesis–stress component, they suggested that people with a style to attribute positive events to stable, global causes should be particularly likely to become hopeful when confronted with a positive event (or a reduction in negative events). Thus, positive events and inferences about them (cause, consequence, self-characteristics) may be particularly important in recovery from hopelessness depression.

Given the logic of the hopelessness theory, relapse or recurrence of hopelessness depression should be predicted by the reappearance of hopelessness because, by definition, a relapse or recurrence is a new onset of hopelessness depression. Thus, the etiological chain hypothesized to culminate in the onset of the symptoms of hopelessness depression also applies directly to the relapse or recurrence of these symptoms. Hence, people with cognitive diatheses will be more likely to have relapses or recurrences of hopelessness depression when confronted with negative life events than people who do not exhibit these diatheses.

Therapy and Prevention

Because the hopelessness theory specifies an etiological chain, each link suggests a point for clinical intervention. A major advantage of using the proximal–distal continuum to order the events that cause hopelessness depression is that it not only suggests points of intervention for reversing current episodes but also suggests points for decreasing vulnerability to future episodes of hopelessness depression.

Treating Current Episodes of Hopelessness Depression

Any therapeutic strategy that undermines hopelessness and restores hopefulness should be effective in remediating current symptoms of hopelessness depression (see also Hollon & Garber, 1980). Hopelessness could be attacked directly. Alternatively, the proximal causes (e.g., stable, global attributions for particular negative life events) that contribute to a person's current hopelessness could be attacked. Insofar as negative events and situational information supporting depressogenic inferences contribute to the maintenance of hopelessness, therapeutic interventions aimed at modifying the hopelessness-inducing environment should be helpful. Finally, if the person's own behavior is, to some degree, contributing to the depressogenic events and situational information he or she encounters, then personal behavior change would be an important therapeutic goal.

Preventing Onset, Relapse, and Recurrence of Hopelessness Depression

According to the hopelessness theory, the three hypothesized cognitive diatheses put people at risk for initial onset, relapse, and recurrence of hopelessness depression. Therefore, modifying cognitive diatheses is an important goal for prevention. Insofar as the cognitive diatheses require negative life events to exert their depressogenic effects, prevention efforts also might be directed toward lessening the stressfulness of events in the environments of cognitively vulnerable people. Finally, "primary prevention" efforts could be aimed at building "nondepressive" cognitive styles and environments.

Relation of Hopelessness Depression to Other Types of Depression and Psychopathology

Does the concept of hopelessness depression map onto any nosological category of affective disorders currently diagnosed (e.g., dysthymic disorder), or does this concept cut across the various nosological categories of affective or even nonaffective disorders currently diagnosed (cf. Halberstadt, Mukherji, Metalsky, Dykman, & Abramson, 1992; Rose, Leff, Halberstadt, Hodulik, & Abramson, 1992; Seligman, 1978)? Hopelessness depression most likely includes subsets of individuals from various currently diagnosed categories of depression (e.g., major depression, dysthymia, etc.) and may even include some depressed individuals who a priori would not be expected to be hopelessness depressives (e.g., some endogenous depressives). Moreover, based on empirical and clinical studies of the comorbidity of anxiety and depression, Alloy, Kelly, Mineka, and Clements (1990) suggested that many hopelessness depressives also may be suffering from anxiety.

A second descriptive psychiatric question is which diagnostic categories of depression, if any, involve etiological processes, and perhaps symptoms and therapy, that are fundamentally different from those involved in hopelessness depression. Klein's (1974) concept of endogenomorphic depression (see also Costello's, 1972, concept of "reinforcer ineffectiveness depression"), which maps closely onto the DSM-III-R category of major depressive episode with melancholia, may be fundamentally distinct from the concept of hopelessness depression. The hypothesized core process in endogenomorphic depressions is impairment in the capacity to experience pleasure rather than hopelessness.

Nondepression

The hopelessness theory offers some predictions about how people maintain a positive emotional state. According to the theory, the occurrence of a negative event provides a "challenge" to a positive emotional state. Making any of the three depressogenic inferences for negative events about cause, consequence, or self should increase the likelihood that hope will be lost and, as a result, the positive emotional state will break down. In contrast, refraining from making these inferences should allow hope to endure and, as a result, the challenge to be withstood and a positive state maintained.

The logic of the hopelessness theory also suggests that a positive event provides an opportunity for the individual to enhance his or her emotional state. Making any of the following inferences when a positive event occurs should facilitate a positive emotional state by restoring or increasing hope: (a) Attributing the positive event to stable, global factors; (b) inferring positive consequences; and/or (c) inferring positive characteristics about the self.

THE SEARCH FOR HOPELESSNESS DEPRESSION: TOWARD AN EVALUATION OF THE HOPELESSNESS THEORY

How might we search for hopelessness depression to see if it exists in nature and conforms to theoretical description? Some of our colleagues have expressed puzzlement and even mystification about how to determine whether a theory-based subtype of depression exists in nature or have suggested that a search for hopelessness depression involves "circular reasoning." In contrast, we suggest that at a conceptual level, the search for hopelessness depression is straightforward and doesn't involve anything spooky. To assert that hopelessness depressions exist in nature is simply to say that the hopelessness theory is true (cf. Clark, 1983). We search for hopelessness depression by testing the hopelessness theory.

A variety of possible methodological approaches exist for searching for hopelessness depressions and distinguishing them from other types of depression. For example, a symptom-based approach would involve determining if a subgroup of depressives exhibits the symptoms hypothesized to be associated with hopelessness depression (e.g., retarded initiation of voluntary responses). A symptom-based approach commonly has been utilized by workers in descriptive psychiatry, where categories of depression traditionally have been formed on the basis of symptom similarity. However, we believed a symptom-based approach alone would be unsatisfactory in the context of work on the hopelessness theory. The basic problem is that some or all the symptoms hypothesized to be characteristic of hopelessness depressions conceivably may be present in other types of depression as well (e.g., endogenomorphic depression; Klein, 1974). In contrast to a purely symptom-based approach, the hopelessness theory of depression points to a *process-oriented* approach for searching for hopelessness depressions.

A search for hopelessness depression involves at least five components:

1. A test of the etiological chain hypothesized to culminate in the manifest symptoms of hopelessness depression.
2. An examination of the hypothesized manifest symptoms of hopelessness depression.
3. A test of theoretical predictions about the course, remission, relapse, and recurrence of hopelessness depression.
4. A test of theoretical predictions about the cure and prevention of hopelessness depression.

5. Delineation of the relationship among hopelessness depression, other subtypes of depression, and other types of psychopathology.

In discussing how to search for hopelessness depression, we note the possibility that future work may not corroborate the existence of hopelessness depression as a bona fide subtype with characteristic cause, symptoms, course, treatment, and prevention. Instead, the etiological chain featured in the hopelessness theory may be one of many pathways to a final common outcome of depression. In this case, it would be more compelling to speak of a hopelessness cause, as opposed to a hopelessness subtype, of depression.

EMPIRICAL VALIDITY OF THE HOPELESSNESS THEORY

Because the theory is relatively new, the evidence about its validity is not all in. Consequently, it is not possible to say definitively whether or not hopelessness depression exists in nature. However, we and others have conducted a number of studies that test the theory and thereby give clues about the existence of hopelessness depression.

Etiological Chain

Proximal Sufficient Cause Component

A key prediction of the hopelessness theory is that hopelessness temporally precedes and is a proximal sufficient cause of the symptoms of hopelessness depression. An alternative hypothesis is that hopelessness has no causal status and, instead, is simply another symptom of depression. Relevant to distinguishing between these two views, Rholes, Riskind, and Neville (1985) conducted a longitudinal study and reported that college students' levels of hopelessness at Time 1 predicted their levels of depression five weeks later at Time 2 over and above the predictive capacity of depression at Time 1. Similarly, in their prospective study, Carver and Gaines (1987) demonstrated that, after controlling statistically for earlier levels of depressive symptoms, dispositional pessimists were more likely to develop postpartum depression than were optimists. Although these results do not establish that hopelessness actually caused depressive symptoms at a later time, they do support the temporal precedence of hopelessness in predicting change in depressive symptoms (see also Riskind, Rholes, Brannon, & Burdick, 1987, for a demonstration that the interaction of attributional style and negative expectations predict future depression).

In addition to the preceding longitudinal studies, a number of cross-sectional studies have examined the relationship between hopelessness and depression. A notable feature of these studies is that they tested whether hopelessness is specific to depression or is a more general feature of psychopathology. Abramson, Garber, Edwards, and Seligman (1978) reported that hospitalized unipolar depressives were more hopeless than both hospitalized nondepressed control subjects and nondepressed schizophrenics. Interestingly, the unipolar depressives also were more hopeless than the depressed schizophrenics. Hamilton and Abramson (1983) found that hospitalized unipolar depressives were more hopeless than a hospitalized nondepressed psychiatric group with mixed diagnoses (e.g., schizophrenia, anxiety disorder, and personality disorders) as well as a nondepressed community control group. Beck, Riskind, Brown, and Steer (1988) found that psychiatric patients suffering from major depression were more hopeless than either patients suffering from generalized anxiety disorder or a group of mixed psychiatric patients (diagnoses other than depression or anxiety). Taken together, these studies suggest that hopelessness is specific to depression and not a general feature of psychopathology.

Although the studies examining the association between hopelessness and depression are promising, they do not provide a wholly adequate test of the proximal sufficient cause component of the theory. As we have argued elsewhere (Abramson, Metalsky, & Alloy, 1988, 1989), insofar as the hopelessness theory postulates a subtype of depression, it is inappropriate simply to lump all depressives together and examine their levels of hopelessness to test the theory. Fortunately, some investigators have begun to examine the relationship between hopelessness and the hypothesized individual symptoms of hopelessness depression and have reported a strong association between hopelessness and suicide attempts and ideation (Beck et al., 1975; Kazdin et al., 1983; Minkoff et al., 1973; Petrie & Chamberlain, 1983).

To what degree must people's cognitions of hopelessness be active to exert an influence on their moods? In this regard, Needles and Abramson (1992) stressed the importance of distinguishing between the *content* and the *activation* of a belief. They showed that among depressed people, changes in depressive mood can be produced by merely changing the level of activation of cognitions of hopelessness without altering the content of these cognitions. These results suggest that future revisions of the hopelessness theory incorporate the distinction between content and activation of beliefs.

Diathesis–Stress and Causal Mediation Components

Relevant to these components, a multitude of cross-sectional and longitudinal studies have examined the relationship between attributional style and depression (see Barnett & Gotlib, 1988; Brewin, 1985; Coyne & Gotlib, 1983; Peterson & Seligman, 1984; and Sweeney, Anderson, & Bailey, 1986, for reviews). Overall, these studies have shown that the tendency to make internal, stable, and global attributions for negative events is associated with severity of concurrent and future depressive symptoms in college student, patient, and other samples. However, the corroborative findings have not always been strong.

We have argued elsewhere that this research strategy is inappropriate to test the diathesis–stress component (Abramson et al., 1988, 1989; Alloy et al., 1988). Recently, a number of studies have been conducted that do provide a more powerful test of the diathesis–stress component (and in some cases the causal mediation component) of the hopelessness theory. In a prospective field study, Metalsky et al. (1987) found that college students who showed a style to attribute negative achievement events to stable, global causes experienced a more enduring depressive mood reaction to a low midterm grade than did students who did not exhibit this style. Consistent with the diathesis–stress component, attributional style for negative achievement events was not associated with students' mood reactions in the absence of the low grade. Interestingly, whereas students' more enduring depressive mood reactions were predicted by the interaction between attributional style and midterm grade (consistent with the diathesis–stress component), their immediate depressive mood reactions were predicted solely by the outcome on the exam (see also Follette & Jacobson, 1987). The results also provided support for the specific vulnerability hypothesis in that attributional style for negative achievement events, but not for negative interpersonal events, interacted with students' outcomes on the exam (an achievement event) to predict their enduring depressive mood reactions. Finally, consistent with the mediation component of the theory, failure students' attributional styles predicted their particular attributions for their midterm grades, which, in turn, completely mediated the relation between attributional style and their enduring depressive mood responses.

Recently, Metalsky, Joiner, Hardin, and Abramson (in press) replicated the Metalsky et al. (1987) findings and further showed that, consistent with the mediation component, students who showed a style to attribute negative achievement events to stable, global causes became more hopeless on receipt of a low grade than did students who did not exhibit this style. This increase in hopelessness, in turn, mediated the enduring depressive reaction to the low grade exhibited by the former group of students. Of importance, Metalsky et al. further tested the mediation component by examining whether changes in depression predicted changes in hopelessness (i.e., the *opposite* causal direction to what is hypothesized in the hopelessness theory). Consistent with the theory, changes in depression did not predict changes in hopelessness. In addition to examining predictions from the hopelessness theory itself, Metalsky et al. also integrated this theory with the self-esteem theories of depression. Qualifying the diathesis–stress predictions of the hopelessness theory, they found that among students who exhibited a style to attribute negative achievement events to stable, global causes, only those who also exhibited low self-esteem developed the hopelessness-mediated enduring depressive mood response to a low grade.

With a design similar to Metalsky et al. (1987), Alloy et al. (1992) used causal modeling techniques to test the diathesis–stress and causal mediation components of the hopelessness theory and obtained support for both components. Alloy et al. additionally reported that the interaction between attributional style and midterm grade predicted change in depressive symptoms as well as in transient depressive mood responses. In a longitudinal study, Nolen-Hoeksema, Girgus, and Seligman (1986) asked whether life events and attributional styles interacted to predict schoolchildren's future depression. They obtained partial support for the diathesis–stress component of the theory with negative life events interacting with attributional style in some analyses but not in others. Sacks and Bugental (1987) tested the diathesis–stress component in a laboratory study involving social failure or success (interaction with an unresponsive or responsive confederate). Supporting the diathesis–stress component, attributional style predicted short-term depressive reactions to the stressful social experience as well as the behaviors accompanying such a reaction.

Recently, Alloy, Lipman, and Abramson (1992) tested the attributional vulnerability component of the hopelessness theory with a retrospective behavioral high-risk paradigm. Consistent with prediction, currently nondepressed, but attributionally vulnerable subjects exhibited more frequent and more severe episodes of past major depressive disorder than did currently nondepressed attributionally invulnerable subjects. Using a prospective version of the behavioral high risk paradigm, Alloy and Just (1992) found that currently nondepressed, attributionally vulnerable subjects exhibited higher levels and greater within-day and across-day variability of depressive symptoms, and of hopelessness depression symptoms in particular, than did nondepressed, attributionally invulnerable subjects.

Related to the diathesis–stress component, Clements and Alloy (1990) tested the theory's prediction that depression-prone students should be particularly likely to exhibit the hypothesized depressogenic attributional style. Consistent with prediction, they found that depression-prone students had more negative attributional styles than students who were not depression-prone, regardless of current depression level.

Insofar as dysfunctional attitudes overlap, in part, with the cognitive diatheses, studies examining dysfunctional attitudes and negative life events in predicting depression are relevant to evaluating the diathesis–stress component. In this regard, Olinger, Kuiper, & Shaw (1987) administered the Dysfunctional Attitudes Scale (DAS; Weissman & Beck, 1979) and DAS-Contractual Contingencies Scale (DAS-CC; Olinger et al., 1987) to subjects. The DAS-CC was designed to measure the presence or absence of life events that impinge on a person's dysfunctional attitudes. Consistent with the diathesis–stress component, subjects who were cognitively vulnerable (high DAS) and experienced negative events impinging on their vulnerability (high DAS-CC) were more depressed than both cognitively vulnerable subjects who did not experience the relevant negative life events (high DAS, low DAS-CC) and subjects who were not cognitively vulnerable (low DAS with either high or low DAS-CC scores).

Similarly, Wise and Barnes (1986) reported that a normal sample of college students who were cognitively vulnerable (high DAS scores) and exposed to negative life events during the past year were more depressed than students who also were cognitively vulnerable but not exposed to a high rate of negative life events as well as students who were not cognitively vulnerable regardless of life events. In a clinical sample, DAS scores and negative life events scores exerted main effects in predicting depression. A limitation of these two studies is that they employed cross-sectional designs.

Related to the mediation component, some investigators (e.g., Brewin, 1985) have questioned whether people's attributional styles predict their causal attributions for particular negative life events. As we previously indicated, in their tests of the causal mediation component of the theory, Metalsky et al. (1987) and Alloy et al. (1992) found that attributional styles did, in fact, predict people's causal attributions for actual life events (see also Follette & Jacobson, 1987, for similar results). Moreover, support for the mediation component of the hopelessness theory challenges the alternative hypothesis that some antecedent or correlate of the cognitive diatheses is actually mediating depressive reactions.

The hopelessness theory predicts that attributions for life events should be influenced by situational information as well as attributional style. Consistent with this prediction, Haack, Metalsky, Dykman, and Abramson (1992) found that both depressed and nondepressed students' causal attributions were influenced by consensus, consistency, and distinctiveness information. Similarly, Crocker, Alloy, and Kayne (1988) found that people's perceptions of consensus information mediated their attributional styles (see also Alloy & Ahrens, 1987).

A further aspect of the mediation component of the hopelessness theory involves whether people's attributions or attributional styles predict the formation of hopelessness. Consistent with this component, in a laboratory study, Alloy and Ahrens (1987) demonstrated that a depressogenic attributional style contributed to depressives' pessimism in predicting future events. More generally, Weiner's (1985) work has demonstrated that people's causal attributions affect their expectancies about future events.

Symptoms

A shortcoming of much of the work testing the hopelessness theory is that it has looked at the symptoms of depression in general as opposed to examining the specific, hypothesized symptoms of hopelessness depression. However, we know of two studies that have examined the symptoms of hopelessness depression in particular. First, Alloy et al. (1992), with their retrospective, high-risk design, further asked whether currently nondepressed, but attributionally vulnerable subjects exhibited more past episodes of the specific constellation of symptoms hypothesized to constitute the syndrome of hopelessness depression than did currently nondepressed attributionally invulnerable subjects. The syndrome of hopelessness depression was diagnosed if the subject experienced a period of at least 2 weeks in which he or she exhibited hopelessness and at least six of the symptoms hypothesized to form the hopelessness depression syndrome. Consistent with the theory, the attributionally vulnerable subjects experienced more past episodes of the specific syndrome of hopelessness depression than did the attributionally invulnerable subjects.

Using a longitudinal design, Alloy and Clements (1991) tested the symptom component of the hopelessness theory with college students. Consistent with the theory, hopelessness was uniquely associated both concurrently and prospectively with depression but not anxiety. Hopelessness prospectively predicted most of the symptoms hypothesized to be part of the hopelessness depression syndrome (e.g., suicidal ideation) and, consistent with the theory, failed to predict depressive symptoms not hypothesized to be part of the syndrome (e.g., appetite disturbance). Of interest, hopelessness also predicted some symptoms of other psychopathologies (e.g., hostility, paranoia, and psychoticism). In addition, the diathesis–stress and mediation hypotheses were supported for the hopelessness depression syndrome. Specifically, college students who both exhibited the depressogenic attributional style and who experienced negative life events were more likely than other students to develop hopelessness and, in turn, the symptoms hypothesized to constitute the hopelessness depression syndrome.

Course

Four studies have tested the course component directly. Consistent with prediction, Needles and Abramson (1990) reported that attributional style for positive outcomes interacted with positive life events to predict recovery from hopelessness. When positive events occurred in their lives, depressed students with a style to attribute positive events to stable, global causes showed a dramatic reduction in hopelessness relative to depressed students who did not exhibit this style. This change in hopelessness was accompanied by a reduction of depressive symptoms. Students who did not experience an increase in positive events, regardless of style, also did not show such dramatic reduction of hopelessness.

In a 2-year follow-up, Evans et al. (1991) reported that patients treated cognitively (cognitive therapy alone or in combination with drugs) showed half the rate of relapse of patients treated with drugs alone who were then withdrawn from medication. Patients kept on medication also showed reduced relapse. Posttreatment attributional style evidenced greater change in cognitively treated patients than in patients treated purely pharmacologically and, consistent with the theory, predicted subsequent relapse when residual depression was partialed out (the other two cognitive diatheses—consequences and self were not assessed). Further analyses suggested that change in attributional style mediated the relapse-preventive effect of cognitive therapy.

In a follow-up of psychiatric patients, Rush, Weissenburger, and Eaves (1986) reported that the presence of dysfunctional attitudes (high DAS scores) at remission from depression predicted the presence of depression 6 months later. Although not statistically significant, a similar pattern was found for attributional style. A limitation of this study was its small sample size ($n = 15$).

Finally, Lewinsohn, Steinmetz, Larson, and Franklin (1981) found that unipolar depressed community volunteers who held negative expectations about the future and perceptions of low control (in our terminology, the two features of hopelessness) at Time 1 were less likely to recover over an 8-month period compared with unipolar depressives who did not exhibit these cognitions, controlling for initial level of depression (see also Eaves & Rush, 1984).

Cure and Prevention

A number of studies have documented the efficacy of cognitive therapy for unipolar depression. The goals of cognitive therapy as currently practiced (cf. Beck, Rush, Shaw, & Emery, 1979) overlap with the goals for treatment and prevention of hopelessness depression. Therefore, empirical work demonstrating the efficacy of cognitive therapy for unipolar depression provides some support for the validity of the hopelessness theory's therapeutic predictions. Future work is needed to examine predictions about treatment of hopelessness depression in particular. In addition, predictions about the prevention of hopelessness depression need to be tested. Finally, the hopelessness theory's novel clinical predictions need to be tested.

Relation of Hopelessness Depression to Other Types of Depression and Psychopathology

Recently, Rose et al. (1992) asked which depressed people exhibit the depressogenic cognitive styles featured in the hopelessness theory and which do not. They used three approaches with a psychiatric inpatient sample to identify subgroups of depressives whose extremely negative cognitive styles distinguished them from other depressives:

1. They examined the cognitive styles of depressives representing all currently diagnosed depression subtypes in their sample.
2. They examined the cognitive styles of depressed patients who spontaneously verbalized cognitions consistent with a negative cognitive style and described characteristics identifying these depressives.
3. They asked whether nonnosological variables such as sex, developmental events, depression history, and severity of depression predicted cognitive styles among depressed inpatients.

These approaches converged on a consistent finding: Borderline personality disorder, developmental maltreatment, and severe depression characterize depressed patients who exhibit extremely negative cognitive styles. These results suggest that hopelessness depression probably does not map onto any currently diagnosed category of depression and instead may cut across currently diagnosed categories of depression and other psychopathologies.

Rose et al. pointed out that the relationship they found between developmental trauma and adult negative cognitive style integrates current work on the hopelessness theory with its precursor, Seligman's (1975) work on learned helplessness in animals. Techniques used to induce helplessness in laboratory animals now seem similar to the traumatic abuse histories of Rose et al.'s depressed research subjects who exhibited markedly negative cognitive styles. Thus, the findings of Rose et al. underscore the importance of incorporating the element of trauma in the hopelessness theory.

CONCLUSION

Does hopelessness depression exist? Work testing the hopelessness theory provides promise that hopelessness depression, or something similar to its theoretical description, indeed may exist in nature. Current research suggests that hopelessness depression probably cuts across currently diagnosed categories of depression and perhaps other currently diagnosed categories of psychopathology not previously linked strongly to depression (e.g., borderline personality disorder, posttraumatic stress disorder). If this speculation is correct, then an integration of the hopelessness theory with descriptive psychiatry will require a reorganization of the existing classification systems to accommodate the inclusion of the theory-based category of hopelessness depression. We look forward to future research that further reveals the nature of this hypothesized disorder.

ACKNOWLEDGMENTS

Preparation of this chapter was supported by NIMH Grant R01MH43866, a Vilas Associate Award, a Graduate School Research Grant, and a Romnes Fellowship to Lyn Y. Abramson and NIMH Grant R01MH48216 to Lauren B. Alloy.

REFERENCES

Abramson, L. Y., Garber, J., Edwards, N. B., & Seligman, M. E. P. (1978). Expectancy changes in depression and schizophrenia. *Journal of Abnormal Psychology, 87,* 49–74.

Abramson, L. Y., Metalsky, G. I., & Alloy, L. B. (1988). The hopelessness theory of depression: Does the research test the theory? In L. Y. Abramson (Ed.), *Social cognition and clinical psychology: A synthesis* (pp. 33–65). New York: Guilford.

Abramson, L. Y., Metalsky, G. I., & Alloy, L. B. (1989). Hopelessness depression: A theory-based subtype of depression. *Psychological review, 96,* 358–372.

Abramson, L. Y., Seligman, M. E. P., & Teasdale, J. (1978). Learned helplessness in humans: Critique and reformulation. *Journal of Abnormal Psychology, 87,* 49–74.

Alloy, L. B. (1982). The role of perceptions and attributions for response-outcome noncontingency in learned helplessness: A commentary and discussion. *Journal of Personality, 50,* 443–479.

Alloy, L. B., & Ahrens, A. (1987). Depression and pessimism for the future: Biased use of statistically relevant information in predictions for self versus others. *Journal of Personality and Social Psychology, 52,* 366–378.

Alloy, L. B., & Clements, C. (1991). *The hopelessness theory of depression: Test of the symptom component in late adolescents.* Paper presented at the meeting of the American Psychological Association, San Francisco, CA.

Alloy, L. B., Clements, C., & Kolden, G. (1985). The cognitive diathesis–stress theories of depression: Therapeutic implications. In S. Reiss & R. Bootzin (Eds.). *Theoretical issues in behavior therapy* (pp. 379–410). New York: Academic Press.

Alloy, L. B., Hartlage, S., & Abramson, L. Y. (1988). Testing the cognitive diathesis–stress theories of depression: Issues of research design, conceptualization, and assessment. In L. B. Alloy (Ed.), *Cognitive processes in depression* (pp. 31–73). New York: Guilford.

Alloy, L. B., & Just, N. (1992). *Attributional style and variability of depressive symptoms: A prospective behavioral high risk paradigm.* Paper presented at the meeting of the Midwestern Psychological Association, Chicago, IL.

Alloy, L. B., Kayne, N. T., Romer, D., & Crocker, J. (1992). *Predicting depressive reactions in the classroom: A test of a cognitive diathesis stress theory of depression with causal modeling techniques.* Manuscript under editorial review.

Alloy, L. B., Kelly, K. A., Mineka, S., & Clements, C. M. (1990). Comorbidity in anxiety and depressive disorders: A helplessness/hopelessness perspective. In J. D. Maser & C. R. Cloninger (Eds.), *Comorbidity in anxiety and mood disorders* (pp. 499–543). Washington, DC: American Psychiatric Press.

Alloy, L. B., Lipman, A. J., & Abramson, L. Y. (1992). Attributional style as a vulnerability factor for depression: Validation by past history of mood disorders. *Cognitive Therapy and Research, 16,* 391–407.

Anderson, C. A., & Arnoult, L. H. (1985). Attributional style and everyday problems in living: Depression, loneliness, and shyness. *Social Cognition, 3,* 16–35.

Anderson, C. A., Horowitz, L. M., & French, R. (1983). Attributional style of lonely and depressed people. *Journal of Personality and Social Psychology, 45,* 127–136.

Barnett, P. A., & Gotlib, I. H. (1988). Psychosocial functioning and depression: Distinguishing among antecedents, concomitants, and consequences. *Psychological Bulletin, 104,* 97–126.

Beck, A. T. (1967). *Depression: Clinical, experimental, and theoretical aspects.* New York: Harper & Row.

Beck, A. T. (1976). *Cognitive therapy and the emotional disorders.* New York: International Universities Press.

Beck, A. T., Kovacs, M., & Weissman, A. (1975). Hopelessness and suicidal behavior: An overview. *Journal of the American Medical Association, 234,* 1146–1149.

Beck, A. T., Riskind, J. H., Brown, G., & Steer, R. A. (1988). Levels of hopelessness in DSM-III disorders: A partial test of content-specificity in depression. *Cognitive Therapy and Research, 12,* 459–469.

Beck, A. T., Rush, A. J., Shaw, B. R., & Emery, G. (1979). *Cognitive therapy of depression.* New York: Guilford.

Bolles, R. C. (1972). Reinforcement, expectancy, and learning. *Psychological Review, 79,* 394–409.

Bower, G. H. (1981). Mood and Memory. *American Psychologist, 36,* 129–148.

Brewin, C. R. (1985). Depression and causal attributions: What is their relation? *Psychological Bulletin, 98,* 297-309.

Brewin, C. T., & Furnham, A. (1987). Dependency, self-criticism and depressive attributional style. *British Journal of Clinical Psychology, 26,* 225–226.

Brown, G. W., & Harris, T. (1978). *Social origins of depression.* New York: Free Press.

Carver, C. S., & Gaines, J. G. (1987). Optimism, pessimism, and postpartum depression. *Cognitive Therapy and Research, 11,* 449–462.

Clark, A. (1983). Hypothetical constructs, circular reasoning, and criteria. *Journal of Mind and Behavior, 4,* 1–12.

Clements, C. M., & Alloy, L. B. (1990). *Depression, depression-proneness and self and other evaluation: Perceiving the self when you believe you are another and others when you believe they are the self.* Manuscript in preparation.

Costello, C. G. (1972). Depression: Loss of reinforcers or loss of reinforcer effectiveness? *Behavior Therapy, 3,* 240–247.

Coyne, J. C., & Gotlib, I. H. (1983). The role of cognition in depression: A critical appraisal. *Psychological Bulletin, 94,* 472–505.

Crocker, J., Alloy, L. B., & Kayne, N. T. (1988). Attributional style, depression, and perceptions of consensus for events. *Journal of Personality and Social Psychology, 54,* 840–846.

Ellis, A. (1977). The basic clinical theory of rational-emotive therapy. In A. Ellis and R. Grieger (Eds.), *Handbook of rational-emotive therapy* (pp. 3–34). New York: Springer.

Evans, M. D., Hollon, S. D., DeRubeis, R. J., Piasecki, J. M., Grove, W. M., Garvey, M. J., & Tuason, V. B. (1991). *Differential relapse following cognitive therapy, pharmacotherapy, and combined cognitive-pharmacotherapy for depression: IV. A 2-year follow-up of the CPT project.* Manuscript submitted for publication.

Follette, V. M., & Jacobson, N. S. (1987). Importance of attributions as a predictor of how people cope with failure. *Journal of Personality and Social Psychology, 52,* 1205–1211.

Gong-Guy, E., & Hammen, C. (1980). Causal perceptions of stressful life events in depressed and nondepressed clinic outpatients. *Journal of Abnormal Psychology, 89,* 662–669.

Haack, L. J., Metalsky, G. I., Dykman, B. M., & Abramson, L. Y. (1992). *Use of situational information and depression: Do depressed students make "unwarranted" causal inferences?* Manuscript in preparation.

Halberstadt, L. J., Mukherji, B. R., Metalsky, G. I., Dykman, B. M., & Abramson, L. Y. (1992). *Cognitive styles among college students: Toward an integration of the cognitive theories of depression with cognitive psychology and descriptive psychiatry.* Manuscript under editorial review.

Hamilton, E. W., & Abramson, L. Y. (1983). Cognitive patterns in major depressive disorder: A longitudinal study in a hospital setting. *Journal of Abnormal Psychology, 92,* 173–184.

Hammen, C., & Cochran, S. (1981). Cognitive correlates of life stress and depression in college students. *Journal of Abnormal Psychology, 90,* 23–27.

Hammen, C., & de Mayo, R. (1982). Cognitive correlates of teacher stress and depressive symptoms: Implications for attributional models of depression. *Journal of Abnormal Psychology, 91,* 96–101.

Hammen, C., Marks, T., Mayol, A., & de Mayo, R. (1985). Depressive self-schemas, life stress, and vulnerability to depression. *Journal of Abnormal Psychology, 94,* 308–319.

Hammen, C., & Mayol, A. (1982). Depression and cognitive characteristics of stressful life-event types. *Journal of Abnormal Psychology, 91,* 165–174.

Hollon, S. D., & Garber, J. (1980). A cognitive-expectancy theory of therapy for helplessness and depression. In J. Garber and M. E. P. Seligman (Eds.), *Human helplessness: Theory and applications* (pp. 173–195). New York: Academic Press.

Ickes, W., & Layden, M. A. (1978). Attributional styles. In J. Harvey, W. Ickes, & R. Kidd (Eds.), *New directions in attribution research* (Vol. 2, pp. 119–152). Hillsdale, NJ: Erlbaum.

Kazdin, A. E., French, N. H., Unis, A. S., Esveldt-Dawson, K., & Sherick, R. B. (1983). Hopelessness, depression, and suicidal intent among psychiatrically disturbed inpatient children. *Journal of Consulting and Clinical Psychology, 51,* 504–510.

Kelley, H. H. (1967). Attribution theory in social psychology. In D. Levine (Ed.), *Nebraska symposium on motivation* (Volume 15, pp. 192–238). Lincoln: University of Nebraska Press.

Kendell, R. E. (1968). *The classification of depression illness.* London: Oxford University Press.

Klein, D. F. (1974). Endogenomorphic depression: Conceptual and terminological revision. *Archives of General Psychiatry, 31,* 447–454.

Klerman, G. L. (1978). The evolution of a scientific nosology. In J. C. Shershow (Ed.), *Schizophrenia: Science and practice* (pp. 99–121). Cambridge, MA: Harvard University Press.

Lewinsohn, P. M., Steinmetz, J. L., Larson, D. W., & Franklin, J. (1981). Depression related cognitions: Antecedent or consequence? *Journal of Abnormal Psychology, 90,* 213–219.

Lloyd, C., Zisook, S., Click, M., Jr., & Jaffe, K. E. (1981). Life events and response to antidepressants. *Journal of Human Stress, 7,* 2–15.

McArthur, L. A. (1972). The how and what of why: Some determinants and consequences of causal attributions. *Journal of Personality and Social Psychology, 22,* 171–193.

McLemore, C. W., & Benjamin, L. S. (1979). Whatever happened to interpersonal diagnosis? A psychosocial alternative to DMS-III. *American Psychologist, 34,* 17–34.

Metalsky, G. I., & Abramson, L. Y. (1981). Attributional styles: Toward a framework for conceptualization and assessment. In P. C. Kendall and S. D. Hollon (Eds.), *Cognitive-behavioral interventions: Assessment methods* (pp. 13–58). New York: Academic Press.

Metalsky, G. I., Abramson, L. Y., Seligman, M. E. P., Semmel, A., & Peterson, C. (1982). Attributional styles and life events in the classroom: Vulnerability and invulnerability to depressive mood reactions. *Journal of Personality and Social Psychology, 43,* 612–617.

Metalsky, G. I., Halberstadt, L. J., & Abramson, L. Y. (1987). Vulnerability to depressive mood reactions: Toward a more powerful test of the diathesis–stress and causal mediation components of the reformulated theory of depression. *Journal of Personality and Social Psychology, 52,* 386–393.

Metalsky, G. I., Joiner, T. E., Jr., Hardin, T. S., & Abramson, L. Y. (in press). Depressive reactions to failure in a naturalistic setting: A test of the hopelessness and self-esteem theories of depression. *Journal of Abnormal Psychology.*

Minkoff, K., Bergman, E., Beck, A. T., & Beck, R. (1973). Hopelessness, depression and attempted suicide. *American Journal of Psychiatry, 130,* 455–459.

Needles, D. J., & Abramson, L. Y. (1990). Positive life events, attributional style, and hopelessness: Testing a model of recovery from depression. *Journal of Abnormal Psychology, 99,* 156–165.

Needles, D. J., & Abramson, L. Y. (1992). *Cognitive and affective consequences of rumination and distraction in response to a depressed mood.* Manuscript under review.

Nolen-Hoeksema, S. (1991). Responses to depression and their effects on the duration of depressive episodes. *Journal of Abnormal Psychology, 100,* 569–582.

Nolen-Hoeksema, S., Girgus, J. S., & Seligman, M. E. P. (1986). Learned helplessness in children: A longitudinal study of depression, achievement, and explanatory style. *Journal of Personality and Social Psychology, 51,* 435–442.

Olinger, L. J., Kuiper, N. A., & Shaw, B. F. (1987). Dysfunctional attitudes and stressful life events: An interactive model of depression. *Cognitive Therapy and Research, 11,* 25–40.

Peterson, C., & Seligman, M. E. P. (1984). Causal explanations as a risk factor for depression: Theory and evidence. *Psychological Review, 91,* 347–374.

Petrie, K., & Chamberlain, K. (1983). Hopelessness and social desirability as moderator variables in predicting suicidal behavior. *Journal of Consulting and Clinical Psychology, 51,* 485–487.

Rholes, W. S., Riskind, J. H., & Neville, B. (1985). The relationship of cognitions and hopelessness to depression and anxiety. *Social Cognition, 3,* 36–50.

Riskind, J. H., Rholes, W. S., Brannon, A. M., & Burdick, C. A. (1987). Attributions and expectations: A confluence of vulnerabilities in mild depression in a college student population. *Journal of Personality and Social Psychology, 53,* 349–354.

Rose, D. T., Leff, G., Halberstadt, L. J., Hodulik, C., & Abramson, L. Y. (1992). *Heterogeneity of cognitive style among inpatient depressives: A search for "negative cognition" depressives.* Manuscript under review.

Rush, A. J., Weissenburger, J., & Eaves, G. (1986). Do thinking patterns predispose depressive symptoms? *Cognitive Therapy and Research, 10,* 225–236.

Sacks, C. H., & Bugental, D. B. (1987). Attributions as moderators of affective and behavioral responses to social failure. *Journal of Personality and Social Psychology, 53,* 939–947.

Seligman, M. E. P. (1975). *Helplessness: On depression, development, and death.* San Francisco: Freeman.

Seligman, M. E. P. (1978). Comment and integration. *Journal of Abnormal Psychology, 87,* 165–179.

Skinner, H. A. (1981). Toward the integration of classification theory and methods. *Journal of Abnormal Psychology, 90,* 68–87.

Sweeney, P. D., Anderson, K., & Bailey, S. (1986). Attributional style in depression: A meta-analytic review. *Journal of Personality and Social Psychology, 50,* 974–991.

Tiger, L. (1979). *Optimism: The biology of hope.* New York: Simon & Schuster.

Weiner, B. (1985). An attributional theory of achievement motivation and emotion. *Psychological Review, 92,* 548–573.

Weissman, A., & Beck, A. T. (1979). *The dysfunctional attitude scale.* Paper presented at the annual meeting of the American Psychological Association, New York.

Wise, E. H., & Barnes, D. R. (1986). The relationship among life events, dysfunctional attitudes, and depression. *Cognitive Therapy and Research, 10,* 257–266.

Zubin, J. E., & Spring, B. (1977). Vulnerability: A new view of schizophrenia. *Journal of Abnormal Psychology, 86,* 103–126.

CHAPTER 10

Psychomotor Agitation and Retardation

MARYLENE CLOITRE, MARTIN M. KATZ, and HERMAN M. VAN PRAAG

INTRODUCTION

Although Hippocrates (4th century B.C.) is said to have given the first medical description of depression, it was Aretaeus of Cappadocia (2nd century A.D.) who first wrote a full description of the syndrome. His description included psychomotor activity as one of the symptoms signaling the onset of depression:

> The characteristic appearances, then, are not obscure; for the patients are dull or stern or unreasonably torpid without any manifest cause: such is the commencement of melancholy. (Quoted from Arieti & Bemporad, 1978)

As recently as the late 19th century, the movement behavior of an organism was considered a highly salient feature in the description of emotional states. The ethologist, Darwin, highlighted the motor movements characteristic of depression by noting that sad people

> no longer wish for action but remain motionless and passive or may occasionally rock themselves to and fro . . . the eyelids droop, the head hangs on the contracted chest, the lips, cheeks, and low jaw all sink downward from their own weight. (Quoted from Widlocher, 1983a)

At about the same time, great debate ensued among psychologists concerning the relationship between body movement and mood state. Some argued that emotional state derived from the awareness of body movements made in response to environmental events (e.g., the James-Lange theory), whereas others viewed emotions as a core defining feature of human experience that determined and/or was expressed by bodily movement.

For the larger portion of the 20th century, the general opinion has been that mood states, that is, sadness or anhedonia, are the core or defining features of depressive syndromes. Psychomotor activity has been viewed as an expression or by-product of mood state and relegated to the periphery of the symptom constellations descriptive of the disorder. One of the reasons for the shift in emphasis from behavioral to more psychological symptoms of psychopathology was the influence of theorists such as Meyer and Freud who focused primarily on the internal psychological mechanisms rather than the behavioral activities associated with depression (see Widlocher, 1983b).

Nevertheless, recent studies that have focused on psychomotor activity in depression have made significant and unique contributions in understanding the onset, course, and treatment assessment of depression. Neurovegetative symptoms such as psychomotor agitation and retardation occur early in the course of depressive disorder, relative to psychological symptoms of depression such as sadness and anhedonia (e.g., Kupfer et al., 1974), and thus provide a signal of the onset of depression. Neurovegetative signs have been useful in distinguishing between types of depression. For example, retardation and increased sleep and appetite are more typical of the depressive phase of bipolar disorder, whereas increased agitation is more typical of unipolar depression (e.g., Kupfer et al., 1974; Teicher, Barber, Lawrence, & Baldessarini, 1989). Finally, the presence of psychomotor retardation is well known to be a good predictor of positive outcome in several pharmacological treatments of depression.

The terms *psychomotor agitation* and *retardation* actually cover a wide range of movement behaviors. According to the *Diagnostic and Statistical Manual of Mental Disorders* (3rd ed.; DSM-III-R; American Psychiatric Association, 1980), psychomotor agitation is indicated by behaviors such as hand wringing, pacing, inability to stand or sit still, pulling or rubbing hair, pressured speech, and outbursts of complaining or shouting. Psychomotor retardation is expressed in behaviors such as slowed speech and body movements; low, monotonous, or impoverished speech; and increased pauses before answering.

One line of research in exploring the character of psychomotor agitation and retardation has relied primarily on the use of clinical measures of general motor activity. This approach involves the therapist's or staff's assessment of the general level of agitation or retardation of the patient on an Likert-type scale (e.g., overall agitation is rated on a scale that may range in values from 0 (no agitation) to 4 (severe agitation)). This type of measure is typically discussed in terms of its relationship to other clinical symptom measures or as a predictor of outcome, which is often measured by a hospital discharge decision or change in diagnostic status.

An alternative approach, which follows ethological principles, involves direct observation, coding, and analysis of specific nonverbal behaviors such as gaze duration, hand movements and body posture in naturalistic settings. Observation is completed by trained raters viewing depressed individuals most often in videotapes of psychiatric interviews, task activities, or social interactions. This approach allows for observation of very specific movement patterns as well as an assessment of the relationships among simultaneously occurring movements. Furthermore, the movements that are observed occur as part of the individual's interaction with the natural environment, allowing an understanding of the relationship of movement behaviors to goals such as affect communication and task completion.

Methodological innovations such as the use of activity monitors and observation of videotapes have significantly advanced ethological approaches to understanding emotional disorders. Activity monitors, small devices that can be unobtrusively attached to an individual's leg or wrist provide information about movement rate and patterns during the course of the day as the individual engages in routine activities (e.g., Kupfer et al., 1974). Video methodology captures a permanent record of expressive and social behaviors allowing a detailed study of movements and their relationships to each other within and across slices of time (e.g., Katz & Itil, 1974; Katz, Wetzler, Koslow, & Secunda, 1989). A predominant number of the studies reviewed in this chapter take an ethological approach and adopt these types of measures.

This chapter first identifies the nonverbal characteristics of depression associated with psychomotor agitation and retardation. The relationship between motor activity and other symptoms of depression is then discussed, especially in relation to general models of depression. Next, global measures of motor activity as well as specific nonverbal behaviors associated with communicative effort are discussed in terms of their ability to predict treatment response. A review of the nonverbal changes that occur during treatment indicates that recovery is associated with a shift from impoverished and disjointed movement behavior to a richer, more coherent and individual presentation of self. Lastly, nonverbal behavior is studied in relation to efforts to discriminate among subtypes of depression and more generally different types of psychiatric disorders.

CHARACTERISTICS OF PSYCHOMOTOR AGITATION AND RETARDATION

Although symptoms of agitation and retardation often influence the clinician's assessment of the presence of depression, the role these symptoms play is often not explicitly acknowledged. One explanation for this circumstance is that psychomotor events are often interpreted as a component of an essentially psychic symptom. Widlocher (1983b), for example, notes that retardation has often been assumed to be a characteristic of sadness, that is, an expression of a psychological state, rather than a symptom in and of itself.

In the past 15 years, research in the area of psychomotor activity has brought this viewpoint into question. This work has assessed the status of nonverbal behaviors as independent variables in the expression of depression and determined the specific movement characteristics that make up the general phenomena of agitation and retardation.

Widlocher (1983b) argues for the centrality of psychomotor symptoms in depression. He notes that psychomotor retardation is, along with self-blame, the most common symptom of depression, that retardation along with early morning awakening is better than mood as a discriminator of anxiety and depressive states (Gurney, Roth, Garside, Kerr, & Shapira, 1972), and that psychomotor change is the symptom most clearly associated with endogenous depression (Nelson & Charney, 1981). Widlocher (1983b) completed a series of studies in which he identified the various behaviors that constitute the global notion of psychomotor retardation and also determined that retardation is a discrete symptom of depression, relatively independent of other symptoms such as sadness. In these studies, clinicians rated depressed inpatients using the Hamilton Rating Scale for Depression (HRSD; Hamilton, 1960) as well as a scale devised to evaluate movements such as gait, posture, and brevity of responses—the Retardation Rating Scale (RRS; Widlocher, 1983b).

Principal component analysis of the RRS items indicated that Factor I accounted for nearly 50% of the variance and that almost all items in the scale (except, e.g., negative items such as "anxious agitation") participated in this factor. These results were taken to indicate a "unity" in the construct of retardation. The correlation between the global scores of the RRS and the HDRS was significant ($r = .68$). However, a principal component analysis of all the items from both scales indicated that the retardation items remained more closely related to each other than to the items of the HRSD. These results confirmed the notion of the unity of the retardation construct and also suggested the relative independence of the retardation from the psychological aspects of depression as measured on the HRSD.

In a similar line of investigation, Katz and colleagues analyzed the structure of the major components of the depressed state as part of the NIMH Collaborative Study on the Psychobiology of Depression (Katz et al., 1984). Eleven components of the state were identified in a sample of approximately 100 major depressive disorders examined at baseline with a battery of clinical rating, self-report inventories, and performance tests. The components included specific disturbed emotions, cognitive impairment, somatic elements, and such psychomotor attributes as motor retardation, agitation, and distressed facial expression. In that study, a second order factor analysis of the intercorrelations of the 11 components resulted in three independent principal components that accounted for 75% of the variance. On the first component, agitation, anxiety, and somatization were highly loaded; on the second, motor retardation and depressed mood.

These results indicate that agitation appears to be one of the major physical correlates of the emotional state of anxiety, whereas motor retardation is more closely associated with true depression. In severe depressive states, then, the affect and a particular type of physical manifestation—agitation or retardation—are closely linked.

A number of studies have evaluated the presence of specific nonverbal behaviors associated with agitation as well as retardation in depressed individuals. Several such studies have shown that retarded depression is associated with reduced looking (Hinchcliffe, Lancashire, & Roberts, 1971; Rutter & Stephenson, 1972; Ulrich & Harms, 1985; Waxer, 1974), reduced speaking (Bouhuys, Jansen, & van den Hoofdakker, 1991; Bouhuys & Mulder-Hajonides van der Meulen, 1984; Greden & Carroll, 1981), increased pausing (Bouhuys & Alberts, 1984; Nilsonne, 1987; Szabadi, Bradshaw, & Besson, 1976), and monotone voice (Nilsonne, 1987; Scherer, 1981). Depressed individuals show agitation by displaying increased levels of restlessness (Ulrich & Harms, 1985), hand movements and self-touching (Eckman & Friesen, 1974; Jones & Pansa, 1979; Ulrich & Harms, 1985) and gesturing (Waxer, 1977).

Specific types of nonverbal behaviors are associated with one type of psychomotor activity but not another. For example, as the preceding review indicates, retardation is associated with changes in speech such as increase in the length of pauses and reduced speaking. Agitation, however, shows no relationship to paraverbal symptoms—there is no evidence of increased speech productivity or changes in voice tone occurring in agitation experienced during depression. Rather, agitation seems to be expressed primarily through movements in the fingers, hands, legs, and torso.

A few studies have identified groups of nonverbal behaviors that occur simultaneously or that cluster together in the expression of agitation or retardation. Ulrich and Harms (1985) identified various simultaneous nonverbal behaviors by repeated viewing of videotapes of 47 endogenously depressed inpatients. From a series of items concerning various aspects of motor activity, three factors emerged, one representing retardation, the other two relevant to agitation. Depressive retardation was expressed primarily in reduced eye movement, reduced facial expression, constricted posture, and low and impoverished speech. One type of depressive agitation was characterized by gross motor movement: body touching directed to various parts of the body such as face or hair. The other type of agitation was characterized by smaller, more constricted movements in the fingers and hands that seemed amorphous or without an intended goal.

In a study of 61 unipolar and bipolar patients, Bouhuys, Jansen, and van den Hoofdakker (1991), using a similar technique, also identified two different types of agitation. One type consisted of light body touching (with only fingers and hands moving) and leg movements, whereas the other type involved object touching (e.g., plucking a chair) and wider movements in which hands were "on their way" to an object. These two types of agitation have some parallels of those described by Ulrich and Harms (1985). Light body touching overlaps with Ulrich and Harms's perceptions of "constricted" agitation in that both factors involve small and contained movements. In contrast, the larger, goal-directed movements resemble the directed body touching to face and hair described by Ulrich and Harms (1979).

The two types of agitation may represent differences in level of severity of depressive illness. For example, Bouhuys et al. (1991) note that *low* levels of baseline light touching (an aspect of "constricted agitation") have been associated with improvement (Bouhuys, Bersma, & van den Hoofdakker, 1987). The second type of agitation, comprising larger, directed movements, occurred more often with other movement factors associated with active listening (e.g., head nodding) and speaking effort (looking, gesticulating). These differences suggest that the presence of the latter type of agitation, reflecting what Bouhuys et al. (1991) called "involvement in conversation," may be a sign of relative health. High levels of movements confined to fingers and hands, in contrast, may indicate a more negative clinical picture, as they are associated with relatively slow improvement.

Although most of the preceding studies have characterized psychomotor retardation and agitation as independent phenomena, a few studies have noted the interrelationship of agitated and retarded movements. Jones and Pansa (1979), for example, have noted that though depressed inpatients exhibit retardation in decreased looking behavior and facial movement, they also show an increase in hand movement. Similarly, Ulrich & Harms (1985), noted the simultaneous appearance of both psychomotor agitation and retardation. Patients showed retardation through reduced eye movement and facial expression yet also showed agitation in larger features such as gross motor restlessness and numerous hand movements. The simultaneous production of elements of both retardation and agitation may contribute to the clinical sense of the patient as discomforted or distressed.

An alternative approach to identifying constellations of specific movement symptoms associated with particular body areas has been developed by Frey and colleagues. Their approach determines broad movement characteristics based on the activities of the whole body, such as overall mobility, complexity, and dynamic activation (Fisch, Frey, & Hirsbrunner, 1983; Frey, Jorns, & Daw, 1980). In this approach, through relatively sophisticated algorithms, specific movement characteristics that occur simultaneously are evaluated and provide the basis for identifying the "gestalt" of the individual's movement changes. In an analysis of 13 depressed inpatients, Fisch et al. (1983) found evidence of diminished mobility (time spent in motion), complexity (degree to which various parts of the body are simultaneously involved in motion), and dynamic activation (swiftness with which movements are initiated or terminated). These findings are consistent with clinical observations that depressed patients have difficulty in initiating movement and that their movement behavior is slowed down, impoverished, and monotonous.

RELATION TO OTHER SYMPTOMS OF DEPRESSION

Very few studies have directly assessed the relationship between psychomotor activities and the range of other symptoms associated with depression such as sadness and guilt. Although several studies obtain HRSD or other symptom scale ratings, the relationship between specific symptom ratings and psychomotor activity is not reported or perhaps simply not computed. Furthermore, few significant relationships do emerge when the appropriate analyses are conducted.

Nilsonne (1987), for example, evaluated the relationship between various speech measures and a global measure of sadness based on the Comprehensive Psychopathological Rating Scale (CPRS; Asberg, Montgomery, Perris, Schalling, & Sedvall, 1978). Only very few voice measures were correlated with those of clinical state. Sadness as well as retardation (but not agitation or muscle tension) were associated with a more monotonous tone of voice that has been named "the voice of depression." This finding does, however, emphasize the importance of vocal characteristics in the expression of sadness.

Bouhuys et al. (1991) studied the relationship between various nonverbal behaviors, Hamilton ratings of retardation and agitation, and a self-report measure of activation assessed by the activation-deactivation checklist (AD-ACL; Thayer, 1967) in 61 endogenously depressed inpatients. The nonverbal behaviors were based on observations of patients during a psychiatric interview and measured speech duration, head and leg movement, and gesturing activities. Patients reported information that allowed discrimination of four different types of subjective states of activation: general activation (patient feels vigorous, peppy), general deactivation (patient feels calm, placid), high activation (patient feels jittery, tense), and deactivation-sleep (patient feels drowsy, tired).

A speech factor (with items such as duration of speech) was negatively correlated with high activation and retardation, indicating that in states of activation and/or retardation, speech is diminished. A positive correlation was obtained between the speech and speech effort factors and general deactivation, suggesting that states of relative calm in depression are associated with increased verbalization and communication. Several other relationships were obtained that reiterate the findings of studies previously mentioned, such as body touching being associated with agitation. The unique contribution of this study concerns the identification of moments of relative calm in depression and their association with more positive experiences. Indeed, high levels of general deactivation were positively correlated with high levels of general activation, suggesting that experiences of calmness may allow for or enhance the experience of high energy in depression.

Finally, studies of animal behavior provide an additional source of information about the clustering of behavioral symptoms of depression. Certain environmental and biochemical manipulations produce behaviors in animals similar to those seen in depressed humans. These studies allow for the possibility of identifying biochemical and environmental causes of depression and the typical symptom clusters associated with them. Teicher et al. (1989) identified at least four independently occurring clusters of behavioral symptoms in animals that may have distinct causes and that resemble disturbances found in depressed humans. One cluster associates prominent psychomotor agitation with decreased appetite and sleep. This cluster has been associated with increases in plasma corticosteriods in animals.

The remaining three clusters are associated with prominent retardation. In one cluster, retardation may be seen with increased appetite and sleep and has been shown to be caused by amphetamine withdrawal. This type of depression in animals is also associated with an inability to perceive or obtain pleasure, as indicated by diminished initiation of self-stimulation of intracranial pleasure centers. The second retardation-based cluster includes diminished sleep and appetite. This cluster is seen in studies in which animals are placed under stress-inducing conditions, such as chronic unpredictable stress, and is associated with decreased reactivity to stress. The last retardation cluster also includes decreased appetite and sleep but is caused by conditions of separation from care figures and is also accompanied by decreased play and social interaction.

According to Teicher et al. (1989), although various circumstances may produce psychomotor agitation in animals, it occurs with the same set of symptoms and is regularly associated with increased corticosteroid levels, suggesting that syndromes in which psychomotor agitation is prominent are fairly homogenous. In contrast, retardation may be associated with three distinct symptom clusters. Teicher et al. draw parallels between the behavior of depressed humans and the three types of retardation depression seen in animals. The expression of retardation associated with lack of pleasure in animals is apparently comparable to the behaviors observed in endogenous depression in humans, such as in seasonal affective disorder or bipolar disorders, and both are presumed to have a strong neurobiological basis.

The other two types of retardation clusters have their source in environmental causes and have direct analogs in human experiences. Humans exposed to uncontrollable stress in laboratory settings have experienced depressed mood with a withdrawal or psychomotor retardation component. This model of depression has been recently described as at least partially induced in the natural environment by the presence of negative life events that the individual feels unable to control or change (see Alloy, Kelly, Mineka, & Clements, 1990). The second environmental model concerns the loss of or separation from a care figure or significant other (see Bowlby, 1980), and the same symptom clusters have been observed in both humans and primates. As Teicher et al. (1989) note, these types of depression are most likely to be viewed as reactive depression or adjustment disorders with depressed mood rather than an endogenous type of depression.

Although a symptom-cluster approach to the study of psychomotor retardation and agitation seems promising, many more studies have focused on the relationship between motor activity and single clinical measures, such as a global measure of improvement or a change in diagnostic status. These studies will be discussed in the next two sections.

PROGNOSTIC VALUE OF PSYCHOMOTOR ACTIVITY

The single most common finding concerning psychomotor activity and clinical assessment of depression is the prognostic value of psychomotor retardation. Several studies have found that the presence of retardation at pretreatment is a strong indicator of good therapeutic response to antidepressant medication (see Joyce & Paykel, 1989). Interestingly, Joyce and Paykel found that the presence of other neurovegetative symptoms such as appetite and sleep disturbance do not predict good response to antidepressants. Furthermore, among those who have failed to improve from antidepressant treatment, the continued presence of retardation along with diminished sleep and appetite are predictors of good response to ECT (Browning & Cowen, 1986). According to Browning and Cowen, these symptoms are also the first to improve following ECT and to indicate overall recovery.

Comprehensive studies of early predictors of good response to the tricyclic amitriptyline have focused on the sequence of behavioral change in depressed patients who recover (Katz et al., 1991; Katz et al., 1989). In these studies, expressive factors were both predictive of treatment response and displayed a kind of sequence of their own during the process of change. During the process of recovery, one of the first "physical" indicators of response to drugs, occurring within the 1st week of treatment, is a lessening of the facial expression of "distress"; only later, at 2 to 3 weeks of tricyclic drug treatment do we see improvement in retardation of motor functions. These effects on physical qualities appeared to reinforce the researchers' conclusions that one of the two initial effects of amitriptyline in treatment-responsive patients is on the anxiety dimension, acting only secondarily on the depressed mood or retardation components.

Several studies have indicated that baseline nonverbal behaviors associated with social or communicative activity also have predictive value. Troisi, Pasini, Bersani, Grispini, and Ciani (1989) found that nonverbal behaviors indicating high levels of assertive and affiliative behavior (e.g., lean forward, nod) predicted poor response to tricyclic medication. This finding seems inconsistent with other studies in which improvement is correlated with increased communication and interpersonal functioning (e.g., Schelde et al., 1988). An alternative interpretation of these findings is that only *low* levels of assertive and affiliative behavior are predictive of *good* response. Although the authors rule out a relationship between affiliative behavior and retardation, low levels of affiliative behavior might be related to severity of depression, or a particular type of depression in which withdrawal is prominent. This suggestion is not testable with the given data, but is consistent with the prognostic studies indicating that the presence of relatively strong maladaptive nonverbal behaviors (e.g., looking away, crouching) at baseline predicts improvement with antidepressants. Although Fossi, Faravelli, and Paoli (1984) found no behavioral predictors of response to tricyclics, Bouhuys et al. (1987) found, consistent with Troisi et al. (1989), that responders showed fewer socially interactive behaviors at baseline than nonresponders.

The preceding studies show that nonverbal behavior provides clinically relevant information concerning prognosis and treatment in ways that complement more traditional psychiatric and psychological assessment measures. An example of the potential for nonverbal measures to provide important clinical information about a patient comes from a report by Schelde et al. (1988). Five patients were followed during hospitalization for depression. At discharge, all patients were viewed as completely recovered according to Hamilton ratings and clinical assessment. One patient, however, who had been judged recovered by clinical ratings, was found to show signs of relapse as judged by his movement behaviors. Following discharge, the patient made a suicide attempt and was rehospitalized. This dramatic anecdote suggests the relative sensitivity of nonverbal measures to changes in depressive state and their potential prognostic value.

CHANGES IN NONVERBAL BEHAVIOR DURING TREATMENT

Several studies have focused on evaluations of movement behavior across time during the length of a hospital stay and have identified patterns of behavior associated with shifts in depressive state.

The treatment modalities implemented in all the studies to be discussed are pharmacological or a blend of drug and psychotherapy treatment. Typically, movement behavior is initially assessed at the end of a washout period, in which the patient is drug free. The patient is then reassessed at regular intervals from point of entry into treatment (e.g., day 1, 14, 24 . . .) until some specified time keyed to the completion of a drug trial or until the patient is determined to be recovered, usually through clinical assessment that includes the Hamilton rating scale or some other symptom measure scale.

Relative to pretreatment observation, patients evaluated as recovered show decreased pause time (Bouhuys & Mulder-Hajonides van der Meulen, 1984;

Greden & Carroll, 1981; Hoffmann, Gonze, & Mendlewicz, 1985; Szabadi, Bradshaw, & Besson, 1976) and self-touching (Jones & Pansa, 1979), and increases in overall activity levels (Kupfer et al., 1974), smiling and gazing (Hinchliffe et al., 1971; Jones & Pansa, 1979) and in amount, diversity and complexity of movement (Fisch et al., 1983; Schelde et al., 1988).

Several studies have found prominent changes in the movement behaviors associated with social and communicative activity. In the Jones and Pansa (1979) study, nonverbal behaviors such as smiling frequency and duration showed greater increases with clinical improvement in interpersonal settings (e.g., during a clinical interview), than in other settings in which smiling behavior was elicited (e.g., looking at an amusing picture). Pedersen et al. (1988) noted that behavior on the ward became more social in parallel with decreases in Hamilton ratings obtained over the course of treatment. With improved clinical status, patients were more likely to get out of bed, look at persons and objects, maintain closer physical contact with others, and send as well as respond to more communication signals. Schelde et al. (1988) determined that the greatest change in nonverbal behavior revolved around social gestures. A time-course analysis identified shifts in which specific behaviors indicated four relatively distinct phases of social or communicative change.

The first phase reflected a period of stupor marked by inactivity. The second phase, labeled the presocial phase, reflected a noticeable shift in motoric activation, as evidenced by the presence of restlessness and agitation. The third phase involved the initiation of tasks that were not directly social but involved activity preparatory to social activity, such as grooming behavior. In the last stage, the social stage, patients showed clear evidence of responding to and sending communicative gestures. This stage coincided with an assessment of clinical recovery in the individual. These findings must be viewed as preliminary because they were based on observation of only five patients. However, the observation that behaviors representing social contact and communication are the most salient features of improvement in depression is consistent with ethologically based theories of depression, which view withdrawal as a core behavioral feature of the disorder (see Klerman, 1977; Rehm, 1989).

Ulrich and Harms (1985) noted an interesting change in what at baseline had been the simultaneous presence of both agitation and retardation in depression, which conveyed an overall impression of distress or discomfort. Observations of videotapes of patients across time indicated that as patients improved, agitated and retarded movements separated in their contemporaneous production, giving the individual a greater appearance of coherence in overall body movement. Thus, the appearance of bodily coherence or well-organized movement behavior may be a hallmark of clinical improvement.

Last, Fisch et al. (1983) noted that as patients improved, complexity of movement not only increased but showed qualitative changes, so that the complexity patterns across patients became more differentiated. Although depressives' movements had a uniform look, perhaps due to their relatively impoverished nature, with improvement, the idiosyncratic or "signature" movement characteristics of the individual emerged.

The preceding several studies present a picture of the depressed individual when he or she is recovered. There appears to be a general activation along several dimensions of movements and an increase in communicative signals, representing greater interpersonal engagement. Furthermore, an overall appearance of movement coherence obtains, and the individual's characteristic movement habits reemerge, revealing more aspects of his or her movement signature or nonverbal personality.

A frequent observation in studies that evaluate indicators of improvement is that the specific behavioral changes across time as well as the size of the changes are quite varied across a patient sample. For example, although Fisch et al. (1983) found that patients recovered from depression spent more time in movement, an equally striking finding concerned the large individual differences within each evaluation period. Some patients, even when depressed, spent more than 50% of observed time in motion, while other subjects, even at recovery, spent less than 25% of their time in motion. Ellgring (1986) found that attempts to generalize over particular aspects of movement as core indicators of change failed. However, subject-by-subject analyses showed movement change readily observable for each individual: One depressed patient might show improvement by increasing gaze frequency; the other by increasing speech-related movements. Similarly, Pedersen et al. (1988) noted that although improvement was associated with increased social signals, there were great individual differences in the specific behavioral elements that changed.

Movement behavior in illness as in health admits of great individual variation. This may suggest that the clinician who wishes to use nonverbal assessment as a signal or predictor change should analyze patients' behaviors idiographically, in a case-by-case manner, using research findings to identify the most likely areas of change.

NONVERBAL BEHAVIOR ACROSS THE DEPRESSIVE SUBTYPES

Various researchers have identified different types of subsyndromes of depression—for example, hysteroid dysphoria, (Liebowitz & Klein, 1979), retarded anhedonia and agitated delusional depression (Nelson & Charney, 1981), and endogenous or reactive types of depression (e.g., Mendels & Cochrane, 1968). Each of these types of depression has been identified as having different symptom clusters, and yet there remains controversy about the validity of these systems because there is substantial overlap in symptoms when the profiles from different symptoms are compared. For purposes of clarity, this section will use the DSM-III system of classification as the reference point in the following discussion. DSM-III identifies the unipolar-bipolar distinctions as the major subtypes of depression. These subtypes are further divided by degree of severity and chronicity, with the unipolar depressions being viewed as either dysthymic or major depressive types, and the bipolar depressions categorized as either cyclothymic or bipolar disorder. Further salient characteristics include the presence of psychotic features or melancholia.

The large majority of movement behavior studies have focused on and lent support to the validity of the bipolar-unipolar distinction. Several studies that have measured overall activity, some using ambulatory activity monitors, have found that depressed bipolar patients are less active than unipolar depressives (e.g., Kupfer et al., 1974; Peery & Ingoldsby, 1980; Teicher et al., 1989; Weiss, Foster, Reynolds, & Kupfer, 1974; Wolff, Putnam, & Post, 1985). Observation of ward activities has indicated that individuals with unipolar depression have higher pacing rates (Beigal & Murphy, 1971), and standardized test evaluations have shown that while unipolar patients did not differ from normal controls in psychomotor tasks (tracing through a maze), bipolar patients were significantly slowed (Blackburn, 1975).

At least one study noted that the bipolar and unipolar patients did not differ in overall clinical severity scores (Blackburn, 1975), suggesting that the movement behavior differences reflected the distinct nature of the subtypes rather than the severity of the illness. Furthermore, movement characteristics noted during the illness disappeared with improvement (Blackburn, 1975; Kupfer et al., 1974), suggesting that these behaviors were specific to the active phase of illness and did not represent stable aspects of the individual's character, nor would they be noted during healthy periods of functioning.

A relatively new area of investigation concerns the monitoring of circadian rhythms in depressed patients (see Teicher et al., 1989). Foster and Kupfer (1975), for example, found that compared with normal controls, depressed patients showed a blunting of activities during the day but a higher than normal activity rate during the night. Distinct patterns of disturbances in the timing of activities have been found among unipolar and bipolar patients. Compared with the daily rhythm of activity level seen in normal controls, bipolar patients are phase advanced (that is, show an activity level expected at a later point in the day), whereas unipolar patients are phase delayed (show an activity level expected earlier in the day) (Teicher et al., 1989; Wolff et al., 1985). Teicher et al. (1989) suggest that daily rhythm rates may be biological markers of distinct subtypes of depression calling for different expectations about course of illness and different treatment recommendations. For example, if phase-advanced activity level is a movement marker of bipolar disorder, it would be expected that observation of this type of activity level would be an indicator for lithium carbonate treatment, whereas the presence of phase-delayed disturbances would not.

Studies of child or adolescent depression are relatively few; however, at least one study has noted a relationship between unipolar and bipolar illness that is mediated by motor activity. Strober and Carlson (1982) found that the presence of psychomotor retardation in adolescents hospitalized for the first time for major depression was one of the strongest predictors of the development of bipolarity three to four years later. This finding is consistent with the adult literature, which finds that motor retardation is a more prominent symptom of bipolar than unipolar depression.

A few studies have investigated potential differences in movement behavior among the subtypes within unipolar depression. Troisi, Pasini, Bersani, Grispini, and Ciani (1990) compared the movement behavior of individuals with DSM-III-R Dysthymia (n = 15), Major Depression with Melancholia (n = 16), and Major Depression without Melancholia (n = 13). Movement behaviors were assessed through a one-way mirror during a psychiatric interview. These behaviors fell into eight different functional categories, which were viewed as ethological in nature (i.e., pertaining to the regulation of affective communication).

The three groups differed in global HRSD score, with the dysthymic group having the lowest score and the melancholic group having the highest. In contrast, there were no differences across the groups in any of the eight functional categories. Thus, DSM-III-R unipolar subtyping was not supported by movement behavior indices. The authors note that the validity of the movement behaviors as indicators of different types of depression had already been established by their success in differentiating between bipolar and unipolar depression. Thus, they conclude that the absence of differences in movement behavior between dysthymia and major depression should prompt a reevaluation of the usefulness and validity of this particular subtyping distinction.

Some studies have found that distinguishing unipolar depression in terms of the relative predominance of agitation or retardation produces distinct movement-related and clinically useful profiles. Peery and Ingoldsby (1980), for example, found that patients with agitated, retarded, and "suicidal" depression all moved less frequently than a manic bipolar patient, as judged by microanalyses of videotapes of head and shoulder activity during a psychiatric interview. Direct comparisons among the unipolar patients showed that the three different types of depression each showed differences in the quantity but not the rate of movement, with the retarded patient moving least frequently and the agitated patient moving most frequently.

Avery and Silverman (1984) found that distinguishing unipolar depression in terms of the relative predominance of agitation or retardation produced a useful clinical profile. For example, agitated depression was associated with a greater likelihood of recovery or marked improvement, shorter hospital stays, and better and faster response to ECT, compared with those patients with retarded depression. Certain demographic characteristics were also associated with these types of depression and thus may ultimately serve as predictors of the course of illness. Psychomotor agitation was found to occur more often in women, old patients, and those with late onset of illness.

In summary, motor activity has supported the validity of the bipolar-unipolar distinction, but not the subtyping within unipolar depression. It appears that unipolar depression is more successfully or usefully classified according to the presence of predominant agitation or retardation. Because only a limited number of studies have been completed on this issue, no definitive conclusion can be reached until the results of more studies, with larger sample sizes, become available.

NONVERBAL BEHAVIOR IN DEPRESSION COMPARED WITH OTHER PSYCHIATRIC DISORDERS

Studies of nonverbal movement across different types of illnesses in relation to depression have focused predominantly on differences across subtypes of the disorder. A few studies have compared the movement behavior of depressives with individuals with other disorders, primarily schizophrenia.

Depressives' nonverbal behaviors tend to be less vague and more goal directed than schizophrenics, and in most cases, depressives' nonverbal expressions of affect are contextually appropriate, whereas those of schizophrenics might not be. Some studies indicate that hand tapping and body focused behavior have more form in depressives than in schizophrenics (Freedman & Hoffman, 1967; Steingart & Freedman, 1975). Jones and Pansa (1979) found that schizophrenics tended to exhibit behaviors that were incongruous to their current context, whereas this was not true of depressives. For example, schizophrenics might increase smiling behavior toward a morbid picture, but depressives, like normal controls, would not.

Depressives and schizophrenics do share certain nonverbal behaviors such as decreased looking and smiling and increased body touching. However, with improvement, these behaviors change in depressives to the point where their behavior appears quite similar to that of normal controls. In contrast, schizophrenics do not show significant change in body movement with clinical improvement (Jones & Pansa, 1979). It is difficult to interpret the meaning of these findings. The differences may point to the episodic or statelike nature of many characteristics of depression compared with what might be the more chronic nature of schizophrenia. Also, differences in the type of medication used and the regularity with which it is taken in the postacute phase of treatment may contribute to some of these differences.

The clinical observation that schizophrenia is associated with "flat affect" is supported by close-range videotape analyses of facial expressions. Schizophrenics show limited facial expression in small movement behaviors such as eyebrow lifting (Jones & Pansa, 1979). This flatness is not seen in depressives, who show a range of facial movement similar to that of healthy subjects but engage in certain types of behavior more or less than they do (e.g., frowning and smiling).

Levin, Hall, Knight, and Albert (1985), however, found striking similarities in the vocal characteristics of depressives and negative-symptom schizophrenics. Recorded segments of depressives and schizophrenics telling sad, happy, and neutral episodes in their lives were filtered so that vocal characteristics but not content could be discriminated. Blind raters found both depressives and negative-symptom schizophrenics to have a "flat" voice tone that showed poor differentiation across the three different types of stories. Interestingly, the depressed patients seemed less accurate than the schizophrenics in the expression of the relevant affect during storytelling, receiving their highest anger scores during the telling of the happy story and their highest happy scores during the angry story.

These findings are inconsistent with those reported by Jones and Pansa (1979), in which affectively incongruous facial expressions were seen more frequently in the schizophrenic than the depressive subjects. It could be that each disorder shows affective inaccuracies in different nonverbal domains (facial expression in schizophrenia and voice tone in depression). Differences in the types of depression and schizophrenia studied as well as differences in methodology may also contribute to differences in findings. An understanding of the sources of this inconsistency can be attained only through systematic investigation of the similarities and differences in nonverbal behaviors of these disorders.

CONCLUSION

The studies reviewed in this chapter indicate that nonverbal behaviors have clinical utility and complement more traditional methods of assessment. Movement behavior is useful in predicting response to pharmacological treatments and change in clinical status, and is contributing to the resolution of controversies concerning the categorization of subtypes of depression and its relationship to other disorders.

The relationship of nonverbal behaviors to other symptoms of depression requires further study. Research to date has concentrated on the relationship between nonverbal behaviors and global measures of depression such as "discharge from hospital." Although many studies indicate that traditional symptom measures such as the HRSD are taken contemporaneously with nonverbal behaviors and discharge decisions, this information is rarely presented. Presentation of these results, even if they do not show any relationship with other indicators, would allow some determination of relevant symptom patterns and establish directions for future research. Studies of the relationship between motor activity and other symptoms of depression might be facilitated by the development and use of more greatly elaborated theoretical models of depression. Much of the research conducted thus far has been primarily descriptive and atheoretic. Sufficient data are now available to allow biological (e.g., neuroendocrine) models and psychosocial models of depression (e.g., chronic stress, separation-despair) to guide the selection of variables for study and to predict potential relationships among them.

Finally, to expand our understanding of the functional relationship between psychomotor agitation and retardation and other aspects of depression, it would seem useful to study further the nonverbal behaviors of relatively healthy individuals in positive and sad mood states. Nonverbal behavioral change is likely to occur on a continuum, and observations of changes from the healthy to the sad to the despairing might contribute to the development of a more coherent picture of the involvement of nonverbal behaviors in affect regulation. Another promising area of research concerns the study of nonverbal behavior during social interactions because so much of nonverbal behavior appears to involve the monitoring and communication of affective state.

REFERENCES

Alloy, L. B., Kelly, K. A., Mineka, S., & Clements, C. M. (1990). Comorbidity of anxiety and depressive disorders: A helplessness–hopelessness perspective. In J. D. Maser and C. R. Cloninger (Eds.), *Comorbidity of mood and anxiety disorders* (pp. 123–137). Washington, DC: American Psychiatric Press.

American Psychiatric Association (1980). *Diagnostic and statistical manual of mental disorders* (3rd ed.). Washington, DC: Author.

Arieti, S., & Bemporad, J. (1978). *Severe and mild forms of depression: The psychotherapeutic approach.* New York: Basic Books.

Asberg, M., Montgomery, S. A., Perris, C., Schalling, D., & Sedvall, G. (1978). A comprehensive psychopathological rating scale. *Acta Scandinavica Psychiatrica, Suppl. 271,* 5–27.

Avery, D., & Silverman, J. (1984). Psychomotor retardation and agitation in depression. Relationship to age, sex, and response to treatment. *Journal of Affective Disorders, 7,* 67–76.

Beigel, A., & Murphy, D. L. (1971). Unipolar and bipolar affective illness, differences in clinical characteristics accompanying depression. *Archives of General Psychiatry, 24,* 215–220.

Blackburn, I. M. (1975). Mental and psychomotor speed in depression and mania. *British Journal of Psychiatry, 126,* 329–335.

Bouhuys, A. L., & Alberts, E. (1984). An analysis of the organization of looking and speech-pause behavior of depressive patients. *Behavior, 89,* 269–298.

Bouhuys, A. L., Bersma, D. G. M., & van den Hoofdakker, R. H. (1987). Observed behaviors during clinical interviews predict improvement in depression. *Journal of Psychopathology and Behaviour, 9,* 13–23.

Bouhuys, A. L., & Mulder-Hajonides van der Meulen, W. R. E. H. (1984). Speech timing measures of severity, psychomotor retardation and agitation in endogenously depressed patients. *Journal of Communication Disorders, 17,* 277–288.

Bouhuys, A., Jansen, C. J., & van den Hoofdakker, R. H. (1991). Analysis of observed behaviors displayed by depressed patients during a clinical interview; relationships between behavioral factors and clinical concepts of activation. *Journal of Affective Disorders, 21,* 79–88.

Bowlby, J. (1980). *Attachment and loss: Vol. 3. Loss: Sadness and depression.* New York: Basic Books.

Browning, S. M., & Cowen, P. J. (1986). Changes in mood, appetite and psychomotor retardation in depressed patients. *British Journal of Psychiatry, 149,* 371–373.

Eckman, P., & Friesen, W. V. (1969). The repertoire of nonverbal behavior—Categories, origins, usage and coding. *Semiotica, 1,* 49–98.

Ellgring, H. (1986). Nonverbal expression of psychological states in psychiatric patients. *European Archives of Psychiatry and Neurological Sciences, 236,* 31–34.

Fisch, H. U., Frey, S., & Hirsbrunner, H. P. (1983). Analyzing nonverbal behavior in depression. *Journal of Abnormal Psychology, 92,* 307–318.

Fossi, L., Faravelli, C., & Paoli, M. (1984). The ethological approach to the assessment of depressive disorders. *Journal of Nervous and Mental Disease, 172,* 332–341.

Foster, F. G., & Kupfer, D. J. (1975). Psychomotor activity as a correlate of depression and sleep in acutely disturbed psychiatric inpatients. *American Journal of Psychiatry, 132,* 928–931.

Freedman, N., & Hoffman, S. P. (1967). Kinetic behavior in altered clinical states: Approach to objective analysis of motor behavior during clinical interviews. *Perceptual and Motor Skills, 24,* 527–539.

Frey, S., Jorns, U., & Daw, W. A. (1980). A systematic description and analysis of nonverbal interaction between doctors and patients in a psychiatric interview. In S. A. Corson (Ed.), *Ethology and nonverbal communication in mental health.* (pp. 213–258), New York: Pergamon.

Greden & Carroll (1981). Psychomotor functioning in affective disorders: An overview of new monitoring techniques. *American Journal of Psychiatry, 138,* 1441–1448.

Gurney, C., Roth, M., Garside, R. F., Kerr, T. A., & Shapira, K. (1972). Studies in the classification of affective disorders. The relationship between anxiety states and depressive illnesses. II: *British Journal of Psychiatry, 121,* 162–166.

Hamilton, M. (1960). A rating scale for depression. *Journal of Neurological and Neurosurgical Psychiatry, 23,* 56–62.

Hinchliffe, M. K., Lancashire, M., & Roberts, F. J. (1971). A study of eye-contact changes in depressed and recovered psychiatric patients. *British Journal of Psychiatry, 119,* 213–215.

Hoffmann, G. M. A., Gonze, J. C., & Mendlewicz, J. (1985). Speech pause time as a method for the evaluation of psychomotor retardation in depressive illness. *British Journal of Psychiatry, 146,* 535–538.

Jones, I. H., & Pansa, H. M. (1979). Some nonverbal aspects of depression and schizophrenia occurring during the interview. *Journal of Nervous and Mental Disease, 167,* 402–409.

Joyce, P. R., & Paykel, E. S. (1989). Predictors of drug response in depression. *Archives of General of Psychiatry, 46,* 89–99.

Katz, M. M., & Itil, T. M. (1974). Video methodology for research in psychopathology and psychopharmacology. *Archives of General Psychiatry, 31,* 204–210.

Katz, M. M., Koslow, S. H., Berman, N., Secunda, S., Mass, J. W., Casper, R., Kocsis, J., & Stokes, P. (1984). A multi-vantaged approach to measurement of behavioral and affect states for clinical and psychobiological research. *Psychological Reports,* Monograph Supplement 1-V55, 619–671.

Katz, M. M., Koslow, S. H., Maas, J. W., Frazer, A., Kocisi, J., Secunda, S., Bowden, C. L., & Casper, R. C. (1991). Identifying the specific clinical actions of amitriptyline: Interrelationships of behavior, affect and plasma levels in depression. *Psychological Medicine, 21,* 599–611.

Katz, M. M., Wetzler, S., Koslow, S., & Secunda, S. (1989). Video methodology in the study of the psychopathology and treatment of depression. *Psychiatric Annals, 19,* 372–381.

Klerman, G. (1977). Anxiety and depression. In G. Burrows (Ed.), *Handbook of studies on depression.* New York: Excerpta Medica.

Kupfer, D. J., Weiss, B. L., Foster, F. G., Detre, T. P., Delagado, J., McPartland, R., & Pittsburgh, M. E. E. (1974). Psychomotor activity in affective states. *Archives of General Psychiatry, 30,* 765–768.

Levin, S., Hall, J. A., Knight, R. A., & Albert, M. (1985). Verbal and nonverbal expression of affect in speech of schizophrenic and depressed patients. *Journal of Abnormal Psychology, 94,* 487–497.

Liebowitz, M. R., & Klein, D. F. (1979). Hysteroid dysphoria. *Psychiatric Clinics of North America, 2,* 240–248.

Mendels, J., & Cochrane, C. (1968). The nosology of depression. The endogenous reactive concept of major depressive illness. *American Journal of Psychiatry, 124,* 1–11.

Nelson, J. C., & Charney, D. S. (1981). The symptoms of major depressive illness. *American Journal of Psychiatry, 138,* 1–13.

Nilsonne, A. (1987). Acoustic analysis of speech variables during depression and after improvement. *Acta Psychiatrica Scandinavica, 76,* 235–245.

Pedersen, J., Schelde, J. T. M., Hannibal, E., Behnke, K., Nielsen, B. M., & Hertz, M. (1988). An ethological description of depression *Acta Scandinavica Psychiatrica, 78,* 320–330.

Peery, J. C., & Ingoldsby, B. B. (1980). Body activity, psychological state, and psychiatric diagnosis. *Hillside Journal of Clinical Psychiatry, 2,* 87–94.

Rehm, L. P. (1989). Behavioral models of anxiety and depression. In P. C. Kendell & D. Watson (Eds.), *Anxiety and depression: Distinctive and overlapping features* (pp. 55–79). New York: Academic Press.

Rutter, D. R., & Stephenson, G. M. (1972). Visual interaction in a group of schizophrenic and depressive patients. *British Journal of Social and Clinical Psychology, 11,* 57–65.

Schelde, J. T., Pedersen, J., Hannibal, E., Behnke, K., Nielsen, B. M., & Hertz, M. (1988). An ethological analysis of depression: Comparison between ethological recording and Hamilton rating of five endogenously depressed patients. *Acta Psychiatrica Scandinavica, 78,* 331–340.

Scherer, K. R. (1981). Speech and emotional states. In J. K. Darby (Ed.), *Speech evaluation in psychiatry* (pp. 189–220). New York: Grune & Strutton.

Steingart, I., & Freedman, N. (1975). The organization of body-focused kinesic behavior and language construction in schizophrenic and depressed states. *Psychoanalysis and Contemporary Science, 4,* 423–450.

Strober, M., & Carlson, G. (1982). Bipolar illness in adolescents with major depression. Clinical, genetic, and psychopharmacologic predictors in a three to four year prospective follow-up investigation. *Archives of General Psychiatry, 39,* 549–555.

Szabadi, E., Bradshaw, C. M., & Besson, J. A. O. (1976). Elongation of pause-time in speech: A simple, objective measure of motor retardation of depression. *British Journal of Psychiatry, 129,* 592–597.

Teicher, M. H., Barber, M. I., Lawrence, J. M., & Baldessarini, R. J. (1989). Motor activity and antidepressant drug: A proposed approach to categorizing depression syndromes and their animal models. In G. F. Koob, C. L. Ehlers, & D. J. Kupfer (Eds.), *Animal models of depression.* Boston: Birkhauser.

Thayer, R. E. (1967). Measurement of activation through self-report. *Psychological Reports, 20,* 663–678.

Troisi, A., Pasini, A., Bersani, G., Grispini, A., & Ciani, N. (1989). Ethological predictors of amitriptyline response in depressed outpatients. *Journal of Affective Disorders, 17,* 129–136.

Troisi, A., Pasini, A., Bersani, G., Grispini, A., & Ciani, N. (1990). Ethological assessment of the DSM-III subtyping of unipolar depression. *Acta Psychiatrica Scandinavia, 81,* 560–564.

Ulrich, G., & Harms, K. (1979). Video-analytic study of manual kinesics and its lateralization in the course of treatment of depressive syndromes. *Acta Psychiatrica Scandinavia, 59,* 481–492.

Ulrich, G., & Harms, K. (1985). A video analysis of the nonverbal behaviour of depressed patients before and after treatment. *Journal of Affective Disorders, 9,* 63–67.

Waxer, P. H. (1977). Nonverbal cues for anxiety: An examination of emotional leakage. *Journal of Abnormal Psychology, 86,* 306–314.

Waxer, P. H. (1974). Nonverbal cues for depression. *Journal of Abnormal Psychology, 83,* 319–322.

Weiss, B. L., Foster, G., Reynolds, C. F., & Kupfer, D. J. (1974). Psychomotor activity in mania. *Archives of General Psychiatry, 31,* 379–383.

Widlocher, D. J. (1983a). Psychomotor retardation: Clinical, theoretical and psychometric aspects. In H. S. Akiskal (Ed.), *The psychiatric clinics of North America, 6,* 27–40.

Widlocher, D. J. (1983b). Retardation: A basic emotion? In J. M. Davies & J. W. Maas (Eds.), *The Affective Disorders* (pp. 99–107). Washington, DC: American Psychiatric Press.

Wolff, E. A., Putnam, F. W., & Post, R. M. (1985). Motor activity and affective illness: The relationship of amplitude and temporal distribution to changes in affective state. *Archives of General Psychiatry, 42,* 288–294.

CHAPTER 11

Eating Problems

GEORGE C. PATTON

INTRODUCTION

Body weight changes in psychiatric illnesses have long attracted attention, but nowhere has this interest been more marked than in patients with affective disorders (Kalinowsky, 1948; Post, 1956). Indeed, these body weight changes were often so greatly in excess of what could be viewed as normal that researchers earlier in this century took them to reflect an underlying physiological dysfunction in weight control intricately associated with the origins of the disorder rather than arising secondary to eating change (Altstroem, 1943). In a key review of this literature, Post noted the methodological weaknesses in early reports of weight change in depression and pointed out that no researcher had pursued the obvious course of measuring food intake and metabolic exchanges in recurrent melancholics. He furthermore suggested that the study of eating and appetite changes in the course of psychiatric disorders would be a more promising area for further inquiry than the pursuit of elusive endogenous changes in weight control. It is perhaps surprising that modern researchers have been slow to pursue this clear recommendation. Despite this lack of enthusiasm, some modest progress in developing measurement instruments and delineating the eating changes of depression has been made.

APPROACHES TO THE MEASUREMENT OF EATING IN DEPRESSION

Progress in elucidating relationships between eating change and depression is necessarily limited by the quality of instruments available for the assessment of dietary intake and its putative determinants. Such determinants might include the following:

1. Physiological responses to food—appetite, hunger, satiety, and thirst.
2. Perceptual changes—taste and smell.

3. Attitudinal changes—psychological significance of food in terms of its effect on appearance, body weight, or health.
4. Other symptoms of depression, such as social withdrawal, anxiety.
5. Premorbid eating habits.

For the most part, these potential determinants of eating in depression have not been explored. Further, some of these items, for example, change in appetite, have often been taken as a measure of eating in depression rather than being viewed as one of its determinants, albeit a probably important one. In examining the methods that have been adopted to study eating in depression, there is variation in a number of respects: in the type of information sought, in the time frame considered, and in methods used to elicit information.

Direct Measurement

Direct observation of food intake in metabolic wards offers the most sensitive and accurate means for the evaluation of eating. Such settings allow accurate measurement of nutrient intake either by developing special apparatuses to deliver food or more usually by measuring food consumed (Jordan, Wieland, Zebley, Stellar, & Stunkard, 1966). In this way, interrelationships between subjective states (e.g., hunger, palatability, or food preference), behavioral and physiological responses to dietary status can be examined. However, direct measurement is intrusive and cannot be easily extended beyond the strictly controlled environment of a metabolic ward. Naturalistic settings would be of greater interest in the study of depression. To date, there have been no studies of eating in depressed subjects using direct measurement approaches.

Indirect Measures

The evaluation of eating disturbances in depression has usually been undertaken through indirect indices of eating derived from the traditional psychiatric assessment. Typically, these are based on perceived appetite and reported weight change.

Reported Appetite

As appetite is an intrinsically subjective entity, measurement relies on self-report.

DEPRESSION INVENTORIES. Appetite loss is the usual index of eating in standardized instruments for evaluating depression. In the Montgomery-Asberg Depression rating scale (Montgomery & Asberg, 1979), designed to be sensitive to change, it is rated on a 7-point scale ranging from "a normal or increased appetite" to "needing persuasion to eat at all." On the Beck

Depression Inventory (Beck, Ward, Mendelson, Mock, & Erbaugh, 1961), it is rated on a 4-point scale ranging from "appetite being no worse than usual" to "having no appetite at all."

SPECIFIC APPETITE SCALES. Adequate measures of appetite should assess not only loss but increase in appetite. Although this approach was earlier used to evaluate appetite in other settings (Jordan et al., 1966), Paykel (1977) was the first to devise a scale for general use in depressed patients. He combined scales for both decrease and increase in appetite into a 13-point bipolar scale ranging from "little food eaten" to "severe increase in intake and preoccupation with food." The scale was rated at initial psychiatric interview with the rating made on the basis of reported appetite at the height of illness. No reference was made to validity of the measure for either instrument.

A better evaluated measure of appetite was developed by Robinson, McHugh, and Folstein (1976), who used visual analog scales to facilitate self-report. Thirty-two psychiatric inpatients with varied diagnoses and 18 staff responded to the question "How is your appetite right now?" on a scale ranging from their greatest to poorest appetites. The scale was found to have satisfactory test–retest reliability under constant conditions. Further it was shown to be predictive of crude measures of actual food intake in both groups. For the patient group, scale scores before a meal showed a high correlation with food eaten; and for the staff group, modest correlations were found with the amount of money spent at the cafeteria. This is one of the few attempts made to examine the predictive validity of reported appetite as a measure of eating.

Reported Weight Change

Next to reported loss of appetite, weight loss is the clinical item most used to evaluate eating changes in depression. Weight change has the potential advantage of being easily amenable to external validation. In a prospective design, Fernstrom, Krowinski, and Kupfer (1987), for example, studied reported weight in 50 outpatients with unipolar depression over a 4-month period of treatment with imipramine. They found that 96% of the self-reported weights were within 4 pounds of clinic weight. The accuracy of patient report of weight over the 4-month period was calculated to be 92% ± 2%. The findings suggested that, in such a setting, reported weight and by implication weight change are valid measures of true weight.

Weight loss, however, is a less satisfactory measure of eating than subjective appetite change for two reasons. First, weight change may not be manifest for some period of weeks after eating change even where the latter is marked. More importantly, weight change is a function not only of food intake but also of energy expenditure, which is likely to change in some depressed states. Nevertheless, it is commonly used in standardized assessments of depression. On the Hamilton Rating Scale (Hamilton, 1967), for example, it is evaluated on three points: no weight loss, probably weight loss during present illness, and definite weight loss.

Reports of Food Consumed

Two approaches have been commonly used in the evaluation of diet in clinical and epidemiological studies in medicine: recall and records of food consumed (Lee-Han, McGuire, & Boyd, 1989). Dietary records can be used where motivated subjects are being studied within a prospective design. Typically, subjects are asked to either estimate food and beverages consumed over a specified period or alternatively weigh and measure all food and beverages consumed. This approach does not appear to have been used in the study of eating change in depression.

For depressed subjects, the more usual approach to assessing food eaten had been recall of food eaten in recent days, assessed either at the interview or using self-report. Fernstrom et al. (1987) used this approach in the assessment of food preferences in depression. These authors devised the Pittsburgh Appetite Test (PAT), a self-report assessment, based on the subjects' recall of eating food from six nutritional classes in the week before assessment. Frequency of eating was recorded on a 5-point scale ranging from never to more than 4 times/day. This appears to be the only attempt to evaluate eating in depression beyond ratings of reported appetite and weight. Unfortunately, the authors have not provided details of validity and reliability of the instrument.

Progress in developing appropriate instruments for evaluating eating in depression has been slow. The evaluation of possible determinants of eating in depression has received scant attention, with most relevant dimensions remaining unstudied. Neither the range of possible methods of dietary evaluation nor the validity of those so far examined has received sufficient scrutiny. Assessing the validity of instruments for measuring recall of eating is by no means easy. Nevertheless, validation through comparison with eating records kept over a defined period, with biochemical indices of food consumed (e.g., 24-hour urine and fecal nitrogen, serum carotene) or by testing instruments on groups known to differ in food intake and strategies that might be adopted.

EATING IN DEPRESSION

Reported Appetite and Weight Change in Depression

Kraepelin (1921) viewed weight loss as a pathognomic sign of depression and its reversal as an early sign of recovery. Later workers suggested that it was predominantly in endogenous depression that weight loss was marked with weight loss being either trivial or absent in neurotic depressions (Kalinowsky, 1948; Post, 1956).

Early systematic studies of the symptoms in depression concurred with Kraepelin's view that anorexia with accompanying weight loss was the usual disturbance found in depression. Woodruff, Murphy, and Herjanic (1967), for example, used a structured interview to systematically evaluate symptom frequencies in 54 patients with a diagnosis of primary affective disorder drawn from an inpatient unit in St. Louis. Anorexia was reported by 87% and weight loss by 78%. In contrast, weight gain was reported by only 7%.

Paykel's (1977) study of 208 patients referring to a variety of settings in one American city was the first specifically to address appetite changes in depression. He used recall of appetite at the height of illness as the principal measure. Of these patients, 37% described marked appetite loss and a further 29%, milder appetite loss. In contrast, only 14% reported an increase in appetite, the majority of these being women. Relationships between loss of appetite and both severity and endogenous pattern of illness, as judged by the Hamilton Rating Scale, supported earlier views that decreased eating was typical of severe endogenous depressions.

More recent studies have provided diverging views on the typical eating changes found in depression. Casper et al. (1985) used measures that included the Schedule for Affective Disorder and Schizophrenia interview (SADS) (Endicott & Spitzer, 1978), the Hopkins Symptom Checklist (Derogatis, Lipman, Rickels, & Uhlenhoth, 1976), and Hamilton Rating Scale (Hamilton, 1967) to study the frequency of somatic symptoms in 85 patients with recurrent unipolar depression and a further 47 with bipolar disorder. Loss of appetite was reported by 65% of the unipolar depressives and 45% of bipolar depressives, a difference that reached statistical significance. An increase in appetite was reported by 13% of unipolar and 23% of bipolar depressives, similar rates to those of earlier studies. The difference between the two types of depression apparently resulted from the age difference between the groups, loss of appetite and weight being more common in older patients. Severity of depression was also associated with greater reported weight and appetite loss. In contrast, an increase in appetite was most common in young women, particularly those with bipolar disorders. The authors commented that the rate and level of the classic somatic symptoms of depression was a function of the severity of disorder and a patient's age.

These findings contrast with those from other recent studies of weight change in depression. Weissenburger, Rush, Giles, and Stunkard (1986) studied reported weight change in 109 outpatients from a psychiatric unit in Texas with a special interest in affective disorders. During the course of an episode of depression, weight change ranged from a loss of 33 lbs to a gain of 50 lbs. Forty percent of subjects described a mean weight gain of 17 lbs. In contrast, only 30% of this group reported a mean weight loss of 11 lbs. No gender relationship was observed, but weight loss was associated with higher scores on the Hamilton scale.

Stunkard, Fernstrom, Price, Frank, and Kupfer (1990) examined weight change over two episodes of recurrent depression in 68 patients from the Pittsburgh Maintenance Therapy project. Weight gain was prominent, with 18 of 53 patients classed as weight gainers during the initial episode as opposed to 27 of 53 who were classed as weight losers. Only 8 of 53 patients remained unchanged. The direction of weight change between episodes remained stable in that very few subjects changed the direction of weight change in the earlier episode. The variables most highly correlated with weight change were reported appetite and the body mass index as a measure of a patient's weight. The heavier the patient, the greater the weight gain. Duration of episode was found to relate to the overall degree of weight change, but no relationship between weight loss and an endogenous pattern was found. Similarly, no association was found between severity of illness and either absolute weight change or appetite.

These contrasting findings suggest that there is now less agreement about typical eating changes in depression. In large part, however, these apparently inconsistent findings might be explained by methodological differences between studies. First, differences in the study populations on dimensions such as age gender and severity of depression, which seem likely to influence the eating change in depression, might account for the varying rates of particular eating disturbances. Second, neither the relationship between these commonly used indices of eating (i.e., reported appetite and weight change) and actual dietary intake nor between these indices themselves are clear. Those studies using weight change as a central measure tend to report an increase as opposed to those with a focus on appetite where loss is more common. Because weight change is influenced by food intake but also energy expenditure, which may be altered in depression, it is understandable that changes in weight will not necessarily parallel those in appetite.

Appetite and Weight Change in Depressive Subtypes

The influence of clinical subtypes on appetite and weight change is illustrated by two suggested subtypes of depression: seasonal affective disorder (Rosenthal et al., 1984) and atypical depression (Davidson & Turnbull, 1986; Paykel, Rowan, Parker, & Bhat, 1982). In both subtypes, patterns of eating and weight change have been viewed as different from those found in typical endogenous depression.

Rosenthal et al. (1984), in the description of the seasonal affective disorder syndrome, described overeating and carbohydrate craving along with hypersomnia as typical symptoms in the depressed phase; later smaller studies have generally concurred with this view. Garvey, Wesner, and Godes (1988) reported that 67% of those with seasonal periodicity reported carbohydrate craving compared with only 23% of those without a seasonal pattern. Similarly Kräuchi and Wirz-Justice (1988) compared 28 outpatients with seasonal affective disorder (SAD) with 26 volunteers regarding food intake over the previous 12 months and found that women with SAD reported a higher carbohydrate consumption during the winter months. A later intervention study of 36 volunteers with seasonal affective disorder indicated that phototherapy diminished food craving in those subjects with a relatively high carbohydrate intake (Kräuchi, Wirz-Justice, & Graw, 1990).

Those subjects who show a good response to monoamine oxidase inhibitors have been described as atypical depressives, with a symptom constellation of increased appetite in association with evening worsening of mood and increased sleep (Davidson & Turnbull, 1982; Paykel, Rowan, Parker, & Bhat, 1982). Casper et al. (1985) described a small subgroup of 10, from a larger sample of 132 patients with either unipolar or bipolar affective disorder, in whom the features of increased appetite and increased sleeping occurred together in the depressed phase. These atypical depressives were distributed across both unipolar and bipolar groups. However, they were noted to be a young group, all under 35 years of age, and differed in having high ratings on depression and hostility but lower ratings on agitation than typical depressives.

Food Preferences in Depression

Fernstrom et al. (1987) broadened the focus of studies of eating in depression with a study of food preferences in 50 depressed outpatients, examined during 16 weeks of treatment with imipramine and psychotherapy. The Pittsburgh Appetite Test, a self-report measure based on the recall of the frequency of intake of specified foods, was used to ascertain preferred food categories. During the depressed phase, subjects reported modest increases in their preferences for high calorie/high carbohydrate foods. The authors concluded that food preferences in depression were determined by the taste rather than the nutritional value of food or a subject's appetite in that the sweetness of the high calorie/high carbohydrate foods appeared to be the key element.

In summary, it seems that eating and weight change are common in depression but that there is considerable variability in the nature of these changes between patients. There are indications that weight gain and increased appetite are particularly common in young women, whereas anorexia and weight loss, for long considered typical indicators of changed eating in depression, are more likely in the severe depressions of the elderly. It is probably wise to be cautious in the interpretation of these findings as methodological differences between studies are likely to have influenced findings. Most patients so far studied have been derived from psychiatric inpatient or outpatient facilities, and the symptoms observed are therefore more likely to be typical of severe and chronic disorders. However, depression is more likely to be present in a primary care setting (Goldberg & Huxley, 1980). So far there have been no reports of the frequency of eating changes found in depression in this or general population settings. It is therefore difficult to draw conclusions about the eating changes that may occur in less severe forms of depression.

DEPRESSION IN EATING DISORDERS

The relationship between symptoms of depression and eating disturbance has also been studied from the perspective of depression arising in the course of patients with eating disorders. In contrast to the relative neglect of studies of eating changes in depression, there has been considerable interest in this area (Halmi, 1985; Levy, Dixon, & Stern, 1989; Swift, Andrews, & Barklage, 1986; Szmukler, 1987). In part, this interest arises from the high prevalence rates of major depression in underweight patients with anorexia nervosa, estimated to lie between 40% and 60% (Hendren, 1983; Herzog, 1984; Laessle, Kittle, Fichter, Wittchen, & Pirke, 1987; Piran, Kennedy, Garfinkel, & Owens, 1985). Further, a higher rate of affective disorder in family members and similarities in the neuroendocrine profile have further raised interest in the relationships between the two disorders.

In general, a close relationship exists between the severity of weight loss and the prominence of depressive symptoms. Eckert, Goldberg, Halmi, and Casper (1982), for example, studied 105 women with anorexia nervosa prior to their joining an inpatient treatment program. Using self-report and nurse ratings, they found mild-to-moderate levels of depression, which correlated with indices of the severity of eating disorder. Similarly, Herpetz-Dahlmann and Remschmidt (1989) demonstrated the resolution of depression with effective treatment for weight loss, providing support for a view of depression being secondary to weight loss. Of some importance for the interpretation of symptoms of depression in subjects where weight loss is marked are the difficulties in distinguishing between the manifestations of starvation and those of depression.

Yet more attention has been focused on depression in simple bulimia and bulimia nervosa, where again high rates have been reported. Russell (1979), in his delineation of the syndrome, noted that 37% of his series described previous suicide attempts. Rates of depression ranging from 24% (Herzog, 1986) to 79% (Viesselman & Roig, 1985) have been subsequently reported, with the mood disorder sometimes preceding the eating disorder. The close relationship between depressive symptoms and eating disorder is further supported by a cohort study in adolescent girls where the development of milder bulimic disorders was accompanied by higher scores on measures of depression and neurotic symptoms (Patton, Johnson-Sabine, Wood, Mann, & Wakeling, 1990). However, as yet, the nature of this relationship between the depression and eating disturbance in bulimia nervosa is uncertain.

DETERMINANTS OF EATING CHANGES IN DEPRESSION

There has been little attempt to study the determinants of eating change in depression. To a large extent, this could be viewed as a result of a focus on indirect measures of dietary intake and a subsequent confounding of influences (e.g., appetite) and consequences (weight change).

Dietary Restraint

The concept of dietary restraint derives from Schachter's hypothesis (1971) that the eating patterns of the obese are stimulus bound and they are therefore more likely to rely on conscious dietary restraint to control their food intake. Dietary restraint encompasses common dieting behaviors such as eating small amounts, counting calories, not eating to satiation, and avoiding fattening foods. This restraint was viewed as fragile and liable to break down in situations of high emotional arousal such as is likely to occur during anxiety or depression. Although there is no doubt that dietary restraint and obesity are causally related, there is evidence that subjects who exhibit dietary restraint differ from others in their eating patterns. Ruderman (1985), for example, studied eating in 105 female students, assessing specifically the influence of dietary restraint on eating when a dysphoric mood state was experimentally induced. The potential importance of dietary restraint on eating was supported in that restrained eaters ate comparatively more, after earlier food consumption, when drinking alcohol and—most relevantly—during the dysphoric state.

A link between dietary restraint and the weight change of depression was suggested by Polivy and Herman (1976) in a small study of depressed outpatients. The findings indicated that unrestrained eaters lost weight when depressed, whereas restrained eaters tended to gain. This hypothesis was examined in a further study using Stunkard and Messick's Eating Questionnaire (1985; Weissenburger et al., 1986). This self-report questionnaire distinguishes three dimensions of eating: restraint, disinhibition, and hunger. Self-reported weight changes during a current episode of depression were estimated by 109 depressed outpatients. Weight gain was reported by 39% of subjects and weight loss by 30%. Depressives who gained weight were found to score more highly on each dimension of the Eating Questionnaire, with the influence of disinhibition being most prominent. However, as these patients were evaluated during a depressive episode it is not possible to ascertain to what extent these eating constructs were long-standing or secondary to the subjects' depressed mood state.

Later studies of eating during experimentally induced unpleasant mood states have also supported a role for previous dietary restraint in determining the amount of food eaten during dysphoria and depression. Frost, Goolkasian,

Ely, and Blanchard (1982) examined 68 female psychology undergraduate volunteers for food consumption during a dysphoric mood state. Restrained eaters consumed more food during the dysphoric state. Further experimental evidence for the influence of dietary restraint was provided by Ruderman (1985), who suggested that concern with dieting specifically was the best predictor of the amount of food consumed during an induced dysphoric state. Although the relevance of these studies for the understanding of eating disturbances in other abnormal mood states is not proven, the findings are consistent with a role for earlier dietary restraint in determining a subject's pattern of eating during depression.

Loss of Taste

Changes in food preference linked to changes in taste have been suggested in both depressed subjects and in animal models of depression. In rats subject to unpredictable mild stresses over a 5- to 9-week period, a reduction in sucrose preference has been noted (Willner, Towell, Sampson, Sophokleous, & Muscat, 1987). It was, however, unclear whether this represented a specific effect due to change in taste or results from a more general anhedonia. It is noteworthy that such changes were reversed after 2 to 4 weeks of treatment with a tricyclic antidepressant.

In their study of 50 depressed outpatients, Fernstrom et al. (1987) suggested that the preference for high-carbohydrate/high-fat foods appeared related to the taste rather than nutrient content of this type of food. However, this finding contrasts with those of Settle, Doty, Abelman, and Winokur (1987), who studied taste and odor recognition in depression. Although no differences between depressed subjects and controls emerged on tests of smell, the intensity of sucrose taste was diminished in depressed subjects, a factor these authors suggested could be related to diminished appetite in depression.

Eating Disturbance as Cause of Depression

A number of sources suggest that not only may depression affect dietary intake but that conversely eating disturbance may affect mood state. First, the high rates of depression found in eating disorders usually arise secondary to the eating change and tend to reverse with resolution of the eating difficulties. Similarly, early studies of patients undergoing strict dietary treatment for obesity indicated that depression commonly occurred after around 10 days of treatment or a weight loss of about 8 kg (Stunkard & Rush, 1974).

Perhaps the most convincing demonstration of the effect of starvation on mood state comes from Keys (1950), who studied conscientious objectors, placed on a semistarvation diet over a period of months. As weight loss progressed, these young men exhibited increasing symptoms of depression, irritability, nervousness, and emotional instability. Other symptoms commonly found in depression—social withdrawal, narrowing of interests, loss of sexual drive, and difficulty in concentration—became prominent. The overlap with symptoms of depression is striking and the symptom reversal with reinstatement of a normal diet further demonstrates the causal role of food deprivation in inducing mood changes in this group. It further demonstrates the difficulties that may arise in disentangling whether symptoms arise from a primary affective disorder or from starvation-related changes in subjects where weight loss is pronounced.

Animal experimentation provides further evidence that diet may affect mood. It also indicates that this effect may be mediated through brain monoamine pathways. A carbohydrate-rich, protein-poor diet fed to fasting rats reduces the levels of large neutral amino acids (e.g., leucine, isoleucine, and valine) but not tryptophan, a precursor of 5-hydroxy tryptamine. Because tryptophan competes with these amino acids for uptake into the brain, there is a consequent accelerated production and release of 5-HT. In animals, this produces a reduced awareness of environmental stimuli. A high-protein meal after fasting has the opposite effect on tryptophan uptake in rats.

This putative model has been tested in humans. Spring, Maller, Wurtman, Digman, and Cozolino (1983) studied the effects of protein and carbohydrate meals at various times of the day in 184 adults. Subjects were assigned to either protein or carbohydrate meal types that were consumed at either breakfast or lunch. Sleepiness was assessed with the Stanford Sleepiness Scale and mood with both the Profile of Mood States (POMS) and visual analog scales. Performance was evaluated using auditory reaction time, and dichotic shadowing approaches were used. Gender and age differences in response to the meals were noted. Carbohydrates were associated with postprandial sleepiness in women and calmness in men. Older subjects reported feeling tenser and less calm after a protein meal. In contrast, a high-carbohydrate lunch was found to bring about poorer concentration and lapses in attention in order subjects.

Studies of obese subjects also support an effect of carbohydrate consumption on mood. Lieberman, Wurtman, and Chew (1986) administered a test meal to two groups of obese subjects: 23 subjects with and 14 without a history of high-carbohydrate consumption. In the latter group, a high-carbohydrate test meal was accompanied by an increase in fatigue, sleepiness, and diminished alertness. In the high-consumption carbohydrate group, the opposite was observed, leading these workers to propose a hypothesis that a high-carbohydrate meal, in leading to changes in tryptophan uptake, could in some subjects be viewed as a form of self-medication. This might explain the carbohydrate craving observed in some depressed subjects.

In summary, evidence has emerged that diet may have a short-lived effect on mood state, possibly mediated through brain monoamine activity. Where eating difficulties persist, more pervasive changes in mood may occur. The extent to which such changes may be clinically significant in accentuating the symptoms of depression is as yet unclear.

Antidepressants and Eating

The role of antidepressant medication both in reversing the eating changes found in depression and in causing abnormal eating has received attention. Paykel, Mueller, and De la Vergne (1973), examined appetite and craving for carbohydrates in 51 depressed women during a trial of maintenance therapy with amitriptyline. The group continuing with amitriptyline gained on average 2.5 kg more than the placebo group over 6 months. This weight gain was found to be dose related. Ratings of overall appetite did not differ, but craving for carbohydrates was significantly greater in the maintenance group. Both findings remained significant when level of persisting depression was considered as a covariate.

In a study examining shorter term weight and appetite changes during a 6-week course of a treatment for depression, Harris, Young, and Hughes (1984) examined 168 depressed outpatients, who received seven different antidepressant regimens. Weight was recorded at the outset and at 6 weeks, appetite assessed on a 7-point scale, and consumption of carbohydrate-containing foods on a 3-point scale. A greater weight increase occurred in the group treated with an isocarboxazid and trimipramine combination, though differences between regimens were not great. Determinants of weight change over the 6-week treatment period included low weight, diminished appetite, and less carbohydrate craving at presentation. Absence of a previous history of tending to eat when stressed was similarly predictive of weight gain. Patients presenting with normal appetite rating tended to remain stable in weight after 6 weeks of treatment. The authors concluded that in the short term the depression itself and secondary loss of restraint are the most important determinants of eating. In the longer term, it remains possible the antidepressant therapy will become a more important determinant of weight change.

COURSE AND OUTCOME OF EATING PROBLEMS IN DEPRESSION

Apart from studies examining weight and eating changes associated with antidepressant treatment, the course of eating changes in depression has received little attention. Similarly little has been written on the onset of eating changes in relation to other symptoms of depression. However, Kraepelin's (1921) view that a return to normal eating is an early sign of recovery in depression has been borne out in recent studies. In their study of appetite and food preference changes in 50 depressed outpatients during a 4-month course of imipramine treatment, Fernstrom et al. (1987) found that in patients presenting with appetite loss, recovery of appetite took place usually within the 1st month of treatment with imipramine. By comparison, weight increase was often delayed to the 2nd or 3rd month.

TREATMENT OF EATING PROBLEMS IN DEPRESSION

Despite evidence that depressive symptoms may develop secondary to eating disturbance and that tryptophan may be a useful adjunct to treatment in depression there have been no studies examining the efficacy of measures to correct dietary insufficiencies found in depressed subjects. However, animal studies suggest that food deprivation resulting in moderate weight loss can attenuate the ability of tricyclic antidepressants to reverse depressive-like behaviors. Soubrié, Martin, Massol, and Gaudel (1988) examined the capacity of imipramine to reverse the behavioral changes brought about in rats previously exposed to uncontrollable stress and found this to be diminished for rats that had been mildly starved. The most likely explanation appeared to be a reduction in receptor sensitivity; the authors suggested that such considerations may be relevant in studies examining the efficacy of antidepressants and, specifically, treatment resistance in humans.

FUTURE DIRECTIONS

Although modest steps have been taken to delineate the eating changes that occur in depression, researchers have in large part failed to follow Post's (1956) recommendations. This would seem to be the result of methodological problems that still need to be addressed.

Measurement Issues

Too little attention has been paid to the distinction between eating change and its determinants. Measures so far used are generally indirectly related to an underlying construct of eating change. Such relationships require clarification, and further measures might extend beyond those so far examined to include evaluations of physiological responses to food, perceptual changes relevant to eating, attitudinal change, and further evaluation of previous eating habits and their influence on eating in the depressed state.

Study Populations

To date, most studies have taken place in selected groups often with severe depressions. To allow generalization of findings, future studies of eating disturbance in depression might include more representative subjects.

Study Design

Most studies of eating in depression have used a cross-sectional retrospective methodology to evaluate the relationship. Future studies might adopt cohort designs to better elucidate issues such as the influence of the aforementioned determinants on eating, time course of the relationship between eating changes and mood, and the significance of eating changes prognostically and as early indicators of relapse.

REFERENCES

Altstroem, C. H. (1943). Über Gewichtsschwankungen bei Geisteskranken. *Acta Psychiatrica et Neurologica.* Supplement 26.

Amsterdam, J. A., Settle, R. G., Doty, R. L., Abelman, E., & Winokur, A. (1987). Taste and smell perception in depression. *Biological Psychiatry, 22,* 1481–1485.

Beck, A. T., Ward, C. H., Mendelson, M., Mock, J., & Erbaugh, J. (1961). An inventory for measuring depression. *Archives of General Psychiatry, 4,* 561–571.

Casper, R. C., Redmond, E., Katz, M. M., Schaffer, C. B., Davis, J. M., & Koslow, S. H. (1985). Somatic symptoms in primary affective disorder. *Archives of General Psychiatry, 42,* 1098–1105.

Davidson, J., & Turnbull, C. D. (1986). Diagnostic significance of vegetative symptoms in depression. *British Journal of Psychiatry, 148,* 442-446.

Davidson, J. T. R., & Turnbull, C. D. (1982). Loss of appetite and weight associated with the MAO inhibitor isocarboxazid. *Journal of Clinical Pharmacology, 2,* 263–266.

Derogatis, L. R., Lipman, R. S., Rickels, K., Uhlenhoth, E. H. (1976) in "Psychological Measures in Psychopharmacology" (Ed. P. Pichot). Koryer Baset.

Eckert, E. D., Goldberg, S. C., Halmi, K. A., Casper, R. C., & Davis, J. M. (1982). Depression in anorexia nervosa. *Psychological Medicine, 12,* 115–122.

Endicott, J., & Spitzer, R. L. (1978). The Schedule for Affective Disorders and Schizophrenia. *Archives of General Psychiatry, 35,* 373–382.

Fernstrom, M. H., Krowinski, R. L., & Kupfer, D. J. (1987). Appetite and food preference in depression: Effects of imipramine treatment. *Biological Psychiatry, 22,* 529–539.

Frost, R. O., Goolkasian, G. A., Ely, R. J., & Blanchard, F. A. (1982). Depression, restraint and eating behaviour. *Behaviour Research and Therapy, 20,* 113–121.

Garvey, M. J., Wesner, R., & Godes, M. (1988). Comparison of seasonal and nonseasonal affective disorders. *American Journal of Psychiatry, 145,* 100–102.

Goldberg, D., & Huxley, P. (1980). *Mental illness in the Community: The pathways to psychiatric care.* London and New York: Tavistock.

Halmi, K. A. (1985). Relationship of the eating disorders to depression. *International Journal of Eating Disorders, 4,* 667–680.

Hamilton, M. (1967). Development of a rating scale for primary depressive illness. *British Journal of Social and Clinical Psychiatry, 6,* 278–296.

Harris, B., Young, J., & Hughes, B. (1984). Changes occurring in appetite and weight during short-term antidepressant treatment. *British Journal of Psychiatry, 145,* 645–648.

Hendren, R. L. (1983). Depression in anorexia nervosa. *Journal of the American Academy of Child and Adolescent Psychiatry, 22,* 59–62.

Herpetz-Dahlmann, B., & Remschmidt, H. (1989). Anorexia nervosa und Depression. *Nervenarzt, 60,* 490–495.

Herzog, D. B. (1984). Are anorexia and bulimia nervosa patients depressed? *American Journal of Psychiatry, 141,* 1594–1597.

Jordan, H. A., Wieland, W. F., Zebley, S. P., Stellar, E., & Stunkard, A. J. (1966). Direct measurement of food intake in man: A method for the objective study of eating behaviour. *Psychosomatic Medicine, 28,* 836–842.

Kalinowsky, L. B. (1948). Variation of body weight and mental illness and their relation to shock treatments. *Journal of Nervous and Mental Diseases, 108,* 423.

Keys, A. (1950). *The biology of human starvation.* Minneapolis: University of Minnesota Press.

Kraepelin, E. (1921). *Manic-depressive insanity and paranoia.* Edinburgh: Livingstone.

Kräuchi, K., & Wirz-Justice, A. (1988). The four seasons: Food intake frequency in seasonal affective disorder. *Psychiatry Research, 25,* 323–338.

Kräuchi, K., Wirz-Justice, A., & Graw, P. (1990). The relationship of affective state to dietary preference: Winter depression and light therapy as a model. *Journal of Affective Disorders, 20,* 43–53.

Laessle, R. G., Kittle, S., Fichter, M. M., Wittchen, H. U., & Pirke, K. M. (1987). Major affective disorder in anorexia nervosa and bulimia—A descriptive diagnostic study. *British Journal of Psychiatry, 151,* 785–789.

Lee-Han, H., McGuire, V., & Boyd, N. F. (1989). A review of the methods used by studies of dietary measurement. *Journal of Clinical Epidemiology, 42,* 269–279.

Lieberman, H. R., Wurtman, J. J., & Chew, B. (1986). Changes in mood after carbohydrate consumption among obese individuals. *American Journal of Clinical Nutrition, 44,* 772–778.

Levy, A. B., Dixon, K. N., & Stern, S. L. (1989). How are depression and bulimia related? *American Journal of Psychiatry, 146,* 162–169.

Montgomery, S., & Asberg, M. (1979). A new depression rating scale designed to be sensitive to change. *British Journal of Psychiatry, 134,* 382–389.

Patton, G. C., Johnson-Sabine, E., Wood, K., Mann, A. H., & Wakeling, A. (1990). Abnormal eating attitudes in London schoolgirls—A prospective epidemiological study: Outcome at twelve month follow-up. *Psychological Medicine, 20,* 383–394.

Paykel, E. S. (1972). Correlates of a depressive typology. *Archives of General Psychiatry, 27,* 203–210.

Paykel, E. S. (1977). Depression and appetite. *Journal of Psychosomatic Research, 21,* 401–407.

Paykel, E. S., Mueller, P. S., & De la Vergne, P. M. (1973). Amitriptyline, weight gain and carbohydrate craving: A side effect, *British Journal of Psychiatry, 123,* 501–507.

Paykel, E. S., Rowan, P. R., Parker, R. R., & Bhat, A. V. (1982). Merponie to phenelzine and amitriptyline in subtypes of outpatient depression. *Archives of General Psychiatry, 39,* 527–534.

Piran, P. D., Kennedy, S., Garfinkel, P. E., & Owens, M. (1985). Affective disturbance in eating disorders. *Journal of Nervous and Mental Disease, 173,* 395–400.

Polivy, J., & Herman, C. P. (1976). Clinical depression and weight change: A complex relation. *Journal of Abnormal Psychology, 85,* 338–340.

Post, F. (1956). Body-weight changes in psychiatric illness: A critical survey of the literature. *Journal of Psychosomatic Research, 1,* 219–226.

Robinson, R. G., McHugh, P. R., & Folstein, M. F. (1976). Measurement of appetite disturbances in psychiatric disorders. *Journal of Psychiatric Research, 12,* 59–65.

Rosenthal, N. E., Sack, D. A., Gillin, J. C., Lewy, A. J., Goodwin, F. K., Davenport, Y., Mueller, P. S., Newsome, D. A., & Wehr, T. A. (1984). Seasonal affective disorder. *Archives of General Psychiatry, 41,* 71–80.

Ruderman, A. J. (1985). Dysphoric mood and overeating: A test of the restraint theory's disinhibition hypothesis. *Journal of Abnormal Psychology, 94,* 78–85.

Russell, G. F. M. (1979). Bulimia nervosa: An ominous variant of anorexia nervosa. *Psychological Medicine, 9,* 429–443.

Schachter, S. (1971). Some extraordinary facts about obese humans and rats. *American Psychologist, 26,* 129–144.

Soubrié, P., Martin, P., Massol, J., & Gaudel, G. (1988). Attenuation of response to antidepressants in animals by reduction in food intake. *Psychiatry Research, 27,* 149–159.

Spring, B., Maller, O., Wurtman, J., Digman, L., & Cozolino, L. (1983). Effects of protein and carbohydrate meals on mood and performance: Interactions with age and sex. *Journal of Psychiatric Research, 17,* 155–167.

Stunkard, A. J., Fernstrom, M. H., Price, A., Frank, E., & Kupfer, D. J. (1990). Direction of Weight Change in Recurrent Depression. *Archives of General Psychiatry, 47,* 857–860.

Stunkard, A. J., & Messick, S. (1985). The Three-Factor Eating Questionnaire to measure dietary restraint, disinhibition and hunger. *Journal of Psychosomatic Research, 29,* 71–81.

Stunkard, A. J., & Rush, J. (1974). Dieting and depression reexamined. *Annals of Internal Medicine, 81,* 526–533.

Swift, W. J., Andrews, D., & Barklage, N. E. (1986). The relationship between affective disorder and eating disorders. *American Journal of Psychiatry, 143,* 290–299.

Szmukler, G. I. (1987). Some comments on the link between anorexia nervosa and affective disorder. *International Journal of Eating Disorders, 6,* 181–189.

Viesselman, J. O., & Roig, M. (1985). Depression and suicidality in eating disorders. *Journal of Clinical Psychiatry, 46,* 118–124.

Weissenburger, J., Rush, J. A., Giles, D. E., & Stunkard, A. J. (1986). Weight change in depression. *Psychiatry Research, 17,* 275–283.

Willner, P., Towell, A., Sampson, D., Sophokleous, S., & Muscat, R. (1987). Reduction of sucrose preference by chronic unpredictable mild stress and its restoration by a tricyclic antidepressant. *Psychopharmacology, 93,* 358–364.

Woodruff, R. A., Murphy, G. E., & Herjanic, M. (1967). The natural history of affective disorders: Symptoms of 72 patients at the time of index hospital admission. *Journal of Psychiatric Research, 5,* 255–263.

CHAPTER 12

Sleeping Problems

ROSALIND D. CARTWRIGHT

INTRODUCTION

A sleep disturbance almost nightly is one of a group of nine symptoms, any five of which are required to make a diagnosis of a major depressive episode according to the *Diagnostic and Statistical Manual of Mental Disorders* (3rd ed.-rev.; DSM IIIR; American Psychiatric Association, 1987). The subjective experience of this disturbance is likely to be one of poor quality of the night's sleep and/or inadequate total amount of sleep, leaving the patient feeling disturbed at night and unrefreshed in the morning. Typically, patients describe their difficulty as one of initiating sleep, middle of the night awakenings, and early morning awakenings. In other words, initial, middle, and terminal insomnias are all part of the subjective experience common in the affective disorders. At the other end of the spectrum, a few patients report being sleepy all the time despite longer than normal time asleep at night. This is more likely to be the case in those with bipolar, than in those with unipolar depression (Detre et al., 1972). The rough proportions of those reporting too little sleep and too much sleep are about 85% to 15%.

With the advent of laboratories for the continuous monitoring of sleep on an all-night basis, it became possible to detail the specific nature of the sleep disturbances associated with depressive disorders on a more objective basis. This literature is now extensive and somewhat controversial in many of its aspects. Reynolds and Kupfer (1987) have reviewed it recently.

One area of debate arises because the criteria for measuring the distinctive features of the sleep associated with the depressive disorders have not been standardized and, as a consequence, results have not always been comparable from study to study. Knowles, MacLean, and Cairns (1982) have addressed this problem directly by comparing the differences in results arising from scoring the same group of patient records by five different criteria currently in use. This brought the problem to the attention of those concerned but did not resolve the issues.

The sleep abnormality associated with major depression that has proved to be most robust has to do with the timing of rapid eye movement (REM) sleep and the distribution within REM of the phasic events (the number of rapid eye movements per 30-second epoch). The strongest of these findings is that REM sleep begins too early in the night. This is known as a reduced, or short, REM latency. This has been reported by many laboratories to be a characteristic of the sleep of a large proportion, but not all, medication-free patients while they are diagnosably depressed. What is more, this has been found to be characteristic of many different types of patients with depressive disorders, outpatients as well as inpatients (e.g., Akiskal, 1984; Coble, Gordon, & Kupfer, 1976; Duncan, Pettigrew, & Gillin, G., 1979; Kupfer, 1976; Rush, Giles, Roffwarg, & Parker, 1982; Schulz, Lund, Cording, & Dirlich, 1979), although the proportion of patients showing this sign is higher (80%) among inpatients than outpatients (30%–50%), suggesting that it may relate to the severity of the depression.

Not only has the first REM sleep period of the night been found to begin too early in the sleep of the depressed in comparison with age-matched normals, this period often lasts too long—up to double the length of a first REM period in nondepressed individuals. In addition, some investigators have reported that this early, long, first REM also contains more rapid eye movements than expected (Kupfer, Foster, Coble, McPartland, & Ulrich, 1978). Cartwright (1983) also reported that the expected sequence of increasing eye movements from REM to REM across the night is not present in the depressed.

Another abnormality of the REM system has to do with the distribution of REM time across the night. Vogel (1981) found that the first half of the night appears to contain a disproportionate amount of REM sleep in comparison with the normal proportion of one third. In the depressed individual, half or more of the total REM sleep may occur in the first half of the night (see Table 12.1 and Figures 12.1 and 12.2).

TABLE 12.1. Difference Between REM Sleep in Depressed and Normal Persons

Variable	Normal Group	Depressed Group
First REM		
Latency	80–120 min	< 60 min
Eye movement density	< 1.5 per min	> 1.5 per min
Duration	8–12 min	20 min
All night		
REM distribution in first half of night	1/3	1/2
Eye movement distribution	Successively higher with each REM stage	Sequence irregular

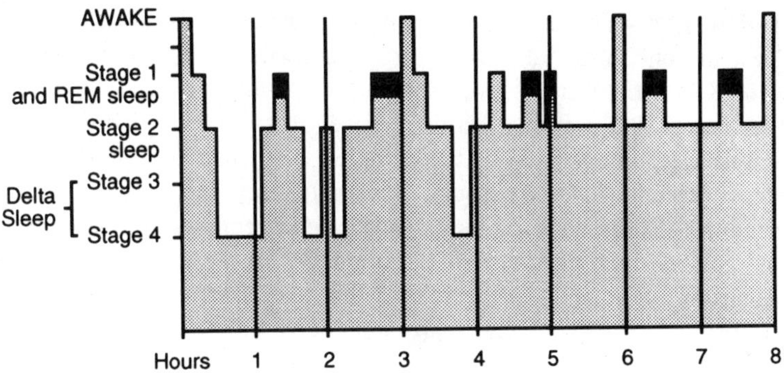

Figure 12.1. Normal sleep architecture.

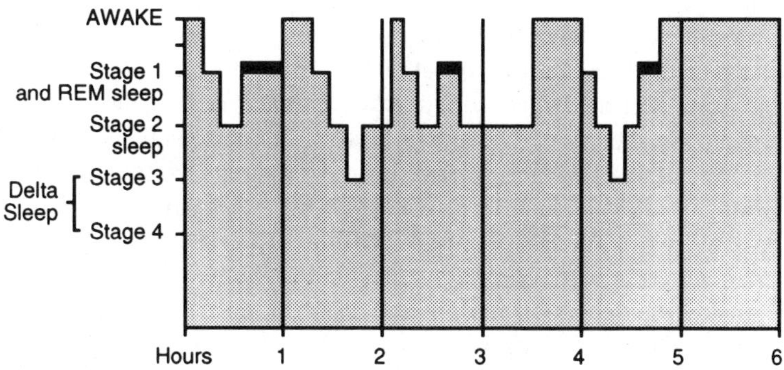

Figure 12.2. Depressed sleep architecture.

THE SENSITIVITY AND SPECIFICITY OF THE SLEEP DISTURBANCE

That these REM-related differences are found in most, but not all, depressed patients raised several questions about their sensitivity. Carroll (1979) and Kupfer and Thase (1983) have each reviewed many studies using the two most prominent sleep signs, a reduced REM latency and increased eye movement density (REM activity), to determine their sensitivity in characterizing the sleep of depressed patients. They report that the sensitivity ranges from 61% to 90%. Are the reported inconsistencies from study to study due to differences in measurement? For example, how short does a REM latency need to be to be considered short? This criterion is sometimes set at less than 60 minutes, whereas other studies use a cutoff of 65 minutes. In some studies, the first night is discarded, while in others it is averaged in with a second night. These are only a few of the sleep-scoring differences that may give rise to differences in sensitivity.

Another factor that may lead to differences in findings is inconsistencies in the diagnostic homogeneity of the samples, or to age differences. Childhood depressions appear to be associated with different sleep signs than those found in adults. Here the shortened REM latency follows remission rather than being episode-related. The depressed elderly are also different from the other two groups. There is now evidence that age is an important factor to take into account in interpreting depression sleep signs (Gillin et al., 1981; Puig-Antich et al., 1983).

Aside from the measurement issues, there is a second area of controversy about the uniqueness of these disturbances of sleep to the depressed. This has to do with the specificity of these findings to this diagnosis. Are the REM abnormalities limited to depression or are these shared by patients with other psychiatric disorders, sleep disorders, or some other diagnosis? A number of studies have also addressed this question.

Two groups—Gillin, Duncan, Pettigrew, Frankel, and Snyder (1979) and Vogel, Vogel, McAbee, and Thurmond (1980)—have studied the question of overlap between the REM sleep measures in depressed patients and those suffering from chronic insomnia. Both studies showed clear differences between the sleep troubles of these two groups. Gillin et al. (1979) and Vogel et al. (1980) both report shorter REM latencies and higher eye movement density in REM among the depressed than in age-matched normals or chronic insomniac patients. Depressed sleep is not just bad sleep; it is more specifically a REM-sleep-related problem. This is potentially a very interesting psychological finding since REM is so closely associated with dreaming, and dreaming is so closely associated with affect, and depression with dysphoric affect. When something is wrong with REM, it may well relate to the affect problems characteristic of depression.

Other psychiatric populations have been studied with the same measures to discover if they, too, show a REM sleep disturbance. Zarcone, Benson, and Berger (1987) reported that schizophrenic and major depressive disorder patients did not differ in REM latency, although these were shorter for both patient groups than normal controls. A study by Keshavan et al. (1990) showed that schizophrenics with a family history of affective disorder have significantly shorter latencies to the first REM than those whose family history shows no affective disorder.

Obsessive-compulsive patients, too, have been reported to have a lower REM latency than normals (Insel et al., 1982) as do some borderline patients (Akiskal, 1981; Bell, Lycaki, Jones, Kewala, & Sitaram, 1983). Although there is some overlap of the short REM latency sign with some other psychiatric disorders, none appear to show the same constellation of REM signs, the prolonged first REM period, increased REM density, and higher proportion of REM sleep in the first half of the night as well.

The specificity question must include this aspect: Not only do other disorders share the same sleep findings but also do some disorders that might be expected to share these findings fail to produce them? Sleep studies have been done in two other psychiatric conditions with disturbed affect: patients with panic disorder (Akiskal, 1981, 1984) and generalized anxiety disorder (Reynolds, Shaw, Newton, Coble, & Kupfer, 1983). Neither show the REM sleep markers. Taken together, the REM sleep of the depressed appears to be uniquely affected.

In addition to the sensitivity and specificity issues, researchers have also questioned whether the sleep abnormalities are stable physiological traits, markers of some biological vulnerability to depression that are present during symptom-free periods, or whether these are part of the disruption of many vegetative systems, characteristic of the depressed state, and remit when the patient is between episodes. Studies by Cartwright (1983), Rush et al. (1986), and Hauri, Chernick, Hawkins, and Mendels (1974) all show the persistence of the sleep signs into periods of remission.

Here the literature on family studies has added to the evidence of the short REM being possibly a genetic, traitlike characteristic. Giles, Roffwarg, and Rush (1987) report that "first degree relatives with similar depressions have similar REM latencies" (p. 911). In a later study, Giles, Biggs, Rush, and Roffwarg (1988) found that the relatives of depressed patients have a greatly increased risk of developing a depressive disorder if they share a reduced REM latency over that of relatives with normal REM latencies.

CURRENT THEORIES OF THE CAUSES OF THE REM SLEEP DYSFUNCTION

The findings of REM sleep abnormalities both during an episode of depression and periods of remission, as well as its presence in first-degree relatives of depressed patients, makes this an interesting area for speculation about the cause. Here theories abound. These vary from neurochemical models to those based on biological rhythms, and causation ranges from genetic to psychological.

Schulz and Lund (1985) compared three competing explanations of early REM. These authors start with two major findings concerning the first sleep cycle of the night in depressed patients: (a) It often shows less delta (Stages 3 and 4) sleep than is usual (Gillin et al., 1979), and (b) there is a reduced time to the first REM period (Kupfer, 1976). Although reduced delta can occur in other groups (e.g., normal aged persons; Gillin et al., 1979, 1981, 1985) and early REM can occur in nondepressed persons with shifts in sleep schedule (Weitzman et al., 1974), persons with free-running sleep–wake cycles

(Czeisler, Weitzman, Moore-Ede, Zimmerman, & Knauer, 1980) and persons recovering from REM sleep deprivation (Dement, 1960), nonetheless these two signs occur together more regularly in depression.

The first explanation of these findings entertained by these authors is a circadian phase shift hypothesis. This suggests that in depression there is a phase advance of the REM sleep, the body temperature cycle, and the cortisol cycle (Wehr, Gillin, & Goodwin, 1983). This proposal rests on the hypothesis that the REM sleep rhythm is time locked to the body temperature rhythm. However, Schulz and Lund did not find support for this in their data on the timing of REM sleep onset and the time of the lowest rectal temperature of a group of 15 depressed patients, in comparison with 12 patients who were in remission, and 10 normal controls.

The second hypothesis they considered is that there is an interaction of the delta sleep and REM sleep rhythms. This derives from a model developed by Borbely (1982) that sleep is regulated by two processes. The first, *C,* is a circadian process that governs subjective sleepiness. The second, *S,* is a sleep-dependent process revealed by the production of delta waves. If *C* is intact but *S* is deficient, REM sleep is allowed to move forward in the night to occupy an earlier time for a longer duration (Borbely & Wirz-Justice, 1982). Both these models, the phase advance and the two-process model, can account for the early morning awakenings typical of depression by arguing that REM, which ordinarily is predominant at the end of the night, has been completed too early. However, the second hypothesis also fails to meet a series of tests of a predicted relation between REM latency and amount of delta. These two appear to be independently controlled. The authors conclude an early REM is not caused by deficient delta sleep that night.

The third explanation investigated by Schulz and Lund (1985) is a variation on the circadian hypothesis. It suggests that in depression there is a flattened amplitude of the circadian "arousal cycle." Their test of this is to anticipate a very small variation in core body temperature around the 24-hour mean value in these patients. A dampening of the circadian arousal cycle, they suggest, lowers the threshold for REM sleep allowing it to occur early. Their data on the difference between the minimum and maximum rectal temperature plotted against REM latency appears to support this. They found that sleep onset REM periods occur in those patients with the lowest differences in core temperature around the clock. This has led to some exploratory work on lowering the core body temperatures in the depressed before sleep (Sewitch, Kittrell, Kupfer, & Reynolds, 1986).

Kupfer and Ehlers (1989) developed a somewhat more differentiated model to explain the relation of sleep and depression. They call this "two roads to rapid eye movement latency" (see Figure 12.3). On the first road, they argue that REM sleep appears early because the first nonrapid eye movement (NREM) sleep, particularly delta, terminates early. On the other road, REM occurs sooner after sleep onset because the propensity for REM is

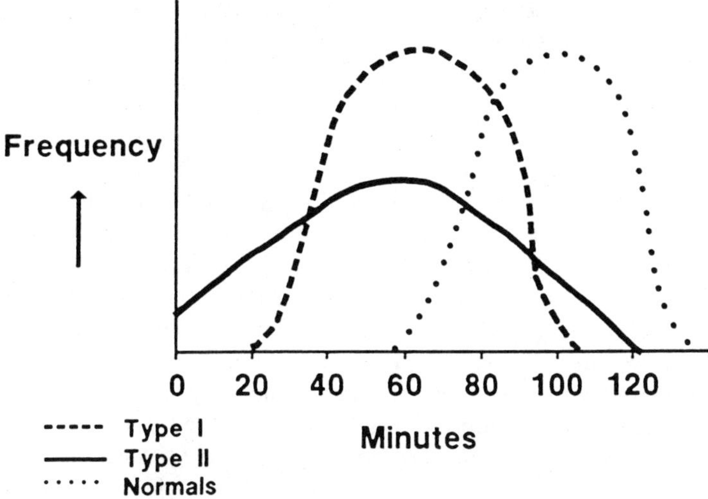

Figure 12.3. Adapted from "Two Roads to Rapid Eye Movement Latency" by D. Kupfer & C. Ehlers, (1989), *Archives of General Psychiatry, 46,* 947.

unusually stronger. The first blames a weak delta system for early REM, the second, an exaggerated REM "need."

In the first type, REM occurs sooner but is not more active, nor more prolonged. In Type 2, the other indications of an overly strong REM system are also apparent. This type is thought to be episode-related rather than trait-like, and to respond better to antidepressant medication. Type 1 is thought to be age related and family history related. This two-type model leads to a clear set of hypotheses that can be tested to see if it is supported; although Type 1 was not supported in the Schulz and Lund study, they did not stratify their sample appropriately to segregate patients by those meeting the "weak delta" criterion.

Aside from the physiological and biological rhythm theories, there are psychological explanations of depression that relate to the sleep disruption that is part of the symptom picture.

Akiskal and McKinney (1973) recognize that depressions represent interactions among biological, psychological, and sociological factors but relate all these to the impairment of the biogenic amines system. In one grand summary, they state:

> Melancholia is a psychobiological state that is the final common pathway of processes involving interpersonally induced states of mind in which the individual sees himself as losing control over his fate (hopelessness), increased psychic turmoil, increased neuronal excitability and hyperarousal, disturbances of genetically vulnerable neuronal circuits in the diencephalon, depletion of biogenic

> amines, impairment of the neurophysiological substrates of reinforcement, further decrements in coping mechanisms, and a vicious cycle of more hopelessness, psychic turmoil and hyperarousal. (p. 27)

In other words, psychosocial stress in a person with a genetic vulnerability can lead to neurochemical changes that are responsible for the symptoms of depression. Where does the sleep disruption fit into this model?

Recently, Ford and Kamerow (1989) investigated sleep complaints and psychiatric symptoms by a questionnaire survey in a large catchment area. Among the 7,954 respondents, 10.2% reported insomnia using the Diagnostic Interview Schedule. The question that elicited the insomnia response was: "Have you ever had a period of two weeks or more when you had trouble falling asleep, staying asleep, or with waking too early?" Only those with this symptom within the preceding 6 months were included in the count. Higher insomnia rates were experienced by persons who could be described as under more stress: women, separated or widowed persons, the unemployed, and those in the lowest socioeconomic status. Of those with insomnia, 40% had a psychiatric disorder when first interviewed. One year later when reinterviewed, most insomnias had resolved, but an additional 17% of those whose insomnia persisted now met the diagnostic criteria for a psychiatric disorder. The diagnosis of depressive disorder had a strong relation to insomnia. Of those with insomnia complaints, 14% met the full diagnostic criteria for depression. Most interesting was the finding at follow-up of those with persisting insomnia developing a new diagnosis of a major depression. These authors suggest that a sleep disturbance may be an early symptom in the progression to a full major depression episode, and if so, this represents an opportunity for early intervention. Unfortunately without a sleep study, they did not know whether the subjective report of "insomnia" manifested itself as low delta and early REM. However, the strong suggestion is that a sleep disruption precedes waking symptoms of depression.

From a laboratory study of volunteers undergoing marital separation with the expectation of divorce, there is some support of the Ford and Kamerow speculation (Cartwright & Wood, 1991). Sixty-one subjects, of whom 38 were originally diagnosed with a major depression and 23 were not depressed, returned 1 year later for follow-up sleep tests. Originally both depressed and nondepressed had lower delta than age-matched controls. Those who were depressed also had a shorter REM latency than those not depressed. Among those who were not depressed originally and who were still not yet divorced at the follow-up point, delta sleep remained low. In addition, REM latency was not shortened to the range characteristic of depression. This suggests that under long-term stress from a situation over which the individual is helpless to effect a resolution, a reduced REM latency may occur and herald an episode of depression. This suggestion has some support from studies tracking REM latency over the course of a depression and into periods of remission

(Rush et al., 1986; Kupfer, Frank, Grochocinski, Gregor, & McEachran, 1988). The model here is that an extended period of continued stress, and a failure of adaptation, may be a precursor of one type of depression, the kind Kupfer & Ehlers refer to as Type 2.

Giles, Roffwarg, Schlesser, and Rush (1986) looked into the question of what waking symptoms of depression were related to the reduced REM latency sign among depressed patients. Point-biserial correlations between endogenous symptoms and REM latency as a continuous variable showed loss of appetite, unreactive mood, and distinct quality of the mood were all significantly inversely related to REM latency. Using a cutoff of 65 minutes as short, worsening of mood in the morning, psychomotor activity change, significant weight loss, excessive self-reproach, or loss of interest did not discriminate between those with short or not-short REM latency, although the depression of those with short REM latencies was always rated as more severe. Pervasive anhedonia and terminal insomnia did discriminate the short REM latency group, along with unreactive mood. Since it is the more psychological and affect-related symptoms that are distinctive to the shortened REM latency depressives, dream content should be examined to discover if this reflects some disturbance in mood regulatory function. For example, it may show some lack of working through of negative affect from dream to dream across the night, specific to short REM latency.

The search for a function for dreaming had been almost given up as a lost cause, too difficult to pursue with experimental rigor, when a study by Vogel et al., (1975) revitalized the issue. In this landmark study, 34 hospitalized endogenously depressed patients were treated by hand awakenings to prevent REM from occurring. This manipulation had originally been used by Dement (1960) in hopes of revealing what function dreaming plays in normal subjects. This proved difficult to carry out for more than a few nights, and these few had little effect. Healthy young normal volunteers appeared to tolerate some REM sleep deprivation without becoming psychotic or dysphoric, without hallucinating, or even without losing much mental acuity except what might be anticipated from sleep loss. The main finding was that REM sleep has an insistent needlike characteristic. This was demonstrated by the increasing number of awakenings needed throughout the night to prevent REM from occurring and by the observation that when allowed ad lib sleep once more, REM begins earlier, and increases in total amount as if to make up for the previous loss. Since at the time Vogel undertook his study of the effects of REM deprivation in the depressed, most antidepressant medications were severe REM sleep suppressors, he argued that their therapeutic action might be due to the elimination of the abnormal early REM and the buildup of REM pressure.

The study was heroic, both on the part of the patients and staff. The design involved a crossover with half the patients deprived of REM sleep by keeping them awake for three minutes each time they attempted to get into REM sleep for six nights in a row or up to 30 awakenings each night before one night of ad lib sleep was permitted. This was continued an average of three weeks. The intermittent full night of sleep made it possible for subjects to tolerate the deprivation for a longer period. The control subjects received an equal number of non-REM awakenings after which the subjects were crossed over into the other arm of the study. Ten of the experimental subjects and three of the controls improved on the Hamilton Scale after the first half of the project. By the end, half the patients, 17 of the 34, improved sufficiently to be discharged with no other treatment. The other half of the sample, who did not improve on this manipulation, were then tried on imipramine. Only one improved sufficiently for discharge. Vogel et al. suggested that if direct REM suppression was not effective, antidepressants that suppress REM sleep would also be ineffective. This proved to be supported in other studies that have shown that unless the REM latency is short, tricyclic antidepressant medications are not effective in treating the depression (Rush et al., 1989; Svendsen & Christensen, 1981).

In the latter study, 80% of those with a two-night mean REM latency of less than 65 minutes responded to amitriptyline or disipramine, whereas only 50% of those with normal REM latency responded. A reduced REM latency is a positive sign for response to tricyclics. It also has been shown to be a positive sign for spontaneous recover (Cartwright, Kravitz, Eastman, & Wood, 1991). Dividing a group of maritally separated volunteer subjects who meet research diagnostic criteria for major depression into those with short (< 60 minutes) REM latency on a two-night mean, and those with normal REM latency, all those with traitlike short REM latency over a 1-year period were no longer depressed at follow-up, whereas only a third of those with stable normal REM latency recovered without treatment. There is some suggestion that Type 2 early REM may be associated with a more episodic course, however, and these persons may get into trouble again with future trauma. It is possible that those with normal latency might profit from the buildup of early REM pressure by REM deprivation because those in the study by Vogel, Vogel, McAbee, & Thurmond (1980) have had a good long-term follow-up history. This suggests that early REM may be an adaptive response to an increase in affective load.

One function of dreaming that has been suggested by many authors is that it is involved with affective information processing (Breger, 1969) and further that dreams have an adaptive function in relation to emotion-arousing events. If so, depression might represent an overloaded or even damaged dream system. This is suggested by the correlation of short REM latency and unreactive mood in the study by Giles et al. (1986). In a recent study, Cartwright (1991) showed that dreams of the depressed are more unpleasant in mood than those of nondepressed subjects going through the same stressful life event. In the same study, those depressed persons who incorporated the person central to the stressful event into their dreams recovered and made a good waking adjustment 1 year later significantly more often than those who did not. In this study, unfortunately, the numbers of incorporators with and without reduced REM latency were too small for any further analysis. These findings support those of Greenberg et al., (1990) that dreams of depressed patients relate to their response to treatment. These authors report that depressed patients with an absence of other people or the self in their dreams and poor dream story structure are less likely to recover.

Rotenberg (1984) suggests that REM sleep has a search activity function and that when this is renounced, it resembles the hopelessness or learned helplessness of depression. During heightened search, REM pressure may increase, shortening the latency; and during renunciation, normal or long latencies may be seen. These are the depressed who appear to need a more vigorous intervention to increase the pressure for REM or work directed to their dreams to revitalize them to deal with the people and problems involved.

RECOMMENDATIONS

The study of the sleep of the depressed needs to involve attention both to the timing and activity of REM and to the dream content that accompanies it. Researchers need to look into the differences between those with normal REM, those with stable short REM latency, and those whose reduced REM latency is episode-related, by conducting longitudinal studies. These are expensive and tedious to carry out but crucial to our understanding of the prognostic value of the sleep for the development and resolution of a depressive episode.

Manipulative studies that reduce REM by hand awakenings need to be carried out specifically for those who maintain normal REM latency while depressed to discover if they can be induced to build REM pressure and, if so, whether this will precipitate an improvement of symptoms. Since REM deprivation at the animal level has been found to increase activity levels in the cat as well as appetite and sex drive (Dement, 1969), it seems that this may also be beneficial to the depressed if carried out on a sustained basis, as Vogel et al. (1975) were able to do with their patients. Since those with poor dreams are poor treatment responders (Greenberg et al., 1990) and do not "work" on the interpersonal problems in their dreams (Cartwright, 1991), perhaps therapists might well return to dream work with these patients in an attempt to have these become more active in searching for solutions to emotional problems.

Sleep studies need to be integrated with waking studies to estimate the effect of particular kinds of nighttime sleep on morning mood. Little has been done to test the mood regulatory effect of different kinds of nights of REM sleep and dream patterns. I proposed such a model (Cartwright, 1979), but it has only begun to be tested. Dream sequences from REM to REM across the night can be progressive in problem solving, repetitive, or "stuck," or can become increasingly dysfunctional. Knowing these patterns may be very useful to the therapist who attempts to help patients learn to cope with their emotional problems. The REM sleep of the depressed and their dreams represent a clearer window into the affective difficulties of the patients than they may be able to convey in waking. This is an opportunity not to be overlooked.

REFERENCES

Akiskal, H. (1981). Subaffective disorders: Dysthymic, cyclothymic and bipolar II disorders in the "borderline" realm. *Psychiatric Clinics of North America, 4,* 25–46.

Akiskal, H. (1984). Interface of chronic depression with personality and anxiety disorders. *Psychopharmacology Bulletin, 20,* 393–398.

Akiskal, H., & McKinney, W. (1973). Depressive disorders: Toward a unified hypothesis. *Science, 182,* 20–29.

American Psychiatric Association. 1987. *Diagnostic and statistical manual of mental disorders* (3rd ed.-rev.). Washington, DC: Author.

Bell, J., Lycaki, H., Jones, D., Kewala, S., & Sitaram, N. (1983). Effect of preexisting borderline personality disorder on clinical and EEG sleep correlates of depression. *Psychiatry Research, 9,* 115–123.

Borbely, A. (1982). A two-process model of sleep regulation. *Human Neurobiology, 1,* 195–204.

Borbely, A., & Wirz-Justice, A. (1982). Sleep, sleep deprivation and depression: A hypothesis derived from a model of sleep regulation. *Human Neurobiology, 1,* 205–210.

Breger, L. (1969). Dream function: An information processing model. In L. Breger (Ed.), *Clinical Cognitive Psychology* (pp. 182–227). Englewood Cliffs, NJ: Prentice-Hall.

Carroll, B. (1979). Implications of biological research for the diagnosis of depression. In J. Mendlewicz (Ed.) *New advances in the diagnosis and treatment of depressive illness* (pp. 85–107). Amsterdam: Excerpta Medica.

Cartwright, R. (1979). The nature and function of repetitive dreams: A survey and speculation. *Psychiatry, 42,* 131–137.

Cartwright, R. (1983). Rapid eye movement sleep characteristics during and after mood-disturbing events. *Archives of General Psychiatry, 40,* 197–201.

Cartwright, R. (1991). Dreams that work: The relation of dream incorporation to adaptation to stressful events. *Dreaming, 1,* 3–9.

Cartwright, R., Kravitz, H., Eastman, C., & Wood, E. (1991). REM latency and the recovery from depression: Getting over divorce. *American Journal of Psychiatry.*

Cartwright, R., & Wood, E. (1991). Adjustment disorders of sleep: The sleep effects of a major stressful event and its resolution. *Psychiatry Research.*

Coble, P., Gordon, F., & Kupfer, D. (1976). Electronephalographic sleep diagnosis of primary depression. *Archives of General Psychiatry, 33,* 1124–1127.

Czeisler, C., Weitzman, E., Moore-Ede, M., Zimmerman, J., & Knauer, R. (1980). Human sleep: Its duration and organization depend on its circadian phase. *Science, 210,* 1264–1267.

Dement, W. (1960). The effect of dream deprivation. *Science, 131,* 1705–1707.

Dement, W. (1969). The biological role of REM sleep (circa 1968). In A. Kales (Ed.), *Sleep, physiology & pathology* (pp. 245–265). Philadelphia, PA: J. B. Lippincott.

Detre, T., Himmelhoch, J., Swartzburg, M., Anderson, C., Byck, R., & Kupfer, D. (1972). Hypersomnia and manic-depressive disease. *American Journal of Psychiatry, 128,* 1303–1305.

Duncan, W., Pettigrew, K., & Gillin, J. (1979). REM architecture changes in bipolar and unipolar depression. *American Journal of Psychiatry, 136,* 1424–1427.

Ford, D., & Kamerow, D. (1989). Epidemiologic study of sleep disturbances and psychiatric disorders. *JAMA, 262,* 1479–1484.

Giles, D., Biggs, M., Rush, J., & Roffwarg, H. (1988). Risk factors in families of unipolar depression: I. Psychiatric illness and reduced REM latency. *Journal of Affective Disorders, 14,* 51–59.

Giles, D., Roffwarg, H., & Rush, J. (1987). REM latency concordance in depressed family members. *Biological Psychiatry, 22,* 910–914.

Giles, D., Roffwarg, H., Schlesser, M., & Rush, J. (1986). Which endogenous depressive symptoms relate to REM latency reduction? *Biological Psychiatry, 21,* 473–482.

Gillin, C., Duncan, W., Murphy, D., Post, R., Wehr, T., Goodwin, F., Wyatt, R., & Bunney, W. (1981). Age-related changes in sleep in depressed and normal subjects. *Psychiatry Research, 4,* 73–78.

Gillin, C., Duncan, W., Pettigrew, K., Frankel, B., & Snyder, F. (1979). Successful separation of depressed, normal, and insomniac subjects by EEG sleep data. *Archives of General Psychiatry, 36,* 85–90.

Gillin, J. C., & Borbely, A. (1985). Sleep: A neurobiological window on affective disorders. *Trends in Neuroscience, 8,* 537–542.

Greenberg, R., Pearlman, C., Blacher, R., Katz, H., Sashin, J., & Gottlieb, P. (1990). Depression: Variability of intrapsychic and sleep parameters. *Journal of American Academy of Psychoanalysis, 18,* 233–246.

Hauri, P., Chernick, D., Hawkins, D., & Mendels, J. (1974). Sleep of depressed patients in remission. *Archives of General Psychiatry, 31,* 386–391.

Insel, T., Gillin, J., Moore, A., Mendelson, W., Lowenstein, R., & Murphy, D. (1982). The sleep of patients with obsessive compulsive disorder. *Archives of General Psychiatry, 39,* 1372–1377.

Keshavan, M., Reynolds, C., Ganguli, R., Brar, J., Houck, P., & Kupfer, D. (1990). EEG sleep in familial subgroups of schizophrenia. *Sleep Research, 19,* 330.

Knowles, J., MacLean, A., & Cairns, J. (1982). Definitions of REM latency: Some comparisons with particular reference to depression. *Biological Psychiatry, 17,* 993–1002.

Kupfer, D. (1976). REM latency: A psychobiologic marker for primary depressive disease. *Biological Psychiatry, 11,* 159–174.

Kupfer, D., & Ehlers, C. (1989). Two roads to rapid eye movement latency. *Archives of General Psychiatry, 46,* 945–948.

Kupfer, D., Foster, F., Coble, P., McPartland, R., & Ulrich, R. (1978). The application of EEG sleep for the differential diagnosis of affective disorders. *American Journal of Psychiatry, 135,* 69–74.

Kupfer, D., Frank, E., Grochocinski, V., Gregor, M., & McEachran, A. (1988). Electroencephalographic sleep profiles in recurrent depression: A longitudinal investigation. *Archives of General Psychiatry, 45,* 678–681.

Kupfer, D., & Thase, M. (1983). The use of the sleep laboratory in the diagnosis of affective disorders. *Psychiatric Clinics of North America, 6,* 3–25.

Puig-Antich, J., Goetz, R., Hanlon, C., Tabrizi, M., Davies, M., & Weitzman, E. (1983). Sleep architecture and REM sleep measures in prepubertal major depressives: Studies during recovery from the depressive episode in a drug-free stage. *Archives of General Psychiatry, 40,* 187–192.

Reynolds, C., & Kupfer, D. (1987). Sleep research in affective illness: State of the art circa 1987. *Sleep, 10,* 199–215.

Reynolds, C., Shaw, D., Newton, T., Coble, P., & Kupfer, D. (1983). EEG sleep in outpatients with generalized anxiety: A preliminary comparison with depressed outpatients. *Psychiatry Research, 8,* 81–89.

Rotenberg, V. (1984). Search activity in the context of psychosomatic disturbances of brain monoamines and REM sleep function. *Pavlovian Journal of Biological Science, 19,* 1–15.

Rush, J., Erman, M., Giles, D., Schlesser, M., Carpenter, G., Vasavada, N., & Roffwarg, H. (1986). Polysomnographic findings in recently drug-free and clinically remitted depressed patients. *Archives of General Psychiatry, 43,* 878–884.

Rush, J., Giles, D., Jarrett, R., Feldman-Koffler, F., Debus, J., Weissenburger, J., Orsulak, P., & Roffwarg, H. (1989). Reduced REM latency predicts response to Tricyclic medication in depressed out-patients. *Biological Psychiatry, 26,* 61–72.

Rush, J., Giles, D., Roffwarg, H., & Parker, C. (1982). Sleep EEG and dexamethasone suppression test findings in outpatients with unipolar major depressive disorders. *Biological Psychiatry, 17,* 327–341.

Schulz, H., & Lund, R. (1985). On the origin of early REM episodes in the sleep of depressed patients: A comparison of three hypotheses. *Psychiatry Research, 16,* 65–77.

Schulz, H., Lund, R., Cording, C., & Dirlich, G. (1979). Bimodal distribution of REM sleep latencies. *Biological Psychiatry, 14,* 595–600.

Sewitch, D., Kittrell, E., Kupfer, D., & Reynolds, C. (1986). Body temperature and sleep architecture in response to a mild cold stress in women. *Physiology and Behavior, 36,* 951–957.

Svendsen, K., & Christensen, P. (1981). Duration of REM latency as a predictor of effect of antidepressant therapy: A preliminary report. *Acta Psychiatrica Scandinavica, 64,* 238–243.

Vogel, G. (1981). The relationship between endogenous depression and REM sleep. *Psychiatric Annals, 11,* 423–428.

Vogel, G., Thurmond, A., Gibbons, P., Sloan, K., Boyd, M., & Walker, M. (1975). REM sleep reduction effects on depression syndromes. *Archives of General Psychiatry, 32,* 765–777.

Vogel, G., Vogel, F., McAbee, R., & Thurmond, A. (1980). Improvement of depression by REM sleep deprivation. *Archives of General Psychiatry, 37,* 247–253.

Wehr, T., Gillin, C., & Goodwin, F. (1983). Sleep and circadian rhythms in depression. In M. Chase & E. Weitzman (Eds.), *Sleep disorders: Basic and clinical research* (pp. 195–225). New York: Spectrum.

Weitzman, E., Nogeire, C., Perlow, M., Fukushima, D., Sassin, J., McGregor, P., Gallagher, T., & Hellman, L. (1974). Effects of a prolonged 3-hour sleep-wake cycle on sleep states, plasma cortisol, growth hormone and body temperature in man. *Journal of Clinical Endocrinology and Metabolism, 38,* 1018.

Zarcone, V., Benson, K., & Berger, P. (1987). Abnormal rapid eye movement latencies in schizophrenia. *Archives of General Psychiatry, 44,* 45–48.

CHAPTER 13

Suicide Attempts

ROY F. BAUMEISTER

INTRODUCTION

Does depression cause suicide? The question has been very important to psychology, and large amounts of information have been collected. At present, the best available answer is "Not really." That is, it is undeniably true that depressed people attempt suicide at much higher rates than nondepressed people. But the depression itself is apparently not responsible for the suicide. Two facts are particularly telling. First, the vast majority of depressed people never attempt to kill themselves, so it cannot be argued simply that depression causes suicide. Second, when measures of hopelessness are included, depression fails to predict suicide independently (Bedrosian & Beck, 1979; Cole, 1988; Drake & Cotton, 1986; Dyer & Kreitman, 1984; Ellis & Ratliff, 1986; Petrie & Chamberlain, 1983; Platt & Dyer, 1987). Depression and hopelessness often go together (see Abramson, Metalsky, & Alloy, Chapter 9, this volume), but it is the hopelessness, not the depression, that leads to suicide.

Nonetheless, depressed people do show elevated rates of suicide compared with nondepressed people. Suicide may be a rare outcome, but it is a significant matter when it occurs, not only for the individual who attempts it but also for his or her family, relatives, friends, co-workers—and therapist. Although suicide is not strictly speaking a particular symptom of depression, its increased rate of occurrence among depressed people makes it critical for anyone who works with depressed people to understand something about the causes and mental processes that lead to a suicide attempt.

THEORIES OF SUICIDE

A great deal has been written about suicide; in fact, suicide research may be older than modern psychology itself. Durkheim's (1897/1963) book on suicide is often regarded as the beginning of modern social science methods and sometimes even of sociology. Shortly thereafter, Freud (1916, 1920) developed a theory of suicide from his psychodynamic perspective. Subsequent theories of suicide have generally been shaped by Freud's and Durkheim's views.

Freud

Freud (1916, 1920) regarded suicide as aggression turned inward. Thus, the person has a violent wish to murder someone, but the aggressive impulse is checked by the superego (using guilt) and redirected against the self. The individual therefore murders himself or herself as a substitute for murdering the originally intended victim. Freud's theory was widely appealing to many psychologists but has gradually been discredited by the accumulation of data. A direct test by Levenson and Neuringer (1970) looked for evidence that suicidal individuals were more intropunitive (that is, feeling that they were guilty and deserved to suffer) than control subjects, but this view was not supported. Cantor (1976) showed that suicidal people tended to aim their aggression outward, contrary to the Freudian view that suicide results from aggression turned inward. Farmer (1987) likewise found that suicidals surpassed control subjects in outward, but not inward, directed aggression. Thus, the evidence about the direction of aggressive impulses does not fit Freud's theory of suicide.

In support of Freud's hypothesis, his supporters have long cited that suicide rates decrease during wartime. They have interpreted this as evidence that war fosters the outward expression of aggression, thereby reducing the quantity of aggression that has to be turned inward and hence reducing the suicide rate. This interpretation has been seriously challenged by new findings, however. Rojcewicz (1970) found that the wartime decrease in suicide occurs in neutral countries and even in ones occupied by enemy forces, where outward expression of aggression is often severely curtailed. Thus, the effects of war on suicide must be explained on some other basis than the refocusing of aggressive impulses away from the self.

A last bit of evidence pertaining to Freudian suicide theory concerns the combination murder-suicides. Their very existence offers a challenge to Freud's theory, for if an individual has just murdered someone else, he or she should not need another aggressive outlet (i.e., in suicide). One Freudian explanation has been that the murderer feels overcome with guilt and desire for punishment and so commits suicide as a means of punishing the self. In these views, the murder is the primary act and the suicide is a consequence or afterthought. The available evidence about murder-suicide combinations suggests the opposite, however. Most often, the suicide is the primary act and the murder is secondary. Often the murderer appears to be taking revenge for his or her own death on the person who has, in the murderer's view, caused his or her suffering (see Hendin, 1982; Rhine & Mayerson, 1973; also Allen, 1983; Berman, 1979; Palmer & Humphrey, 1980). More generally, suicides seem to regard themselves (and succeed in inducing their intimates to regard them) as victims rather than as murderers. Thus, Freud's view that the suicide is a murderer first and a victim second does not fit the evidence currently available.

Durkheim

Durkheim's (1897/1963) work focused on the hypothesis of social integration. As an early sociologist, he sought to understand suicide as the product of the social system, and he proposed that suicide results when people feel left out or excluded from society. People who are well integrated into society should be far less likely to commit suicide than marginal people. Any loss of social integration, whether through divorce, loss of employment, or severing of interpersonal ties, should increase the likelihood of suicide. Current evidence indicates that Durkheim's hypothesis is correct, as far as it goes (Trout, 1980; see also Douglas, 1967; Hendin, 1982). It fails to explain why many marginal individuals do not commit suicide, and it fails to clarify the subjective processes that people experience en route to a suicide attempt, so it is not currently regarded as a complete explanation of suicide. There is little dispute, however, that suicide rates rise among people who lack or lose social ties.

Others

A variety of other theories have been proposed. Powell's (1958) contribution built on Durkheim's view but added that a sense of personal impotence and a lack of self-validation mediated between social integration and suicide. Although Powell's work was frustratingly vague on most psychological issues, it must be considered an important step between Durkheim and the theory I shall propose, because it assigns central importance to the self.

An updated Freudian theory was proposed by Henry and Short (1954), who invoked the relation between frustration and aggression to explain suicide. In their view, the self is blamed for frustrating failure, and so the person attacks himself or herself. Unfortunately, the failure of the data to support hypotheses of intropunitiveness are as damaging to Henry and Short's theory as they are to Freud's original version. Henry and Short also offered an extended discussion of internal and external restraints, but their concepts have been thoroughly criticized elsewhere (see Douglas, 1967; Maris, 1969).

For a time, the concept of a "cry for help" was popular among clinicians and theorists seeking to understand suicide (e.g., Farberow & Shneidman, 1961; Stengel & Cook, 1958). Unfortunately, this phrase has been interpreted in a variety of different ways (see Farberow & Shneidman, 1961, for an assortment), suggesting that its appeal was based more on expressive simplicity than on articulate, theoretical coherence. Although the notion of a cry for help has proven inadequate as a theory to generating research hypotheses and interpreting empirical findings, it may prove useful as a heuristic for clinicians in helping people cope with the aftermath of an insincere suicide attempt.

Escape theory, my own contribution to suicide theory, arises from my research on the self and self-awareness theory. It treats suicide as resulting from frustrated efforts to escape from aversive self-awareness (see Baumeister, 1990a, 1991a). This "escape theory" offers a viable framework for organizing and understanding the immense quantity of empirical findings about suicide. Escape theory is particularly relevant to depression, because depressed people show high rates of self-awareness, particularly an unpleasant self-awareness that persists after failure, rejection, or personal disappointment (Greenberg & Pyszczynski, 1986).

ESCAPE THEORY

The escape theory of suicide can be summarized in six main steps. These should be considered as choice points in a decision tree. At each step, one path leads toward suicide. A person will attempt to kill him- or herself only after resolving all six steps in the appropriate direction. That helps explain why suicide attempts are, in general, so rare.

The first step is a major disappointment; that is, events fall far short of expectations or other standards. This disappointment may arise because expectations are too high or because events and circumstances are very negative, or both. What matters is the discrepancy between the standard and reality. The recent experience of a large, major discrepancy sets the suicidal process in motion.

The second step involves the individual's interpretation of recent or current problems in a way that attributes primary responsibility to the self. If the person can blame other people or external circumstances, suicide is less likely (Henry & Short, 1954). Attributions exist at a high (or broad) level of meaning, because they generalize: An attribution begins with a single event at one point in time, and from that it infers a stable trait or disposition that in principle characterizes the person continually across months or even years, invoking many possible situations, actions, and feelings (e.g., Jones, 1979). It is one thing to say "a bad thing just happened," but it is far more ominous and meaningful to conclude "I am a bad person," because the latter has implications for many things that may have happened in the past and are likely to continue happening in the future. Moreover, because the suicidal process involves causal attributions for disappointing events, attributions to self will necessarily invoke unflattering characterizations of the self as having stable, undesirable traits. In other words, the negative evaluation of recent events now applies to the self too.

The third step is high self-awareness. Self-awareness theory has long emphasized the comparison of self against relevant standards (e.g., Carver, 1979;

Carver & Scheier, 1981; Duval & Wicklund, 1972). In the previous two steps of the presuicidal process, events have fallen short of standards and have been blamed on the self; hence the self too is seen as falling short of standards. The presuicidal individual thus becomes aware of self as incompetent, unattractive, guilty, or inadequate in other ways. Although such characterizations of self may characterize depressed people, they do not yet amount to a suicidal mental state.

Two types of standards deserve special mention because they are particularly relevant to suicide. First, the status quo is nearly always taken as one standard, such that people compare subsequent events with the way things were before. If the self gets worse—loses attractiveness or competence in some crucial way—this may furnish the aversive self-awareness that satisfies this step in the presuicidal process. The second type of standards lies in the expectations of other people. People who feel that they cannot live up to what family, co-workers, or others expect of them should be more likely than others to attempt suicide.

The fourth step involves emotional distress. Anxiety, depressed mood, anger, and other states of negative affect may arise from evaluating the self in an unfavorable fashion (cf. Higgins, 1987). Such states are acutely unpleasant and it is safe to assume that people will want to escape from them as soon as possible.

The fifth step is a common mental response to the dilemma of negative affect associated with aversive self-awareness. It can be described with the technically precise term of *cognitive deconstruction* (Baumeister, 1990a, 1990b) or with the metaphorical but less formidable term of *mental narrowing* (Baumeister, 1991a). It encompasses what has been described as low levels of action identification (Vallacher & Wegner, 1985, 1987), low levels of self-awareness (Carver & Scheier, 1981; Powers, 1973), or low level thinking (Pennebaker, 1989). A deconstucted or low-level mental state entails being aware of self and action in concrete, short-term ways focusing on movements and sensations rather than action and experience, thinking only of proximate, immediate tasks and goals, and generally rejecting meaning and meaningful thought.

This response of mental narrowing is common because it removes the person's capacity to feel negative affect. As previously noted, attributions are broad meaningful constructs that subsume many possible single actions into a general disposition; the prevention of meaningful thought will remove such attributions from the mind and hence undercut the basis for feeling bad. Likewise, emotion is itself based on evaluation of circumstances and self, so mental narrowing removes emotion (cf. Pennebaker, 1989). And the comparison of self with standards (i.e., the essence of self-awareness) is another meaningful calculation that disappears when meaningful thought is curtailed.

The mentally narrow state is thus an effective escape from emotional distress associated with high, aversive self-awareness. It can be regarded as a kind of mental and emotional numbness, and as such it is preferable to painful distress. Unfortunately, evidence indicates that such low-level or narrow mental states are generally unstable and hard to sustain (e.g., Baumeister, 1991a; Vallacher & Wegner, 1985), and so the individual finds it difficult to remain thus numb. But each time the mind attempts to resume meaningful thought and broader awareness, the distressing thoughts and feelings return.

Ideally, people who reach this numb, deconstructed state gradually return to meaningful awareness by making sense of their recent problems and rebuilding their positive views of self and world (e.g., Silver, Boon, & Stones, 1983; Taylor, 1983). They move back to higher, broader meanings, assisted perhaps by ideologies that show how to see their troubles in the context of divine plans and the like. For people who are unable to reconstruct self and world, however, the remaining choice is between trying to stay numb (which is often an empty, boring state) and acute emotional distress. They may grasp at increasingly strong and desperate means to prevent the recurrence of the aversive self-awareness and its attendant emotional suffering. Suicide can be considered an extreme means of achieving such oblivion and numbness.

The sixth step involves several consequences of mental narrowing that may increase the appeal of suicide. Mental narrowing removes inhibitions, because inhibitions are based on meaningful evaluations (such as moral principles) and self-awareness. A mental vacuum may result from the rejection of meaning, and this vacuum may increase the person's receptiveness to bizarre or irrational ideas. Passivity and lack of emotion also result from mental narrowing, and they will tend to shape the person's interest in suicide.

Suicide is not the only form of escape from self, and indeed it should be considered atypical of escapes in that its outcome is so extremely maladaptive. Elsewhere, I have listed three widely separate pathways that can motivate the person to want to escape from self-awareness (Baumeister, 1991a). The first is the abrupt occurrence of a personal calamity, and it leads to extreme reactions and the quest for powerful means of escape (such as suicide). As a response to a crisis, this pattern of escape may be unusual and may disregard considerations of safety and repeatability. The second pathway, in contrast, involves people who desire to escape self-awareness more frequently, and such escapes (such as sexual masochism or controlled alcohol use) often show careful patterning and prudent consideration of safety and repeatability. The third pathway is the quest for powerful, ecstatic experiences and other benefits that accrue to the escape from selfhood. Religious spirituality, such as embodied in powerful mystical experiences, is one example of such a pattern. These escapes from self have features in common with suicide but differ in other respects. The suicide attempt can thus be seen in a context of many other means of losing oneself. One approach to treating suicidal individuals, therefore, is to raise awareness of alternative methods for escaping from self-awareness, in order to steer the individual away from the most drastic and destructive method.

Two qualifications must be made. First, I am not suggesting that all suicides follow this process, for a variety of processes can lead to suicide (see Baechler, 1979). Escape does however appear to be the most common motive or meaning of suicide, indeed more common than all others combined (Smith & Bloom, 1985; see also Bancroft, Skrimshire, & Simkins, 1976; Hawton, Cole O'Grady, & Osborn, 1982; Loo, 1986; Parker, 1981). It may also be the pattern most relevant to depression, for other patterns (such as honor suicide and altruistic suicide) are of less concern to theorists, researchers, and clinicians interested in depression.

Second, escape theory is concerned with explaining why people attempt suicide rather than why some succeed better than others at it. Researchers have noted some differences between successful and unsuccessful suicide attempters (e.g., Drake, Gates, & Cotton, 1986; Goldney, 1981; Hendin, 1982; Maris, 1981; Pallis, Barraclough, Levey, Jenkins, & Sainsbury, 1982; Shneidman & Farberow, 1961, 1970). The difference between successful and unsuccessful suicide may often be due to the effectiveness and speed of various means (e.g., guns vs. pills), luck (being found in time), or the presence of a competing wish to live, all of which are irrelevant to escape theory. Escape theory is a theory of suicide *attempts.* In that connection, even an unsuccessful suicide attempt may be an effective escape. The survivor of a suicide attempt may be hospitalized, thereby removing him or her from having to deal with personal troubles and practical concerns. Hospital staff, friends, and family may treat this individual with gentle, concerned, nurturant solicitude, which again may provide escape from interpersonal conflicts and other problems.

With that as a framework, I shall now review a substantial body of empirical evidence about suicide.

DISAPPOINTMENT

The first step concerns a severely disappointing experience, which can be produced by excessively high standards and expectations, by strongly negative outcomes, or both. Some findings emphasize the high standards whereas others emphasize the poor outcomes, but the important point is the discrepancy between standards and outcomes.

A professional who begins to read the suicide literature is first disturbed by the seemingly contradictory welter of findings that point alternately to good and bad circumstances as predictive of suicide. It is particularly ironic that favorable circumstances could increase the suicide rate, but that conclusion is indisputable. It appears, however, that the favorable circumstances that foster suicide do so by generating high expectations, especially because they tend to be stable and chronic conditions. In contrast, the unfavorable circumstances that increase suicide tend to be recent and acute problems. This is relevant to predicting suicide from depression. Some evidence suggests that the indications of depression among suicidal people tend to be of fairly recent origin (Barraclough, Bunch, Nelson, & Sainsbury, 1974). Therapists, therefore should be most concerned and vigilant with clients who have recently become depressed, rather than with those who have been depressed for years.

Places with high standards of living tend to have high suicide rates. The positive correlation between living standards and suicide rate has been shown by comparing different nations (Argyle, 1987; Lester, 1984) and even by comparing different states within the United States (Lester, 1987). On the other hand, suicide rates rise when the economy takes a turn for the worse, such as occurs in the onset of a depression (Araki & Murata, 1987; Argyle, 1987; Holinger, 1978; Wasserman, 1984). Putting these findings together, the maximum risk of suicide is created by becoming accustomed to prosperity but then experiencing a severe economic decline.

Suicide rates are higher in areas that have better weather (Lester, 1986), and generally they tend to rise during the months with the best weather, such as late spring and summer (Nayha, 1982; Parker & Walter, 1982). It is not plausible that weather conditions per se cause suicide; rather, good weather may produce generalized expectations for happiness, which then form a painful contrast for individuals whose lives are marked by misfortune. When external conditions are good, people may develop higher expectations for happiness, which are thus more easily disappointed.

Suicide rates are higher among college students than among people of the same age who are not in college (Hendin, 1982). College must be regarded as a desirable environment in many ways, especially compared with working in shops or other settings that do not require college education. But college also undoubtedly raises expectations. It is instructive to examine the academic performance of suicidal individuals: In terms of their entire college career, suicidal students, perhaps surprisingly, have better grade point averages than nonsuicidal students (Braaten & Darling, 1962). On the other hand, during the semester preceding the suicide attempt, their grades were below average (P. Davis, 1983; also Hendin, 1982). The suicidal pattern is thus marked by a long-term pattern of good performance but a recent deterioration. Other evidence suggests that suicidal students may often have unusually high expectations, sometimes associated with demanding parents, for academic success (Braaten & Darling, 1962; Hendin, 1982).

The recent lives of suicide attempters have been found to be marked by aversive, stressful events (Cochrane & Robertson, 1975; Paykel, Prusoff, & Myers, 1975; Power, Cooke, & Brooks, 1985; Schotte & Clum, 1982). Several particular changes for the worse, such as imprisonment or bereavement, have been associated with suicide, but the evidence repeatedly implicates the *recency* of these events in suicide. Different researchers have used different times frames for examining recency, but their findings consistently suggest that the likelihood of suicide diminishes with the passage of time following a trauma. Most suicides in prison occur within the first month following imprisonment (Backett, 1987). Suicides in mental hospitals are most likely during the first week of institutionalization (Copas & Robin, 1982). Suicide among widows and widowers is most likely within the first two years after bereavement (Bunch, 1972; McMahon & Pugh, 1965). (It is possible that bereavement is a little slower than institutionalization to produce suicide, because in the immediate aftermath of bereavement many people receive social support from family and friends and do not suffer the full impact until that support drops off.) I noted earlier that the status quo is nearly always a salient standard, and so when things take a sharp turn for the worse, the downward shift is most acutely suffered in the days or weeks immediately following it. Once the individual grows accustomed to the new status quo, apparently, the risk of suicide diminishes.

An exception to this pattern concerns loss of employment. Evidence suggests that job loss produces a *delayed* increase in suicide; that is, people are more likely to commit suicide several months after losing their jobs, rather than immediately afterward (Platt, 1986). The explanation for this may lie in some delayed emergence of self-blame; I shall return to this in the next section.

Many researchers have sought to establish a link between socioeconomic status and suicide rates, but the results have been inconsistent and inconclusive. Such comparisons have several methodological problems; for example, wealthy families may exert influence to prevent a member's death from being classified as suicide. The largest problem, however, may be that many suicides are preceded by an abrupt change in socioeconomic status. Downward social mobility produces a marked increase in suicide rates (Breed, 1963; Maris, 1969, 1981). Suicide does not arise from being poor throughout life, whereas a fall from relative affluence into relative poverty produces a sharp increase in frequency of suicide (Farberow, 1975). This fits the notion of disappointed expectations. The status quo is always a salient standard, and then subsequent events are compared against it. If a person has always been poor, further poverty does not foster suicide, but if he or she has been accustomed to comfort or affluence, poverty is experienced as an abrupt and shocking disappointment.

The single, unmarried state is in some ways parallel to financial poverty. Single people do have slightly higher suicide rates than married people, consistent with Durkheim's hypothesis of social integration (e.g., Rothberg & Jones, 1987; Trout, 1980), but the difference is small. A much bigger effect is seen in comparing the recently divorced or separated with married people (e.g., Rothberg & Jones, 1987). Thus, it is not being single all through life, but moving abruptly into the single state from the more desirable married state, that fosters suicide. More generally, any recent and substantial deterioration in intimate relationships can apparently produce an increase in suicidal tendencies (Berlin, 1987; Bourque, Kraus, & Cosand, 1983; Conroy & Smith, 1983; Hendin, 1982; Loo, 1986; Maris, 1981; Stephens, 1985; Tishler, McKenry, & Morgan, 1981).

Some evidence associates a particular pattern or relationship disappointment with suicide. (Although the evidence is not as strong as for other points, its potential clinical relevance makes it worth considering, and it is consistent with the general pattern.) Certain people have relatively few social contacts and may feel they have few chances for romantic relationships. When such lonely individuals do find a partner, they may invest all their hopes and feelings in that relationship, even to the extent of withdrawing from other social contacts; and if it breaks up, the emotional impact is much stronger than for other people. Homosexuals, lonely adolescents, shy people, and any others who have a reduced range of possible partners may be vulnerable for this pattern (P. Davis, 1983; Hendin, 1982; Ringel, 1976). More generally, some evidence suggests that suicidal people are not true loners but in fact have unusually strong desires for affiliation, nurturance, and social belonging, and so isolation is especially painful to them (Cantor, 1976; Neuringer, 1972).

The study of intimate relationships of suicidal individuals has yielded especially clear evidence that it is the discrepancy between expectations and reality that leads to suicide. Stephens (1985) found two relationship patterns to be most common among suicidal women. In one pattern, the woman's expectations for intimate communion were unrealistically high, and her husband's relatively normal level of intimate sharing was experienced as severely disappointing. In the other pattern, the woman's expectations for intimacy were normal, but her mate tended to be aloof, cold, and withdrawn. Hence either the expectations or the reality can be out of line, and either departure can lead to suicidal tendencies. What matters is the size of the gap between them.

Several other suicidal predictors fit the pattern of recent departure from favorable standards. Substantial deterioration in health has been shown to increase suicidal tendencies, perhaps especially among the elderly (Bourque et al., 1983) and alcoholics (Motto, 1980). People who have recently learned that they have cancer are twice as likely as others to commit suicide (Marshall, Burnett, & Brasurel, 1983). Likewise, a major change for the worse in occupational circumstances can lead to increased suicidal tendencies. Such changes include an increased workload, raised standards or expectations, reduced salary or other rewards, reduced status, loss of privileges, perceived loss of personal skill or capability (as due to aging), and failure of anticipated promotion or simply a reduction in perceived chances for advancement (Blachly, Disher, & Roduner, 1968; Brodsky, 1977; Hendin, 1982; Loo, 1986; Maris, 1981). Many of these patterns share the common theme of finding that the demands of the job have become excessive and impossible (Brodsky, 1977).

Even temporal patterns fit the notion that gaps between expectations and reality contribute to suicidal tendencies. Contrary to some clinical stereotypes, suicide rates actually decline with the approach of major holidays, and they stay low for the holidays themselves. After a major holiday, however, there is a small rise in suicide (Phillips & Liu, 1980; Phillips & Wills, 1987). Similarly, suicide rates appear to drop with the approach of the weekend and rise after it, so that suicides are least likely on Friday and most often reported on Monday (Rothberg & Jones, 1987). Although these temporal patterns are not unambiguous, they are consistent with the hypothesis that the approach of a holiday (or weekend) raises encouraging expectations for happiness; whereas if the outcome is disappointing, a suicide attempt may be likely afterward.

IMPLICATING THE SELF

The second step involves pointing the finger of blame at oneself. Everyone experiences misfortunes and disappointments, but those who can comfortably attribute their problems to luck, external circumstances, or other people should be less likely to commit suicide than people who blame themselves.

It is quite clear that the problems and sufferings of suicidal individuals invoke unflattering implications for their self-concepts. One large-scale survey found that self-blame was the single most common distinguishing factor among attempted suicides and close to the most common factor among completed suicides (Maris, 1981). Nor is this confined to modern Western cultures; Palmer (1971) found condemnation to self to be far and away the most common motive for suicide among nonliterate cultures. Breed (1972) proposed that a general suicidal syndrome involves low self-esteem resulting from failure to live up to high expectations.

Low self-esteem has been implicated in several studies of suicide. Suicidal people often regard themselves as worthless and inadequate, and they blame others' rejection of them on their own lack of desirable attributes (Bonner & Rich, 1987; Rosen, 1976; Rothberg & Jones, 1987; Stephens, 1987; Tishler, McKenry, & Morgan, 1981). Further evidence suggests that recent loss of self-esteem, or other changes for the worse in self-concept, are associated with increases in suicidal tendencies (Gerber, Nehemkis, Farberow, & Williams, 1981; Kaplan & Pokorny, 1976).

Self-blame and loss of self-esteem may constitute a hidden factor in other suicidal patterns, even though direct evidence is lacking. The effects of some economic factors may be mediated by self-esteem changes. The preceding section cited Platt's (1986) evidence that unemployment produces an increase in suicide after a delay. The reason may be that job loss initially can be blamed on external circumstances, but if no satisfactory new job is found while family finances continue to deteriorate, the individual may increasingly blame himself or herself. Consistent with that, Newman (1988) concluded that executives who lost their jobs initially blamed the economy, office politics, and other factors, but after some months of unemployment, they began to think that they themselves must be at fault. Platt (1986) also found a curvilinear relationship between the unemployment rates and suicide rates (in Great Britain), such that initial increases in unemployment bring increases in suicide but further increases in unemployment bring reductions in the suicide rate. Platt's conclusions implicate self-blame. The first people to lose their jobs during an economic downturn probably blame themselves, but once the downturn is widely recognized as a nationwide problem, people cease to hold themselves individually responsible for losing their jobs. A similar conclusion emerged from a study of suicide in Japan, which found that the increase in suicide rates preceded the general recognition of an economic depression (Araki & Murata, 1987).

HIGH SELF-AWARENESS

I have already noted that suicide rates tend to be high among groups known to have high self-awareness. This relationship obtains among adolescents (Hendin, 1982; Simmons, Rosenberg, & Rosenberg, 1973; Tice, Buder, & Baumeister, 1985), among depressed people (e.g., Barraclough et al., 1974; Greenberg & Pyszczynski, 1986; Vandivert & Locke, 1979; Wilson, 1981), among alcoholics (Hendin, 1982; Hull, 1981; Hull, Young, & Jouriles, 1986; Maris, 1981; McKenry & Kelley, 1983; Roy & Linnoila, 1986), and among members of cultures that espouse individualistic values or emphasize self-focusing emotions such as pride and shame (Farberow, 1975; Smith & Hackathorn, 1982). Another form of evidence, namely a review of laboratory studies, has linked high self-awareness with a variety of self-destructive behavior patterns (Baumeister & Scher, 1988). Thus, a variety of indirect evidence links high self-awareness to suicide.

Direct evidence is hard to come by, but what exists is consistent with the hypothesis that suicidal people are highly focused on themselves. Careful quantitative analyses of suicide notes have revealed that suicidal people refer to themselves more often than writers of other documents and even more often than people facing involuntary death (Henken, 1976; also Ogilvie, Stone, & Shneidman, 1983). The high rate of self-references is commonly interpreted as a sign of self-awareness (e.g., Davis & Brock, 1975; Wegner & Giulano, 1980). These analyses also suggest that suicidal people conceptualize their interpersonal relationships in terms of separate, isolated individuals with discrepant or even opposed interests, in contrast to other groups who describe their relationships in "we" terms of mutuality and common interests.

EMOTION

Direct evidence of unpleasant emotional states associated with suicidal tendencies is surprisingly weak. One important reason may be that the most common methodology for studying suicide is to use people who have attempted suicide but survived and who are hospitalized after the event. By this point, the emotion may have subsided. Another reason may be that the presuicidal mental state features processes aimed at escaping from emotion, and so there is an emotional calm even during the period immediately preceding the suicide attempt. I shall return to the suppression of emotion in a later section.

The empirical links between negative affect and suicide are mostly indirect. People who might be expected to be having a great deal of negative affect are also prone to increased suicide rates. People who are temperamentally or dispositionally prone to anxiety have high suicide rates (Bhagat, 1976; Mehrabian & Weinstein, 1985). Likewise, people inclined toward feelings of depression and hopelessness have high rates of suicide (e.g., Kovacs, Beck, & Weissman, 1975; Platt & Dyer, 1987; Schotte & Clum, 1982).

A smattering of evidence has implicated other emotions. There is some suggestion of elevated levels of guilt among suicidal people (Maris, 1981; Miller & Chabrier, 1987; Palmer, 1971), and studies of mothers who commit child abuse have found both guilt and suicidal tendencies, although the relation between the two appears to be indirect (Hawton, Roberts, & Goodwin, 1985; Roberts & Hawton, 1980). Several studies have found evidence that anger filled the presuicidal period in a substantial minority of cases (Bancroft et al., 1976; Birtchnell & Alarcon, 1971; Bonnar & McGee, 1977; Hawton et al., 1982). Sadness, depressed feelings, worry, and loneliness have been observed too (Bancroft et al., 1976; Barraclough et al., 1974; Birtchnell & Alarcon, 1971; Maris, 1981).

Still, the evidence is far from overwhelming. Researchers can say with much greater confidence that suicidal people have recently had experiences that seemingly ought to bring a great deal of negative emotion. As we have seen, romantic rejection, divorce, loss of employment, deterioration in health, career disappointment, loss of freedom, and other major personal setbacks are often found to have preceded suicide attempts, and most people would suffer emotional distress from any of these. From that perspective, what is surprising is not the periodic evidence of unpleasant emotion, but rather the absence of overwhelming indications of emotion. To understand the absence of emotion, it is perhaps necessary to examine the mental state that is apparently adopted by presuicidal individuals in response to their personal crises.

MENTAL NARROWING

One way to respond to the combination of personal calamity, self-blame, aversive high self-awareness, and negative affect is to become mentally and emotionally numb. By avoiding meaningful thought, the individual can stop realizing the distressing implications of recent events, thereby removing the basis for both self-awareness and the resulting emotion. The cognitive shift is one of deconstruction, in the sense of dismantling meaning into fragments. The person focuses narrowly on the here and now, on physical movements and sensations, rather than engaging in the full range of complex information processing (see Baumeister, 1989, 1990a, b, 1991a).

One sign of mental narrowing is a restricted time perspective. For the person who has just blamed himself or herself for a distressing personal calamity, the past is painful to recall, and the future is clouded with very troubling implications. Only the immediate present moment offers a refuge from meaning and emotion. The present orientation of suicidal individuals, or the relative absence of past and future orientations, has been documented in various ways, including their inability to envision any future or particularly any happy future for themselves, and even a pronounced tendency for their speech patterns to lack past and future tense verbs (Greaves, 1971; Hendin, 1982; Iga, 1971; Melges & Weisz, 1971; Yufit & Benzies, 1973). Their present orientation is also a factor in their distorted sense of time flow. Laboratory studies have verified the subjective distortions in the flow of time among suicidal individuals, whose estimates of time intervals are far more inaccurate than those of normal or psychiatric control subjects (Neuringer & Harris, 1974; see also Brockopp & Lester, 1970; Greaves, 1971). The presuicidal mental state resembles that of acutely bored people—it is an empty, dull, unemotional immersion in the present, unredeemed by reflective memory of the past or interest in the future. Time seems to drag, and when the individual checks the clock, he or she is surprised at how little time has actually passed. It is noteworthy that depression is similarly characterized by such an immersion in the present (Wyrick & Wyrick, 1977).

This transformation of temporal perspective is important for understanding suicide. When I first began to study suicide, it was in the hope that it would contribute valuable insights to my research on how people find meaning in life (Baumeister, 1991b; see also Klinger, 1977). I hoped that suicide would show me what makes people reject life, and that that would shed light on what is needed to make life acceptably meaningful. But apparently suicide is not a rejection of life as a whole; it is a rejection mainly of the present moment, which is intolerable. Past and future have been banished from awareness. Most suicides therefore do not shed much light on the issue of life's meaning, because the presuicidal mental state has ceased to think in such long-term, integrative patterns as involve the meaning of the person's life as a whole.

A second feature of mental narrowing is that thought and speech become austerely concrete. This has been shown most effectively by studying suicide notes. The stereotype of the suicide note is profound, reflective, possibly emotional, and often philosophical, as the person explains his or her reasons for rejecting life. The reality is quite different, however, for actual suicide notes tend to be banal and specific. They are devoid of abstract terms, "thinking words," and other expressions of higher mental awareness (Henken, 1976). They tend to focus on specific practical matters and arrangements, such as bills, care for relatives or pets, and occasionally funeral requests (Ogilvie et al., 1983). Compared with simulated suicide notes, actual notes have a greater frequency of references to physical objects and fewer references to awareness, cognitive processes, and mental states (Gottschalk & Gleser, 1960). All in all, "Suicide notes are *not* the insightful documents we would like them to be," in the words of one researcher (Henken, 1976, p. 36).

Cognitive rigidity is another indication of the rejection of meaning, insofar as the individual clings to fixed ideas and interpretations rather than being open to exploring new thoughts. Such rigidity is marked by stereotyped, inflexible, one-sided, black-and-white thinking, with an absence of creativity or spontaneity. Many studies have demonstrated the cognitive rigidity of suicidal individuals (Arffa, 1983; Beall, 1969; Iga, 1971; Levenson & Neuringer, 1971; Neuringer, 1964, 1967; Patsiokas, Clum & Luscomb, 1979; Vinoda, 1966). The inability of suicidal people to engage in divergent thinking, especially in relation to exploring multiple possible solutions to problems, was shown by Schotte and Clum (1987; also Asarnow, Carson, & Guthrie, 1987). Suicidal people are not stupid, and they can probably do math problems or draw deductive conclusions as well as anyone else. But if they are asked to find multiple solutions to an open-ended problem, or if they are asked to find an alternative pathway or method toward some end, or if they are challenged to rethink basic assumptions, they have difficulty and tend to perform poorly.

For years, cognitive rigidity was regarded as a personality trait that constituted a risk factor in suicide, but recent evidence has suggested that cognitive rigidity may be a state rather than a trait. Perrah and Wichman (1987) replicated the usual patterns of cognitive rigidity among people who were tested right after a suicide attempt, but similar individuals tested after a delay of several months showed no differences from control subjects (see also Schotte & Clum, 1982; Shneidman, 1981). This finding fits escape theory, which regards the mental narrowing as a response to a recent personal crisis rather than a stable personality trait.

CONSEQUENCES OF MENTAL NARROWING

Several of the consequences of mental narrowing are relevant to suicide. A first consequence is a reduction in inhibitions. This does not mean that suicidal people become uninhibited in the sense of being spontaneous, creative individuals. Rather, it just means that many internal barriers cease to operate, and so people become willing to do things that they normally would not consider doing. Inhibitions are based on meaningful evaluations of actions and their implications, and the reduction or cessation of meaningful thought entails that people cease to think about possible actions in that way. That mental narrowing removes such internal barriers is evident in other escapes from self, such as alcohol intoxication (Steele & Southwick, 1985; see also Hull, 1981), sexual masochism (Baumeister, 1989), and binge eating (Heatherton & Baumeister, 1991).

Probably the most important form of disinhibition is the suicide attempt itself. Most people would not attempt suicide most of the time, and violent self-destructive impulses would be restrained by a variety of considerations and inhibitions. For people to attempt to kill themselves, something must overcome those restraints.

Still, a variety of other evidence supports the disinhibition hypothesis. Some studies have characterized suicidal people as impulsive, and impulsive action can be regarded as one form of action that evades inhibitions. Early studies treated impulsiveness as a personality trait that predisposed people to suicide (Bhagat, 1976; Cantor, 1976), but like mental rigidity, impulsiveness has come to look more like a feature of the presuicidal state than a stable personality dimension (Patsiokas et al., 1979).

A person's willingness to take risks and gamble with his or her life reflects a suspension of normal inhibitions and self-preservation tendencies. Although the evidence is not entirely consistent, it appears that suicidal people show some elevated willingness to take such risks (Adams, Giffen, & Garfield, 1973; Taylor, 1978). Once again, this willingness to take risks appears to be a matter of the presuicidal mental state (Adams et al., 1973) rather than a stable aspect of personality (Silberfeld, Streiner, & Ciampi, 1985). Many suicide attempts apparently take the form of dangerously risky behavior rather than deliberate, unambiguous efforts at self-destruction (Taylor, 1978).

Murder-suicide combinations may also be relevant to disinhibition. Most individuals who commit murder and suicide have no prior criminal record and indeed differ markedly from typical demographic profiles of murderers and other criminals (e.g., Allen, 1983). The most common murderer-suicide is a white middle-class adult male who kills his wife or girlfriend, and the next most common is a woman who kills her mate or children or both; such murders would be highly taboo under most circumstances, and their occurrence therefore reflects a suspension of powerful inhibitions. As noted earlier in this chapter, the suicide appears to be the main event in such episodes (e.g., Rhine & Mayerson, 1973), and the murder may therefore be a consequence of the disinhibited state that precedes suicide. To look at this another way: Hendin (1982) calculated that suicidal individuals commit murder at a much higher rate than the general population, which attests to disinhibition.

Passivity is another consequence of mental narrowing, although the term "consequence" may not be fully appropriate, because the passivity may appeal to people as a means of achieving and sustaining escape from self

(Baumeister, 1991a). Conscious, deliberate, intentional action implicates the self by requiring it to plan, decide, and initiate acts and (hence) by conferring responsibility on the self. To use and implicate the self in such a fashion is the last thing a person would want to do if his or her goal is to escape from selfhood. Escape from self therefore fosters passivity with regard to any meaningful acts or involvements. Such individuals may prefer to do nothing or may act in impulsive, random, meaningless, or trivial ways.

A variety of evidence points to the importance and appeal of passivity among suicidal individuals. Several researchers have specifically characterized suicidal individuals as passive (Mehrabian & Weinstein, 1985; Ringel, 1976; Simon & Lumry, 1968; see also Neuringer, 1964). Suicidal people are prone to deny responsibility for their actions (Gerber et al., 1981). The language of suicide notes contains an unusually high frequency of constructions indicating passivity and passive submission to fate (Henken, 1976); for example, instead of "I have tried to make our marriage work," the person might say, "Our marriage has not worked" or even "Nothing can be done to make our marriage work." Suicidal tendencies are linked to a decreased sense of internal control over events (Gerber et al., 1981; Melges & Weisz, 1971; Topol & Reznikoff, 1982). Indeed, the passive sense of lacking control and responsibility may extend to feelings of helplessness, which has often been noted as a feature of the presuicidal state (Connor, Daggett, Maris, & Weiss, 1973; Maris, 1985; Neuringer, 1974; Ringel, 1976; Stephens, 1985). Studies of coping strategies have also indicated that suicidal individuals tend to cope passively rather than actively (Asarnow et al., 1987; Linehan, Camper, Chiles, Strosahl, & Shearin, 1987; Spirito, Stark, Williams, & Guevremont, 1987). Passive coping strategies, such as emotional withdrawal, are generally considered less effective than active, problem-solving strategies.

An apparent paradox is that suicide requires the active taking of a person's own life, and such an active stance seemingly conflicts with the passive orientation of the suicidal mental state. My sense is that this is often a difficult personal problem for suicidal individuals. Their orientation toward passivity may be one reason that they perceive themselves (and convince others close to them to see them) in the passive role of victim rather than in the active role of murderer (e.g., Buksbazen, 1976; Counts, 1987; Douglas, 1967; Stengel, 1967). The avoidance of an active role and responsibility may be a further reason that many suicide attempts appear as impulsive acts (Patsiokas et al., 1979) or risk taking (Taylor, 1978) rather than as deliberately planned and executed sequences. Nor is this dilemma unique to suicide, for the same active-passive struggle is apparent in other escapes from self. Sexual masochists struggle to obtain and orchestrate the experiences they crave, which are ironically based on their total loss of control and responsibility (Baumeister, 1989); binge eaters, ranging from lapsing dieters to bulimics, regard such episodes of intense eating as losses of control, even though they must take some active initiative to put food in their mouths (Heatherton &

Baumeister, 1991). In all these, the individual searches for ways to disguise and minimize his or her personal initiative while emphasizing the resultant passivity and helplessness.

Emotion represents another area of seeming contradiction. Affectively charged experiences are instrumental in setting the suicidal process in motion and creating the wish to die, but many studies of suicidal individuals have turned up only scattered, fragmentary, and surprisingly weak evidence of emotion among suicidal individuals. Escape theory offers one resolution, which is that traumatic or disappointing events have generated the basis for emotional distress, but the person struggles (via mental narrowing) to keep the emotion out of awareness.

In this connection, an important study by Williams and Broadbent (1986) is enlightening. These researchers used a cued-recall task to elicit emotional memories. Contrary to their predictions, they found that suicidal individuals responded more slowly than control subjects to cues for positive emotion and did not differ from control subjects in speed of responding to cues for negative emotion. Even more important, perhaps, was the finding that suicidal subjects surpassed controls in cue refusals, that is, in being unable to come up with any personal memory that fit the requested emotion. These results depict suicidal individuals as people who have lost touch with their emotional systems or indeed have tried to shut these systems down. To ask them for personal associations in response to emotional cues runs diametrically opposite to what mental narrowing is designed to accomplish, namely to divest themselves of emotion. The seeming emotional incapacity that they showed in this study fits the view of people who are avoiding emotion (see also Geller & Atkins, 1978).

A last consequence of cognitive narrowing is a vulnerability to irrational thought, bizarre belief, and unusual fantasy. Rationality is maintained by constructive thought such as checking ideas against other beliefs and common sense; the deconstructive process in mental narrowing removes the basis for such rationality and leaves the person vulnerable to ideas that he or she would normally reject. A variety of studies have found evidence suggesting irrationality, unrealistic thinking, or fantasies of magical solutions in the thought processes of suicidal individuals (Bonner & Rich, 1987; Ellis & Ratliff, 1986; Iga, 1971). In particular, Neuringer (1972) noted that, prior to suicide, many individuals may withdraw into fantasy for solace and refuge from the disappointing state of their interpersonal relationships. Irrational or fantasied imagining among suicidal individuals of their death and its effects on others has been noted by several researchers (Douglas, 1967; Ringel, 1976). Other evidence, however, suggests that these may be minority patterns because most suicidal people simply give very little thought to the consequences of their act (Bancroft et al., 1976; Weiss, 1957).

Another relatively uncommon, but theoretically revealing and important, pattern of irrational thought among suicidal individuals involves the fantasy of identity change. Maris (1981) found that a substantial minority of suicidal individuals (but no nonsuicidal individuals) endorsed a wish that they could be someone else. The fantasy of or wish for identity change is a relatively unambiguous indication of the desire to escape from self and provides a valuable confirmation of the hypothesis that such escapism is indeed a driving force behind suicide. It parallels similar wishes or fantasies in other forms of escape from self. Sexual masochists enact dramas of thoroughgoing identity change, including alteration of name, gender, occupation, residence, and/or status, such as might be involved in becoming someone's full-time sex slave (Baumeister, 1989). Among binge eaters, the fantasied identity changes may be less complete, but often the desire for transformation into a new, slender, glamorous individual is powerful and is linked to a sense that the change would make all troubles vanish (Heatherton & Baumeister, 1991). If a person could become someone else, of course, all his or her troubles would indeed vanish. (Most likely the individual would have a new set of troubles, but fantasies may not recognize this.) People who blame their troubles on the self may find the fantasy of identity change especially appealing because the central source of their problems—the self—would be removed. To a person with such a wish, suicide may appeal because it too means that all his or her troubles will vanish.

RECOMMENDATIONS FOR CLINICIANS AND RESEARCHERS

Making recommendations is not simple or straightforward, because as previously noted, suicide is not a result of depression, although depression must be considered a risk factor insofar as it is statistically correlated with suicide. Depression researchers may not need to concern themselves directly with issues of suicide. For clinicians, the great problems that arise when a patient attempts suicide may override concern with theoretical issues such as that suicide was not caused by depression.

Researchers concerned with suicide will have noted that several steps in the escape theory could benefit from further research. Most of what exists is consistent with escape theory, but further studies and prospective tests of escape hypotheses would be highly desirable. The issues of self-awareness and emotion are particular areas that need further study. If it could be shown that an increased preoccupation with self (especially an aversive preoccupation with the self's failings and shortcomings) precedes a suicide attempt, that would provide valuable confirmation of escape theory. The view of suicidal individuals as struggling to become emotionally numb in order to suppress emotional distress is likewise consistent with current evidence but needs further study and verification.

Moreover, escape theory holds that the person proceeds to the suicide attempt because he or she is unable to sustain the mentally narrow state and to keep the problematic views of self and world effectively deconstructed. The mind inevitably tries to resume meaningful, integrative thought, and whenever it does so, it returns to the person's recent problems and their distressing implications. To ward them off, the person grasps desperately at any available means, and suicide offers the promise of peaceful, untroubled oblivion. It promises to divest the person of the self that is regarded as the source and cause of his or her troubles. This account, however, rests presently more on inference and speculation than on hard evidence, and it would be extremely valuable to have some direct evidence of such internal struggles among presuicidal individuals. To be sure, this problem is not unique to escape theory and its hypotheses; the issue of how the individual moves from the causal background of troubles and other predisposing factors to the actual making of the suicide attempt is a central challenge for all suicide research. Methodological difficulties are likely to continue to hamper research on such issues, for such work seeks to study the sequence of events occurring when people actually decide and undertake to end their own lives, and at such a point most professionals (if they were present at all) would feel obliged to make intervention rather than dispassionate observation their first priority. Still, the events and subjective processes during those crucial moments are particularly important for research to illuminate.

In addition, I have emphasized that escape theory is aimed at explaining why people *attempt* to kill themselves. It would be a valuable extension of the theory to investigate whether any of the factors I have covered help predict or determine why some people succeed more than others at suicide.

Clinicians are, of course, less urgently concerned with developing and refining the theory of suicide. Their concerns are probably focused on two main issues: how to predict a suicide attempt and how to prevent it from happening. If the attempt does take place, then a third issue arises: how to help the individual cope with it and its aftermath.

Predicting suicide is far from an exact science. Considering the ambiguity, it is not surprising that clinicians have evolved a variety of lore, superstitions, and rules of thumb. Despite their appeal and despite the inevitable fact that individual cases may occasionally fit such generalizations, it is recommended that clinicians remain skeptical about them and instead keep an eye on the research literature to determine the true predictors of suicide. I have already noted the clinical belief that suicides are most common during major holidays, which appears to be entirely wrong; even the rise in suicides *after* a holiday is not as substantial as the decrease in suicides preceding and during the holiday, so the net effect of the entire holiday season is a decrease in suicides (Phillips & Wills, 1987). Various hypotheses about effects of lunar cycles on suicide can probably be dismissed; initial support for such notions in various data sets apparently were artifacts of day-of-the-week effects. There does appear to be a decrease in suicides through the workweek to the weekend, whereas the end of the weekend and Monday's return to work are associated with rises in suicides (e.g., Rothberg & Jones, 1987). Another notion holds that highly depressed people are too inactive to kill themselves, but suicide becomes likely as depression begins to subside. This is plausible, and to my knowledge, it has neither been confirmed nor denied by research, probably because a careful empirical test would be extremely difficult; still, it may be best to be skeptical about this notion unless it can be verified. (Some evidence suggests that the transition from a nondepressed to a depressed state *has* been associated with an increase in suicidal tendencies; see Barraclough et al., 1974). The same may be said for the various, competing notions that suicide attempts only occur among people who have, or have not, spoken about suicide recently to other people.

In place of such superstitious generalizations, it seems preferable to rely on research findings to predict suicide. Once again, it must be acknowledged that single research findings simply show small shifts in the very small odds of a suicide attempt, and most people with one or more risk factors will never attempt suicide. If a combination of risk factors is present, there is perhaps reason for particular vigilance, but even so the likelihood of a suicide attempt is small.

One approach to predicting suicide may be to use the steps in escape theory, as presented in this chapter, as a kind of checklist for an individual's progress through the presuicidal mental state. The mere occurrence of a setback or trauma (i.e., the first step in the theory) should not cause alarmed concern about the possibility of suicide. If, however, the individual responds to the trauma by blaming himself or herself, becoming preoccupied with personal deficiencies, and struggling to shut out emotions, then some cautious vigilance may be warranted. Once mental narrowing and its consequences are observed, the individual may be reaching a state at which a suicide attempt is possible, and increased vigilance or even preventive intervention may be warranted. But as long as individuals are earnestly blaming their troubles on other people, cultivating a philosophical attitude, or struggling toward pragmatic solutions to their problems, suicide is unlikely.

Any suggestions for treatment would be largely speculative, but some suggestions follow plausibly from the work presented in this chapter. Once the suicidal crisis begins to become acute, as indicated by the individual reaching the later steps in the presuicidal process, some interventions probably work better than others. Psychodynamic approaches that fix the client's attention on the problems and their causes could even be counterproductive at that point, for they increase the painful awareness of the problems from which the person is trying to escape, and the desire to escape may therefore become more desperate. At that point, insight may be more threatening and harmful than helpful. Instead of striving for insight, therefore, the therapist may find it helpful in the short run to teach some cognitive skills such as thought-stopping. If the person can successfully stop these aversive, distressing trains of thought, he or she may feel less need to grasp for extreme and dangerous means (such as suicide).

Thought-stopping therapy should be regarded as a crisis intervention rather than a long-term solution, for in effect it simply offers a technique for facilitating the numbness that is sought in mental narrowing. In the long run, it is necessary to help the individual find ways of dealing with the precipitating crisis, such as rebuilding an ordered life and adequate sense of self. Ultimately, to go on living, the person must be able to think in broad, meaningful terms about the events in his or her life without being overwhelmed by emotional distress. That capacity may require learning how to interpret or frame past events in ways that allow for optimism, self-acceptance, and pragmatism in the face of future challenges. Indeed, a first step may be for the individual to realize that past problems, however severe, do not condemn him or her to a bleak, empty, painful, or otherwise useless future. The inability to envision future happiness is one factor leading to suicide, and exercises in imagining a desirable future may therefore be useful.

I have also cited evidence that the presuicidal state is marked by the least effective coping styles, such as passive withdrawal. Clinicians may want to attend particularly to the coping styles of their suicidal clients in order to foster the development of active, problem-solving ones. Even if the person survives the current crisis, the next setback may bring a recurrence if withdrawal remains the preferred style of coping. An active style of coping allows people to solve their problems or, when the damage is irreparable, to believe at least that the next time things will be different.

The discussion of coping raises the third concern of clinicians, namely, how to deal with the aftermath of an unsuccessful suicide attempt. A rule of thumb to keep in mind is that the suicide attempt may have successfully allowed the individual to escape from his or her problems and may therefore be reinforcing, which could raise the likelihood of similar responses in the future. The popular notion of suicide as a "cry for help," despite its therapeutic heuristic value, should probably not be used to encourage indiscriminate supportiveness for suicide attempters. Instead, these individuals must be led to see that attempting suicide is not a solution, and that even when the particular crisis is passed and discharge from the hospital is imminent, the causes of the life crisis may remain unchanged. Changes in self and environment are probably necessary. If family and friends have been gentle and supportive during the period of institutionalization after the suicide attempt, the individual may not see the need for further changes, and it may be necessary to be forceful and clear that these attitudes of others probably do not reflect long-term changes but simply a sympathetic response to the attempt.

The suicide attempt may in fact exacerbate problems. Bonnar and McGee (1977) studied a sample of women who had survived suicide attempts. These women hoped that their suicide attempt would lead to a new intimacy and improved communication with their husbands, but the husbands tended to regard the suicide attempt as a cheap, manipulative ploy and hence to withdraw further. If intimate relationships do deteriorate as the result of a suicide attempt, the immediate future promises that things will be getting worse, not better, and clinicians should be ready to deal with such eventualities. Some clinicians and researchers have regarded suicide as a form of communication, but it is necessary to recognize that it is often a poor and counterproductive form of communication.

CONCLUSION

Decades of research have yielded a wealth of empirical findings about suicide, although areas of unclarity remain. Dozens of variables have been shown to predict suicide attempts. It is necessary either to assume that suicide can result from a vast assortment of unrelated causes or to attempt to erect some integrative framework that shows how these multiple causes may work in tandem. Escape theory is one such integrative framework. It does not propose to explain all suicides or to explain every aspect of suicidal behavior, but it does seem capable of integrating a large number of empirical findings in a plausible sequence that can lead to a suicide attempt.

Escape theory holds that suicide attempts follow from recent disappointments that may be triggered by unrealistically high standards and expectations, severe misfortunes and setbacks, or both. These disappointments are blamed on the self, leading to a preoccupation with the self as deficient, undesirable, or worthless, which in turn is linked with a proneness to emotional distress. In response, the person seeks to create a state of mental narrowing, characterized by a rejection of meaningful thought, deconstruction of generalizations about the self, and emphatic focus on the here and now. People struggle to remain rigidly in this narrow, empty state, which is itself mildly unpleasant but seems preferable to the acute emotional distress that accompanies a meaningful examination of recent events and their unflattering implications about the self. The consequences of this state make the person receptive to suicide, for they include the suspension of normal inhibitions, the suspension of common sense and rational thought, and a reluctance to intervene actively to change life circumstances.

Other theories about suicide have presented its appeal as an aggressive outlet, in which the individual's murderous impulses are expressed toward the self, as an effort to communicate with others, or as a form of self-punishment. In contrast, escape theory proposes that the appeal of suicide is its offer of oblivion. Attempting suicide is an escalation of means in the quest for peace that is begun by seeking mental narrowing. Suicide offers to make the person's problems go away and frees him or her from facing the troubling implications of recent events about the self.

The effort to escape from self-awareness is not inherently bad. Indeed, I have emphasized elsewhere that many great thinkers and religious traditions throughout history have regarded egotism and self-orientation as major barriers to wisdom and spiritual attainment (Baumeister, 1991a). Suicide is thus only one manifestation of the wish to escape from self. But it is the most maladaptive one, chosen by people who are not thinking clearly and are responding to personal crises. Suicide is a desperate means toward a desirable end. From religious exercises to thought-stopping, other means are available for escaping the self, and these means hold out hope that troubled individuals can be diverted from suicide.

ACKNOWLEDGMENTS

The preparation of this chapter was facilitated by a fellowship granted by the Alexander von Humboldt Foundation.

REFERENCES

Adams, R. L., Giffen, M. B., & Garfield, F. (1973). Risk-taking among suicide attempters. *Journal of Abnormal Psychology, 82,* 262–267.

Allen, N. H. (1983). Homicide followed by suicide: Los Angeles, 1970–1979. *Suicide and Life-Threatening Behavior, 13,* 155–165.

Araki, S., & Murata, K. (1987). Suicide in Japan: Socioeconomic effects on its secular and seasonal trends. *Suicide and Life-Threatening Behavior, 17,* 64–71.

Arffa, S. (1983). Cognition and suicide: A methodological review. *Suicide and Life-Threatening Behavior, 13,* 109–122.

Argyle, M. (1987). *The psychology of happiness.* London, England: Methuen.

Asarnow, J. R., Carson, G. A., & Guthrie, D. (1987). Coping strategies, self-perceptions, hopelessness, and perceived family environments in depressed and suicidal children. *Journal of Consulting and Clinical Psychology, 55,* 361–366.

Backett, S. A. (1987). Suicide in Scottish prisons. *British Journal of Psychiatry, 151,* 218–221.

Baechler, J. (1979). *Suicides.* New York: Basic Books. (Original work published 1975)

Bancroft, J., Skrimshire, A., & Simkins, S. (1976). The reasons people give for taking overdoses. *British Journal of Psychiatry, 128,* 538–548.

Barraclough, B., Bunch, J., Nelson, B., & Sainsbury, P. (1974). A hundred cases of suicide: Clinical aspects. *British Journal of Psychiatry, 125,* 355–373.

Baumeister, R. F. (1989). *Masochism and the self.* Hillsdale, NJ: Erlbaum.

Baumeister, R. F. (1990a). Suicide as escape from self. *Psychological Review, 97,* 90–113.

Baumeister, R. F. (1990b). Anxiety and deconstruction: On escaping the self. In J. M. Olson & M. P. Zanna (Eds.), *Self-inference processes: The Ontario Symposium (Vol. 6,* pp. 259–291). Hillsdale, NJ: Erlbaum.

Baumeister, R. F. (1991a). *Escaping the self: Alcoholism, Spirituality, Masochism, and other flights from the burden of selfhood.* New York: Basic Books.

Baumeister, R. F. (1991b). *Meanings of life.* New York: Guilford.

Baumeister, R. F., & Scher, S. J. (1988). Self-defeating behavior patterns among normal individuals: Review and analysis of common self-destructive tendencies. *Psychological Bulletin, 104,* 3–22.

Beall, L. (1969, March). The dynamics of suicide: A review of the literature, 1897–1965. *Bulletin of Suicidology,* 2–16.

Bedrosian, R. C., & Beck, A. T. (1979). Cognitive aspects of suicidal behavior. *Suicide and Life-Threatening Behavior, 9,* 87–96.

Berlin, I. N. (1987). Suicide among American Indian adolescents: An overview. *Suicide and Life-Threatening Behavior, 17,* 218–232.

Berman, A. L. (1979). Dyadic death: Murder-suicide. *Suicide and Life-Threatening Behavior, 9,* 15–23.

Bhagat, M. (1976). The spouses of attempted suicides: A personality study. *British Journal of Psychiatry, 128,* 44-46.

Birtchnell, J., & Alarcon, J. (1971). The motivational and emotional state of 91 cases of attempted suicide. *British Journal of Medical Psychology, 44,* 42–52.

Blachly, P. H., Disher, W., & Roduner, G. (1968, December). Suicide by physicians. *Bulletin of Suicidology,* 1–18.

Bonnar, J. W., & McGee, R. K. (1977). Suicidal behavior as a form of communication in married couples. *Suicide and Life-Threatening Behavior, 7,* 7–16.

Bonner, R. L., & Rich, A. R. (1987). Toward a predictive model of suicidal ideation and behavior: Some preliminary data in college students. *Suicide and Life-Threatening Behavior, 17,* 50–63.

Bourque, L. B., Kraus, J. F., & Cosand, B. J. (1983). Attributes of suicide in females. *Suicide and Life-Threatening Behavior, 13,* 123–138.

Braaten, L. J., & Darling, C. D. (1962). Suicidal tendencies among college students. *Psychiatric Quarterly, 36,* 665–692.

Breed, W. (1963). Occupational mobility and suicide among white males. *American Sociological Review, 28,* 179–188.

Breed, W. (1972). Five components of a basic suicide syndrome. *Life-Threatening Behavior, 2,* 3–18.

Brockopp, G. W., & Lester, D. (1970). Time perception in suicidal and nonsuicidal individuals. *Crisis Intervention, 2,* 98–100.

Brodsky, C. M. (1977). Suicide attributed to work. *Suicide and Life-Threatening Behavior, 7,* 216–229.

Buksbazen, C. (1976). Legacy of a suicide. *Suicide and Life-Threatening Behavior, 6,* 106–122.

Bunch, J. (1972). Recent bereavement in relation to suicide. *Journal of Psychosomatic Research, 16,* 361–366.

Cantor, P. C. (1976). Personality characteristics found among youthful female suicide attempters. *Journal of Abnormal Psychology, 85,* 324–329.

Carver, C. S. (1979). A cybernetic model of self-attention processes. *Journal of Personality and Social Psychology, 37,* 1251–1281.

Carver, C. S., & Scheier, M. F. (1981). *Attention and self-regulation: A control-theory approach to human behavior.* New York: Springer-Verlag.

Cochrane, R., & Robertson, A. (1975). Stress in the lives of parasuicides. *Social Psychiatry, 10,* 161–171.

Cole, D. (1988). Hopelessness, social desirability, depression, and parasuicide in two college student samples. *Journal of Consulting and Clinical Psychology, 56,* 131–136.

Connor, H. E., Daggett, L., Maris, R. W., & Weiss, S. (1973). Comparative psychopathology of suicide attempts and assaults. *Life-Threatening Behavior, 3,* 33–50.

Conroy, R. W., & Smith, K. (1983). Family loss and hospital suicide. *Suicide and Life-Threatening Behavior, 13,* 179–194.

Copas, J. B., & Robin, A. (1982). Suicide in psychiatric in-patients. *British Journal of Psychiatry, 141,* 503–511.

Counts, D. A. (1987). Female suicide and wife abuse: A cross-cultural perspective. *Suicide and Life-Threatening Behavior, 17,* 194–204.

Davis, D., & Brock, T. C. (1975). Use of first person pronouns as a function of increased objective self-awareness and prior feedback. *Journal of Experimental Social Psychology, 11,* 381–388.

Davis, P. A. (1983). *Suicidal adolescents.* Springfield, IL: Thomas.

Douglas, J. D. (1967). *The social meanings of suicide.* Princeton, NJ: Princeton University Press.

Drake, R. E., & Cotton, P. G. (1986). Depression, hopelessness, and suicide in chronic schizophrenia. *British Journal of Psychiatry, 148,* 554–559.

Drake, R. E., Gates, C., & Cotton, P. G. (1986). Suicide among schizophrenics: A comparison of attempters and completed suicides. *British Journal of Psychiatry, 149,* 784–787.

Durkheim, E. (1963). *Suicide.* New York: Free Press. (Original work published 1897).

Duval, S., & Wicklund, R. A. (1972). *A theory of objective self-awareness.* New York: Academic Press.

Dyer, J. A. T., & Kreitman, N. (1984). Hopelessness, depression and suicidal intent in parasuicide. *British Journal of Psychiatry, 144,* 127–133.

Ellis, T. E., & Ratliff, K. G. (1986). Cognitive characteristics of suicidal and nonsuicidal psychiatric inpatients. *Cognitive Therapy and Research, 10,* 625–634.

Farberow, N. L. (1975). Cultural history of suicide. In N. L. Farberow (Ed.), *Suicide in different cultures* (pp. 1–16). Baltimore, MD: University Park Press.

Farberow, N. L., & Shneidman, E. S. (1961). *The cry for help.* New York: McGraw-Hill.

Farmer, R. (1987). Hostility and deliberate self-poisoning: The role of depression. *British Journal of Psychiatry, 150,* 609–614.

Freud, S. (1916). Trauer und Melancholie. *Gesammelte Werke, 10* (pp. 427–446). London: Imago.

Freud, S. (1920). Ueber die psychogenese eines Falls von weiblicher Homosexualitaet. *Gesammelte Werke, 12* (pp. 269–302). London: Imago.

Geller, A. M., & Atkins, A. (1978). Cognitive and personality factors in suicidal behavior. *Journal of Consulting and Clinical Psychology, 46,* 860–868.

Gerber, K. E., Nehemkis, A. M., Farberow, N. L., & Williams, J. (1981). Indirect self-destructive behavior in chronic hemodialysis patients. *Suicide and Life-Threatening Behavior, 11,* 31–42.

Goldney, R. D. (1981). Attempted suicide in young women: Correlates of lethality. *British Journal of Psychiatry, 139,* 382–390.

Gottschalk, L. A., & Gleser, G. C. (1960). An analysis of the verbal content of suicide notes. *British Journal of Medical Psychology, 33,* 195–204.

Greaves, G. (1971). Temporal orientation in suicidals. *Perceptual and Motor Skills, 33,* 1020.

Greenberg, J., & Pyszczynski, T. (1986). Persistent high self-focus after failure and low self-focus after success: The depressive self-focusing style. *Journal of Personality and Social Psychology, 50,* 1039–1044.

Hawton, K., Cole, D., O'Grady, J., & Osborn, M. (1982). Motivational aspects of deliberate self-poisoning in adolescents. *British Journal of Psychiatry, 141,* 286–291.

Hawton, K., Roberts, J., & Goodwin, G. (1985). The risk of child abuse among mothers who attempt suicide. *British Journal of Psychiatry, 146,* 486–489.

Heatherton, T. F., & Baumeister, R. F. (1991). Binge eating as escape from self-awareness. *Psychological Bulletin, 110,* 86–108.

Hendin, H. (1982). *Suicide in America.* New York: Norton.

Henken, V. J. (1976). Banality reinvestigated: A computer-based content analysis of suicidal and forced-death documents. *Suicide and Life-Threatening Behavior, 6,* 36–43.

Henry, A. F., & Short, J. F. (1954). *Suicide and homicide: Some economic, sociological and psychological aspects of aggression.* Glencoe, IL: Free Press.

Higgins, E. T. (1987). Self-discrepancy: A theory relating self and affect. *Psychological Review, 94,* 319–340.

Holinger, P. C. (1978). Adolescent suicide: An epidemiological study of recent trends. *American Journal of Psychiatry, 135,* 754–756.

Hull, J. G. (1981). A self-awareness model of the causes and effects of alcohol consumption. *Journal of Abnormal Psychology, 90,* 586–600.

Hull, J. G., Young, R. D., & Jouriles, E. (1986). Applications of the self-awareness model of alcohol consumption: Predicting patterns of use and abuse. *Journal of Personality and Social Psychology, 51,* 790–796.

Iga, M. (1971). A concept of anomie and suicide of Japanese college students. *Life-Threatening Behavior, 1,* 232–244.

Jones, E. E. (1979). The rocky road from acts to dispositions. *American Psychologist, 34,* 107–117.

Kaplan, H. B., & Pokorny, A. D. (1976). Self-attitudes and suicidal behavior. *Suicide and Life-Threatening Behavior, 6,* 23–35.

Klinger, E. (1977). *Meaning and void: Inner experience and the incentives in people's lives.* Minneapolis, MN: University of Minnesota Press.

Kovacs, M., Beck, A. T., & Weissman, A. (1975). Hopelessness: An indicator of suicidal risk. *Suicide, 5,* 98–103.

Lester, D. (1984). The association between the quality of life and suicide and homicide rates. *Journal of Social Psychology, 124,* 247–248.

Lester, D. (1986). Suicide and homicide rates: Their relationship to latitude and longitude and to the weather. *Suicide and Life-Threatening Behavior, 16,* 356–359.

Lester, D. (1987). Suicide, homicide, and the quality of life: An archival study. *Suicide and Life-Threatening Behavior, 16,* 389–392.

Levenson, M., & Neuringer, C. (1970). Intropunitiveness in suicidal adolescents. *Journal of Projective Techniques and Personality Assessment, 34,* 409–411.

Levenson, M., & Neuringer, C. (1971). Problem solving behavior in suicidal adolescents. *Journal of Consulting and Clinical Psychology, 37,* 433–436.

Linehan, M. M., Camper, P., Chiles, J. A., Strosahl, K., & Shearin, E. (1987). Interpersonal problem solving and parasuicide. *Cognitive Therapy and Research, 11,* 1–12.

Loo, R. (1986). Suicide among police in a federal force. *Suicide and Life-Threatening Behavior, 16,* 379–388.

Maris, R. (1969). *Social forces in urban suicide.* Homewood, IL: Dorsey.

Maris, R. (1981). *Pathways to suicide: A survey of self-destructive behaviors.* Baltimore, MD: Johns Hopkins University Press.

Maris, R. (1985). The adolescent suicide problem. *Suicide and Life-Threatening Behavior, 15,* 91–100.

Marshall, J. R., Burnett, W., & Brasurel, J. (1983). On precipitating factors: Cancer as a cause of suicide. *Suicide and Life-Threatening Behavior, 13,* 15–27.

McKenry, P. C., & Kelley, C. (1983). The role of drugs in adolescent suicide attempts. *Suicide and Life-Threatening Behavior, 13,* 166–175.

McMahon, B., & Pugh, T. F. (1965). Suicide in the widowed. *American Journal of Epidemiology, 81,* 23–31.

Mehrabian, A., & Weinstein, L. (1985). Temperament characteristics and suicide attempters. *Journal of Consulting and Clinical Psychology, 53,* 544–546.

Melges, F. T., & Weisz, A. E. (1971). The personal future and suicidal ideation. *Journal of Nervous and Mental Disease, 153,* 244–250.

Miller, F., & Chabrier, L. A. (1987). The relation of delusional content in psychotic depression to life-threatening behavior. *Suicide and Life-Threatening Behavior, 17,* 13–17.

Motto, J. A. (1980). Suicide risk factors in alcohol abuse. *Suicide and Life-Threatening Behavior, 10,* 230–238.

Nayha, S. (1982). Autumn incidence of suicides re-examined: Data from Finland by sex, age, and occupation. *British Journal of Psychiatry, 141,* 512–517.

Neuringer, C. (1964). Rigid thinking in suicidal individuals. *Journal of Consulting Psychology, 28,* 54–58.

Neuringer, C. (1967). The cognitive organization of meaning in suicidal individuals. *Journal of General Psychology, 76,* 91–100.

Neuringer, C. (1972). Suicide attempt and social isolation on the MAPS test. *Life-Threatening Behavior, 2,* 139–144.

Neuringer, C. (1974). Attitudes toward self in suicidal individuals. *Life-Threatening Behavior, 4,* 96–106.

Neuringer, C., & Harris, R. M. (1974). The perception of the passage of time among death-involved hospital patients. *Life-Threatening Behavior, 4,* 240–254.

Newman, K. S. (1988). *Falling from grace: The experience of downward mobility in the American middle class.* New York: Free Press.

Ogilvie, D. M., Stone, P. J., & Shneidman, E. S. (1983). A computer analysis of suicide notes. In E. Shneidman, N. Farberow, & R. Litman (Eds.), *The psychology of suicide* (pp. 249–256). New York: Aronson.

Pallis, D. J., Barraclough, B. M., Levey, A., Jenkins, J., & Sainsbury, P. (1982). Estimating suicide risk among attempted suicides: The development of new clinical scales. *British Journal of Psychiatry, 141,* 37–44.

Palmer, S. (1971). Characteristics of suicide in 54 nonliterate societies. *Life-Threatening Behavior, 1,* 178–183.

Palmer, S., & Humphrey, J. A. (1980). Offender–victim relationships in criminal homicide followed by offender's suicide, North Carolina, 1972–1977. *Suicide and Life-Threatening Behavior, 10,* 106–118.

Parker, A. (1981). The meaning of attempted suicide to young parasuicides: A repertory grid study. *British Journal of Psychiatry, 139,* 306–312.

Parker, G., & Walter, S. (1982). Seasonal variation in depressive disorders and suicidal deaths in New South Wales. *British Journal of Psychiatry, 140,* 626–632.

Patsiokas, A., Clum, G., & Luscomb, R. (1979). Cognitive characteristics of suicide attempters. *Journal of Consulting and Clinical Psychology, 47,* 478–484.

Paykel, E. S., Prusoff, A. B., & Myers, J. K. (1975). Suicide attempts and recent life events. *Archives of General Psychiatry, 32,* 327–333.

Pennebaker, J. W. (1989). Stream of consciousness and stress: Levels of thinking. In J. S. Uleman & J. A. Bargh (Eds.), *The direction of thought: Limits of awareness, intention, and control* (pp. 327–350). New York: Guilford.

Perrah, M., & Wichman, H. (1987). Cognitive rigidity in suicide attempters. *Suicide and Life-Threatening Behavior, 17,* 251–262.

Petrie, K., & Chamberlain, K. (1983). Hopelessness and social desirability as moderator variables in predicting suicidal behavior. *Journal of Consulting and Clinical Psychology, 51,* 485–487.

Phillips, D. P., & Liu, J. (1980). The frequency of suicides around major public holidays: Some surprising findings. *Suicide and Life-Threatening Behavior, 10,* 41–50.

Phillips, D. P., & Wills, J. S. (1987). A drop in suicides around major national holidays. *Suicide and Life-Threatening Behavior, 17,* 1–12.

Platt, S. D. (1986). Parasuicide and unemployment. *British Journal of Psychiatry, 149,* 401–405.

Platt, S. D., & Dyer, J. A. T. (1987). Psychological correlates of unemployment among male parasuicides in Edinburgh. *British Journal of Psychiatry, 151,* 27–32.

Powell, E. H. (1958). Occupation, status, and suicide: Toward a redefinition of anomie. *American Sociological Review, 23,* 131–139.

Power, K. G., Cooke, D. J., & Brooks, D. N. (1985). Life stress, medical lethality, and suicidal intent. *British Journal of Psychiatry, 147,* 655–659.

Powers, W. T. (1973). *Behavior: The control of perception.* Chicago: Aldine.

Rhine, M. W., & Mayerson, P. (1973). A serious suicidal syndrome masked by homicidal threats. *Life-Threatening Behavior, 3,* 3–10.

Ringel, E. (1976). The presuicidal syndrome. *Suicide and Life-Threatening Behavior, 6,* 131–149.

Roberts, J., & Hawton, K. (1980). Child abuse and attempted suicide. *British Journal of Psychiatry, 137,* 319–323.

Rojcewicz, S. J. (1970). War and suicide. *Life-Threatening Behavior, 1,* 46–54.

Rosen, D. H. (1976). Suicide survivors: Psychotherapeutic implications of egocide. *Suicide and Life-Threatening Behavior, 6,* 209–215.

Rothberg, J. M., & Jones, F. D. (1987). Suicide in the U. S. Army: Epidemiological and periodic aspects. *Suicide and Life-Threatening Behavior, 17,* 119–132.

Roy, A., & Linnoila, M. (1986). Alcoholism and suicide. *Suicide and Life-Threatening Behavior, 16,* 244–273.

Schotte, D. E., & Clum, G. A. (1982). Suicide ideation in a college population: A test of a model. *Journal of Consulting and Clinical Psychology, 50,* 690–696.

Schotte, D. E., & Clum, G. A. (1987). Problem-solving skills in suicidal psychiatric patients. *Journal of Consulting and Clinical Psychology, 55,* 49–54.

Shneidman, E. S. (1981). Suicide thoughts and reflections, 1960–1980. *Suicide and Life-Threatening Behavior, 11,* 197–360.

Shneidman, E. S., & Farberow, N. L. (1961). Statistical comparisons between attempted and committed suicides. In N. L. Farberow & E. S. Shneidman (Eds.), *The cry for help* (pp. 19–47). New York: McGraw-Hill.

Shneidman, E. S., & Farberow, N. L. (1970). Attempted and committed suicides. In E. S. Shneidman, N. L. Farberow, & R. E. Litman (Eds.), *The psychology of suicide* (pp. 199–225). New York: Science House.

Silberfeld, M., Streiner, B., & Ciampi, A. (1985). Suicide attempters, ideators, and risk-taking propensity. *Canadian Journal of Psychiatry, 30,* 274–277.

Silver, R. L., Boon, C., & Stones, M. H. (1983). Searching for meaning in misfortune: Making sense of incest. *Journal of Social Issues, 39,* 81–102.

Simmons, R., Rosenberg, F., & Rosenberg, M. (1973). Disturbance in the self-image at adolescence. *American Sociological Review, 38,* 553–568.

Simon, W., & Lumry, G. K. (1968). Suicide among physicians. *Journal of Nervous and Mental Disease, 147,* 105–112.

Smith, D. H., & Hackathorn, L. (1982). Some social and psychological factors related to suicide in primitive societies: A cross-cultural comparative study. *Suicide and Life-Threatening Behavior, 12,* 195–211.

Smith, G. W., & Bloom, I. (1985). A study in the personal meaning of suicide in the context of Baechler's typology. *Suicide and Life-Threatening Behavior, 15,* 3–13.

Spirito, A., Stark, L. J., Williams, C. A., & Guevremont, D. C. (1987, November). *Common problems and coping strategies reported by normal adolescents and adolescent suicide attempters.* Paper presented to the Association for the Advancement of Behavior Therapy, Boston, MA.

Steele, C. M., & Southwick, L. (1985). Alcohol and social behavior: I. The psychology of drunken excess. *Journal of Personality and Social Psychology, 48,* 18–34.

Stengel, E. (1967, December). The complexity of motivations to suicide attempts. *Bulletin of Suicidology,* 35–40.

Stengel, E., & Cook, N. G. (1958). *Attempted suicide.* London: Oxford University Press.

Stephens, B. J. (1985). Suicidal women and their relationships with husbands, boyfriends, and lovers. *Suicide and Life-Threatening Behavior, 15,* 77–89.

Stephens, B. J. (1987). Cheap thrills and humble pie: The adolescence of female suicide attempters. *Suicide and Life-Threatening Behavior, 17,* 107–118.

Taylor, S. (1978). The confrontation with death and the renewal of life. *Suicide and Life-Threatening Behavior, 8,* 89–98.

Taylor, S. E. (1983). Adjustment to threatening events: A theory of cognitive adaptation. *American Psychologist, 38,* 1161–1173.

Tice, D. M., Buder, J., & Baumeister, R. F. (1985). Development of self-consciousness: At what age does audience pressure disrupt performance? *Adolescence, 20,* 301–305.

Tishler, C. L., McKenry, P. C., & Morgan, K. C. (1981). Adolescent suicide attempts: Some significant factors. *Suicide and Life-Threatening Behavior, 11,* 86–92.

Topol, P., & Reznikoff, M. (1982). Perceived peer and family relationships, hopelessness, and locus of control as factors in adolescent suicide attempts. *Suicide and Life-Threatening Behavior, 12,* 141–150.

Trout, D. L. (1980). The role of social isolation in suicide. *Suicide and Life-Threatening Behavior, 10,* 10–23.

Vallacher, R. R., & Wegner, D. M. (1985). *A theory of action identification.* Hillsdale, NJ: Erlbaum.

Vallacher, R. R., & Wegner, D. M. (1987). What do people think they're doing: Action identification and human behavior. *Psychological Review, 94,* 3–15.

Vandivert, D. S., & Locke, B. Z. (1979). Suicide ideation: Its relation to depression, suicide, and suicide attempts. *Suicide and Life-Threatening Behavior, 9,* 205–218.

Vinoda, K. S. (1966). Personality characteristics of attempted suicides. *British Journal of Psychiatry, 112,* 1143–1150.

Wasserman, I. M. (1984). The influence of economic business cycles on United States suicide rates. *Suicide and Life-Threatening Behavior, 14,* 143–156.

Wegner, D. M., & Giulano, T. (1980). Arousal-induced attention to self. *Journal of Personality and Social Psychology, 38,* 719–726.

Weiss, J. M. A. (1957). The gamble with death in attempted suicide. *Psychiatry, 20,* 17–25.

Williams, J. M., & Broadbent, K. (1986). Autobiographical memory in suicide attempters. *Journal of Abnormal Psychology, 95,* 144–149.

Wilson, M. (1981). Suicidal behavior: Toward an explanation of differences in female and male rates. *Suicide and Life-Threatening Behavior, 11,* 131–140.

Wyrick, R. I., & Wyrick, L. (1977). Time experience during depression. *Archives of General Psychiatry, 34,* 1441–1443.

Yufit, R. I., & Benzies, B. (1973). Assessing suicidal potential by time perspective. *Life-Threatening Behavior, 3,* 270–282.

CHAPTER 14

From Symptoms of Depression to Syndromes of Depression

CHARLES G. COSTELLO

INTRODUCTION

There is no need for all psychopathologists to direct their research into finding a way from our knowledge of symptoms of depression into the creation of syndromes of depression, and not all clinicians may await impatiently the creation of those syndromes. The biologically oriented and particularly the psychologically oriented clinicians may believe that it will be more useful to concentrate therapeutic efforts on specific symptoms such as motor retardation or anhedonia rather than on a syndrome that, for example, forms the basis of a diagnosis of major depression. As for researchers, those who do not seek justification of their research strategies in the likely payoff for clinicians might argue that, for their purposes, concentrating efforts on a specific symptom is more likely to bear fruit.

It is true, as the review in Chapter 1 demonstrated, that our currently defined syndromes of depression are unsatisfactory, and it seems that important clinical problems cannot be solved because of this poor state of affairs. For instance, Guscott and Grof's (1991) review of the data on refractory depression indicates that the resistant problems associated with trying to understand the nature of refractory depression stems to some extent from problems in the diagnosis of depression.

But both clinical observation and research using multivariate statistical procedures, including new ones such as latent class analysis that appear more sound than factor analysis and cluster analysis (e.g., Eaton, Dryman, Sorenson, & McCutcheon, 1989), strongly suggest that symptoms of depression do occur in clusters (Blashfield & Morey, 1979; Grove & Andreason, 1989). Therefore, one important source of information for the understanding of a specific symptom would seem to be the way in which it is related to the other symptoms in the cluster.

This apparent clustering of symptoms also suggests that there are some underlying processes, whether biological or psychological or a mixture of both, that cause these symptom clusters to occur and that these underlying processes are the proper targets for therapy. This would suggest, in turn, that improvements in clinical work await improvements in our knowledge of the nature of syndromes of depression.

A particularly questionable research strategy would seem to be one that aims to understand the nature of depressive syndromes by investigating the nonsymptom correlates of one specific symptom of depression. For instance, a considerable amount of research has been done on memory biases associated with depressed moods (see Blaney, 1986, for a thorough review). But these memory biases may have nothing to do with the functional relationships between depressed mood and other symptoms of depression including even subjective complaints of memory impairment. It would seem to be a better strategy to study the relationships between two or more symptoms. For instance, Cartwright, in Chapter 12, argued for the promise of research on the relationships between sleep disturbance and daily moods. The problem of researching symptoms in isolation from other symptoms has been discussed further in Costello (1992, in press a).

Although multivariate statistical procedures have been of value in that, by revealing clusters of symptoms, (a) they give us some confidence that valid syndromes of depression will be discovered and (b) they indicate what the nature of these syndromes may be (e.g., that they are caused primarily by biological processes or primarily by psychological processes), they can probably do no more than they have done. It is unlikely that they can help us find the source of the syndromes. The most sophisticated current approach to the use of multivariate statistics to identify the source of syndromes of schizophrenia is Meehl's taxometric methodology (Meehl & Golden, 1982) but, as Golden (1991) has pointed out, "It is sad but true, that almost 30 years after Meehl's initial insights, no gene, virus or any other kind of such a dichotomous causal factor has been discovered by use of bootstrapping taxometrics" (p. 264). It would seem that the further search for syndromes must start from a more thorough understanding of each symptom and from the testing of theories concerning the relationships between symptoms.

One reason that multivariate statistical procedures may be limited as far as providing us with knowledge of syndromes is that they use cross-sectional symptom data. It is unlikely that we can gain much knowledge about symptoms and their interrelationships without investigating them over time. As we have seen in Chapter 2, even the basic biological process of circadian rhythms shows intraindividual temporal variability. Strauss (1986) has noted:

> A disease is a manifestation of some kind of pathologic process. The nature of the process may be identified and understood by attending to its course and to

> the variables that influence it. In essence, the principle is that when exploring and trying to understand a mysterious object, one valid approach is to see the way the object responds to a variety of situations and events. If the object changes over time, studying its evolution provides further crucial information about its nature. (p. 258)

If a researcher decides to investigate how a particular, or focal, symptom is related to others, which other symptoms should be chosen for investigation? And what about the researcher who does not have a focal symptom in mind but wishes to select one? What should guide this selection?

Obviously, to maintain the symptom approach being advocated in this book, the researcher cannot simply select in some arbitrary manner one symptom in an apparent cluster to be the focal symptom and begin to investigate its relationship with all the other symptoms in the cluster because then the research will have slipped into the syndrome approach. The researcher can only maintain the symptom approach if he or she selects a focal symptom on some rational grounds and investigates its relationship to one other, or at most to begin with, two other symptoms.

The best possible way to choose a focal symptom for investigation is on the basis of some theory about the nature of depression and the role played by the symptom in the natural history of depression. Similarly, the best possible way to choose the other one or two symptoms for investigation is on the basis of a theory as to how the symptoms are related to one another and to the underlying causal processes.

But how are we going to generate promising theories? Are there any empirical data on the symptoms of depression that might guide the generation of theories? Four sorts of data might be considered, keeping in mind that the assessments of symptoms in the generation of these data have not come to grips with the complexities of the phenomena as detailed in the previous chapters: (a) the prevalence of specific symptoms; (b) the relative convergent and discriminant validity of symptoms; (c) the temporal sequence of symptoms in the onset of and recovery from a depressive episode; (d) stability of symptoms over episodes of depression.

At the expense of being called a naive inductive empiricist, I shall present what data are available in relation to the preceding four factors. They have not led me to a promising theory, but they may provide useful fodder for the reader with more imagination.

PREVALENCE OF SPECIFIC SYMPTOMS

There would seem to be some value in beginning our research with the most prevalent of the symptoms of depression as long as they are not equally prevalent in other disorders. Putting aside the question of the discriminant validity of the symptoms for a later section, what are the data on prevalence? I shall not consider the prevalences of depressed mood because it either occurs in 100% of the cases studied when it is a necessary symptom as in the Present State Examination (PSE) or the prevalence is hidden as in the Diagnostic Interview Schedule (DIS) where cases of depression must answer "yes" to the question "In your lifetime, have you ever had two weeks or more during which you felt sad, blue, depressed or when you lost all interest or pleasure in things that you usually cared about or enjoyed?"

If clearly nonspecific symptoms such as irritability and muscular tension are omitted, the three most prevalent PSE symptoms of depression in 23 depressed inpatients studied by Wing, Mann, Leff, and Nixon (1978) were hopelessness and lack of self-confidence, both occurring in 70% of the patients, and subjective anergia (61%). The three most prevalent symptoms in 14 depressed outpatients were hopelessness (83%), suicidal ideas (83%), and subjective anergia (75%); and in 23 cases identified in a community study, the most prevalent symptoms were lack of self-confidence (41%), hopelessness (36%), and subjective anergia (32%).

Eaton et al. (1989) reported that, in 49 DIS/DSM-III cases of major depressive disorder, sleep problems and poor concentration were among the most prevalent symptoms (84% and 73% prevalences, respectively). Loss of pleasure in sex and feelings of worthlessness were relatively infrequent (20%, 49%). In a study of the prevalence of physical symptoms in 51 depressed patients, Mathew, Weinman, and Mirabi (1981) found that poor concentration was the most frequent symptom, occurring in 83.6% of the patients.

Costello (in press b) presented data on (a) the prevalences of specific DIS symptoms in the worst episode of depression for women with current major depressive episodes in 3 clinic and 7 community samples, and (b) the prevalences of specific PSE symptoms in the current episode of depression for women in 3 clinic samples and 5 community samples.

With respect to the DIS, worthlessness was among the three most prevalent symptoms in all three clinic samples with an average prevalence across the samples of 88%. But this symptom was only among the three most prevalent in two of the seven community samples where the average prevalence of the symptom across all seven samples was 60%. Loss of sleep was among the three most prevalent symptoms in all three clinic samples (M = 83%) and all seven community samples (M = 75%). Poor concentration was among the three most prevalent symptoms in the three clinic samples (M = 84%) but in only two of the community samples (M = 59%).

With respect to the PSE symptoms that were rated as moderate in intensity, hopelessness was among the three most prevalent symptoms in two of the three clinic samples (M = 67%) and in three of the five community samples (M = 40%). Poor concentration was among the three most prevalent symptoms of moderate intensity in all the clinic samples (M = 70%) but in only one of the five community samples (M = 34%).

With respect to the PSE symptoms that were rated severe, only morning depression was among the three most prevalent symptoms in an appreciable number of samples—all three clinic samples (M = 39%) and three of the five community samples (M = 17%).

The data for only two small samples of depressed men, one clinic sample and one community sample, were presented in Costello (in press b). The three most prevalent symptoms in the 20 men of the clinic sample were morning depression (95%), poor concentration (85%), and inefficient thinking (70%). The three most prevalent symptoms in the 22 men of the community sample were morning depression (59%), hopelessness (55%), and subjective anergia (55%). Whereas poor concentration was reported by 85% of the depressed men in the clinic sample, it was reported by only 50% of the depressed men in the community sample. This was the only symptom that differed significantly in prevalence between the two samples.

These data, which must be approached with great caution, suggest three conclusions: (a) Problems with sleep are quite prevalent in both clinic and community samples of depressed individuals; (b) certain symptoms are more prevalent among clinic samples of depressed patients than among community samples of depressed individuals; namely, hopelessness, suicidal ideas, and poor concentration (the high proportion of depressed patients who report poor concentration and feelings of hopelessness was also documented in Chapters 6 and 9 of this book); (c) loss of interest is not as prevalent as might have been expected in either clinic or community samples.

Readers should probably be particularly wary of the third conclusion. The data presented by Eaton et al. (1989) and some of the data I presented in a previous study (Costello, in press b) were obtained with the DIS, and this interview does not have a question specifically and solely dealing with loss of interest. The symptom also may be difficult to measure, particularly in less severe depressions. In five community samples for which symptom data were reported (Costello, in press b), the prevalence of loss of interest for currently depressed women ranged from 9% to 57%. In the three clinic samples, the prevalences were closer: 47%, 48%, and 58%. In Chapter 3, Klinger noted that among a sample of Beck's severely depressed patients, 92% reported a loss of gratification and 86% a loss of motivation. Klinger also noted that research with the BDI indicated that loss of interest was one of the best discriminators between individuals high and low in depression.

It is somewhat disheartening that more convincing data on the relative prevalence of symptoms are not available. But, as the authors of the chapters in this book have documented, the data are inconsistent, and one of the main reasons for this state of affairs is that measurement techniques are so underdeveloped.

CONVERGENT AND DISCRIMINANT VALIDITY OF SYMPTOMS

The symptoms of depression that seem particularly worthy of initial research attention are those that not only frequently occur in depressed people but that also show regular associations with other symptoms of depression and few or no associations with the symptoms of other disorders.

Clark (1989) reviewed six studies that reported the prevalence of symptoms of depression in patients with depressive disorders or anxiety disorders. Unfortunately, not all the symptoms of depression were included in all the studies. However, among the symptoms that were included in all of them, the following were significantly more prevalent in the depressed patients in a majority of the studies: pessimism, brooding, and self-pity (5/6 studies); anhedonia (4/5 studies); suicidal behavior (3/4 studies); psychomotor retardation (2/3 studies); early morning awakening (2/3 studies).

Clark's (1989) review of the factor-analytic studies of clinical data indicated that the studies have produced either a broad factor that includes both symptoms of depression and symptoms of anxiety and that appears to be measuring something similar to the general personality disposition of Negative Affectivity, or a specific factor that appears to measure something similar to what has been variously called endogenous or melancholic depression and on which the following symptoms have high loadings: anhedonia, hopelessness, and suicidal tendencies.

Clark and Watson's (1991) review of self-report measures of depression and anxiety indicated that the Beck inventories: Beck Depression Inventory (BDI; Beck, Ward, Mendelson, Mock, & Erbaugh, 1961), and the Beck Anxiety Inventory (BAI; Beck, Epstein, Brown, & Steer, 1988) and the Costello–Comrey anxiety and depression scales (CC-A, CC-D; Costello & Comrey, 1967) exhibited somewhat better convergent and discriminant validity patterns than other measures they examined. Their analysis suggested that the discriminant validity of the Beck inventories stems largely from the content specificity of the BAI. Both the CC-D and the CC-A appear to have appreciable discriminant validity. In the case of the CC-D this may be because it focused on the symptoms of depressed mood, loss of interest or pleasure, and worthlessness and did not assess physiological or vegetative changes, fatigue, or suicidal ideation. Clark and Watson suggested that the CC-D appears to be measuring the absence of Positive Affectivity (Watson & Tellegen, 1985). The 15 items of the self-report inventory of depression that de Bonis, Lebeaux, de Boeck, Simon, and Pichot (1991) found had a satisfactory fit for both items and persons as defined by the Rasch model (Rasch, 1980) also seem to be measuring predominantly depressed mood, loss of interest, and feelings of worthlessness.

In summary, it seems that hopelessness and suicidal ideas as well as being very prevalent among clinic cases of depression tend not to be associated with symptoms of anxiety and do not occur with such frequency in anxiety-disordered patients. But there are also symptoms that may not occur in large numbers of depressed patients but are significantly less prevalent in anxiety disorder patients; namely, anhedonia, psychomotor retardation, and early morning awakening.

TEMPORAL SEQUENCE OF SYMPTOMS

There are two alternative ways of viewing data on the temporal sequence of symptoms. One view is to consider symptoms that occur early in the development of depression to be closer to the causes of depressive disorders than those that occur later and therefore particularly worthy of research attention. Research on such early symptoms has to come to grips with the problem of whether or not they are indeed best considered to be symptoms of depression or proximal causes of depression, a problem that has been discussed with respect to self-esteem in Chapter 7 and with respect to hopelessness in Chapter 9.

The alternative view is to consider symptoms that occur later to be part of the transition from a subclinical state of depression to a clinical state and therefore to be more pathognomic of depressive disorders and particularly worthy of research attention.

The second view would seem to be more consistent with the clinical view that a certain minimum number of symptoms are required before an individual can be given a diagnosis of depression. But the matter of which symptoms have greater etiological importance is likely to be resolved only by research on the symptoms themselves. Consequently, data on the temporal sequence of symptoms are unlikely to provide much guidance in our selection of symptoms for priority research investigation.

In any case, there would seem to be little research data available on the temporal sequence of depressive symptoms. Young and Grabler (1985) examined the temporal sequence of symptoms in seven patients for whom it took more than 4 weeks to develop a full RDC major depressive syndrome. The mean number of symptoms that occurred before each specific symptom were as follows: depressed mood—a mean of 1.00 symptoms occurred beforehand; loss of pleasure—1.43; appetite/weight change—2.29; decreased energy—2.71; increased/decreased sleep—3.29; impaired concentration—4.26; suicidal ideation—4.71.

Young, Watel, Lahmeyer, and Eastman (1991) found that three symptoms—fatigue, hyersomnia, and increased appetite and weight—occurred early in the onset of episodes of winter seasonal affective disorder (SAD). But these findings may not be generalizable to other kinds of depressions.

In a somewhat related study by Dryman and Eaton (1991), 9,295 individuals in the ECA study who did not have a life history of major affective disorder, as determined by an initial DIS interview, were interviewed on a second occasion one year later. The researchers examined the strength of association between the occurrence of depressive symptoms for 2 weeks or longer, as reported in the first interview, and the onset of a major depressive episode over the 1-year follow-up period. For both women and men, the symptoms most strongly associated with onset were diminished sexual drive, feelings of worthlessness or excessive guilt, and trouble concentrating or thinking. For women, sleep disturbance was also strongly associated and, for men, fatigue. In Chapter 12 of this book, Cartwright also has presented data indicating that sleep disturbance may be an early symptom in the progression to a full major depressive episode.

STABILITY OF SYMPTOMS OVER EPISODES OF DEPRESSION

There may be important individual differences in the manner with which depressive disorders are manifested, and with respect to each individual's core symptoms of depression, there is likely to be stability across episodes of depression. Therefore, symptoms that show stability might be given research priority. Unfortunately there are few research data.

Paykel, Prusoff, and Tanner (1976) examined the temporal stability of symptom patterns for 33 depressed patients studied initially at the height of their disorder and again some months later in a relapse following earlier recovery. They found significant, but not particularly high, correlations across the two episodes for depressed mood ($r = .46$), morning depression (.38), hopelessness (.46), anorexia (.47), and increased appetite (.41).

Young, Fogg, Scheftner, and Fawcett (1990) examined the concordance of symptoms in 201 patients who (a) met RDC criteria for a major affective disorder and were subjects in the NIMH Collaborative Study of the Psychobiology of Depression and (b) had two episodes of depression over a 5-year observation period. Of these patients, 93 had a bipolar disorder and 108 had a unipolar disorder; the data were analyzed for the two groups separately. Measuring concordance with kappa (Cohen, 1960), no one symptom showed significant concordance when the analyses were done for all the bipolar and all the unipolar patients. However, for the 22 bipolar patients who had an equal number of symptoms in the two episodes, the k for four symptoms was equal to or greater than 0.70: fatigue, $k = 1.00$; loss of interest/pleasure, 0.72; morning depression, 0.70; agitation, 1.00. For the 18 unipolar patients who had equal numbers of symptoms in the two episodes, high k values were found for loss of interest/pleasure ($k = 1.00$) and agitation ($k = 1.00$).

CONCLUSION

Healy (1990) has suggested distinguishing between symptoms of depression that reflect changes in the brain underlying the disorder and symptoms that reflect psychological reactions to the disorder. For instance, fatigue and poor concentration may be symptoms of the first kind, whereas hopelessness, worthlessness, and lack of self-confidence are symptoms of the second kind.

It may then be useful to investigate two or three symptoms of depression as a means of discovering the necessary biological processes responsible for their emergence and contribution to the syndrome of depression. This is likely to be the wish of the psychopathologist who seeks to understand the fundamental nature of depression. This researcher would have little interest in developing therapies that simply work in some unknown way but would focus only on therapies that strike at the biological heart of the matter in a known and perhaps preventive way. This researcher might want to begin investigations with symptoms that show discriminant validity and stability across episodes, and that appear with little disguise in different cultures and different demographic groups.

On the other hand, a psychopathologist may be interested in how the symptoms of depression are manifested in different ways in different demographic groups and cultures. The data from such a researcher might be of immediate help to clinicians who are unable to wait until the fundamental necessary processes causing depression are found and who wish to help people recover from their depressions by understanding the particular forms their symptoms take. Data from the five sources of information that we have reviewed will do little or nothing to guide such a researcher in selecting symptoms for investigation. On the contrary, the researcher may very well choose to investigate symptoms of the most chameleon sort appearing in different forms in different cultures and demographic groups; perhaps even being a symptom of anxiety in one context and a symptom of depression in another; perhaps showing no concordance over episodes.

It would be a mistake to assume that only those symptoms reflecting biological disturbances are worthy of research attention. Hopelessness is a psychological symptom but obviously deserves investigation. Its importance with respect to suicidal thoughts and attempts is well established. A number of cross-sectional studies have found that hopelessness is significantly correlated with suicidal intent, even after controlling for severity of depression, whereas depression and suicidal intent are not significantly correlated after controlling for levels of hopelessness (e.g., Beck, Kovacs, & Weissman, 1975; Dyer & Kreitman, 1984). Prospective studies have found that individuals who commit suicide had higher prior levels of hopelessness than those who do not commit suicide (e.g., Beck, Brown, Berchick, Stewart, & Steer, 1990; Fawcett et al., 1987).

I have distinguished between researchers who are primarily interested in biological symptoms and those who have a focus on psychological symptoms. But research need not be restricted to one kind of symptom or the other. In Chapter 4, Willner reviewed data indicating that anhedonia (usually considered more biological than psychological) is associated with both hopelessness and suicidal ideation and highly predictive of successful suicide. In Chapter 2, Healy noted that disturbances in circadian rhythms (biological) may disrupt social functioning (psychological).

The psychopathologists who are working on the fourth version of one of the most commonly used diagnostic systems, namely, the American Psychiatric Association's *Diagnostic and Statistical Manual of Mental Disorders,* are doing their best to establish the diagnoses on a more scientific basis (see, e.g., the account by Pincus, Frances, Davis, First, & Widiger, 1992). But it is hard not to feel that DSM-IV will be the product of yet another attempt to clear turbid solutions by pouring them continually from one glass to another. It would seem that meaningful syndromes of depression will only arise from a more thorough understanding of the symptoms of depression, from better methods for measuring the symptoms, and from demonstrations of theoretically meaningful links between the symptoms.

REFERENCES

Beck, A. T., Brown, G., Berchick, R. J., Stewart, B. L., & Steer, R. A. (1990). Relationships between hopelessness and ultimate suicide: A replication with psychiatric outpatients. *American Journal of Psychiatry, 147,* 190–195.

Beck, A. T., Epstein, N., Brown, G., & Steer, R. (1988). An inventory for measuring clinical anxiety: Psychometric properties. *Journal of Consulting and Clinical Psychology, 56,* 893–897.

Beck, A. T., Kovacs, N., & Weissman, A. (1975). Hopelessness and suicidal behavior: An overview. *Journal of the American Medical Association, 234,* 1146–1149.

Beck, A. T., Ward, C. H., Mendelson, M., Mock, J. E., & Erbaugh, J. K. (1961). An inventory for measuring depression. *Archives of General Psychiatry, 4,* 561–571.

Blaney, P. H. (1986). Affect and memory: A review. *Psychological Bulletin, 99,* 229–246.

Blashfield, R. K., & Morey, L. C. (1979). The classification of depression through cluster analysis. *Comprehensive Psychiatry, 20,* 516–527.

Clark, L. A. (1989). The anxiety and depressive disorders: Descriptive psychopathology and differential diagnosis. In P. C. Kendall & D. Watson (Eds.), *Anxiety and depression: Distinctive and overlapping features* (pp. 83–129). New York: Academic Press.

Clark, L. A., & Watson, D. (1991). Tripartite model of anxiety and depression: Psychometric evidence and taxonomic implications. *Journal of Abnormal Psychology, 100,* 316–336.

Cohen, J. (1960). A coefficient of agreement for nominal scales. *Educational and Psychological Measurement, 20,* 37–46.

Costello, C. G. (1992). Conceptual problems in current research on cognitive vulnerability to psychopathology. *Cognitive Therapy and Research, 16,* 379–390.

Costello, C. G. (in press a). Cognitive causes of psychopathology. In C. G. Costello (Ed.), *Basic issues in psychopathology.* New York: Guilford.

Costello, C. G. (in press b). The similarities and dissimilarities between community and clinic cases of psychopathology. In C. G. Costello (Ed.), *Basic issues in psychopathology.* New York: Guilford.

Costello, C. G., & Comrey, A. L. (1967). Scales for measuring depression and anxiety. *Journal of Psychology, 6,* 303–313.

de Bonis, M., Lebeaux, M. O., de Boeck, P., Simon, M., & Pichot, P. (1991). Measuring the severity of depression through a self-report inventory. *Journal of Affective Disorders, 22,* 55–64.

Dryman, A., & Eaton, W. W. (1991). Affective symptoms associated with the onset of major depression in the community: Findings from the U. S. National Institute of Mental Health Epidemiologic Catchment Area Program. *Acta Psychiatrica Scandinavica, 84,* 1–5.

Dyer, J. A. T., & Kreitman, N. (1984). Hopelessness, depression and suicidal intent in parasuicide. *British Journal of Psychiatry, 144,* 127–133.

Eaton, W. W., Dryman, A., Sorenson, A., & McCutcheon, A. (1989). DSM-III major depressive disorder in the community: A latent class analysis of data from the NIMH Epidemiologic Catchment Area programme. *British Journal of Psychiatry, 155,* 48–54.

Fawcett, J., Scheftner, W., Clark, D., Hedeker, D., Gibbons, R., & Coryell, W. (1987). Clinical predictors of suicide in patients with major affective disorders: A controlled prospective study. *American Journal of Psychiatry, 144,* 35–40.

Golden, R. R. (1991). Bootstrapping taxometrics: On the development of a method for detection of a single major gene. In W. M. Grove & D. Cicchetti (Eds), *Thinking clearly about psychology, Vol. 2. Personality and psychopathology* (pp. 259–294). Minneapolis: University of Minnesota Press.

Grove, W. M., & Andreason, N. C. (1989). Quantitative and qualitative distinctions between psychiatric disorders. In L. N. Robins & J. E. Barrett (Eds.), *The validity of psychiatric diagnoses* (pp. 127–138). New York: Raven.

Guscott, R., & Grof, P. (1991). The clinical meaning of refractory depression: A review for the clinician. *American Journal of Psychiatry, 148,* 695–704.

Healy, D. (1990). *The suspended revolution: Psychiatry and psychotherapy re-examined.* London: Faber & Faber.

Mathew, R. J., Weinman, N. L., & Mirabi, N. (1981). Physical symptoms of depression. *British Journal of Psychiatry, 139,* 293–296.

Meehl, P. E., & Golden, R. R. (1982). Taxometric methods. In J. N. Butcher & D. C. Kendall (Eds.), *The handbook of research methods in clinical psychology* (pp. 127–181). New York: Wiley.

Paykel, E. S., Prusoff, B. A., Tanner, J. (1976). Temporal stability of symptom patterns in depression. *British Journal of Psychiatry, 128,* 369–374.

Pincus, H. A., Frances, A., Davis, W. W., First, M. B., & Widiger, T. A. (1992). DSM-IV and new diagnostic categories: Holding the line on proliferation. *American Journal of Psychiatry, 149,* 112–117.

Rasch, G. (1980). *Probabilistic models for some intelligence and attainment tests.* Chicago: Chicago University Press.

Strauss, J. S. (1986). Psychiatric diagnosis: A reconsideration based on longitudinal processes. In T. Millon & G. L. Klerman (Eds.), *Contemporary directions in psychopathology: Towards the DSM-IV* (pp. 257–263). New York: Guilford.

Watson, D., & Tellegen, A. (1985). Toward a consensual structure of mood. *Psychological Bulletin, 98,* 219–235.

Wing, J. K., Mann, S. A., Leff, J. P., & Nixon, J. P. (1978). The concept of a "case" in psychiatric population surveys. *Psychological Medicine, 8,* 203–217.

Young, M. A., Fogg, L. F., Scheftner, W. A., & Fawcett, J. A. (1990). Concordance of symptoms in recurrent depressive episodes. *Journal of Affective Disorders, 20,* 79–85.

Young, M. A., & Grabler, P. (1985). Rapidity of symptom onset in depression. *Psychiatry Research, 16,* 309–315.

Young, M. A., Watel, L. G., Lahmeyer, H. W., & Eastman, C. I. (1991). The temporal onset of individual symptoms in winter depression: Differentiating underlying mechanisms. *Journal of Affective Disorders, 22,* 191–197.

Author Index

Subject Index